AF574124

The God Who Serves

Books in the Masters of the Word series

C. H. Spurgeon on Matthew
THE KING HAS COME

Alexander Maclaren on Mark
THE GOD WHO SERVES

G. Campbell Morgan on Luke
THE GOD WHO CARES

F. B. Meyer on John
THE LIFE OF LOVE

Lawrence O. Richards, editor for the Gospels

le unless otherwise

the Bible.

ny

e

od

o

es

eral Editor

Company
Jersey

All Scripture quotations are from the King James Version of the B noted.

Scripture quotations identified RV are from the Revised Version (

Maclaren, Alexander, 1826–1910.
The God who serves.

(Masters of the Word)
Reprint. Originally published; He came to serve. 1894.
1. Bible. N.T. Mark—Criticism, interpretation,
etc. 1. Bible. N.T. Mark. 1987. II. Title.
III. Series.
BS2585.M23 1987 226′.3077 87-13045
ISBN 0-8007-1544-6

Published by the Fleming H. Revell Company,
Old Tappan, New Jersey 07675
Printed in the United States of America

The God Who Serves

Larry Richards, General Editor

Fleming H. Revell Company
Old Tappan, New Jersey

All Scripture quotations are from the King James Version of the Bible unless otherwise noted.

Scripture quotations identified RV are from the Revised Version of the Bible.

Maclaren, Alexander, 1826–1910.
The God who serves.

(Masters of the Word)
Reprint. Originally published; He came to serve. 1894.
1. Bible. N.T. Mark—Criticism, interpretation, etc. 1. Bible. N.T. Mark. 1987. II. Title. III. Series.
BS2585.M23 1987 226'.3077 87-13045
ISBN 0-8007-1544-6

Published by the Fleming H. Revell Company,
Old Tappan, New Jersey 07675
Printed in the United States of America

Contents

Contents

Introduction

Mark's Gospel vibrates with a sense of urgency and power. This vivid, impetuous narrative, so filled with energy, is clearly, Mark announces, "about Jesus Christ [as] the Son of God" (1:1).

Yet from earliest times Mark's Gospel has troubled readers. Why is the description so clipped and spare? Why hasn't Mark included a fuller report of Jesus' ethical teachings and his parables? Why does the order of the events differ from the order in the other, fuller Gospels?

Papias, around AD 140, answers by saying that Mark reported the teaching of Peter, who "adapted his instruction as necessity required." Peter's telling of Gospel history had pastoral and evangelistic intent. He was not concerned with chronology or "a compilation of the Lord's oracles." This Gospel, then, must not be contrasted with the other three, but should be viewed from the perspective of its special purpose. What distinctives of Mark help us sense the writer's purpose?

First, Mark emphasizes the authority of Jesus. This is done through a straightforward report of Jesus' confrontations with demons, disease, and death. Eighteen miracles of Christ are reported, but only four parables! As the writer boldly describes Christ's acts of power and records Christ's claims, the reader is confronted with evidence that compels response. The Jesus Mark describes is far too bold and vital a figure to be dismissed or ignored.

Second, Mark vividly describes human emotions. He reports the amazement of those who saw what Jesus did (see 1:22; 2:12; 5:20; 9:15). Mark highlights the disciples' failures and puzzlement (see 4:13; 6:52; 8:17; 9:10; 19:26). And Mark emphasizes Jesus' own emotions: his quick compassion (1:41; 8:2); his disgust and anger (1:43; 8:33; 10:14); his moments of sorrow and distress (7:34; 14:33–34). Jesus, the Son of God, is no stranger to the human condition. And, because of who Jesus is, our own response to him is of utmost importance.

Third, the Gospel story as Mark tells it moves quickly, urgently, to its climax in Cross and Resurrection. This may explain the writer's elimination of everything extraneous to his purpose. Peter, whose preaching Mark reflects, intended to confront his listeners with a compelling picture of Jesus as Lord. Yet he hurries, constantly using the word "straightway" (KJV) or "immediately" (RSV/NIV) to carry the reader along with Christ to the cross. As Christ himself emphasizes (8:31; 9:3; 10:33–34), the one God sent into the world hurries toward sure suffering and death.

Mark's portrait of Jesus as one with all authority stands in such contrast to his death that all becomes clear: that death *must* have been purposive. It must have been deliberately planned by God Himself to accomplish a divine purpose.

Understanding these distinctives, we see how appropriately this briefest of Gospels has been shaped by its evangelistic and pastoral intent.

A strong tradition of the Early Church identifies John Mark as the writer of this Gospel. Tradition also suggests that it was written near the end of the Apostle Peter's life (possibly AD 57–59), although another line of tradition assigns it to a date after Peter's death. However, the early church fathers agree that it was written in Rome, and primarily for Gentile believers.

Much evidence within Mark's Gospel supports the accepted view. Jewish customs are explained (see 7:3–4; 15:42), Aramaic expressions are translated for Greek speakers (cf 3:17; 5:41; 9:43; 14:36), and few references to the Old Testament or to prophecy are included. In addition Mark chooses to use the Roman rather than the Jewish terms for timekeeping (see 6:48; 13:35).

Many find evidence that this Gospel was written primarily for Christians in Mark's tendency to explain the meaning for believers of several of Jesus' sayings and actions (see 2:10, 28; 7:19).

Another feature of Mark's Gospel suggests that its pastoral intent is at least as strong as the evangelistic. Again and again Mark portrays the interaction between Jesus and his disciples. In Mark's 16 chapters there are no less than 59 references to the disciples, and many of Christ's recorded words contain instructions to them.

This emphasis may have been especially precious to John Mark himself. As a youth Mark traveled with Paul and Barnabas on their first missionary journey (Acts 12:25; 13:5). But he abandoned the team at Pamphylia (13:13). Later Paul and Barnabas disagreed so intensely about giving Mark another chance that the two friends separated. Paul took another partner. Barnabas took John Mark and set out on his own mission. The tenderhearted Barnabas proved wiser: later John Mark came to be valued by Paul as a trustworthy companion (Colossians 4:10; Philemon 24; 2 Timothy 4:11), and Peter looked on Mark, whom he had known as a child in Jerusalem (Acts 12:12), as a much loved son (1 Peter 5:13).

How significant then this Gospel's blunt portrayal of the faults and failings of the first disciples. And how wonderful the firm commitment of Jesus to teach and train the Twelve. They, like Mark himself, stumbled often. But Jesus, who had died for each, remained faithful. Through growth in relationship with Jesus, any believer—like the Twelve and like John Mark himself—can grow to the place of spiritual victory and full commitment to the Lord.

It is this intent that Alexander Maclaren (1826–1910), the great Scottish expositor, captures in his study of Mark. Maclaren, known for his careful observation of the biblical text and his penetrating analysis, was a pastor as well as a leader of England's Baptist Union and first president of the Baptist World Alliance (1905). Maclaren, whose preaching drew great crowds and whose illustrations drawn from nature and from life have been widely imitated since, examines Mark incident by reported incident, sharing insights and carefully applying all he finds to the lives of contemporary disciples. For all who share the pastoral concern of Mark and his expositor, this work is a practical treasurehouse.

LAWRENCE O. RICHARDS

The God Who Serves

1

The Strong and Gentle Son

What "The Gospel" Is

The beginning of the gospel of Jesus Christ. MARK 1:1.

The word *gospel* is never used in Luke, and only twice in the Acts of the Apostles, both times in quotations. The Apostle John never employs it, either in his "Gospel" or in his epistles, and in the Apocalypse the word is only once found, and then it may be a question whether it refers to the Good News of salvation in Jesus Christ. We search for the expression in vain in the epistles of James, Jude, and to the Hebrews. Thrice it is used by Peter. The great bulk of the instances of its occurrence are in the writings of Paul, who, if not the first to use it, at any rate is the source from which the familiar meaning of the phrase, as describing the sum total of the revelation in Jesus Christ, has flowed.

The various connections in which the word is employed are remarkable and instructive. We can but touch lightly on the more important lessons which they are fitted to teach.

1. The Gospel is the "Gospel of Christ." On our Lord's own lips and in the records of His life we find the phrase "the gospel of the kingdom"—the Good News of the establishment on earth of the rule of God in the hearts and lives of men. The person of the King is not yet defined by it. The diffused dawn floods the sky, and upon them that sit in darkness the greatness of its light shines, before the sun is above the horizon. The message of the forerunner proclaimed, like a herald's clarion, the coming of the Kingdom, before he could say to a more receptive few, "Behold the Lamb of God." The order is first the message of the Kingdom, then the discovery of the King. And so that earlier phrase falls out of use, and when once Christ's life had been lived, and His death died, the Gospel is no longer the message of an impersonal revolution in the world's attitude to God's will, but the biography of Him who is at once first subject and monarch of the Kingdom of Heaven, and by whom alone we are brought into it. The standing expression comes to be "the gospel of Christ."

It is His, not so much because He is the author, as because He is the subject of it. It is the Good News about Christ. He is its contents and great theme. And so we are led up at once to the great central peculiarity of Christianity, namely that it is a record of historical fact, and that all the world's life and blessedness lie in the story of a human life and death. Christ is Christianity. His biography is the Good News for every child of man.

All that the world needs lies in that story. Out of it have come peace and gladness to the soul, light for the understanding, cleansing for the conscience, renovation for the will, which can be made strong and free by submission, a resting place for the heart, and a starting point and a goal for the loftiest flights of hope. Out of it have come the purifying of family and civic life, the culture of all noble social virtues, the sanctity of the household, and the elevation of the state. The thinker has found the largest problems raised and solved therein. The setting forth of a loftier morality, and the enthusiasm which makes the foulest nature aspire to and reach its heaven-touching heights, are found together there. To it poet and painter, architect and musician, owe their noblest themes. The Good News of the world is the story of Christ's life and death. Let us be thankful for its form; let us be thankful for its substance.

2. The Gospel of Christ is the "Gospel of God." This form of the expression, though by no means so frequent as the other, is found throughout Paul's epistles, thrice in the earliest—Thessalonians (1 Thessalonians 2:8), once in the great Epistle to the Romans (1:1), once in Corinthians (2 Corinthians 11:7), and once in a modified form in the pathetic letter from the dungeon, which the old man addressed to his "son Timothy" (1 Timothy 1:11). It is also found in the writings of Peter (1 Peter 4:17). In all these cases the phrase, "the Gospel of God," may mean the Gospel which has God for its author or origin, but it seems rather to mean "which has God for its subject."

It was, as we saw, mainly designated as the Good News about Jesus Christ, but it is also the Good News about God. So in one and the same set of facts we have the history of Jesus and the revelation of God. They are not only the biography of a man, but they are the unveiling of the heart of God. These Scripture writers take it for granted that their readers will understand that paradox, and do not stop to explain how they change the statement of the subject matter of their message, in this extraordinary fashion, between their Master who had lived and died on earth, and the Unseen Almightiness throned above all heavens. How comes that to be?

It is not that the Gospel has two subjects, one of which is the matter of one portion, and the other of another. It does not sometimes speak of

Christ, and sometimes rise to tell us of God. It is always speaking of both, and when its subject is most exclusively the man Christ Jesus, it is then most chiefly the Father God. How comes that to be?

Surely this unconscious shifting of the statement of their theme, which these writers practice as a matter of course, shows us how deeply the conviction had stamped itself on their spirits, "He that hath seen Me hath seen the Father," and how the point of view from which they had learned to look on all the sweet and wondrous story of their Master's life and death, was that of a revelation of the deepest heart of God.

And so must we look on that whole career, from the cradle to the cross, from Calvary to Olivet, if we are to know its deepest tenderness and catch its gladdest notes. That such a man has lived and died is beautiful, and the portrait will hang forever as that of the fairest of the children of men. But that in that life and death we have our most authentic knowledge of what God is, and that all the pity and truth, the gentleness and the brotherliness, the tears and the self-surrender, are a revelation to us of God; and that the cross, with its awful sorrow and its painful death, tells us not only how a man gave himself for those whom he loved, but how God loves the world and how tremendous is His law—this is Good News of God indeed.

3. The Good News of Christ and of God is the Gospel of our salvation and peace. That Good News about Christ and God brings to a man salvation, if he believes it. To know and feel that I have a loving Father who has so cared for me and all my brethren that He has sent His Son to live and die for me, is surely enough to deliver me from all the bonds and death of sin, and to quicken me into humble consecration to His service. And such emancipation from the burden and misery of sin, from the gnawing consciousness of evil and the weakening sense of guilt, from the dominion of wrong tastes and habits, and from the despair of ever shaking them off which is only too well grounded in the experience of the past, is the beginning of salvation for each of us.

Substantially the same set of facts is included under that other expression, "the Gospel of peace." The Hebrew use of the word "peace" as a kind of shorthand for all good is probably to be remembered. But even in the narrower sense of the word, how great are the blessings set forth by it! All inward serenity and outward calm, the tranquility of a soul free from the agitations of emotion and the storms of passions and the tumults of desire, as well as the security of a life guarded from the assaults of foes and girded about with an impregnable barrier which nothing can destroy and no enemy overleap, are ours, if we take the Good News about God to our heart. They are ours in the measure in which we take it. Clearly such truths as those which the Gospel brings have a plain tendency to give peace. They give peace with God, with the world, and with ourselves. They fill the past, the present, and the future with the loving Father's presence, and brighten life and death with the Saviour's footsteps—and so to live is calm, and to die is to lay ourselves down in peace and sleep, quiet by His side, like a child by its mother. The Good News about God and Christ is the Good News of our salvation and of our peace.

4. The Good News about Christ and God is *the* Gospel. This message is emphatically *the* Good News. It is the tidings which men most of all want. It stands alone; there is no other like it. If this is not the glad tidings of great joy for the world, then there are none.

The life and death of Jesus Christ for the sins of the world, His resurrection and continuous life for the saving of the world—these are the truths, without which there can be no Gospel. They may be apprehended in different ways, set forth in different perspective, proclaimed in different dialects, explained in different fashion, associated with different accompaniments, drawn out into different consequences, and yet, through all diversity of tones, the message may be one. Sounded on a ram's horn or a silver trumpet, it may be the same saving and joy-bringing proclamation, and it will be, if Christ and His life and death are plainly set forth as the beginning and ending of all. But if there be an omission of that mighty name, or if a Christ be proclaimed without a Cross, a salvation without a Saviour, or a Saviour without a Sacrifice, all the adornments of genius and sincerity will not prevent such a half-gospel from falling flat. Only when you speak of a Christ who has died for our sins, will you cause the heavy heart of the world to sing for joy. Only that old, old message is the Good News which men want.

There is no second Gospel. There is but one genuine; all others are counterfeits. Our own salvation depends on our firm grasp of that one message, and the clear decisiveness with which our lips ring it out determines whether we shall be blessings or curses to our generation. There is a Babel of voices now preaching other messages which promise good tidings of good. Let us cleave with all our hearts to Christ alone, and let our tongues not falter in proclaiming, "Neither is there salvation in any other." The Gospel of thc Christ who died for our sins, is *the* Gospel.

And what we have for ourselves to do with it is told us in that pregnant phrase of the apostle's, "my Gospel," and "our Gospel"; meaning not merely the message which he was charged to proclaim, but the Good News which he and his brethren had made their own. So we have to make it ours. It is of no use to us, unless we do.

Make it yours by trusting your whole self to the Christ of whom it tells you. The reliance of heart and will on Jesus who has died for me makes it "my Gospel." There is one God, one Christ, one Gospel which tells us of them, and one faith by which we lay hold upon the Gospel, and upon the loving Father and the ever-helpful Saviour of whom it tells.

The Strong Forerunner and the Stronger Son

The beginning of the Gospel of Jesus Christ, the Son of God; 2.
As it is written faith by which we lay holden in the prophets, Behold,
I send My messenger before Thy face, which shall prepare Thy way
before Thee. 3. *The voice of one crying in the wilderness, Prepare*
ye the way of the Lord, make His paths straight. 4. *John did*
baptize in the wilderness and preach the baptism of repentance for
the remission of sins. 5. *And there went out unto him all the land*
of Judea, and they of Jerusalem, and were all baptized of him in the
river of Jordan, confessing their sins. 6. *And John was clothed*
with camel's hair, and with a girdle of a skin about his loins; and he
did eat locusts and wild honey; 7. *And preached, saying, There*
cometh One mightier than I after me, the latchet of whose shoes I am
not worthy to stoop down and unloose. 8. *I indeed have baptized*
you with water; but He shall baptize you with the Holy Ghost. 9.
And it came to pass in those days, that Jesus came from Nazareth of
Galilee, and was baptized of John in Jordan. 10. *And straightway*
coming up out of the water, He saw the heavens opened, and the
Spirit like a dove descending upon Him: 11. *And there came a*
voice from heaven, saying, Thou art My beloved Son, in whom I am
well pleased. MARK 1:1–11.

The theme of Mark's Gospel is the "strong Son of God" whom he sets forth in his rapid, impetuous narrative. His theme is not the King, as in Matthew; nor the Son of Man, as in Luke; nor the eternal Word manifested in flesh, as in John. Therefore he neither begins by tracing His kingly lineage, as does the first evangelist; nor by dwelling on the humanities of wedded life and the sacredness of the family since He has been born; nor by soaring to the abysses of the eternal abiding of the Word with God, as the agent of creation, the medium of life and light; but plunges at once into his subject, and begins the Gospel with the mission of the forerunner, which melts immediately into the appearance of the Son.

Mark considers that *John's mission* is the beginning of the Gospel. Here are two noteworthy points,—his use of that well-worn word, "the Gospel," and his view of John's place in relation to it. The Gospel is the narrative of the facts of Christ's life and death. The very name "Good News" necessarily implies that the Gospel is, primarily, history; but we cannot exclude from the meaning of the word the statement of the significance of the facts, without which the facts have no message of blessing. Mark adds the dogmatic element when he defines the subject of the Gospel as being "Jesus Christ, the Son of God." In the remainder of the book the simple name "Jesus" is used; but here, in starting, the full, solemn title is given, which unites the contemplation of Him in His manhood, in His office as fulfiller of prophecy and crown of revelation, and in His mysterious, divine nature.

Whether we regard verses 2 and 3 as connected grammatically with the preceding or the following verses, they equally refer to John, and define his position in relation to the Gospel. The Revised Version restores the true reading, "in Isaiah the prophet," which some unwise and timid transcriber has, as he thought, mended into "the prophets," for fear that an error should be found in Scripture. Of course, verse 2 is not Isaiah's, but Malachi's; but verse 3, which is Isaiah's, was uppermost in Mark's mind, and his quotation of Malachi is, apparently, an afterthought, and is plainly merely introductory of the other, on which the stress lies. The remarkable variation in the Malachi quotation, which occurs in all three Evangelists, shows how completely they recognized the divinity of our Lord, in their making words which, in the original, are addressed by Jehovah to Himself, to be addressed by the Father to the Son. There is a difference in the representation of the office of the forerunner in the two prophetic passages. In the former he himself prepares the way of the coming Lord; in the latter he calls upon his hearers to prepare it. In fact, John prepared the way, as we shall see presently, just by calling on men to do so. In Mark's view, the first stage in the Gospel is the mission of John. He might have gone further back—to the work of prophets of old, or to the earliest beginnings in time of the self-revelation of God, as the writer of the Epistle to the Hebrews does; or he might have ascended even higher up the stream—to the true "beginning," from which the fourth Evangelist starts. But his distinctly practical genius leads him to fix his gaze on the historical fact of John's mission, and to claim for it a unique position, which he proceeds to develop.

So we have, next, the strong servant and forerunner (verses 4–8). The abruptness with which the curtain is drawn, and the gaunt figure of the desert-loving ascetic shown us, is very striking. It is like the way in which Elijah, his prototype, leaps, as it were, full-armed, into the arena. The parallel passage in Matthew links his appearance with the events which it has been narrating by the phrase "in these days," and calls him "the Baptist." Mark has no such words, but lets him stand forth in his isolation. The two accounts may profitably be compared. Their likenesses suggest that they rest on a common basis, probably of oral tradition, while their differences are, for the most part, significant. Mark differs in his arrangement of the common matter, in omissions, and in some variations of expression. Each account gives a general summary of John's teaching at the beginning; but Matthew puts emphasis on the Baptist's proclamation that the kingdom of heaven was at hand, to which nothing in Mark corresponds. His Gospel does not dwell on the royalty of Jesus, but rather represents Him as the Servant than as the King. Mark begins with describing John as baptizing, which only appears later in Matthew's account. Mark omits all reference to the Sadducees and Pharisees, and to John's sharp words to them. He has nothing about the axe laid to the trees, nothing about the children of Abraham, nothing about the fan in the hand of the great Husbandman. All the theocratic aspect of the Messiah, as proclaimed by John, is absent; and, as there is no reference to the fire which destroys, so neither is there to the fire of the Holy Ghost, in which He baptizes. Mark reports only John's preaching and baptism of repentance, and his testimony to Christ as stronger than he, and as baptizing with the Holy Ghost.

So, on the whole, Mark's picture brings out prominently the following traits in John's personality and mission: First, his preparation for Christ by preaching repentance. The truest way to create in men a longing for Jesus, and to lead to a true apprehension of His unique gift to mankind, is to evoke the penitent consciousness of sin. The preacher of guilt and repentance is the herald of the bringer of pardon and purity. That is true in reference to the relation of Judaism and Christianity, of John and Jesus, and is as true today as ever it was. The root of maimed conceptions of the work and nature of Jesus Christ is a defective sense of sin. When men are roused to believe in judgment, and to realize their own evil, they are ready to listen to the blessed news of a Saviour from sin and its curse. The Christ whom John heralds is the Christ that men need; the Christ whom men receive, without having been out in the wilderness with the stern preacher of sin and judgment, is but half a Christ—and it is the vital half that is missing.

Again, Mark brings out John's personal asceticism. He omits much; but he could not leave out the picture of the grim, lean solitary, who stalked among soft-robed men, like Elijah come to life again, and held the crowds by his self-chosen privations no less than by his fierce, fiery eloquence. His desert life and contempt for ease and luxury spoke of a strength of character and purpose which fascinated commoner men, and make the next point the more striking—namely, the utter humility with which this strong, self-reliant, fiery rebuker of sin, and despiser of rank and official dignities, flings himself at the feet of the coming One. He is strong, as his life and the awestruck crowds testified; how strong must that Other be! He feared not the face of man, nor owned inferiority to any; but his whole soul melted into joyful submission, and confessed unworthiness even to unlace the sandals of that mightier One. His transitional position is also plainly marked by our Evangelist. He is the end of prophecy, the beginning of the Gospel, belonging to neither and to both. He is not merely a prophet, for he is prophesied of as well; and he stands so near Him whom he foretells, that his prediction is almost fact. He is not an Evangelist, nor, in the closest sense, a servant of the coming Christ; for his lowly confession of unworthiness does not imply merely his humility, but accurately defines the limits of his function. It was not for him to bear or to loose that Lord's sandals. There were those who did minister to Him, and the least of those, whose message to the world was "Christ has come," had the honor of closer service than that greatest among women-born, whose task was to run before the chariot of the King and tell that He was at hand.

We have the gentle figure of the stronger Son. The introduction of Jesus is somewhat less abrupt than that of John; but if we remember whom Mark believed Him to be, the quiet words which tell of His first appearance are sufficiently remarkable. There is no mention of His birth or previous years. His deeds will tell who He is. The years before His baptism were of no moment for Mark's purpose. Nor has he any report of the precious conversation of Jesus with John, when the forerunner testified to Christ's purity, which needed no washing nor repentance, and acknowledged at once his own sinfulness and the Lord's cleansing power, and when Christ accepted the homage, and, by implication, claimed the character, purity, and power which John attributed to Him. The omission may be accounted for on a principle which seems to run through all this Gospel—of touching lightly or omitting indications of our Lord's dignity, and dwelling by preference on His acts of lowliness and service. The baptism is recorded; but the conversation, which showed that the King of Israel, in submitting to it, acknowledged no need of it for Himself, but regarded it as "fulfilling righteousness," is passed by. The sinlessness of Jesus, and the special meaning of His baptism, are sufficiently shown by the descending Spirit and the approving voice. These Mark does record; for they warrant the great name by which, in his first verse, he has described Jesus as "the Son of God."

The brief account of these is marked by the Evangelist's vivid pictorial faculty, which we shall frequently have to notice as we read his Gospel. Here he puts us, by a word, in the position of eyewitnesses of the scene as it is passing, when he describes the heavens as "being rent asunder"—

a much more forcible and pictorial word than Matthew's "opened." He says nothing of John's share in the vision. All is intended for the Son. It is Jesus who sees the rending heavens and the descending dove. The voice which Matthew represents as speaking *of* Christ, Mark represents as speaking *to* Him.

The baptism of Jesus, then, was an epoch in His own consciousness. It was not merely His designation to John or to others as Messiah, but for Himself the sense of Sonship and the sunlight of divine complacency filled His spirit in new measure or manner. Speaking as we have to do from the outside, and knowing but dimly the mysteries of His unqiue personality, we have to speak modestly and little. But we know that our Lord grew, as to His manhood, in wisdom, and that His manhood was continually the receiver, from the Father, of the Spirit; and the reality of His divinity, as dwelling in His manhood from the beginning of that manhood, is not affected by the belief that when the dovelike Spirit floated down on His meek head, glistening with the water of baptism. His manhood then received a new and special consciousness of His Messianic office and of His Sonship.

While that voice was for His sake, it was for others too; for John himself tells us (John 1) that the sign had been told him beforehand, and that it was his sight of the descending dove which heightened his thoughts and gave a new turn to his testimony, leading him to know and to show "that this is the Son of God." The rent heavens have long since closed, and that dread voice is silent; but the fact of that attestation remains on record, that we, too, may hear through the centuries God speaking of and to His Son, and may lay to heart the commandment to us, which naturally follows God's witness to Jesus, "Hear ye Him."

The symbol of the dove may be regarded as a prophecy of the gentleness of the Son. Thus early in His course the two qualities were harmonized in Him, which so seldom are united, and each of which dwelt in Him in divinest perfection, both as to degree and manner. John's anticipations of the strong coming One looked for the manifestations of His strength in judgment and destruction. How strangely his images of the axe, the fan, the fire, are contrasted with the reality, emblemed by this dove dropping from heaven, with sunshine on its breast and peace in its still wings! Through the ages, Christ's strength has been the strength of gentleness, and His coming has been like that of Noah's dove, with the olive branch in its beak, and the tidings of an abated flood and of a safe home in its return. The ascetic preacher of repentance was strong to shake and purge men's hearts by terror; but the stronger Son comes to conquer by meekness, and reign by the omnipotence of love. The beginning of the Gospel was the anticipation and the proclamation of strength like the eagle's, swift of flight, and powerful to strike and destroy. The Gospel, when it became a fact, and not a hope, was found in the meek Jesus, with the dove of God, the gentle Spirit, which is mightier than all, nestling in His heart, and uttering soft notes of invitation through His lips.

Mighty in Word and Deed

And they went into Capernaum; and straightway on the Sabbath day He entered into the synagogue, and taught. 22. And they were astonished at His doctrine: for He taught them as one that had authority, and not as the scribe. 23. And there was in their synagogue a man with an unclean spirit; and he cried out, 24. Saying, Let us alone; what have we to do with Thee, Thou Jesus of Nazareth? art Thou come to destroy us? I know Thee who Thou art, the Holy One of God. 25. And Jesus rebuked him, saying, Hold thy peace, and come out of him. 26. And when the unclean spirit had torn him, and cried with a loud voice, he came out of him. 27. And they were all amazed, insomuch that they questioned among themselves, saying, What thing is this? what new doctrine is this? for with authority commandeth He even the unclean spirits, and they do obey Him. 28. And immediately His fame spread abroad throughout all the region round about Galilee. 29. And forthwith, when they were come out of the synagogue, they entered into the house of Simon and Andrew, with James and John. 30. But Simon's wife's mother lay sick of a fever, and anon they tell Him of her. 31. And He came and took her by the hand, and lifted her up; and immediately the fever left her, and she ministered unto them. 32. And at even, when the sun did set, they brought unto Him all that were diseased, and them that were possessed with devils. 33. And all the city was gathered together at the door. 34. And He healed many that were sick of divers diseases, and cast out many devils; and suffered not the devils to speak, because they knew Him. MARK 1:21–34.

None of the incidents in this section are peculiar to Mark, but the special stamp of his Gospel is on them all; and, both in the narration of each and in the swift transition from one to another, the impression of Christ's strength and unpausing diligence in filial service is made. The short hours of that first Sabbath's ministry are crowded with work; and Christ's energy bears Him through exhausting physical labors, and enables Him to turn with unwearied sympathy and marvelous celerity to each new form of misery, and to throw Himself with freshness undiminished into the relief of each. The homely virtue of diligence shines out in this lesson no less clearly than superhuman strength that tames demons and heals all manner of sickness. There are four pictures here, compressed and yet vivid. Mark can condense and keep all the essentials, for his keen eye and sure hand go straight to the heart of his incidents.

1. The strong Son of God teaching with authority. They enter; we see the little group, consisting of Jesus and of the two pairs of brothers, in whose hearts the mighty conviction of His Messiahship had taken root. Simon and Andrew were at home in Capernaum; but we may, perhaps, infer from the manner in which the sickness of Peter's wife's mother is mentioned, that Peter had not been to his house till after the synagogue service. At all events, these four were already detached from ordinary life and bound to Him as disciples. We meet here with our first instance of Mark's favorite "straightway," the recurrence of which, in this chapter, so powerfully helps the impression of eager and yet careful swiftness with which Christ ran His course, "unhasting, unresting." From the beginning Mark stamps his story with the spirit of our Lord's own words, "I must work the works of Him that sent me, while it is day: the night cometh." And yet there is no hurry, but the calm, equable rapidity with which planets move. The unostentatious manner of Christ's beginning is noteworthy. He seeks to set Himself in the line of the ordinary teaching of the day. He knew all the faults of the synagogue and the rabbis, and He had come to revolutionize the very conception of religious teaching and worship; but He prefers to intertwine the new with the old, and to make as little disturbance as possible. It is easy to get the cheap praise of "originality" by brushing aside existing methods. It is harder and nobler to use whatever methods may be going, and to breathe new value and life into them. Drowsy, hair-splitting disputations about nothings and endless casuistry were the staple of the synagogue talk; but when He opened His mouth there, the weary formalism went out of the service, and men's hearts glowed again when they once more heard a Voice that lived, speaking from a Soul that saw the invisible. Mark has no mission to record many of our Lord's sayings. His Gospel deals more with deeds. The sermon he does not give, but the hearer's comment he does. Matthew has the same words at the close of the Sermon on the Mount, from which it would seem that they were part of the oral tradition which underlies the written Gospels; but Mark probably has them in their right place. Very naturally, the first synagogue discourse in Capernaum would surprise. Deeper impressions might be made by its successors, but the first hearing of that voice would be an experience that could never be repeated.

The feature of His teaching which astonished the villagers most was its "authority." That fits in with the impression of strength which Mark wishes to make. Another thing that struck them was its unlikeness to the type of synagogue teaching to which they had been accustomed all their lives. They had got so accustomed to the droning dreariness and trivial subtleties of the rabbis, that it had never entered their heads that there could be any other way of teaching religion than boring men with interminable pedantries about trifles of ritual or outward obedience. This new Teacher would startle all, as an eagle suddenly appearing in a Sanhedrin of owls. He would shock many; He would fascinate a few. Nor was it only the dissimilarity of His teaching, but also its authority, that was strange. The scribes spoke with authority enough of a sort lording it over the despised common people—"men of the earth," as they called them—and exacting punctilious obedience and much obsequiousness; but authority over the spirit they had none. They pretended to no power but as expositors of a law; and they fortified themselves by citations of what this, that, and the other rabbi had said, which was all their learning. Christ quoted no one. He did not even say, "Moses has said." He did not even preface His commands with a "Thus saith the Lord." He spoke of His own authority: "Verily, I say unto you." Other teachers explained the law; He is a lawgiver. Others drew more or less pure waters from cisterns; He is in Himself a well of water, from which all may draw. To us, as to these rude villagers in the synagogue of the little fishing-town, Christ's teaching is unique in this respect. He does not argue; He affirms. He seeks no support from others' teachings; He alone is sufficient for us. He not only speaks the truth, which needs no other confirmation than His own lips, but He is the truth. We may canvas other men's teachings, and distinguish their insight from their errors; we have but to accept His. The world outgrows all others; it can only grow up towards the fullness of His. Us and all the ages He teaches with authority, and the guarantee for the truth of His teaching is Himself. "Verily, verily, I say unto you." No other man has a right to say that to me. But Christ dominates the race, and the strong Son of God is the world's Teacher.

2. The strong conqueror of demons. Again we have "straightway." The language seems to imply that this wretched sufferer burst hurriedly into the synagogue and interrupted the utterance of astonishment by giving it new good. Perhaps the double consciousness of the demoniac may be recognized, the humanity being drawn to Jesus by some disturbed longings, the demoniac consciousness, on the other hand, being repelled. It is no part of my purpose to discuss demon possession. I content myself with remarking that I, for one, do not see how Christ's credit as a divine Teacher is to be saved without admitting its reality, nor how such phenomena as the demoniac's knowledge of His nature are to be accounted for on the hypothesis of disease or insanity. It is assuming rather too encyclopediacal a knowledge to allege the impossibility of such possession. There are facts enough around us still, which would be at least as satisfactorily accounted for by it as by natural causes; but as to the incident before us, Mark puts it all into three sentences, each of which is pregnant with suggestions. There is, first, the demoniac's shriek of hatred and despair. Christ had said nothing. If, as we suppose, the man had broken in on the worship, drawn to Jesus, he is no sooner in His presence than the other power that darkly lodged in him overpowers him, and pours out fierce passions from his reluctant lips. There is a dreadful meaning in the preposition here used, "a man in an unclean spirit," as if his human self was immersed in that filthy flood. The words embody three thoughts—the fierce hatred which disowns all connection with Jesus; the wild terror, which asks or affirms Christ's destructive might over all foul spirits (for the "us" means not the man and the demon, but the demon and his fellows); and the recognition of Christ's holiness, which lashes unholiness into a paroxysm of mingled despair and hate. Does this sound like a madman, or an epileptic, or like a spirit which knew more than men knew, and trembled and hated more than they could do? There is nothing more terrible than the picture, self-drawn in these spasmodic words, of a spirit which, by its very foulness, is made shudderingly sensitive to the disturbing presence of purity, and would fain have nothing to do with Him whom it recognizes for the Holy One of God, and therefore its destroyer. Foul things that lurk under stones hurry out of the light when you lift the covering. Spirits that love the darkness are hurt by the light. It is possible to recognize Jesus for what He is, and to hate Him all the more. What a miserable state that is, to hope that we shall have nothing to do with Him! These wild utterances, seething with evil passions and fierce detestation, do point to the possible terminus for men. A black gulf opens in them, from which we are meant to start back with the prayer, "Preserve me from going down into that pit!"

What a contrast to the tempest of the demoniac's wild and whirling words is the calm speech of Christ! He knows His authority, and His word is imperative, curt, and assured: "Hold thy peace!" literally, "Be muzzled," as if the creature were a dangerous beast, whose raving and snapping must be stopped. Jesus wishes no acknowledgments from such lips. They who bear the vessels of the Lord must be clean. He had taught with authority, and now He in like manner commands. His teaching rested on His own assurance. His miracle is done by His own power. That power is put forth by His simple word; that is to say, the bare exercise or expression of His will is potent.

The third step in the narrative is the immediate obedience of the demon. Reluctant but compelled, malicious to the last, doing the house which he has to leave all the harm he can, and though no longer venturing to speak, yet venting his rage and mortification, and acknowledging his defeat by one parting howl, he comes out.

Again, we are bid to note the impression produced. The interrupted buzz of talk begins once more, and is vividly reported by the fragmentary sentences of verse 27, and by the remark that it was "among themselves" that they compared notes. Two things startled the people: first, the "new teaching"; and second, the authority over demons, into which they naturally generalize the one instance. The busy tongues were not silenced when they left the synagogue. Verse 28 shows what happened, in one direction, when the meeting broke up. With another "straightway," Mark paints the swift flight of the rumor over all the district, and somewhat overleaps the strict line of chronology, to let us hear how far the echo of such a blow sounded. This first miracle recorded by him is as a duel between Christ and the "strong man armed," who "keeps his house." The shield of the great oppressor is first struck in challenge by the champion, and His first essay at arms proves Him mightiest. Such a victory well heads the chronicle.

3. The tenderness of the strong Son. We come back to the strict order of succession with another "straightway," which opens a very different scene. The Authorized Version gives three "straightways" in the three verses as to the cure of Peter's mother-in-law. "Immediately" they go to the house; "immediately" they tell Jesus of her; "immediately" the fever leaves her; and even if we omit the third of these, as the Revised Version does, we cannot miss the rapid haste of the narrative, which reflects the unwearied energy of the Master. Peter and Andrew had apparently been ignorant of the sickness till they reached the house, from which the inference is not that it was a slight attack which had come on after they went to the synagogue, but that the two disciples had so really left house and kindred, that though in Capernaum, they had not gone home till they took Jesus there for rest and quiet and food after the toil of the morning. The owners would naturally first know of the sickness, which would interfere with their hospitable purpose; and so Mark's account seems more near the details than Matthew's, inasmuch as the former says that Jesus was "told" of the sick woman, while Matthew's version is that He "saw" her. Luke says that they "besought Him for her." No doubt that was the meaning of "telling" Him; but Mark's representation brings out very beautifully the confidence already beginning to spring in their hearts that He needed but to know in order to heal, and the reverence which hindered them from direct asking. The instinct of the devout heart is to tell Christ all its troubles, great or small; and He does not need beseeching before He answers. He did not need to be told either, but He would not rob them or us of the solace of confiding all griefs to Him.

Their confidence was not misplaced. No moment intervened unused between the tidings and the cure. "He came," as if He had been in some outer room, or not yet in the house, and now passed into the sick chamber. Then comes one of Mark's minute and graphic details, in which we may see the keen eye and faithful memory of Peter. He "took her by the hand, and lifted her up." Mark is fond of telling of Christ's taking by the hand; as, for instance, the little child whom He set in the midst, the blind man whom He healed, the child with the dumb spirit. His touch has power. His grasp means sympathy, tenderness, identification of Himself with us, the communication of upholding, restoring strength. It is a picture, in a small matter, of the very heart of the Gospel. "He layeth not hold of angels, but He layeth hold of the seed of Abraham." It is a lesson for all who would help their fellows, that they must not be too dainty to lay hold of the dirtiest hand, both metaphorically and literally, if they want their sympathy to be believed. His hand banishes not only the disease, but its consequences. Immediate convalescence and restoration to strength follow; and the strength is used, as it should be, in ministering to the Healer who, notwithstanding His power, needed the humble ministration and the poor fare of the fisherman's hut. What a lesson for all Christian homes is here! Let Jesus know all that troubles them, welcome Him as a guest, tell Him everything, and He will cure all diseases and sorrows, or give the light of His presence to make them endurable. Consecrate to Him the strength which He gives, and let deliverances teach trust, and inflame grateful love, which delights in serving Him who needs no service but delights in all.

4. The strong Son, unwearied by toil and sufficient for all the needy. Each incident in this lesson has a note appended of the impression it made. Verses 32–34 give the united result of all, on the people of Capernaum. They wait till the Sabbath is past, and then, without thought of His long day of work, crowd round the house with their sick. The sinking sun brought no rest for Him, but the new calls found Him neither exhausted nor unwilling. Capernaum was but a little place, and the whole city might well be "gathered together at the door," some sick, some bearing the sick, all curious and eager. There was no depth in the excitement. There was earnestness enough, no doubt, in the wish for healing, but there was no insight into His message. Any travelling missionary with a medicine chest can get the same kind of following. These people, who hung upon Him thus, were those of whom He had afterwards to say that it would be "more tolerable for Sodom, in the day of judgment, than for them." But though He knew the shallowness of the impression, He was not deaf to the misery; and, with power which knew no weariness, and sympathy which had no limit, and a reservoir of healing virtue which the day's draughts had not emptied by a hairsbreadth, He healed them all. Remarkable is the prohibition of the demons' speech. They knew Him, while men were ignorant; for they had met Him before today. He would have no witness from them; not merely, as has been said, because their attestation would hinder, rather than further, His acceptance by the people, nor because they may be supposed to have spoken in malice, but because a divine decorum forbade that He should accept acknowledgments from such tainted sources.

So ended this first of "the days of the Son of Man," which our Evangelist records. It was a day of hard toil, of merciful and manifold self-revelation. As teacher and doer, in the synagogue, and in the home, and in the city; as Lord of the dark realms of evil and of disease; as ready to hear hinted and dumb prayers, and able to answer them all; as careless of His own ease, and ready to spend Himself for others' help,—Jesus showed Himself, on that Sabbath day, strong and tender, the Son of God and the servant of men.

Healing and Service

Simon's wife's mother lay sick of a fever; and straightway they tell Him of her: 31. And He came and took her by the hand, and raised her up; and the fever left her, and she ministered unto them. MARK 1:30, 31 RV.

This miracle is told us by three of the four Evangelists, and the comparison of their brief narratives is very interesting and instructive. We all know, I suppose, that the common tradition is that Mark was, in some sense, Peter's mouthpiece in this Gospel. The truthfulness of that ancient statement is borne out by little morsels of evidence that crop up here and there throughout the Gospel. There is one of them in this context. The other two Evangelists tell us that our Lord, with His four attendant disciples, "entered into the house of Simon"; Mark knows that Simon's brother Andrew shared the house with him. Who was likely to have told him such an insignificant thing as that? We seem to hear the Apostle himself recounting the whole story to his amanuensis.

Then, further, Mark's narrative is distinguished from that of the other two Evangelists in very minute and yet interesting points, which will come out as we go along. So I think we may fairly say that we have here Peter himself telling us the story of his mother-in-law's cure. Now, one thing that strikes one is that this is a very small miracle. It is by no means—if we can apply the words "great" and "small" to these miraculous events—one of the more striking and significant. Another point to note is that it was done evidently without the slightest intention of vindicating Christ's mission, or of preaching any truth whatever, and so it starts up into a new beauty as being simply and solely a manifestation of His love. I think, when some people are so busy in denying, and others in proving, the miraculous element in Scripture, and others in drawing doctrinal or symbolical lessons out of it, that there is great need to emphasize this, that the first thing about all Christ's miracles, and most conspicuously about this one, is that they were the welling out of His loving heart which responded to the sight of human sorrow—I was going to say instinctively; but I will find a better word, and say divinely. The deed that had no purpose whatsoever except to lighten the burden upon a disciple's heart, and to heal the passing physical trouble of one poor old woman is great, just because it is small; and full of teaching, although to the superficial eye, it teaches nothing.

The first thing in the story is, as it seems to me—

1. The disciple's intercession. I wonder if Peter knew that his wife's mother was ill, when he said to Jesus Christ, after that exciting morning in the synagogue, "Come home, and rest in our house"? Probably not. One can scarcely imagine hospitality proffered under such circumstances, or with a knowledge of them. And if we look a little more closely into the preceding narrative we shall see that it is at least possible that Peter and his brother had been away from home for some time; so that the old woman might easily have fallen ill during their temporary absence. But be that as it may, they expect to find rest and food, and they find a sick woman.

There must have been at least two rooms in that humble house, because they "come to Jesus Christ and tell Him of her." Now if we turn to the other Evangelists, we shall find that Matthew says nothing about any message being communicated to Jesus, but brings Him at once, as it were, to the side of the sickbed. That is evidently an incomplete account. And then we find in Luke's Gospel that, instead of the simple "tell Him of her" of Mark, he intensifies the telling into "they besought Him for her." Now, I think that Mark's is plainly the more precise story, because he lets us see that Jesus Christ did not commit such a breach of courtesy, due to the humblest home, as to go to the woman's bedside without being summoned, and he also lets us see that the "beseeching" was a simple intimation to Him. They did not ask; they tell Him; being, perhaps, restrained from definite petitioning partly by reverence, and partly, no doubt, by hesitation in these early days of their discipleship—for this incident occurred at the very beginning, when all the subsequent manifestations of His character were yet waiting to be flashed upon them—as to whether it might be in accordance with their new Teacher's very little known disposition and mind to help. They knew that He could, because He had just healed a demoniac in the synagogue, but one can understand how, at the beginning of their discipleship, there was a little faltering of confidence as to whether they should go so far as to ask Him to do such a thing. So they "tell Him of her," and do you not think that the tone of petition vibrated in the intimation, and that there looked out of the eyes of the impulsive, warmhearted Peter, an unspoken prayer? So Luke was perfectly right in his interpretation of the incident, though not precise in his statement of the external fact, when, instead of saying "they tell Him of her," he translated that telling into what it meant, and put it, "they besought Him for her."

Ah! dear brethren, there are a great many things in our lives which, though we ought to know Jesus Christ better than the first disciples at first did, scarcely seem to us fit to be turned into subjects of petition, partly because we have wrong notions as to the sphere and limits of prayer, and partly because they seem to be such transitory things that it is a shame to trouble Him about such insignificant matters. Well, go and tell Him, at any rate. I do not think that Christians ought to have anything in their heads or hearts that they do not take to Jesus Christ, and it is an uncommonly good test—and one very easily applied—of our hopes, fears, purposes, thoughts, deeds, and desires—"Should I like to go and make a clean breast of it to the Master?"

"They tell Him of her," and that meant petition, and Jesus Christ can interpret an unspoken petition, and an unexpressed desire appeals to His sympathetic heart. Although the words be but "O Lord! I am troubled, perplexed; and I do not know what to do," He translates them into "Calm Thou me; enlighten Thou me; guide Thou me"; and be sure of this, that as in the story before us, so in our lives, He will answer the unspoken petition in so far as may be best for us.

The next thing to note in this incident is—

2. The Healer's method. There again, the three stories diverge, and yet are all one. Matthew says, "He touched her"; Luke says, "He *stood*"—or rather, as the Greek means, "He *bent over her*—and rebuked the fever." Perhaps Peter was close to the pallet, and saw and remembered that there were not a standing over and rebuking the fever only, but that there was the going out of His tender sympathy to the sufferer, and that if there were stern words as of indignation and authority addressed to the disease as if to an unlawful intruder, there were also compassion and tenderness for the victim. For Mark tells that it was not a touch only, but that "He took her by the hand and lifted her up," and the grasp banished sickness and brought strength.

Now the most precious of the lessons that we can gather from the variety of Christ's methods of healing is this: that all methods which He used were in themselves equally powerless, and that the curative virtue was in neither the word nor the touch, nor the spittle, nor the clay, nor the bathing in the pool of Siloam, but was purely and simply in the outgoing of His will. The reasons for the wonderful variety of ways in which He communicated His healing power are to be sought partly in the respective moral, and spiritual, and intellectual condition of the people to be healed, and partly in wider reasons and considerations. Why did He stoop and touch the woman, and take her by the hand and gently lift her up? Because His heart went out to her, because He felt the emotion and sympathy which makes the whole world kin, and because His heart was a heart of love, and bade Him come into close contact with the poor fever-ridden woman. Unless we regard that hand-clasp as being such an instinctive attitude and action of Christ's sympathetic love, we lose the deepest significance of it. And then, when we have given full weight to that, the simplest and yet the most blessed of all the thoughts that cluster round the deed, we can venture further to say that in that small matter we see mirrored, as a wide sweep of country in a tiny mirror, or the sun in a bowl of water, the great truth: "He took not hold of angels, but He took hold of the seed of Abraham, wherefore it behoved Him to be made in all things like unto His brethren." The touch upon the fevered hand of that old woman in Capernaum was as a condensation into one act of the very principle of the Incarnation and of the whole power which Christ exercises upon a fevered and sick world. For it is by His touch, by His lifting hand, by His sympathetic grasp, and by our real contact with Him, that all our sicknesses are banished, and health and strength come to our souls.

So let us learn a lesson for our own guidance. We can do no man any real good unless we make ourselves one with him, and benefits that we bestow will hurt rather than help, if they are flung down upon men as from a height, or as people cast a bone to a dog. The heart must go with them; and identification with the sufferer is a condition of succor. If we would take lepers and blind beggars and poor old women by the hand—I mean, of course, by giving them our sympathy along with our help—we should see larger results from, and be more Christ-like in, our deeds of beneficence.

The last point is—

3. The healed sufferer's service. "She arose"—yes, of course she did, when Christ grasped her. How could she help it? "And she ministered to them,"—how could she help that either, if she had any thankfulness in her heart? What a lovely, glad, awestricken meal that would be, to which they all sat down in Simon's house, on that Sabbath night, as the sun was setting! It was a humble household. There were no servants in it. The convalescent old woman had to do all the ministering herself, and that she was able to do it was, of course, as everybody remarks on reading the narrative, the sign of the completeness of the cure. But it was a great deal more than that. How could she sit still and not minister to Him who had done so much for her? And if you and I, dear friends, have any living apprehension of Christ's healing power, and understand and respond at all to "that for which we have been laid hold of" by Him, our thankfulness will take the same shape, and we, too, shall become His servants. Up yonder, amidst the blaze of the glory, He is still capable of being ministered to by us. The woman who did so on earth had no monopoly of this sacred office, but it continues still. And every housewife, as she goes about her duties, and every domestic servant, as she moves round her mistress's dinner table, and all of us, in our secular avocations, as people call them, may indeed serve Christ, if only we have regard to Him in the doing of them. There is also a yet higher sense in which that ministration, incumbent upon all the healed, and spontaneous on their part if they have truly been recipients of the healing grace, is still possible for us. "When saw we Thee . . . in need . . . and served Thee?" "Inasmuch as ye did it unto one of the least of these My brethren, ye did it unto Me."

A Parable in a Miracle

And there came a leper to Him, beseeching Him, and kneeling down to Him, and saying unto Him, If Thou wilt, Thou canst make me clean. 41. And Jesus, moved with compassion, put forth His hand, and touched him, and saith unto him, I will; be thou clean. 42. And as soon as He had spoken, immediately the leprosy departed from him, and he was cleansed. MARK 1:40–42.

Christ's miracles are called wonders—that is, deeds which, by their exceptional character, arrest attention and excite surprise. Further, they are called "mighty works"—that is, exhibitions of superhuman power. They are still further called "signs"—that is, tokens of His divine mission. But they are signs in another sense, being, as it were, parables as well as miracles, and representing on the lower plane of material things the effects of His working on men's spirits. Thus, His feeding of the hungry speaks of His higher operation as the Bread of Life. His giving sight to the blind foreshadows His illumination of darkened minds. His healing of the diseased speaks of His restoration of sick souls. His stilling of the tempest tells of Him as the Peacebringer for troubled hearts; and His raising of the dead proclaims Him as the Lifegiver, who quickens with the true life all who believe on Him. This parabolic aspect of the miracles is obvious in the case before us. Leprosy received exceptional treatment under the Mosaic law, and the peculiar restrictions to which the sufferer was subjected, as well as the ritual of his cleansing, in the rare cases where the disease wore itself out, are best explained by being considered as symbolic rather than as sanitary. It was taken as an emblem of sin. Its hideous symptoms, its rotting sores, its slow, stealthy, steady progress, its defiance of all known means of cure, made its victim only too faithful a walking image of that worse disease. Remembering this deeper aspect of leprosy, let us study this miracle before us, and try to gather its lessons.

1. First, then, notice the leper's cry. Mark connects the story with our Lord's first journey through Galilee, which was signalized by many miracles, and had excited much stir and talk. The news of the Healer had reached the isolated huts where the lepers herded, and had kindled a spark of hope in one poor wretch, which emboldened him to break through all regulations, and thrust his tainted and unwelcome presence into the shrinking crowd. He seems to have appeared there suddenly, having forced or stolen his way somehow into Christ's presence. And there he was, with his horrible white face, with his tightened, glistening skin, with some frowsy rag over his mouth, and a hunted look as of a wild beast in his eyes. The crowd shrank back from him; he had no difficulty in making his way to where Christ is sitting, calmly teaching. And Mark's vivid narrative shows him to us, flinging himself down before the Lord, and, without waiting for question or pause, interrupting whatever was going on, with his piteous cry. Misery and wretchedness make short work of conventional politeness.

Note the keen sense of misery that impels to the passionate desire for relief. A leper with the flesh dropping off his bones could not suppose that there was nothing the matter with him. His disease was too gross and palpable not to be felt; and the depth of misery measured the earnestness of desire. The parallel fails us there. The emblem is all insufficient, for here is the very misery of our deepest misery, that we are unconscious of it, and sometimes even come to love it. There are forms of sickness in which the man goes about, and to each inquiry says, "I am perfectly well," though everybody else can see death written on his face. And so it is with this terrible malady that has laid its corrupting and putrefying finger upon us all. The worse we are, the less we know that there is anything the matter with us; and the deeper the leprosy has struck its filthy fangs into us, the more ready we are to say that we are sound. We preachers have it for one of our first duties to try to rouse men to the recognition of the facts of their spiritual condition, and all our efforts are too often—as I, for my part, sometimes half-despairingly feel when I stand in the pulpit—like a firebrand dropped into a pond, which hisses for a moment and then is extinguished. Men and women sit in pews listening contentedly and quietly, who, if they saw themselves, I do not say even as God sees them, but as others see them, would know that the leprosy is deep in them, and the taint patent to every eye. I do not charge you, my brother, with gross transgressions of plain moralities; I know nothing about that. I know this: "As face answereth to face in a glass," so doth the heart of man to man, and I bring this message, verified to me by my own consciousness, that we have all gone astray, and "wounds and bruises and putrefying sores" mark us all. If the best of us could see himself for once, in the light of God, as the worst of us will see himself one day, the cry would come from the purest lips, "Oh! wretched man that I am! who shall deliver me from the body of this death?"—this life in death, rotting and smelling foul to Heaven, that I carry about with me, wheresoever I go.

Note, further, this man's confidence in Christ's power: "Thou canst make me clean." He had heard all about the miracles that were being wrought up and down over the country, and he came to the Worker, with nothing of the nature of religious faith in Him, but with entire confidence, based upon the report of previous miracles, in Christ's ability to heal. I do not suppose that in its nature it was very different from the trust with which savages will crowd round a traveller who has a medicine chest with him, and expect to be cured of their diseases. But still it was real confidence in our Lord's power to heal. As a rule, though not without exceptions, He required (we may perhaps say He needed) such confidence as a condition of His miracle-working power.

If we turn from the emblem to the thing signified, from the leprosy of the body to that of the spirit, we may be sure of Christ's omnipotent ability to cleanse from the extremest severity of the disease, however inveterate and chronic it may have become. Sin dominates men by two opposite lies. I have said how hard it is to get people's consciences awakened to see the facts of their moral and religious condition; but then, when they are waked up, it is almost as hard to keep them from the other extreme. The devil, first of all, says to a man, "It is only a little sin. Do it; you will be none the worse. You can give it up when you like, you know." That is the language before the act. Afterwards, his language is, first, "You have done no harm, never mind what people say about sin. Make yourself comfortable," and then, when that lie wears itself out, the mask is dropped, and this is what is said: "I have got you now, and you cannot get away. Done is done! What thou hast written thou hast written; and neither thou nor anybody else can blot it out." Hence the despair into which awakened consciences are apt to drop, and the feeling, which dogs the sense of evil like a specter, of the hopelessness of all attempts to make oneself better. Brethren, they are both lies; the lie that we are pure is the first; the lie that we are too black to be purified is the second. "If we say that we have no sin, we deceive ourselves and make God a liar," but if we say, as some of us, when once our consciences are stirred, are but too apt to say, "We have sinned, and it cleaves to us for ever," we deceive ourselves still worse, and still more darkly and doggedly contradict the sure word of God. Christ's blood atones for all past sin, and has power to bring forgiveness to every one. Christ's vital Spirit will enter into any heart, and, abiding there, has power to make the foulest clean.

Note, again, the leper's hesitation. "If Thou wilt"—he had no right to presume on Christ's good will. He knew nothing about the principles upon which His miracles were wrought and His mercy extended. He supposed, no doubt, as he was bound to suppose, in the absence of any plain knowledge, that it was a mere matter of accident, of caprice, of monetary inclination and good nature, to whom the gift of healing should come. And so he draws near with the modest "If Thou wilt"; not pretending to know more than he knew, or to have a claim which he had not. But his hesitation is quite as much entreaty as hesitation. What do we mean when we say about a man, "He can do it, if he likes," but to imply that it is so easy to do it, that it would be cruel not to do it? And so, when the leper said, "If Thou wilt, Thou canst," he meant, "There is no obstacle standing between me and health but Thy will, and surely it cannot be Thy will to leave me in this life in death." He, as it were, throws the responsibility for his health or disease upon Christ's shoulders and thereby makes the strongest appeal to that loving heart.

We stand on another level. The leper's hesitation is our certainty. We know the principle upon which His mercy is dispensed; we know that it is a universal, all-embracing love; we know that no caprice nor passing spasm of good nature lies at the bottom of it. We know that if any men are not healed, it is not because Christ will not, but because they will not. If ever there springs in our hearts the dark doubt "If Thou wilt," which was innocent in this man in the twilight of his knowledge, but is wrong in us in the full noontide of ours, we ought to be able to banish it at once, and to lay none of the responsibility of our continuing unhealed on Christ, but all on ourselves. He has laid it there, when He lamented, "How often would I—and ye would not!" Nothing can be more in accordance with the will of God, of which Jesus Christ is the embodiment, than to deliver men from sin, which is the opposite of His will.

2. Notice, secondly, the Lord's answer. Mark's record of this incident puts the miracle in very small compass, and dilates rather upon the attitude and mind of Jesus Christ preparatory to it. As if, apart altogether from the supernatural element and the lessons that are to be drawn from it, it was worth our while to ponder, for the gladdening of our hearts and the strengthening of our hopes, that lovely picture of sheer simple compassion and tenderheartedness. "Jesus, *moved with compassion*"—a clause which occurs only in Mark's account—"put forth His hand and touched him, and said, I will; be thou clean."

Note, then, three things—the compassion, the touch, the word.

As to the first, is it not a precious boon for us, in the midst of our many wearinesses and sorrows and sicknesses, to have that picture of Jesus Christ bending over the leper, and sending, as it were, a gush of pitying love from His heart to flood away all his miseries? It is a true revelation of the heart of Jesus Christ. Simple pity is its very core. That pity is eternal, and subsists as He sits in the calm of the heavens, even as it was manifest whilst He sat teaching in the humble house in Galilee. For "we have not a High Priest which cannot be touched with a feeling of our infirmities." The pitying Christ is near us all. Nor let us forget that it is this swift shoot of pity which underlies all that follows—the touch, the word, and the cure. Christ does not wait to be moved by the prayers that come from these leprous lips, but He is moved by the leprous lips themselves. The sight of the man affects His pitying heart, which sets in motion all the wheels of His healing powers. So we may learn that the impulse to which His redeeming activity owes its origin wells up from His own heart. Show Him sorrow, and He answers it by a pity of such a sort that it is restless till it helps and assuages. We may rise higher. The pity of Jesus Christ is the summit of His revelation of the Father, and, looking upon that gentle heart, into whose depths we can see as through a little window by these words of my text, we must stand with hushed reverence as beholding not only the compassion of the Man, but therein manifested the pity of the God who, "Like as a father pitieth his children, pitieth them that fear Him,'' and pities yet more the more miserable men who fear and love Him not. The Christian's God is no impassive Being, indifferent to mankind, but ''One who in all our afflictions is afflicted, and, in His love and in His pity,'' redeems and bears and carries.

Note, still further, the Lord's touch. With swift obedience to the impulse of His pity, Christ thrusts forth His hand and touches the leper. There was much in that touch, but whatever more we may see in it, we should not be blind to the loving humanity of the act. Remember that the man kneeling there had felt no touch of a hand for years; that the very kisses of his own children and his wife's embrace of love were denied him. And now Jesus puts out His hand, and, without thinking of Mosaic restrictions and ceremonial prohibitions, yields to the impulses of His pity, and gives assurance of His sympathy and His brotherhood, as He lays His pure fingers upon the rotting ulcers. All men that help their fellows must be contented thus to identify themselves with them and to take them by the hand, if they would seek to deliver them from their evils.

Remember, too, that according to the Mosaic law it was forbidden to any but the priest to touch a leper. Therefore, in this act, beautiful as it is in its uncalculated humanity, there may have been something intended of a deeper kind. Our Lord thereby does one of two things—either He asserts His authority as overriding that of Moses and all his regulations, or He asserts His sacerdotal character. Either way there is a great claim in the act.

Further, we may take that touch of Christ's as being a parable of His whole work. It was a piece of wonderful sympathy and condescension that He should put out His hand to touch the leper; but it was the result of a far greater and more wonderful piece of sympathy and condescension that He had a hand to touch him with. For the ''sweet human hands and lips and eyes'' which He wore in this world were assumed by Him in order that He might make Himself one with all sufferers and bear the burden of all their sins. So His touch of the leper symbolizes His identifying of Himself with mankind, the foulest and the most degraded; and in this connection there is a profound meaning in one of the ordinarily trivial legends of the Rabbis, who, founding upon a word of the fifty-third chapter of Isaiah, tell us that when Messiah comes He will be found sitting amongst the lepers at the gate of the city. So He was numbered amongst the transgressors in His life, and ''with the wicked in His death.'' He touches, and, touching, contracts no impurity, cleansing as the sunlight and the fire do, by burning up the impurity, and not by receiving it into Himself.

Note the Lord's word, ''I will; be thou clean.'' It is shaped, convolution for convolution, so to speak, to match the man's prayer. He ever molds His response according to the feebleness and imperfection of the petitioner's faith. But, at the same time, what a ring of autocratic authority and conscious sovereignty there is in the brief, calm, imperative word, "I will; be thou clean!" He accepts the leper's ascription of power; He claims to work the miracle by His own will, and therein He is either guilty of what comes very near arrogant blasphemy, or He is rightly claiming for Himself a divine prerogative. If His word can tell as a force on material things, what is the conclusion? He who "spake and it was done" is Almighty and Divine.

3. Lastly, note the immediate cure. Mark tells us, with his favorite word "straightway," how as soon as Christ had spoken, the leprosy departed from the leper. And to turn from the symbol to the fact, the same sudden and complete cleansing is possible for us. Our cleansing from sin must depend upon the present love and present power of Jesus Christ. On account of Christ's sacrifice, whose efficacy is eternal and lies at the foundation of all our blessedness and our purity until the heavens shall be no more, we are forgiven our sins and our guilt is taken away. By the present indwelling of that cleansing Spirit of the everliving Christ, which will be given to us each if we seek it, we are cleansed day by day from our evil. "The blood of Jesus Christ cleanseth from all sin," not only when shed as propitiatory, but when applied as sanctifying. We must come to Christ, and there must be a real living contact between us and Him through our faith, if we are to possess either the forgiveness or the cleansing which are wrapped up inseparable in His gift.

Further, the suddenness of this cure and its completeness may be reproduced in us. People tell us that to believe in sudden conversion is fanatical. This is not the place to argue that question. It seems to me that such suddenness is in accordance with analogy. And I, for my part, preach with full belief and in the hope that the words may not be spoken altogether in vain to every man, woman, and child listening to me, irrespective of their condition, character, and past, that there is no reason why they should not go to Him straightway; no reason why He should not put out His hand straightway and touch them; no reason why their leprosy should not pass from them straightway, and they lie down to sleep tonight "accepted in the Beloved" and cleansed in Him. Trust Him and He will do it.

Only remember, it was of no use to the leper that crowds had been healed, that floods of blessing had been poured over the land. What he wanted was that a rill should come and refresh his own lips. If you wish to have Christ's cleansing you must make personal work of it, and come with this prayer, "On *me* be all that cleansing shown!" You do not need to go to Him with an "If" nor a prayer, for His gift has not waited for our asking, and He has anticipated us by coming with healing in His wings. The parts are reversed, and He prays you to receive the gift, and stands before each of us with the gentle remonstrance upon His lips, "Why will ye die when I am here ready to cure you?" Take Him at His word, for He offers to us all, whether we desire it or no, the cleaning which we need. Take Him at His word, trust Him wholly, trust to His death for forgiveness, to His sanctifying Spirit for cleansing, and "straightway" your "leprosy will depart from you," and your flesh shall become like the flesh of a little child, and you shall be clean.

Christ's Touch

Jesus put forth His hand, and touched him. MARK 1:41.

"Behold the servant of the Lord" might be the motto of this Gospel, and "He went about doing good and healing" the summing up of its facts. We have in it comparatively few of our Lord's discourses, none of His longer, and not very many of His briefer ones. It contains but four parables. This Evangelist gives no miraculous birth as in Matthew, no angels adoring there as in Luke, no gazing into the secrets of Eternity, where the Word who afterwards became flesh dwelt in the bosom of the Father, as in John. He begins with a brief reference to the Forerunner, and then plunges into the story of Christ's life of service to man and service for God.

In carrying out his conception the Evangelist omits many things found in the other Gospels, which involve the idea of dignity and dominion, while he adds to the incidents which he has in common with them not a few fine and subtle touches to heighten the impression of our Lord's toil and eagerness in His patient, loving service. Perhaps it may be an instance of this that we find more prominence given to our Lord's touch as connected with His miracles than in the other Gospels, or perhaps it may merely be an instance of the vivid portraiture, the result of a keen eye for externals, which is so marked a characteristic of this Gospel. Whatever the reason, the fact is plain, that Mark delights to dwell on Christ's touch. The instances are these—first, He puts out His hand, and "lifts up" Peter's wife's mother, and immediately the fever leaves her (1:31); then, unrepelled by the foul disease, He lays His pure hand upon the leper, and the living mass of corruption is healed (1:41); again, He lays His hand on the clammy marble of the dead child's forehead, and she lives (5:41). Further, we have the incidental statement that He was so hindered in His mighty works by unbelief that He could only lay His hands on a few sick folk and heal them (6:5). We find next two remarkable incidents, peculiar to Mark, both like each other and unlike our Lord's other miracles. One is the gradual healing of that deaf and dumb man whom Christ took apart from the crowd, laid His hands on him, thrust His fingers into his ears as if He would clear some impediment, touched his tongue with saliva, said to him, "Be opened"; and the man could hear (7:34). The other is, the gradual healing of a blind man whom our Lord again leads apart from the crowd, takes by the hand, lays His own kind hands upon the poor, sightless eyeballs, and with singular slowness of progress effects a cure, not by a leap and a bound as He generally does, but by steps and stages; tries it once and finds partial success, has to apply the curative process again, and then the man can see (8:23). In addition to these instances there are two other incidents which may also be adduced. It is Mark alone who records for us the fact that He took little children in His arms, and blessed them. And it is Mark alone who records for us the fact that when He came down from the Mount of Transfiguration He laid His hand upon the demoniac boy, writhing in the grip of his tormentor, and lifted him up.

There is much taught us, if we will patiently consider it, by that touch of Christ's, and I wish to try to bring out its meaning and power.

1. Whatever diviner and sacreder aspect there may be in these incidents, the first thing, and in some senses the most precious thing, in them is that they are the natural expression of a truly human tenderness and compassion. Now we are so accustomed, and as I believe quite rightly, to look at all Christ's life down to its minutest events as intended to be a revelation of God, that we are sometimes apt to think about it as if His motive and purpose in everything was didactic. So an unreality creeps over our conceptions of Christ's life, and we need to be reminded that He was not always acting and speaking in order to convey instruction, but that words and deeds were drawn from Him by the play of simple human feelings. He pitied not only in order to teach us the heart of God, but because His own man's heart was touched with a feeling of men's infirmities. We are too apt to think of Him as posing before men with the intent of giving the great revelation of the Love of God. It is the love of Christ Himself, spontaneous, instinctive, without the thought of anything but the suffering that it sees, which gushes out and leads Him to put forth His hand to the outcast beggars, the blind, the deaf, the lepers. That is the first great lesson we have to learn from this and other stories—the swift human sympathy and heart of grace and tenderness which Jesus Christ had for all human suffering, and has today as truly as ever.

There is more than this instinctive sympathy taught by Christ's touch, but it is distinctly taught. How beautifully that comes out in the story of the leper! That wretched man had long dwelt in his isolation. The touch of a friend's hand or the kiss of loving lips had been long denied him. Christ looks on him, and before He reflects, the spontaneous impulse of pity breaks through the barriers of legal prohibitions and of natural repugnance, and leads Him to lay His holy and healing hand on his foulness.

True pity always instinctively leads us to seek to come near those who are its objects. A man tells his friend some sad story of his sufferings, and while he speaks, unconsciously his listener lays his hand on his arm, and, by a silent pressure, speaks his sympathy. So Christ did with these men—not only in order that He might reveal God to us, but because He was a man, and therefore felt ere He thought. Out flashed from His heart the swift sympathy, followed by the tender pressure of the loving hand—a hand that tried through flesh to reach spirit, and come near the sufferer that it might succor and remove the sorrow.

Christ's pity is shown by His touch to have this true characteristic of true pity, that it overcomes disgust. All real sympathy does that. Christ is not turned away by the shining whiteness of the leprosy, nor by the eating pestilence beneath it; He is not turned away by the clammy marble hand of the poor dead maiden, nor by the fevered skin of the old woman gasping on her pallet. He lays hold on each, the flushed patient, the loathsome leper, the sacred dead, with the all-equalizing touch of a universal love and pity, which disregards all that is repellent, and overflows every barrier and pours itself over every sufferer. We have the same pity of the same Christ to trust to and to lay hold of today. He is high above us and yet bending over us; stretching His hand from the throne as truly as He put it out when here on earth; and ready to take us all to His heart in spite of our weakness and wickedness, our failings and our shortcomings, the fever of our flesh and hearts' desires, the leprosy of our many corruptions, and the death of our sins—and to hold us ever in the strong, gentle clasp of His divine, omnipotent, and tender hand. This Christ lays hold on us because He loves us, and will not be turned from His compassion by the most loathsome foulness of ours.

2. And now take another point of view from which we may regard this touch of Christ: namely, as the medium of His miraculous power. There is nothing to me more remarkable about the miracles of our Lord than the royal variety of His methods of healing. Sometimes He works at a distance, sometimes He requires, as it would appear for good reasons, the proximity of the person to be blessed. Sometimes He works by a simple word: "Lazarus, come forth!" "Peace be still!" "Come out of him!'' sometimes by a word and a touch, as in the instances before us; sometimes by a touch without a word; sometimes by a word and a touch and a vehicle, as in the saliva that was put on the tongue and in the ears of the deaf, and on the eyes of the blind; sometimes by a vehicle without a word, without a touch, without His presence, as when He said, ''Go wash in the pool of Siloam, and he washed and was clean.'' So the divine worker varies infinitely and at pleasure, yet not arbitrarily but for profound, even if not always discoverable, reasons, the methods of His miracle-working power, in order that we may learn by these varieties of ways that He is tied to no way; and that His hand, strong and almighty, uses methods and tosses aside methods according to His pleasure, the methods being vitalized when they are used by His will, and being nothing at all in themselves.

The very variety of His methods, then, teaches us that the true cause in every case is His own bare will. A simple word is the highest and most adequate expression of that will. His word is all-powerful: and that is the very signature of divinity. Of whom has it been true from of old that ''He spake and it was done, He commanded and it stood fast''? Do you believe in a Christ whose bare will, thrown among material things, makes them all plastic, as clay in the potter's hands, whose mouth rebukes the demons and they flee, rebukes death and it looses its grasp, rebukes the tempest and there is a calm, rebukes disease and there comes health?

But this use of Christ's touch as apparent means for conveying His miraculous power also serves as an illustration of a principle which is exemplified in all His revelation, namely, the employment in condescension to men's weakness, of outward means as the apparent vehicles of His spiritual power. Just as by the material vehicle sometimes employed for cure, He gave these poor sensebound natures a ladder by which their faith in His healing power might climb, so in the manner of His revelation and communication of His spiritual gifts, there is provision for the wants of us men, who ever need some body for spirit to make itself manifest by, some form for the ethereal reality, some ''tabernacle'' for the ''sun.'' ''Sacraments,'' outward ceremonies, forms of worship, are vehicles which the Divine spirit uses in order to bring His gifts to the hearts and the minds of men. They are like the touch of the Christ which heals, not by any virtue in itself, apart from His will which chooses to make it the apparent medium of healing. All these externals are nothing, as the pipes of an organ are nothing, until His breath is breathed through them, and then the flood of sweet sound pours out.

Do not despise the material vehicles and the outward helps which Christ uses for the communication of His healing and His life, but remember that the help that is done upon earth, He does it all Himself. Even

Christ's touch is nothing if it were not for His own will which flows through it.

3. Consider Christ's touch as a shadow and symbol of the very heart of His work. Go back to the past history of this man. Ever since his disease declared itself no human being had touched him. If he had a wife he had been separated from her, if he had children their lips had never kissed his, nor their little hands found their way into his hard palms. Alone he had been walking with the plague-cloth over his face, and the cry "Unclean!" on his lips, lest any man should come near him. Skulking in his isolation, how he must have hungered for the touch of a hand. Every Jew was forbidden to approach him but the priest, who, if he were cured, might pass his hand over the place and pronounce him clean. And here comes a Man who breaks down all the restrictions, stretches a frank hand out across the walls of separation, and touches him. What a reviving assurance of love not yet dead must have come to the man as Christ grasped his hand, even if he saw in Him only a stranger who was not afraid of him and did not turn from him!

But beside this thrill of human sympathy, which came hope-bringing to the leper, Christ's touch has much significance, if we remember that, according to the Mosaic legislation, the priest and the priest alone was to lay his hands on the tainted skin and pronounce the leper whole. So Christ's touch was a priest's touch. He lays His hand on corruption and is not tainted. The corruption with which He comes in contact becomes purity. Are not these really the profoundest truths as to His whole work in the world? What is it all but laying hold of the leper and the outcast and the dead—His sympathy leading to His identification of Himself with us in our weakness and misery?

That sympathetic life-bringing touch is put forth once for all in His Incarnation and Death. "He taketh hold of the seed of Abraham," says the Epistle to the Hebrews, looking at our Lord's work under this same metaphor, and explaining that His laying hold of men was His being "made in all points like unto His brethren." Just as he took hold of the fevered woman and lifted her from her bed; or, as He thrust His fingers into the deaf ears of that poor man stopped by some impediment, so, in analogous fashion, He becomes one of those whom He would save and help. In His assumption of humanity and in His bowing of His hand to death, we behold Him laying hold of our weakness and entering into the fellowship of our pains and of the fruit of sin.

Just as He touches the leper and is unpolluted, or the fever patient and receives no contagion, or the dead and draws no chill of mortality into His warm hand, so He becomes like His brethren in all things, yet without sin. Being found in "the likeness of sinful flesh," He knows no sin, but wears His manhood unpolluted and dwells among men "blameless and harmless, the Son of God, without rebuke." Like a sunbeam passing through foul water untarnished and unstained; or like some sweet spring rising in the midst of the salt sea, which yet retains its freshness and pours it over the surrounding bitterness, so Christ takes upon Himself our nature and lays hold of our stained hands with the hand that continues pure while it grasps us, and will make us purer if we grasp it.

Brethren, let your touch answer to His; and as He lays hold of us, in His incarnation and His death, let the hand of our faith clasp His outstretched hand, and though our hold be as faltering and feeble as that of the trembling, wasted fingers which one timid woman once laid on His garment's hem, the blessing which we need will flow into our veins from the contact. There will be cleansing for our leprosy, sight for our blindness, life driving out death from its throne in our hearts, and we shall be able to recount our joyful experience in the old psalmist's triumphant strains—"He sent me from above, He laid hold upon me, He drew me out of many waters."

4. Finally, we may look upon these incidents as being in a very important sense a pattern for us. No good is to be done by any man to his fellows except at the cost of true sympathy which leads to identification and contact. The literal touch of your hand would do more good to some poor outcasts than much solemn advice, or even much material help flung to them as from a height above them. A shake of the hand might be more of a means of grace than a sermon, and more comforting than ever so many free breakfasts and blankets given superciliously.

And, symbolically, we may say that we must be willing to take those by the hand whom we wish to help; that is to say, we must come down to their level, try to see with their eyes, and to think their thoughts, and let them feel that we do not think our purity too fine to come beside their filth, nor shrink from them with repugnance, however we may show disapproval and pity for their sin. Much work done by Christian people has no effect, nor ever will have, because it has peeping through it a poorly concealed "I am holier than thou." An instinctive movement of repugnance has ruined many a well-meant effort.

Christ has come down to us, and has taken all our nature upon Himself. If there is an outcast and abandoned soul on earth which may not feel that Jesus has laid a loving and healing touch on him, Jesus is not the Saviour for the world. He shrinks from none, He unites Himself with all, therefore "He is able to save to the uttermost all who come unto God by Him." His conduct is the pattern and the law for us. A Church is a poor affair if it is not a body of people whose experience of Christ's pity and gratitude for the life which has become theirs through His wondrous making Himself one with them, compels them to do the like in their degree for the sinful and the outcast. Thank God, there are many in every communion who know that constraint of the love of Christ. But the world will not be healed of its sickness till the great body of Christian people awakes to feel that the task and honor of each of them is to go forth bearing Christ's pity certified by their own.

The sins of professing Christian countries are largely to be laid at the door of the Church. We are idle when we ought to be at work. We ''pass by on the other side'' when bleeding brethren lie with wounds gaping to be bound up by us. And even when we are moved to service by Christ's love, and try to do something for our fellows, our work is often tainted by a sense of our own superiority, and we patronize when we should sympathize, and lecture when we should beseech.

We must be content to take lepers by the hand, if we would help them to purity, and to let every outcast feel the warmth of our pitying, loving grasp, if we would draw them into the forsaken Father's House. Lay your hands on the sinful as Christ did, and they will recover. All your holiness and hope come from Christ's laying hold of you. Keep hold of Him, and make His great pity and loving identification of Himself with the world of sinners and sufferers, your pattern as well as your hope, and your touch, too, will have virtue. Keeping hold of Him who has taken hold of us, you too may be able to say, ''Ephphatha, be opened,'' or to lay your hand on the leper, and he will be cleansed.

2

Joy for the Sorrowing

Christ's Authority to Forgive

And again He entered into Capernaum after some days; and it was noised that He was in the house. 2. And straightway many were gathered together, insomuch that there was no room to receive them, no, not so much as about the door; and He preached the word unto them. 3. And they come unto Him, bringing one sick of the palsy, which was borne of four. 4. And when they could not come nigh unto Him for the press, they uncovered the roof where He was: and when they had broken it up, they let down the bed wherein the sick of the palsy lay. 5. When Jesus saw their faith, He said unto the sick of the palsy, Son, thy sins be forgiven thee. 6. But there were certain of the scribes sitting there, and reasoning in their hearts. 7. Why doth this man thus speak blasphemies? who can forgive sins but God only? 8. And immediately when Jesus perceived in His spirit that they so reasoned within themselves, He said unto them, Why reason ye those things in your hearts? 9. Whether is it easier to say to the sick of the palsy, Thy sins be forgiven thee; or to say, Arise, and take up thy bed, and walk? 10. But that ye may know that the Son of Man hath power on earth to forgive sins, (He saith to the sick of the palsy,) 11. I say unto thee, Arise, and take up thy bed, and go thy way into thine house. 12. And immediately he arose, took up the bed, and went forth before them all; insomuch that they were all amazed, and glorified God, saying, We never saw it on this fashion. MARK 2:1–12.

Mark alone gives Capernaum as the scene of this miracle. The excitement which had induced our Lord to leave that place had been allowed ''some days'' to quiet down, ''after'' which He ventures to return, but does not seem to have sought publicity, but to have remained in ''the house''—probably Peter's. There would be at least one woman's heart there, which would love to lavish grateful service on Him. But ''He could not be hid,'' and, however little genuine or deep the eagerness might be, He will not refuse to meet it. Mark paints vividly the crowd flocking to the humble home, overflowing its modest capacity, blocking the doorway, and clustering round it outside as far as they could hear Christ's voice. ''He was speaking the word to them,'' proclaiming His mission, as He had done in their synagogue, when He was interrupted by the events which follow, no doubt to the gratification of some of His hearers, who wanted something more exciting than ''teaching.''

1. We note the eager group of interrupters. Mark gives one of the minute touches which betray an eyewitness and a close observer when he tells us that the palsied man was carried by four friends—no doubt one at each corner of the bed, which would be some light framework, or even a mere quilt or mattress. The incident is told from the point of view of one sitting beside Jesus; they ''come to Him,'' but ''cannot come near.'' The accurate specification of the process of removing the roof, which Matthew omits altogether, and Luke tells much more vaguely, seems also to point to an eyewitness as the source of the narrative, who would of course, be Peter, who well remembered all the steps of the unceremonious treatment of his property. His house was, probably, one of no great pretensions or size, but like hundreds of poor men's houses in Palestine still—a one-storied building with a low, flat roof, mostly earthen, and easily reached from the ground by an outside stair. It would be somewhat difficult to get a sick man and his bed up there, however low, and somewhat free-and-easy dealing with another man's house to burrow through the roof a hole wide enough for the purpose; but there is no impossibility, and the difficulty is part of the lesson of the incident, and is recognized expressly in the narrative by Christ's notice of their ''faith.'' We can fancy the blank looks of the four bearers, and the disappointment on the sick man's thin face and weary eyes, as they got to the edge of the crowd, and saw that there was no hope of forcing a passage. Had they been less certain of a cure, and less eager, they would have shouldered their burden and carried him home again. They could well have pleaded sufficient reason for giving up the attempt. But ''we cannot'' is the coward's word. ''We must'' is the earnest man's. If we have any real consciousness of our need to get to Christ, and any real wish to do so, it is not a crowd round the door that will keep us back. Difficulties test, and therefore increase, faith. They develop a sanctified ingenuity in getting over them, and bring a rich harvest of satisfaction when at last conquered. These four eager faces looked down through the broken roof, when they had succeeded in dropping the bed right at Christ's feet, with a far keener pleasure than if they had just carried him in by the door. No doubt their act was inconvenient;

for, however light the roofing, some rubbish must have come down on the heads of some of the notabilities below. And, no doubt, it was interfering with property as well as with propriety. But here was a sick man, and there was his Healer; and it was their business to get the two together somehow. It was worth risking a good deal to accomplish. The rabbis sitting there might frown at rude intrusiveness; Peter might object to the damage to his roof; some of the listeners might dislike the interruption to His teaching; but Jesus read the action of the bearers and the consent of the motionless figure on the couch as the indication of "their faith," and His love and power responded to its call.

2. Note the unexpected gift with which Christ answers this faith. Neither the bearers nor the paralytic speak a word throughout the whole incident. Their act and his condition spoke loudly enough. Obviously, all five must have had, at all events, so much "faith" as went to the conviction that He could and would heal; and this faith is the occasion of Christ's gift. The bearers had it, as is shown by their work. It was a visible faith, manifest by conduct. He can see the hidden heart; but here He looks upon conduct, and thence infers disposition. Faith, if worth anything, comes to the surface in act. Was it the faith of the bearers, or of the sick man, which Christ rewarded? Both. As Abraham's intercession delivered Lot, as Paul in the shipwreck was the occasion of safety to all the crew, so one man's faith may bring blessings on another. But if the sick man too had not had faith, he would not have let himself be brought at all, and would certainly not have consented to reach Christ's presence by so strange and, to him, dangerous a way—being painfully hoisted up some narrow stair, and then perilously let down, at the risk of cords snapping, or hands letting go, or bed giving way. His faith, apparently, was deeper than theirs; for Christ's answer, though it went far beyond his or their expectations, must have been molded to meet his deepest sense of need. His heart speaks in the tender greeting "son," or, as the margin has it, "child"—possibly pointing to the man's youth, but more probably an appellation revealing the mingled love and dignity of Jesus, and taking this man into the arms of His sympathy. The palsy may have been the consequence of "fast" living; but, whether it were so or no, Christ saw that, in the dreary hours of solitary inaction to which it had condemned the sufferer, remorse had been busy gnawing at his heart, and that pain had done its best work by leading to penitence. Therefore He spoke to the conscience before He touched the bodily ailment, and met the sufferer's deepest and most deeply felt disease first. He goes to the bottom of the malady with His cure. These great words are not only closely adapted to the one case before Him, but contain a general truth, worthy to be pondered by all philanthropists. It is of little use to cure symptoms unless you cure diseases. The taproot of all misery is sin; and, until it is grubbed up, hacking at the branches is sad waste of time. Cure sin, and you make the heart a temple and the world a paradise. We Christians should hail all efforts of every sort for making men nobler, happier, better physically, morally, intellectually; but let us not forget that there is but one effectual cure for the world's misery, and that it is wrought by Him who has borne the world's sins.

3. Note the snarl of the scribes. "Certain of the scribes," says Mark—not being much impressed by their dignity, which, as Luke tells us, was considerable. He says that they were "Pharisees and doctors of the law . . . out of every village of Galilee and Judæa and Jerusalem" itself, who had come on a formal errand of investigation. Their tempers would not be improved by the tearing up of the roof, nor sweetened by seeing the "popularity" of this doubtful young Teacher, who showed that He had the secret, which they had not, of winning men's hearts. Nobody came crowding to them, nor hung on their lips. Professional jealousy has often a great deal to do in helping zeal for truth to sniff out heresy. The whispered cavillings are graphically represented. The scribes would not speak out, like men, and call on Jesus to defend His words. If they had been sure of their ground, they should have boldly charged Him with blasphemy; but perhaps they were half suspicious that He could show good cause for His speech. Perhaps they were afraid to oppose the tide of enthusiasm for Him. So they content themselves with comparing notes among themselves, and wait for Him to entangle Himself a little more in their nets. They affect to despise Him. "This man" is spoken in contempt. If He were so poor a creature, why were they there, all the way from Jerusalem, some of them? They overdo their part. The short, snarling sentences of their muttered objections, as given in the Revised Version, may be taken as shared among three speakers, each bringing his quota of bitterness. One says, "Why doth He thus speak?" Another curtly answers, "He blasphemeth"; while a third formally states the great truth on which they rest their indictment. Their principle is impregnable. Forgiveness is a divine prerogative, to be shared by none, to be grasped by none, without, in the act, diminishing God's glory. But it is not enough to have one premise of your syllogism right. Only God forgives sins; and if this man says that He does, He, no doubt, claims to be, in some sense, God. But whether He "blasphemeth" or not depends on what the scribes do not stay to ask; namely, whether He has the right so to claim: and, if He has, it is they, not He, who are the blasphemers. We need not wonder that they recoiled from the right conclusion, which is—

the divinity of Jesus. Their fault was not their jealousy for the divine honor, but their inattention to Christ's evidence in support of His claims, which inattention had its roots in their moral condition, their self-sufficiency and absorption in trivialities of externalism. But we have to thank them for clearly discerning and bluntly stating what was involved in our Lord's claims, and for thus bringing up the sharp issue—blasphemer, or "God manifest in the flesh."

4. Note our Lord's answer to the cavils. Mark would have us see something supernatural in the swiftness of Christ's knowledge of the muttered criticisms. He perceived it "straightway" and "in His spirit," which is tantamount to saying by divine discernment, and not by the medium of sense, as we do. His spirit was a mirror, in which looking He saw externals. In the most literal and deepest sense, He does "not judge after the sight of His eyes, neither reprove after the hearing of His ears."

The absence from our Lord's answer of any explanation that He was only declaring the divine forgiveness and not Himself exercising a divine prerogative, shuts us up to the conclusion that He desired to be understood as exercising it. Unless His pardon is something quite different from the ministerial announcement of forgiveness, which His servants are empowered to make to penitents, He willfully led the cavillers into error. His answer starts with a counter-question—another "why?" to their "why?" It then puts into words what they were thinking; namely, that it was easy to assume a power the reality of which could not be tested. To *say,* "Thy sins be forgiven," and to say, "Take up thy bed," are equally easy. To *effect* either is equally beyond man's power; but the one can be verified and the other cannot, and, no doubt, some of the scribes were maliciously saying: "It is all very well to pretend to do what cannot be tested. Let Him come out into daylight, and do a miracle which we can see." He is quite willing to accept the challenge to test His power in the invisible realm of conscience by His power in the visible region. The remarkable construction of the long sentence in verses 10 and 11, which is almost verbally identical in the three Gospels, parentheses and all, sets before us the suddenness of the turn from the scribes to the patient with dramatic force. Mark that our Lord claims "authority" to forgive, the same word which had been twice in the people's mouths in reference to His teaching and to His sway over demons. It implies not only power, but rightful power, and that authority which He wields as "Son of Man" and "on earth." This is the first use of that title in Mark. It is Christ's own designation of Himself, never found on other lips except the dying Stephen's. It implies His Messianic office, and points back to Daniel's great prophecy; but it also asserts His true manhood and His unique relation to humanity, as being Himself its sum and perfection—not *a,* but *the* Son of Man. Now the wonder which He would confirm by His miracle is that such a manhood, walking on earth, has lodged in it the divine prerogative. He who is the Son of Man must be something more than man, even the Son of God. His power to forgive is both derived and inherent, but, in either aspect, is entirely different from the human office of announcing God's forgiveness.

For once, Christ seems to work a miracle in response to unbelief, rather than to faith. But the real occasion of it was not the cavils of the scribes, but the faith and need of the man and His friends; while the silencing of unbelief, and the enlightenment of honest doubt, were but collateral benefits.

5. Note the cure and its effect. This is another of the miracles in which no vehicle of the healing power is employed. The word is enough; but here the word is spoken, not as if to the disease, but to the sufferer; and in His obedience he receives strength to obey. Tell a palsied man to rise and walk when his disease is that he cannot! But if he believes that Christ has power to heal, he will try to do as he is bid; and, as he tries, the paralysis steals out of the long-unused limbs. Jesus makes us able to do what He bids us do. The condition of healing is faith, and the test of faith is obedience. We do not get strength till we put ourselves into the attitude of obedience. The cure was immediate; and the cured man, who was "borne of four" into the healing presence, walked away, with his bed under his arm, "before them all." They were ready enough to make way for him then. And what said the wise doctors to it all? We do not hear that any of them were convinced. And what said the people? They were "amazed," and they "glorified God," and recognized that they had seen something quite new. That was all. Their glorifying God cannot have been very deep-seated, or they would have better learned the lesson of the miracle. Amazement was but a poor result. No emotion is more transient or less fruitful than gaping astonishment; and that, with a little varnish of acknowledgment of God's power, which led to nothing, was all the fruit of Christ's mighty work. Let us hope that the healed man carried his unseen blessing in a faithful and grateful heart, and consecrated his restored strength to the Lord who healed him!

The Publicans' Friend

And he went forth again by the sea side; and all the multitude resorted unto Him, and He taught them. 14. And as He passed by, he saw Levi the son of Alphæus sitting at the receipt of custom, and said unto him, Follow me. And he arose and followed Him. 15.

And it came to pass, that, as Jesus sat at meat in his house, many publicans and sinners sat also together with Jesus and His disciples: for there were many, and they followed Him. 16. And when the scribes and Pharisees saw Him eat with publicans and sinners, they said unto His disciples, How is it that He eateth and drinketh with publicans and sinners? 17. When Jesus heard it, He saith unto them, They that are whole have no need of the physician, but they that are sick: I came not to call the righteous, but sinners to repentance. 18. And the disciples of John and of the Pharisees used to fast: and they come and say unto Him, Why do the disciples of John and of the Pharisees fast, but Thy disciples fast not? 19. And Jesus said unto them, Can the children of the bridechamber fast, while the bridegroom is with them? as long as they have the bridegroom with them, they cannot fast. 20. But the days will come, when the bridegroom shall be taken away from them, and then shall they fast in those days. 21. No man also seweth a piece of new cloth on an old garment: else the new piece that filled it up taketh away from the old, and the rent is made worse. 22. And no man putteth new wine into old bottles: else the new wine doth burst the bottles, and the wine is spilled, and the bottles will be marred: but new wine must be put into new bottles. MARK 2:13–22.

By calling a publican, Jesus shocked ‘‘public opinion and outraged propriety, as the Pharisees and scribes understood it. But He touched the hearts of the outcasts. A gush of sympathy melts souls frozen hard by icy winds of scorn. Levi (otherwise Matthew) had probably had wistful longings after Jesus which he had not dared to show, and therefore he eagerly and instantly responded to Christ's call, leaving everything in his customhouse to look after itself. Mark emphasizes the effect of this advance towards the disreputable classes by Jesus, in his repeated mention of the numbers of them who followed Him. The meal in Matthew's house was probably not immediately after his call. The large gathering attracted the notice of Christ's watchful opponents, who pounced upon His sitting at meat with such ‘‘shady’’ people as betraying His low tastes and disregard of seemly conduct, and, with characteristic Eastern freedom, pushed in as uninvited spectators. They did not carry their objection to Himself, but covertly insinuated it into the disciples' minds, perhaps in hope of sowing suspicions there. Their sarcasm evoked Christ's own ‘‘program’’ of His mission, for which we have to thank them.

1. We have, first, Christ's vindication of His consorting with the lowest. He thinks of Himself as ‘‘a physician,’’ just as He did in another connection in the synagogue of Nazareth. He is conscious of power to heal all soul-sickness, and therefore He goes where He is most needed.

Where should a doctor be but where disease is rife? Is not his place in the hospital? Association with degraded and vicious characters is sin or duty, according to the purpose of it. To go down in the filth in order to wallow there is vile; to go down in order to lift others up is Christ's mission and Christ-like.

But what does He mean by the distinction between sick and sound, righteous and sinners? Surely all need His healing, and there are not two classes of men. Have not all sinned? Yes, but Jesus speaks to the cavillers, for the moment, in their own dialect, saying, in effect, "I take you at your own valuation, and therein find My defense. You do not think that you need a physician, and you call yourselves 'righteous' and these outcasts 'sinners.' So you should not be surprised if I, being the healer, turn away to them, and prefer their company to yours." But there is more than taking them at their own estimate in the great words, for to conceit ourselves "whole" bars us off from getting any good from Jesus. He cannot come to the self-righteous heart. We must feel our sickness before we can see Him in His true character, or be blessed by His presence with us. And the apparent distinction, which seems to limit His work, really vanishes in the fact that we are all sick and sinners, whatever we may think of ourselves, and that, therefore, the errand of the great Physician is to us all. The Pharisee who knows himself a sinner is as welcome as the outcast. The most outwardly respectable, clean-living, orthodoxly religious formalist needs Him as much, and may have Him as healingly, as the grossest criminal, foul with the stench of loathsome disease. That great saying has changed the attitude towards the degraded and unclean, and many a stream of pity and practical work for such has been drawn off from that Nile of yearning love, though all unconscious of its source.

2. We have Christ's vindication of the disciples from ascetic critics. The assailants in the second charge were reinforced by singular allies. Pharisees had nothing in common with John's disciples, except some outward observances, but they could join forces against Jesus. Common hatred is a wonderful unifier. This time Jesus Himself is addressed, and it is the disciples with whom fault is found. To speak of His supposed faults to them, and of theirs to Him, was cunning and cowardly. His answer opens up many great truths, which we can barely mention.

First, note that He calls Himself the "bridegroom,"—a designation which would surely touch some chords in John's disciples, remembering how their Master had spoken of the "bridegroom" and his "friend." The name tells us that Jesus claimed the psalms of the "bridegroom" as prophecies of Himself, and claimed the Church that was to be as His bride. It speaks tenderly of His love and of our possible blessedness.

Next, we note the sweet suggestion of the joyful life of the disciples in intercourse with Him. We perhaps do not sufficiently regard their experience in that light, but surely they were happy, being ever with Him, though they knew not yet all the wonder and blessedness which His presence involved and brought. They were a glad company, and Christians ought now to be joyous, because the bridegroom is still with them, and the more really so by reason of His ascending up where He was before. We have seen Him again, as He promised, and our hearts should rejoice with a joy which no man can take from us.

Next, we note Christ's clear prevision of His death, the violence of which is hinted at in the words, "Shall be taken away from them." Further, we note the great principle that outward forms must follow inward realities, and are genuine only when they are the expression of states of mind and feeling. That is a far-reaching truth, ever being forgotten in the tyranny which the externals of religion exercise. Let the free spirit have its own way, and cut its own channels. Laughter may be as devout as fasting. Joy is to be expressed in religion as well as grief. No outward form is worth anything unless the inner man vitalizes it, and such a mere form is not simply valueless, but may quickly become hypocrisy and conscious make-believe.

3. Jesus adds two similes, which are condensed parables, to deal with a wider question rising out of the preceding principles. The difference between His disciples' religious demeanor and that of their critics is not merely that the former are not now in a mood for fasting, but that a new spirit is beginning to work in them, and therefore it will go hard with a good many old forms besides fasting.

The essential point in both the similes of the raw cloth stitched on to the old, and of the new wine poured into stiff old skins, is the necessary incongruity between old forms and new tendencies. Undressed cloth is sure to shrink when wetted, and, being stronger than the old, to draw its frayed edges away. So, if new truth, or new conceptions of old truth, or new enthusiasms, are patched on to old modes, they will look out of place, and will sooner or later rend the old cloth. But the second simile advances on the first, in that it points not only to harm done to the old by the unnatural marriage, but also to mischief to the new. Put fermenting wine into a hard, unyielding, old wineskin, and there can be but one result,—the strong effervescence will burst the skin, which may not matter much, and the precious wine will run out and be lost, sucked up by the thirsty soil, which matters more. The attempt to confine the new within the limits of the old, or to express it by the old forms, destroys them and wastes it. The attempt was made to keep Christianity within the limits of

Judaism; it failed, but not before much harm had been done to Christianity. Over and over again the effort has been made in the Church, and it has always ended disastrously,—and it always will. It will be a happy day for both the old and the new when we all learn to put new wine into new skins, and remember that ''God giveth it a body as it hath pleased Him, and to every seed his *own* body.''

The Secret of Gladness

And Jesus said unto them, Can the children of the bridechamber fast, while the bridegroom is with them? MARK 2:19.

This is part of our Lord's answer to the question put by John's disciples as to the reason for the omission of the practice of fasting by His followers. The answer is very simple. It is—''My disciples do not fast because they are not sad.'' And the principle which underlies the answer is a very important one. It is this: that all outward forms of religion, appointed by man, ought only to be observed when they correspond to the feeling and disposition of the worshipper. That principle cuts up all religious formalism by the very roots. The Pharisee said, ''Fasting is a good thing in itself, and meritorious in the sight of God.'' The modern Pharisee says the same about many externals of ritual and worship; Jesus Christ says, ''No! The thing has no value except as an expression of the feeling of the doer.'' Our Lord did not object to fasting; He expressly approved of it as a means of spiritual power. But He did object to the formal use of it or of any outward form. The formalist's form is rigid, unbending, and cold, like an iron rod. The true Christian form is elastic, like the stem of a palm tree, which curves and sways and yields to the wind, and has the sap of life in it. If any man is sad, let him fast; ''if any man is merry, let him sing psalms.'' Let his ritual correspond to his spiritual emotion and conviction.

But the point which I wish to consider now is not so much this, as the representation that is given here as the reason why fasting was incongruous with the condition and disposition of the disciples. Jesus says, ''We are more like a wedding party than anything else. Can the children of the bridechamber fast as long as the bridegroom is with them?''

The ''children of the bridechamber'' is but another name for those who were called the ''friends'' or companions ''of the bridegroom.'' According to the Jewish wedding ceremonial it was their business to conduct the bride to the home of her husband, and there to spend seven days in festivity and rejoicing, which were to be so entirely devoted to mirth and feasting that the companions of the bridegroom were by the Talmudic ritual absolved even from prayer and from worship, and had for their one duty to rejoice.

And that is the picture that Christ holds up before the disciples of the ascetic John as the representation of what He and His friends were most truly like. Very unlike our ordinary notion of Christ and His disciples as they walked the earth! The presence of the Bridegroom made them glad with a strange gladness, which shook off sorrow as the down on a sea-bird's breast shakes off moisture, and leaves it warm and dry, though it floats amidst boundless seas. I wish now to meditate on this secret of imperviousness to sorrow arising from the felt presence of the Christ.

There are three subjects for consideration arising from the words of my text: The Bridegroom; the presence of the Bridegroom; the joy of the Bridegroom's presence.

1. Now with regard to the first, a very few words will suffice. The first thing that strikes me is the singular appropriateness and the delicate, pathetic beauty in the employment of this name by Christ in the existing circumstances. Who was it that had first said: "He that hath the bride is the bridegroom, but the friend of the bridegroom that standeth by and heareth him, rejoiceth greatly because of the bridegroom's voice. This my joy therefore is fulfilled"? Why, it was the master of these very men who were asking the question. John's disciples came and said, "Why do not your disciples fast?" and our Lord reminded them of their own teacher's words, when he said, "The friend of the bridegroom can only be glad." And so He would say to them, "In your master's own conception of what I am, and of the joy that comes from My presence, you have an answer to your question. He might have taught you who I am, and why it is that the men that stand around Me are glad."

But this is not all. We cannot but connect this name with a whole circle of ideas found in the Old Testament, especially with that most familiar and almost stereotyped figure which represents the union between Israel and Jehovah, under the emblem of the marriage bond. The Lord is the "husband"; and the nation whom He has loved and redeemed and chosen for Himself, is the "wife"; unfaithful and forgetful, often requiting love with indifference and protection with unthankfulness, and needing to be put away, and debarred of the society of the husband who still yearns for her; but a wife still, and in the new time to be joined to Him by a bond that shall never be broken and a better covenant.

And so Christ lays His hand upon all that old history and says, "It is fulfilled here in Me." A familiar note in Old Testament Messianic prophecy too is caught and echoed here, especially that grand marriage ode of the Forty-fifth Psalm, in which he must be a very prosaic or very deeply prejudiced reader who hears nothing more than the shrill wedding greetings at the marriage of some Jewish king with a foreign princess. Its bounding hopes and its magnificent sweep of vision are a world too wide for such interpretation. The Bridegroom of that psalm is the Messiah, and the Bride is the Church.

I need only refer in a sentence to what this indicates of Christ's self-consciousness. What must He, who takes this name as His own, have thought Himself to be to the world, and the world to Him? He steps into the place of the Jehovah of the Old Testament, and claims as His own all these great and wonderful prophecies. He promises love, protection, communion, the deepest, most mystical union of spirit and heart with Himself; and He claims quiet, restful confidence in His love, absolute, loving obedience to His authority, reliance upon His strong hand and loving heart, and faithful cleaving to Him. The Bridegroom of humanity, the Husband of the world, if it will only turn to Him, is Christ Himself.

2. But a word as to the presence of the Bridegroom. It might seem as if this text condemned us who love an unseen and absent Lord to exclusion from the joy which is made to depend on His presence. Are we in the dreary period when "the Bridegroom is taken away" and fasting appropriate?

Surely not. The time of mourning for an absent Christ was only three days; the law for the years of the Church's history between the moment when the uplifted eyes of the gazers lost Him in the symbolic cloud and the moment when He shall come again is, "Lo, I am with you alway." The absent Christ is the present Christ. He is really with us, not as the memory or the influence of the example of the dead may be said to remain, not as the spirit of a teacher may be said to abide with his school of followers. We say that Christ has gone up on high and sits on "the right hand of God." The right hand of God is His active power. Where is "the right hand of God"? It is wherever His divine energy works. He that sits at the right hand of God is thereby declared to be wherever the divine energy is in operation, and to be Himself the wielder of that divine Power. I believe in a local abode of the glorified human body of Jesus Christ now, but I believe likewise that all through God's universe, and eminently in this world, which He has redeemed, Christ is present, in His consciousness of its circumstances, and in the activity of His influence, and in whatsoever other incomprehensible and unspeakable mode Omnipresence belongs to a divine Person. So that He is with us most really, though the visible, bodily Form is no longer by our sides.

That Presence, which survives, which is true for us here today, may be a far better and more blessed and real thing than the presence of the mere bodily Form in which He once dwelt. We may have lost something by His going away in visible form; I doubt whether we have. We have lost the manifestation of Him to the sense, but we have gained the manifestation of Him to the spirit. And just as the great men, who are only men, need to die and go away in order to be measured in their true magnitude and understood in their true glory; just as when a man is in amongst the mountains, he cannot tell which peak is the dominant one, but when he gets away a little space across the sea and looks back, distance helps to measure magnitude and reveal the sovereign summit which towers above all the rest, so, looking back across the ages with the foreground between us and Him of the history of the Christian Church ever since, and noticing how other heights have sunk beneath the waves and have been wrapped in clouds and have disappeared behind the great round of the earth, we can tell how high this One is; and know better than they knew who it is that moves amongst men in "the form of a servant," even the Bridegroom of the Church and of the world. "It is expedient for you that I go away," and Christ is, or ought to be, nearer to us today in all that constitutes real nearness, in our apprehension of His essential character, in our reception of His holiest influences, than He ever was to them who walked beside Him on the earth.

But, brethren, that presence is of no use at all to us unless we daily try to realize it. He was with these men whether they would or no. Whether they thought about Him or no, there He was; and just because His presence did not at all depend upon their spiritual condition, it was a lower kind of presence than that which you and I have now, and which depends altogether on our realizing it by the turning of our hearts to Him, and by the daily contemplation of Him amidst all our bustle and struggle.

Do you, as you go about your work, feel His nearness and try to keep the feeling fresh and vivid, by occupying heart and mind with Him, by referring everything to His supreme control? By trusting yourselves utterly and absolutely in His hand, and gathering round you as it were, the sweetness of His love by meditation and reflection, do you try to make conscious to yourselves your Lord's presence with you? If you do, that presence is to you a blessed reality; if you do not, it is a word that means nothing and is of no help, no stimulus, no protection, no satisfaction, no sweetness whatever to you. The children of the Bridegroom are glad only when, and as, they know that the Bridegroom is with them.

3. And now a word, last of all, about the joy of the Bridegroom's presence. What was it that made these humble lives so glad when Christ was with them, filling them with strange new sweetness and power? The charm of personal character, the charm of contact with one whose lips were bringing to them fresh revelations of truth, fresh visions of God, whose whole life was the exhibition of a nature beautiful, and noble, and pure, and tender, and sweet, and loving, beyond anything they had ever seen before.

Ah! brethren, there is no joy in the world like that of companionship, in the freedom of perfect love, with one who ever keeps us at our best, and brings the treasures of ever fresh truth to the mind, as well as beauty of character to admire and imitate. That is one of the greatest gifts that God gives, and is a source of the purest joy that we can have. Now we may have all that and much more in Jesus Christ. He will be with us if we do not drive Him away from us, as the source of our purest joy, because He is the all-sufficient Object of our love.

Oh! you men and women who have been wearily seeking in the world for love that cannot change, for love that cannot die and leave you; you who have been made sad for life by irrevocable losses, or sorrowful in the midst of your joy by the anticipated certain separation which is to come, listen to this One who says to you, "I will never leave thee, and My lot shall be round thee for ever"; and recognize this, that there is a love which cannot change, which cannot die, which has no limits, which never can be cold, which never can disappoint, and therefore, in it, and in His presence, there is unending gladness.

He is with us as the source of our joy, because He is the Lord of our lives, and the absolute Commander of our wills. To have One present with us whose loving word it is delight to obey, and who takes upon Himself all responsibility for the conduct of our lives, and leaves us only the task of doing what we are bid—that is peace, that is gladness, of such a kind as none else in the world gives.

He is with us as the ground of perfect joy, because He is the adequate object of all our desires, and the whole of the faculties and powers of a man will find a field of glad activity in leaning upon Him, and realizing His presence. Like the Apostle whom the old painters loved to represent lying with his happy head on Christ's heart, and his eyes closed in a tranquil rapture of restful satisfaction, so if we have Him with us and feel that He is with us, our spirits may be still and in the great stillness of fruition of all our wishes and fulfillment of all our needs, may know a joy that the world can neither give nor take away.

He is with us as the source of endless gladness, in that He is the defense and protection for our soul. And as men live in a victualed fortress, and care not though the whole surrounding country may be swept bare of all provision, so when we have Christ with us we may feel safe, whatsoever befalls, and "in the days of famine we shall be satisfied."

He is with us as the source of our perfect joy, because His presence is the kindling of every hope that fills the future with light and glory. Dark or dim at the best, trodden by uncertain shapes, casting many a deep shadow over the present, that future lies, unless we see it illumined by Christ, and have Him by our sides. But if we possess His companionship, the present is but the parent of a more blessed time to come; and we can look forward and feel that nothing can touch our gladness, because nothing can touch our union with our Lord.

So, dear brethren, from all these thoughts and a thousand more which I have no time to dwell upon, comes this one great consideration, that the joy of the presence of the Bridegroom is the victorious antagonist of all sorrow and mourning. "Can the children of the bridechamber mourn, while the bridegroom is with them?" The answer sometimes seems to be, "Yes, they can." Our own hearts, with their experience of tears, and losses, and disappointments, seem to say, "Mourning is possible, even whilst He is here. We have our own share, and we sometimes think, more than our share, of the ills that flesh is heir to." And we have, over and above them, in the measure in which we are Christians, certain special sources of sorrow and trial, peculiar to ourselves alone; and the deeper and truer our Christianity, the more of these shall we have. But notwithstanding all that, what will the felt presence of the Bridegroom do for these griefs that will come? Well, it will limit them, for one thing; it will prevent them from absorbing the whole of our nature. There will always be a Goshen in which there is "light in the dwelling," however murky may be the darkness that wraps the land. There will always be a little bit of soil above the surface, however weltering and wide may be the inundation that drowns our world. There will always be a dry and warm place in the midst of the winter, a kind of greenhouse into which we may get from out of the tempest and fog. The joy of the Bridegroom's presence will last through the sorrow, like a spring of fresh water welling up in the midst of the sea. We may have the salt and the sweet waters mingling in our lives, not sent forth by one fountain, but flowing in one channel.

Our joy will sometimes be made sweeter and more wonderful by the very presence of the mourning and the pain. Just as the pillar of cloud, that glided before the Israelites through the wilderness, glowed into a pillar of fire as the darkness deepened, so, as the outlook around becomes less and less cheery and bright, and the night falls thicker and thicker, what seemed to be but a thin, grey, wavering column in the blaze of the sunlight will gather warmth and brightness at the heart of it when the midnight comes. You cannot see the stars at twelve o'clock in the day; you have to watch for the dark hours ere heaven is filled with glory. And so sorrow is often the occasion for the full revelation of the joy of Christ's presence.

Why have so many Christian men so little joy in their lives? Because they look for it in all sorts of wrong places, and seek to wring it out of all sorts of sapless and dry things. "Do men gather grapes of thorns?" If you fling the berries of the thorn into the winepress, will you get sweet sap out of them? That is what you are doing when you take gratified earthly affections, worldly competence, fulfilled ambitions, and put them into the press, and think that out of these you can squeeze the wine of gladness. No! No brethren, dry and sapless and juiceless they all are. There is one thing that gives a man worthy, noble, eternal gladness, and that is the felt presence of the Bridegroom.

Why have so many Christians so little joy in their lives? A religion like that of John's disciples and that of the Pharisees is a poor affair. A religion of which the main features are law and restriction and prohibition cannot be joyful. And there are a great many people who call themselves Christians, and have just religion enough to take the edge off worldly pleasures, and yet have not enough to make fellowship with Christ a gladness for them.

There is a cry amongst us for a more cheerful type of religion. I re-echo the cry, but I am afraid that I do not mean by it quite the same thing that some of my friends do. A more cheerful type of Christianity means to many of us a type of Christianity that will interfere less with our amusements; a more indulgent doctor that will prescribe a less rigid diet than the old Puritan type used to do. Well, perhaps they went too far; I do not care to deny that. But the only cheerful Christianity is a Christianity that draws its gladness from deep personal experience of communion with Jesus Christ. There is no way of men being religious and happy except being profoundly religious, and living very near their Master, and always trying to cultivate that spirit of communion with Him which shall surround them with the sweetness and the power of His felt presence. We do not want Pharisaic fasting, but we do want that the reason for not fasting shall be that Christians like eating better, but that their religion must be joyful because they have Christ with them, and therefore cannot choose but sing, as a lark cannot choose but carol. "Religion has no power over us, but as it is our happiness," and we shall never make it our happiness, and therefore never know its beneficent control, until we lift it clean out of the low region of outward forms and joyless service, into the blessed heights of communion with Jesus Christ, "Whom having not seen we love."

I would that Christian people saw more plainly that joy is a duty, and that they are bound to make efforts to obey the command, "Rejoice in the Lord always," no less than to keep other precepts. If we abide in Christ, His joy "will abide in us, and our joy will be full." We shall have in our hearts a fountain of true joy which will never be turbid with earthly stains, nor dried up by heat, nor frozen by cold. If we set the Lord always before us our days may be at once like the happy hours of the ''children of the bridechamber,'' bright with gladness and musical with song; and also saved from the enervation that sometimes comes from joy, because they are also like the patient vigils of the servants who ''wait for the Lord, when He shall return from the wedding.'' So strangely blended of fruition and hope, of companionship and solitude, of feasting and watching, is the Christian life here, until the time comes when His friends go in with the Bridegroom to the banquet, and drink for ever of the new joy of the kingdom.

3

Foes, Friend and Family

Works Which Hallow the Sabbath

And it came to pass, that He went through the corn fields on the Sabbath day; and His disciples began, as they went, to pluck the ears of corn. 24. And the Pharisees said unto Him, Behold, why do they on the Sabbath day that which is not lawful? 25. And He said unto them, Have ye never read what David did, when he had need, and was an hungered, he, and they that were with him? 26. How he went into the house of God in the days of Abiathar the high priest, and did eat the shewbread, which is not lawful to eat but for the priests, and gave also to them which were with him? 27. And He said unto them, The Sabbath was made for man, and not man for the Sabbath: 28. Therefore the Son of Man is Lord also of the Sabbath. MARK 2:23–28.

And He entered again into the synagogue; and there was a man there which had a withered hand. 2. And they watched Him, whether He would heal him on the Sabbath day; that they might accuse Him. 3. And He saith unto the man which had the withered hand, Stand forth. 4. And He saith unto them, Is it lawful to do good on the Sabbath days, or to do evil? to save life, or to kill? But they held their peace. 5. And when He had looked round about on them with anger, being grieved for the hardness of their hearts, He saith unto the man, Stretch forth thine hand. And he stretched it out: and his hand was restored whole as the other. MARK 3:1–5.

These two Sabbath scenes make a climax to the preceding paragraphs, in which Jesus had asserted His right to brush aside Rabbinical ordinances about eating with sinners and about fasting. Here He goes much further, in claiming power over the divine ordinance of the Sabbath. Formalists are moved to more holy horror by free handling of forms than by heterodoxy as to principles. So we can understand how the Pharisees' suspicions were exacerbated to murderous hate by these two incidents. It is doubtful whether Mark puts them together because they occurred together, or because they bear on the same subject. They deal with the two classes of "works" which later Christian theology has recognized as legitimate exceptions to the law of the Sabbath rest; namely, works of necessity and of mercy.

1. Whether we adopt the view that the disciples were clearing a path through standing corn, or the simpler one, that they gathered the ears of corn on the edge of a made path as they went, the point of the Pharisees' objection was that they broke the Sabbath by plucking, which was a kind of reaping. According to Luke, their breach of the Rabbinical exposition of the law was an event more dreadful in the eyes of these narrow pedants; for there was not only reaping, but the analogue of winnowing and grinding, for the grains were rubbed in the disciples' palms. What daring sin! What impious defiance of law! But of what law? Not that of the Fourth Commandment, which simply forbade "labor," but that of the doctors' expositions of the commandment, which expended miraculous ingenuity and hair-splitting on deciding what was labor and what was not. The foundations of that astonishing structure now found in the Talmud were, no doubt, laid before Christ. This expansion of the prohibition, so as to take in such trifles as plucking and rubbing a handful of heads of corn, has many parallels there.

But it is noteworthy that our Lord does not avail Himself of the distinction between God's commandment and men's exposition of it. He does not embarrass himself with two controversies at once. At fit times He disputed Rabbinical authority, and branded their casuistry as binding grievous burdens on men; but here He allows their assumption of the equal authority of their commentary and of the text to pass unchallenged, and accepts the statement that His disciples had been doing what was unlawful on the Sabbath, and vindicates their breach of law.

Note that His answer deals first with an example of similar breach of ceremonial law, and then rises to lay down a broad principle which governed that precedent, vindicates the act of the disciples, and draws for all ages a broad line of demarcation between the obligations of ceremonial and of moral law. Clearly, His adducing David's act in taking the shewbread implies that the disciples' reason for plucking the ears of corn was not to clear a path but to satisfy hunger. Probably, too, it suggests that He also was hungry, and partook of the simple food.

Note, too, the tinge of irony in that "Did ye *never* read?" In all your minute study of the letter of the Scripture, did you never take heed to that page? The principle on which the priest at Nob let the hungry fugitives devour the sacred bread, was the subordination of ceremonial law to men's necessities. It was well to lay the loaves on the table in the Presence, but it was better to take them and feed the fainting servant of God and his followers with them. Out of the very heart of the law which the Pharisees appealed to, in order to spin restricting prohibitions, Jesus drew an example of freedom which ran on all-fours with His disciples' case. The Pharisees had pored over the Old Testament all their lives, but it would have been long before they had found such a doctrine as this in it.

Jesus goes on to bring out the principle which shaped the instance he gave. He does not state it in its widest form, but confines it to the matter in hand—Sabbath obligations. Ceremonial law in all its parts is established as a means to an end—the highest good of men. Therefore, the end is more important than the means; and, in any case of apparent collision, the means must give way that the end may be secured. External observances are not of permanent, unalterable obligation. They stand on a different footing from primal moral duties, which remain equally imperative whether doing them leads to physical good or evil. David and his men were bound to keep these, whether they starved or not; but they were not bound to leave the shewbread lying in the shrine, and starve.

Man is made for the moral law. It is supreme, and he is under it, whether obedience leads to death or not. But all ceremonial regulations are merely established to help men to reach the true end of their being, and may be suspended or modified by his necessities. The Sabbath comes under the class of such ceremonial regulations, and may therefore be elastic when the pressure of necessity is brought to bear.

But note that our Lord, even while thus defining the limits of the obligation, asserts its universality. "The Sabbath was made for man"—not for a nation or an age, but for all time and for the whole race. Those who would sweep away the observance of the weekly day of rest are fond of quoting this text; but they give little heed to its first clause, and do not note that their favorite passage upsets their main contention, and establishes the law of the Sabbath as a possession for the world forever. It is not a burden, but a privilege, made and meant for man's highest good.

Christ's conclusion that He is "Lord even of the Sabbath" is based upon the consideration of the true design of the day. If it is once understood that it is appointed, not as an inflexible duty, like the obligation of truth or purity, but as a means to man's good, physical and spiritual, then He who has in charge all man's higher interests, and who is the perfect realization of the ideal of manhood, has full authority to modify and suspend the ceremonial observance if in His unerring judgment the suspension is desirable.

This is not an abrogation of the Sabbath, but, on the contrary, a confirmation of the universal and merciful appointment. It does not give permission to keep or neglect it, according to whim or for the sake of amusement, but it does draw, strong and clear, the distinction between a positive rite which may be modified, and an unchangeable precept of the moral law which it is better for a man to die than to neglect or transgress.

The second Sabbath scene deals with the same question from another point of view. Works of necessity warranted the supercession of Sabbath law; works of beneficence are no breaches of it. There are circumstances in which it is right to do what is not "lawful" on the Sabbath, for such works as healing the man with a withered hand are always "lawful."

We note the cruel indifference to the sufferer's woe which so characteristically accompanies a religion which is mainly a matter of outside observances. What cared the Pharisees whether the poor cripple was healed or no? They wanted him cured only that they might have a charge against Jesus. Note, too, the strange condition of mind, which recognized Christ's miraculous power, and yet considered Him an impious sinner.

Observe our Lord's purpose to make the miracle most conspicuous. He bids the man stand out in the midst, before all the cold eyes of malicious Pharisees and gaping spectators. A secret espionage was going on in the synagogue. He sees it all, and drags it into full light by setting the man forth and by His sudden, sharp thrust of a question. He takes the first word this time, and puts the stealthy spies on the defensive. His interrogation may possibly be regarded as having a bearing on their conduct, for there was murder in their hearts (verse 6). There they sat with solemn faces, posing as sticklers for law and religion, and all the while they were seeking grounds for killing Him. Was that Sabbath work? Whether would He, if He cured the shrunken arm, or they, if they gathered accusations with the intention of compassing His death, be the Sabbath-breakers?

It was a sharp, swift cut through their cloak of sanctity; but it has a wider scope than that. The question rests on the principle that good omitted is equivalent to evil committed. If we can save, and do not, the responsibility of loss lies on us. If we can rescue, and let die, our brother's blood reddens our hands. Good undone is not merely negative. It is positive evil done. If from regard to the Sabbath we refrained from doing some kindly deed alleviating a brother's sorrow, we should not be inactive, but should have done something by our very not doing, and what we should do would be evil. It is a pregnant saying which has many solemn applications.

No wonder that they "held their peace." Unless they had been prepared to abandon their position, there was nothing to be said. That silence indicated conviction and obstinate pride and rooted hatred which would not be convinced, conciliated, or softened. Therefore Jesus looked on them with that penetrating, yearning gaze, which left ineffaceable remembrances on the beholders, as the frequent mention of it indicates.

The emotions in Christ's heart as He looked on the dogged, lowering faces are expressed in a remarkable phrase, which is probably best taken as meaning that grief mingled with His anger. A wondrous glimpse into that tender heart, which in all its tenderness is capable of righteous indignation, and in all its indignation does not set aside its tenderness!

Mark that not even the most rigid prohibitions were broken by the process of cure. It was no breach of the fantastic restrictions which had been engrafted on the commandment, that Jesus should bid the man put out his hand. Nobody could find fault with a man for doing that. These two things, a word and a movement of muscles, were all. So He did ''heal on the Sabbath,'' and yet did nothing that could be laid hold of.

But let us not miss the parable of the restoration of the maimed and shrunken powers of the soul, which the manner of the miracle gives. Whatever we try to do because Jesus bids us, He will give us strength to do, however impossible to our unaided powers it is. In the act of stretching out the hand, ability to stretch it forth is bestowed, power returns to atrophied muscles, stiffened joints are suppled, the blood runs in full measure through the veins. So it is ever. Power to obey attends on the desire and effort to obey.

The Anger and Grief of Jesus

He looked round about on them with anger, being grieved for the hardness of their hearts. MARK 3:5.

Our Lord goes into the synagogue at Capernaum, where He had already wrought more than one miracle, and there He finds an object for His healing power, in a poor man with a withered hand; and also a little knot of His enemies. The scribes and Pharisees expect Christ to heal the man. So much had they learned of His tenderness and of His power.

But their belief that He could work a miracle did not carry them one step towards a recognition of Him as sent by God. They have no eye for the miracle, because they expect that He is going to break the Sabbath. There is nothing so blind as formal religionism. This poor man's infirmity did not touch their hearts with one little throb of compassion. They had rather that he had gone crippled all his days than that one of their Rabbinical Sabbatarian restrictions should be violated. There is nothing so cruel as formal religionism. They only think that there is a trap laid—and perhaps they had laid it—into which Christ is sure to go.

So, as our Evangelist tells us, they sat there stealthily watching Him out of their cold eyes, whether He would heal on the Sabbath day, that they might accuse Him. Our Lord bids the man stand out into the middle of the little congregation. He obeys, perhaps, with some feeble glimmer of hope playing round his heart. There is a quickened attention in the audience; the enemies are watching Him with gratification, because they hope He is going to do what they think to be a sin.

And then He reduces them all to silence and perplexity by His question—sharp, penetrating, unexpected: "Is it lawful to do good on the Sabbath day, or to do evil? You are ready to blame Me as breaking your Sabbatarian regulations if I heal this man. What if I do not heal him? Will that be doing nothing? Will not that be a worse breach of the Sabbath day than if I heal him?"

He takes the question altogether out of the region of pedantic Rabbinism, and bases His vindication upon the two great principles that mercy and help hallow any day, and that not to do good when we can is to do harm, and not to save life is to kill.

They are silenced. His arrow touches them; they do not speak because they cannot answer; and they will not yield. There is a struggle going on in them, which Christ sees, and He fixes them with that steadfast look of His; of which our Evangelist is the only one who tells us what it expressed, and by what it was occasioned. "He looked round about on them *with anger,* being *grieved.*" Mark the combination of emotions, anger and grief. And mark the reason for both: "the hardness," or as you will see, if you use the Revised Version, "the *hardening*" of their hearts—a process which He saw going on before Him as He looked at them.

Now I do not need to follow the rest of the story, how He turns away from them because He will not waste any more words on them, else He had done more harm than good. He heals the man. They hurry from the synagogue to prove their zeal for the sanctifying of the Sabbath day by hatching a plot on it for murdering Him. I leave all that, and turn to the thoughts suggested by this look of Christ as explained by the Evangelist.

1. Consider then, first, the solemn fact of Christ's anger. It is the only occasion, so far as I remember, upon which that emotion is attributed to Him. Once, and once only, the flash came out of the clear sky of that meek and gentle heart. He was once angry; and we may learn the lesson of the possibilities that lay slumbering in His love. He was only once angry, and we may learn the lesson that His perfect and divine charity "is not easily provoked." These very words from Paul's wonderful picture may teach us that the perfection of divine charity does not consist in its being incapable of becoming angry at all, but only in its not being angry except upon grave and good occasion.

Christ's anger was part of the perfection of His manhood. The man that cannot be angry at evil lacks enthusiasm for good. The nature that is incapable of being touched with generous and righteous indignation is so, generally, either because it lacks fire and emotion altogether, or because its vigor has been dissolved into a lazy indifference and easy good nature which it mistakes for love. Better the heat of the tropics, though sometimes the thunderstorms may gather, than the white calmness of the frozen poles. Anger is not weakness, but it is strength, if there be these three conditions, if it be evoked by a righteous and unselfish cause, if it be kept under rigid control, and if there be nothing in it of malice, even when it prompts to punishment. Anger is just and right when it is not produced by the mere friction of personal irritation (like electricity by rubbing), but is excited by the contemplation of evil. It is part of the marks of a good man that he kindles into wrath when he sees "the oppressor's wrong." If you went out hence tonight, and saw some drunken ruffian beating his wife or ill-using his child, would you not do well to be angry? So it is one of the strengths of man that he shall be able to glow with indignation at evil.

Only all such emotion must be kept well in hand and must never be suffered to degenerate into passion. Passion is always weak, emotion is an element of strength.

> The gods approve
> The depth and not the tumult of the soul.

But where a man does not let his wrath against evil go sputtering off aimlessly, like a box of fireworks set all alight at once, then it comes to be a strength and a help to much that is good.

The other condition that makes wrath righteous and essential to the perfection of a man, is that there shall be in it no taint of malice. Anger may impel to punish and not be malicious, if its reason for punishment is the passionless impulse of justice or the reformation of the wrong-doer. Then it is pure and true and good. Such wrath is a part of the perfection of humanity, and such wrath was in Jesus Christ.

But, still further, Christ's anger was part of His revelation of God. What belongs to perfect man belongs to God in whose image man was made. People are very often afraid of attributing to the divine nature that emotion of wrath, very unnecessarily, I think, and to the detriment of all their conceptions of the divine nature.

There is no reason why we should not ascribe emotion to Him. Passions God has not; emotions the Bible represents Him as having. The god of the philosopher has none. He is a cold, impassive Somewhat, more like a block of ice than a god. But the God of the Bible has a heart that can be touched, and is capable of something like what we call in ourselves emotion. And if we rightly think of God as Love, there is no more reason why we should not think of God as having the other emotion of wrath; for as I have shown you, there is nothing in wrath itself which is derogatory to the perfection of the loftiest spiritual nature. In God's anger there is no self-regarding irritation, no passion, no malice. It is the necessary displeasure and aversion of infinite purity at the sight of man's impurity. God's anger is His love thrown back upon itself from unreceptive and unloving hearts. Just as a wave that would roll in smooth, unbroken, green beauty into the open door of some sea cave is dashed back in spray and foam from some grim rock, so the love of God, meeting the unloving heart that rejects it, and the purity of God meeting the impurity of man, necessarily become that solemn reality, the wrath of the most high God. "A God all mercy were a God unjust." The judge is condemned when the culprit is acquitted; and he that strikes out of the divine nature the capacity for anger against sin, little as he thinks it, is degrading the righteousness and diminishing the love of God.

Oh, dear brethren, I beseech you do not let any easy-going gospel that has nothing to say to you about God's necessary aversion from, and displeasure with, and chastisement of, your sins and mine, draw you away from the solemn and wholesome belief that there is that in God which must hate and war against and chastise our evil, and that if there were not, He would be neither worth loving nor worth trusting. And His Son, in His tears and in His tenderness, which were habitual, and also in that lightning flash which once shot across the sky of His nature, was revealing Him to us. The Gospel is not only the revelation of God's righteousness for faith, but is also "the revelation of His wrath against all ungodliness and unrighteousness of men."

"It is hard for thee to kick against the pricks." The ox, with the yoke on his neck, lashes out with his obstinate heels against the driver's goad. He does not break the goad, but only injures his own limbs. Do not you do that!

2. And now, once more, let me ask you to look at the compassion which goes with our Lord's anger here; "being grieved at the hardness of their hearts." The somewhat singular word rendered here "grieved," may either simply imply that this sorrow co-existed with the anger, or it may describe the sorrow as being sympathy or compassion. I am disposed to take it in the latter application, and so the lesson we gather from these words is the blessed thought that Christ's wrath was all blended with compassion and sympathetic sorrow.

He looked upon these scribes and Pharisees sitting there with hatred in their eyes; and two emotions, which many men suppose as discrepant and incongruous as fire and water, rose together in His heart: wrath, which fell on the evil; sorrow, which bedewed the doers of it. The anger was for the hardening; the compassion was for the hardeners.

If there be this blending of wrath and sorrow, the combination takes away from the anger all possibility of an admixture of these questionable ingredients, which mar human wrath, and make men shrink from attributing so turbid and impure an emotion to God. It is an anger which lies harmoniously in the heart side by side with the tenderest pity—the truest, deepest sorrow.

Again, if Christ's sorrow flowed out thus along with His anger when He looked upon men's evil, then we understand in how tragic a sense He was "a Man of sorrows and acquainted with grief." The pain and the burden and the misery of His earthly life had no selfish basis. They were not like the pain and the burdens and the misery that so many of us howl out so loudly about, arising from causes affecting ourselves. But for Him—with His perfect purity, with His deep compassion, with His heart that was the most sensitive heart that ever beat in a human breast, because it was the only perfectly pure one that ever beat there—for Him to go among men was to be wounded and bruised and hacked by the sharp words of their sins.

Everything that He touched burned that pure nature, which was sensitive to evil, like an infant's hand to hot iron. His sorrow and His anger were the two sides of the medal. His feelings in looking on sin were like a piece of woven stuff with a pattern on either side, on one the fiery threads—the wrath; on the other the silvery tints of sympathetic pity. A warp of wrath, a woof of sorrow, dew and flame married and knit together.

And may we not draw from this same combination of these two apparently discordant emotions in our Lord, the lesson of what it is in men that makes them the true subjects of pity? Ay, these scribes and Pharisees had very little notion that there was anything about them to compassionate. But the thing which in the sight of God makes the true evil of men's condition is not their circumstances but their sins. The one thing to weep for when we look at the world is not its misfortunes, but its wickedness. Ah! brother, that is the misery of miseries; that is the one thing worth crying about in our own lives, or in anybody else's. From this combination of indignation and pity, we may learn how we should look upon evil. Men are divided into two classes in their way of looking at wickedness in this world. One set is rigid and stern, and crackling into wrath; the other set placid and goodnatured, and ready to weep over it as a misfortune and a calamity, but afraid or unwilling to say: "These poor creatures are to be blamed as well as pitied.'' It is of prime importance that we all should try to take both points of view, looking on sin as a thing to be frowned at, but also looking on it as a thing to be wept over; and to regard evildoers as persons that deserve to be blamed and to be chastised, and made to feel the bitterness of their evil, and not to interfere too much with the salutary laws that bring down sorrow upon men's heads if they have been doing wrong, but, on the other hand, to take care that our sense of justice does not swallow up the compassion that weeps for the criminal as an object of pity. Public opinion and legislation swing from the one extreme to the other. We have to make an effort to keep in the center, and never to look round in anger, unsoftened by pity, nor in pity, enfeebled by being separated from righteous indignation.

3. Let me now deal briefly with the last point that is here, namely, the occasion for both the sorrow and the anger. ''Being grieved at the *hardening* of the hearts.'' As I said at the beginning of these remarks, ''hardness,'' the rendering of our Authorized Version, is not quite so near the mark as that of the Revised Version, which speaks not so much of a condition as of a process: ''He was grieved at the hardening of their hearts,'' which He saw going on there.

And what was hardening their hearts? It was He. Why were their hearts being hardened? Because they were looking at Him, His graciousness, His goodness, and His power, and were steeling themselves against Him, opposing to His grace and tenderness their own obstinate determination. Some little gleams of light were coming in at their windows, and they clapped the shutters up. Some tones of His voice were coming into their ears, and they stuffed their fingers into them. They half felt that if they let themselves be influenced by Him it was all over, and so they set their teeth and steadied themselves in their antagonism.

And that is what some of you are doing now. Jesus Christ is never preached to you, even though it is as imperfectly as I do it, but that you either gather yourselves into an attitude of resistance, or, at least of mere indifference till the flow of the sermon's words is done; or else open your hearts to His mercy and His grace.

Oh, dear brethren, will you take this lesson of the last part of my text, that nothing so tends to harden a man's heart to the Gospel of Jesus Christ as religious formalism? If Jesus Christ were to come in here now, and stand where I am standing, and look round about upon this congregation, I wonder how many a highly respectable and perfectly proper man and woman, church- and chapel-goer, who keeps the Sabbath day, He would find on whom He had to look with grief not unmingled with anger, because they were hardening their hearts against Him now. I am sure there are some of such among my present audience. I am sure there are some of you about whom it is true that "the publicans and the harlots will go into the Kingdom of God before you," because in their degradation they may be nearer the lowly penitence and the consciousness of their own misery and need, which will open their eyes to see the beauty and the preciousness of Jesus Christ.

Dear brother, let no reliance upon any external attention to religious ordinances; no interest, born of long habit of hearing sermons; no trust in the fact of your being communicants, blind you to this, that all these things may come between you and your Saviour, and so may take you away into the outermost darkness.

Dear brother or sister, you are a sinner. "The God in whose hand thy breath is, and whose are all thy ways, thou hast not glorified." You have forgotten Him; you have lived to please yourselves. I charge you with nothing criminal, with nothing gross or sensual; I know nothing about you in such matters; but I know this—that you have a heart like mine, that we have all of us the one character, and that we all need the one gospel of that Saviour "who bare our sins in His own body on the tree," and died that whosoever trusts in Him may live here and yonder. I beseech you, harden not your hearts, but today hear His voice, and remember the solemn words which not I, but the Apostle of Love, has spoken: "He that believeth on the Son hath everlasting life, he that believeth not the Son shall not see life, but the wrath of God abideth upon Him." Flee to that sorrowing and dying Saviour, and take the cleansing which He gives, that you may be safe on the sure foundation when God shall arise to do His strange work of judgment, and may never know the awful meaning of that solemn word—"the wrath of the Lamb."

Ambassadors for Christ

6. And the Pharisees went forth, and straightway took counsel
with the Herodians against Him, how they might destroy Him. 7.
But Jesus Christ withdrew Himself with his disciples to the sea; and
a great multitude from Galilee followed Him, and from Judea, 8.
And from Jerusalem, and from Idumea, and from beyond Jordan;
and they about Tyre and Sidon, a great multitude, when they had
heard what great things He did, came unto Him. 9. And He spake
to His disciples, that a small ship should wait on Him because of the
multitude, lest they should throng him. 10. For he had healed
many; insomuch that they pressed upon Him for to touch him, as
many as had plagues. 11. And unclean spirits, when they saw Him,
fell down before Him, and cried, saying, Thou art the Son of

God. 12. And He straitly charged them that they should not make Him known. 13. And He goeth up into a mountain, and calleth unto Him whom He would: and they came unto Him. 14. And He ordained twelve, that they should be with Him, and that He might send them forth to preach. 15. And to have power to heal sicknesses, and to cast out devils: 16. And Simon He surnamed Peter; 17. And James the son of Zebedee, and John the brother of James; and He surnamed them Boanerges, which is, The sons of thunder: 18. And Andrew, and Philip, and Bartholomew, and Matthew, and Thomas, and James the son of Alpheus, and Thaddeus, and Simon the Canaanite, 19. And the Judas Iscariot, which also betrayed Him: and they went into an house.'' MARK 3:6–19.

A common object of hatred cements antagonists into strange alliance. Hawks and kites join in assailing a dove. Pharisees and Herod's partisans were antipodes; the latter must have parted with all their patriotism and much of their religion, but both parties were ready to sink their differences in order to get rid of Jesus, whom they instinctively felt to threaten destruction to them both. Such alliances of mutually repellent partisans against Christ's cause are not out of date yet. Extremes join forces against what stands in the middle between them.

Jesus withdrew from the danger which was preparing, not from selfish desire to preserve life, but because His ''hour'' was not yet come. Discretion *is* sometimes the better part of valor. To avoid peril is right, to fly from duty is not. There are times when Luther's ''Here I stand; I can do nothing else; God help me! Amen,'' must be our motto; and there are times when the persecuted in one city are bound to flee to another. We shall best learn to distinguish between these times by keeping close to Jesus.

But side by side with official hatred, and in some measure the cause of it, was a surging rush of popular enthusiasm. Pharisees took offense at Christ's breaches of law in his Sabbath miracles. The crowd gaped at the wonders, and grasped at the possibility of cures for their afflicted. Neither party in the least saw below the surface. Mark describes two ''multitudes''—one made up of Galileans who, he accurately says, ''followed Him''; while the other ''came to Him'' from further afield. Note the geographical order in the list: the southern country of Judea, and the capital; then the trans-Jordanic territories beginning with Idumea in the south, and coming northward to Perea; and then the northwest bordering lands of Tyre and Sidon. Thus three parts of a circle round Galilee as center are described. Observe, also, how turbid and impure the full stream of popular enthusiasm was.

Christ's gracious, searching, illuminating words had no attraction for the multitude. "The great things He *did*" drew them with idle curiosity or desire for bodily healing. Still more impure was the motive which impelled the "evil spirits" to approach Him, drawn by a strange fascination to gaze on Him whom they knew to be their conqueror, and hated as the Son of God. Terror and malice drove them to His presence, and wrung from them acknowledgment of His supremacy. What intenser pain can any hell have than the clear recognition of Christ's character and power, coupled with fiercely obstinate and utterly vain rebellion against Him?

Note, further, our Lord's recoil from the tumult. He had retired before cunning plotters; He withdrew from gaping admirers, who did not know what they were crowding to, nor cared for His best gifts. It was no fastidious shrinking from low natures, nor any selfish wish for repose, that made Him take refuge in the fisherman's little boat. But His action teaches us a lesson that the best Christian work is hindered rather than helped by the "popularity" which dazzles many, and is often mistaken for success. Christ's motive for seeking to check rather than to stimulate such impure admiration, was that it would certainly increase the ruler's antagonism, and might even excite the attention of the Roman authorities, who had to keep a very sharp outlook for agitations among their turbulent subjects. Therefore, Christ first took to the boat, and then withdrew into the hills above the lake.

In that seclusion He summoned to Him a small nucleus, as it would appear, by individual selection. These would be such of the "multitude" as He has discerned to be humble souls who yearned for deliverance from worse than outward diseases or bondage, and who therefore waited for a Messiah who was more than a physician or a patriot warrior. A personal call and a personal yielding make true disciples. Happy we if our history can be summed up in "He called them unto Him, and they came." But there was an election within the chosen circle.

The choice of the Twelve marks an epoch in the development of Christ's work, and was occasioned, at this point of time, by both the currents which we find running so strong at this point in it. Precisely because Pharisaic hatred was becoming so threatening, and popular enthusiasm was opening opportunities which He singly could not utilize, He felt His need both for companions and for messengers. Therefore He surrounded Himself with that inner circle, and did it then. The appointment of the Apostles has been treated by some as a masterpiece of organization, which largely contributed to the progress of Christianity, and by others as an endowment of the Twelve with supernatural powers which are transmitted on certain outward conditions to their successors, and thereby give effect to sacraments, and are the legitimate channels for grace. But if we take Mark's statement of their function, our view will be much simpler. The number of twelve distinctly alludes to the tribes of Israel, and implies that the new community is to be the true people of God.

The Apostles were chosen for two ends, of which the former was preparatory to the latter. The latter was the more important and permanent, and hence gave the office its name. They were to be "with Christ," and we may fairly suppose that He wished that companionship for His own sake as well as for theirs. No doubt, the primary purpose was their training for their being sent forth to preach. But no doubt, also, the lonely Christ craved for companions, and was strengthened and soothed by even the imperfect sympathy and unintelligent love of these humble adherents. Who can fail to hear tones which reveal how much He hungered for companions in His grateful acknowledgment, "Ye are they which have continued with Me in My temptations"? It still remains true that we must be "with Christ" much and long before we can go forth as His messengers.

Note, too, that the miracle-working power comes last as least important. Peter had understood his office better than some of his alleged successors, when he made its qualification to be having been with Jesus during His life, and its office to be that of being witnesses of His resurrection (Acts 1).

The list of the Apostles presents many interesting points, at which we can only glance. If compared with the lists in the other Gospels and in Acts, it brings out clearly the division into three groups of four persons each. The order in which the four are named varies within the limits of each group; but none of the first four are ever in the lists degraded to the second or third group, and none of these are ever promoted beyond their own class. So there were apparently degrees among the Twelve, depending, no doubt, on spiritual receptivity, each man being as close to the Lord, and gifted with as much of the sunshine of His love, as he was fit for.

Further, their places in relation to each other vary. The first four are always first, and Peter is always at their head; but in Matthew and Luke, the pairs of brothers are kept together, while, in Mark, Andrew is parted from his brother Simon, and put last of the first four. That place indicates the closer relation of the other three to Jesus, of which several instances will occur to everyone. But Mark puts James before John, and his list evidently reflects the memory of the original superiority of James as probably the elder. There was a time when John was known as "James's brother." But the time came, as Acts shows, when John took precedence, and was closely linked with Peter as the two leaders. So the ties of kindred may be loosened, and new bonds of fellowship created by similarity of relation to Jesus. In His kingdom, the elder may fall behind the younger. Rank in it depends on likeness to the King.

The surname of Boanerges, "Sons of Thunder," given to the brothers, can scarcely be supposed to commemorate a characteristic prior to discipleship. Christ does not perpetuate old faults in his servants' new names. It must rather refer to excellences which were heightened and hallowed in them by following Jesus. Probably, therefore, it points to a certain majesty of utterance. Do we not hear the boom of thunderpeals in the prologue to John's Gospel, perhaps the grandest words ever written?

In the second quartet, Bartholomew is probably Nathanael; and, if so, his conjunction with Philip is an interesting coincidence with John 1:45, which tells that Philip brought him to Jesus. All three Gospels put the two names together, as if the two men had kept up their association; but, in Acts, Thomas takes precedence of Bartholomew, as if a closer spiritual relationship had by degrees sprung up between Philip, the leader of the second group, and Thomas, which slackened the old bond. Note that these two, who are coupled in Acts, are two of the interlocutors in the final discourses in the upper room (John 14). Mark, like Luke, puts Matthew before Thomas; but Matthew puts himself last, and adds his designation of "publican"—a beautiful example of humility.

The last group contains names which have given commentators trouble. I am not called on to discuss the question of the identity of the James who is one of its members. Thaddeus is by Luke called Judas, both in his Gospel and in the Acts; and by Matthew, according to one reading, Lebbaeus. Both names are probably surnames, the former being probably derived from a word meaning *breast,* and the latter from one signifying *heart*. They seem, therefore, to be nearly equivalent, and may express largeheartedness.

Simon "the Canaanite" (AV) is properly "the Cananean" (RV). There was no alien in blood among the Twelve. The name is a late Aramaic word meaning *zealot*. Hence Luke translates it for Gentile readers. He was one of the fanatical sect who would not have anything to do with Rome, and who played such a terrible part in the final catastrophe of Israel. The baser elements were purged out of his fiery enthusiasm when he became Christ's man. The hallowing and curbing of earthly passion, the ennobling of enthusiasm, are achieved when the pure flame of love to Christ burns up their dross.

Judas Iscariot closes the list, cold and venomous as a snake. Enthusiasm in him there was none. The problem of his character is too complex to be entered on here. But we may lay to heart the warning that, if a man is not knit to Christ by heart's love and obedience, the more he comes into contact with Jesus the more will he recoil from Him, till at last he is borne away by a passion of detestation. Christ is either a sure foundation or a stone of stumbling.

"He is Beside Himself."

And when His friends heard of it, they went out to lay hold on Him: for they said, He is beside Himself. MARK 3:21.

There had been great excitement in the little town of Capernaum in consequence of Christ's teachings and miracles. It had been intensified by His infractions of the Rabbinical Sabbath law, and by His appointment of the twelve Apostles. The sacerdotal party in Capernaum apparently communicated with Jerusalem, with the result of bringing a deputation from the Sanhedrin to look into things, and see what this new rabbi was about. A plot for His assassination was secretly on foot. And at this juncture the incident of my text, which we owe to Mark alone of the Evangelists, occurs. Christ's friends, apparently the members of His own family—sad to say, as would appear from the context, including His mother—came with a kindly design to rescue their misguided kinsman from danger, and laying hands upon Him, to carry Him off to some safe restraint in Nazareth, where He might indulge His delusions without doing any harm to Himself. They wish to excuse His eccentricities on the ground that He is not quite responsible—scarcely Himself; and so to blunt the point of the more hostile explanation of the Pharisees that He is in league with Beelzebub.

Conceive of that! The Incarnate Wisdom shielded by friends from the accusation that He is a demoniac by the apology that He is a lunatic! What do you think of popular judgment?

But this half-pitying, half-contemptuous, and wholly benevolent excuse for Jesus, though it be the word of friends, is like the words of His enemies, in that it contains a distorted reflection of His true character. And if we will think about it, I fancy that we may gather from it some lessons not altogether unprofitable.

1. The first point, then, that I make, is just this—there was something in the character of Jesus Christ which could be plausibly explained to commonplace people as madness. A well-known modern author has talked a great deal about "the sweet reasonableness of Jesus Christ." His contemporaries called it simple insanity; if they did not say "He hath a devil," as well as "He is mad."

Now, if we try to throw ourselves back to the life of Jesus Christ, as it was unfolded day by day, and think nothing about either what preceded in the revelation of the Old Covenant, or what followed in the history of Christianity, we shall not be so much at a loss to account for such explanations of it as these of my text. Remember that charges like these, in all various keys of contempt or of pity, or of fierce hostility, have been cast against all innovators, against every man that has broken a new path; against all teachers that have cut themselves apart from tradition and encrusted formulas; against every man that has waged war with the conventionalisms of society; against all idealists who have dreamed dreams and seen visions; against every man that has been touched with a lofty enthusiasm of any sort; and, most of all, against all to whom God and their relations to Him, the spiritual world and their relations to it, the future life and their relations to that, have become dominant forces and motives in their lives.

The short and easy way with which the world excuses itself from the poignant lessons and rebukes which come from such lives is something like that of my text, "He is beside himself." And the proof that he is beside himself is that he does not act in the same fashion as these incomparably wise people that make up the majority in every age. There is nothing that commonplace men hate like anything fresh and original. There is nothing that men of low aims are so utterly bewildered to understand, and which so completely passes all the calculus of which they are masters, as lofty self-abnegation. And wherever you get men smitten with such, or with anything like it, you will find all the low-aimed people gathering round them like bats round a torch in a cavern, flapping their obscene wings and uttering their harsh croaks, and only desiring to quench the light.

One of our cynical authors says that it is the mark of a genius that all the dullards are against him. It is the mark of the man who dwells with God that all the people whose portion is in this life with one consent say, "He is beside himself."

And so the Leader of them all was served in His day; and that purest, perfectest, noblest, loftiest, most utterly self-oblivious, and God-and-man-devoted life that ever was lived upon earth, was disposed of in this extremely simple method, so comforting to the complacency of the critics—either "He is beside Himself," or "He hath a devil."

And yet, is not the saying a witness to the presence in that wondrous and gentle career of an element entirely unlike what exists in the most of mankind? Here was a new star in the heavens, and the law of its orbit was manifestly different from that of all the rest. That is what "eccentric" means—that the life to which it applies does not move round the same center as do the other satellites, but has a path of its own. Away out yonder somewhere, in the infinite depths, lay the hidden point which drew it to itself and determined its magnificent and overwhelmingly vast orbit. These men witness to Jesus Christ, even by their half excuse, half reproach, that His was a life unique and inexplicable by the ordinary motives which shape the little lives of the masses of mankind. They witness to His entire neglect of ordinary and low aims; to His complete absorption in lofty purposes, which to His purblind, would-be critics seem to be delusions and fond imaginations that could never be realized. They witness to what His disciples remembered had been written of Him, "The zeal of Thy house hath eaten Me up"; to His perfect devotion to man and to God. They witness to His consciousness of a mission; and there is nothing that men are so ready to resent as that. To tell a world, engrossed in self and low aims, that one is sent from God to do His will, and to spread it among men, is the sure way to have all the heavy artillery and the lighter weapons of the world turned against one.

These characteristics of Jesus seem then to be plainly implied in that allegation of insanity—lofty aims, absolute originality, utter self-abnegation, the continual consciousness of communion with God, devotion to the service of man, and the sense of being sent by God for the salvation of the world. It was because of these that His friends said, "He is beside Himself."

These men judged themselves by judging Jesus Christ. And all men do. There are as many different estimates of a great man as there are people to estimate, and hence the diversity of opinion about all the characters that fill history and the galleries of the past. The eye sees what it brings and no more. To discern the greatness of a great man, or the goodness of a good one, is to possess, in lower measure, some portion of that which we discern. Sympathy is the condition of insight into character. And so our Lord said once, "He that receiveth a prophet in the name of a prophet shall receive a prophet's reward," because he is a dumb prophet himself, and has a lower power of the same gift in him, which is eloquent on the prophet's lips.

In like manner, to discern what is in Christ is the test of whether there is any of it in myself. And thus it is no mere arbitrary appointment which suspends your salvation and mine on our answer to this question, "What think ye of Christ?" The answer will be—I was going to say—the elixir of our whole moral and spiritual nature. It will be the outcome of our inmost selves. This plowshare turns up the depths of the soil. That is eternally true which the gray-bearded Simeon, the representative of the Old, said when he took the Infant in his arms and looked down upon the unconscious, placid, smooth face. "This Child is set for the rise and fall of many in Israel, that the thoughts of many hearts may be revealed." Your answer to that question discloses your whole spiritual condition and capacities. And so to judge Christ is to be judged by Him; and what we think Him to be, that we make Him to ourselves. The question which tests us is not merely, "Whom do men say that I am?" It is easy to answer that; but this is the all-important interrogation, "Whom do *ye* say that I am?" I pray that we may each answer as he to whom it was first put answered it, "Rabbi, Thou art the Son of God, Thou art the King of Israel!"

2. Second, mark the similarity of the estimate which will be passed by the world on all Christ's true followers. The same elements exist today, the same intolerance of anything higher than the low level, the same incapacity to comprehend simple devotion and lofty aims, the same dislike of a man who comes and rebukes by his silent presence the vices in which he takes no part. And it is a great deal easier to say, "Poor fool! enthusiastic fanatic!" than it is to lay to heart the lesson that lies in such a life.

The one thing, or at least the principal thing, which the Christianity of this generation needs is a little more of this madness. It would be a great deal better for us who call ourselves Christians if we had earned and deserved the world's sneer, "He is beside himself." But our modern Christianity, like an epicure's rare wines, is preferred iced. And the last thing that anybody would think of suggesting in connection with the demeanor—either the conduct or the words—of the average Christian man of this day is that his religion had touched his brain a little.

But, dear friends, go in Christ's footsteps and you will have the same missiles flung at you. If a church or an individual has earned the praise of the outside ring of godless people because its or his religion is "reasonable and moderate; and kept in its proper place; and not allowed to interfere with social enjoyments, and political and municipal corruptions," and the like, then there is much reason to ask whether that church or man is Christian after Christ's pattern. Oh, I pray that there may come down on the professing Church of this generation a baptism of the Spirit; and I am quite sure that when that comes, the people that admire moderation and approve of religion, but like it to be "kept in its own place," will be all ready to say, when they hear the "sons and the daughters prophesying, and the old men seeing visions, and the young men dreaming dreams," and the fiery tongues uttering their praises of God, "These men are full of new wine." Would we *were* full of the new wine of the Spirit. Do you think any one would say of your religion that you were "beside yourself," because you made so much of it? They said it about your Master, and if you were like Him it would be said, in one tone or another, about you. We are all desperately afraid of enthusiasm today. It seems to be that it is *the* want of the Christian Church, and that we are not enthusiastic because we don't half believe the truths that we say are our creed.

One more word. Christian men and women have to make up their minds to go on in the path of devotion, conformity to Christ's pattern, self-sacrificing surrender, without minding one bit what is said about them. Brethren, I do not think Christian people are in half as much danger of dropping the standard of the Christian life by reason of the sarcasms of the world, as they are by reason of the low tone of the Church. Don't you take your ideas of what a reasonable Christian life is from the men round you, howsoever they may profess to be Christ's followers. And let us keep so near the Master that we may be able to say, "With me it is a very small matter to be judged of you, or of man's judgment. He that judgeth me is the Lord." Never mind, though they say, "Beside himself!" Never mind, though they say, "Oh! utterly extravagant and impracticable." Better that than to be patted on the back by a world that likes nothing so well as a Church with its teeth drawn, and its claws out; which may be made a plaything and an ornament by the world. And that is what much of our modern Christianity has come to be.

3. Lastly, notice the sanity of the insane. I have only space to put before you three little pictures, and ask you what you think of them. I dare say the originals might be found among us without much search.

Here is one. Suppose a man who, like the most of us, believes that there is a God, believes that he has something to do with Him, believes that he is going to die, believes that the future state is, in some way or other, and in some degree, one of retribution; and from Monday morning to Saturday night he ignores all these facts, and never allows them to influence one of his actions. May I venture to speak direct to this hypothetical person, whose originals are dotted about in my audience? It would be the very same to you if you said, "No" instead of "Yes" to all these affirmations. The fact that there is a God does not make a bit of difference to what you do, or what you think, or what you feel. The fact that there is a future life makes just as little difference. You are going on a voyage next week, and you never dream of getting your outfit. You believe all these things, you are an intelligent man—you are very likely, in a great many ways, a very amiable and pleasant one; you do many things very well; you cultivate congenial virtues, and you abhor uncongenial vices; but you never think about God; and you have made absolutely no preparation whatever for stepping into the scene in which you know that you are to live.

Well, you may be a very wise man, a student with high aims, cultivated understanding, and all the rest of it. I want to know whether, taking into account all that you are, and your inevitable connection with God, and your certain death and certain life in a state of retribution—I want to know whether we should call your conduct sanity or insanity? Which?

Take another picture. Here is a man that believes—really believes—the articles of the Christian creed, and in some measure has received them into his heart and life. He believes that Jesus Christ, the Son of God, died for him upon the Cross, and yet his heart has but the feeblest tick of pulsating love in answer. He believes that prayer will help a man in all circumstances, and yet he hardly ever prays. He believes that self-denial is the law of the Christian life, and yet he lives for himself. He believes that he is here as a "pilgrim" and as a "sojourner," and yet his heart clings to the world, and his hand would fain cling to it, like that of a drowning man swept over Niagara, and catching at anything on the banks. He believes that he is sent into the world to be a "light" of the world, and yet from out of his self-absorbed life there has hardly ever come one sparkle of light into any dark heart. And that is a picture, not exaggerated, of the enormous majority of professing Christians in so-called Christian lands. And I want to know whether we shall call that sanity or insanity?

The last of my little miniatures is that of a man who keeps in close touch with Jesus Christ, and so, like Him, can say, "Lo! I come; I delight to do Thy will, O Lord. Thy law is within my heart." He yields to the strong motives and principles that flow from the Cross of Jesus Christ, and, drawn by the "mercies of God," gives himself a "living sacrifice" to be used as God will. Aims as lofty as the Throne which Christ His Brother fills; sacrifice as entire as that on which his trembling hope relies; realization of the unseen future as vivid and clear as His who could say that He was "*in* Heaven" while He walked the earth; subjugation of self as complete as that of the Lord's, who pleased not Himself, and came not to do His own will—these are some of the characteristics which mark the true disciple of Jesus Christ. And I want to know whether the conduct of the man who believes in the love that God hath to him, as manifested in the Cross, and surrenders his whole self thereto, despising the world and living for God, for Christ, for man, for eternity—whether his conduct is insanity or sanity?

"The fear of the Lord is the beginning of wisdom."

The Mistakes of Christ's Foes and Friends

And the scribes which came down from Jerusalem said, He hath Beelzebub, and by the prince of the devils casteth He out devils. 23.

And He called them unto Him, and said unto them in parables, How
can Satan cast out Satan? 24. And if a kingdom be divided against
itself, that kingdom cannot stand. 25. And if a house be divided
against itself, that house cannot stand. 26. And if Satan rise up
against himself, and be divided, he cannot stand, but hath an
end. 27. No man can enter into a strong man's house, and spoil his
goods, except he will first bind the strong man; and then he will spoil
his house. 28. Verily I say unto you, All sins shall be forgiven unto
the sons of men, and blasphemies wherewith soever they shall blas-
pheme: 29. But he that shall blaspheme against the Holy Ghost
hath never forgiveness, but is in danger of eternal damnation: 30.
Because they said, He hath an unclean spirit. 31. There came then
His brethren and His mother, and, standing without, sent unto Him,
calling Him. 32. And the multitude sat about Him, and they said
unto Him, Behold, Thy mother and Thy brethren without seek for
Thee. 33. And he answered them, saying, Who is my mother, or my
brethren? 34. And He looked round about on them which sat about
Him, and said, Behold My mother and My brethren! 35. For who-
soever shall do the will of God, the same is My brother, and My
sister, and mother. MARK 3:22–35.

We have in this passage three parts,—the outrageous official explanation of Christ and His works, the Lord's own solution of His miracles, and His relatives' well-meant attempt to secure Him, with His answer to it.

1. The scribes, like Christ's other critics, judged themselves in judging Him, and bore witness to the truths which they were eager to deny. Their explanation would be ludicrous, if it were not dreadful. Mark that it distinctly admits His miracles. It is not fashionable at present to attach much weight to the fact that none of Christ's enemies ever doubted these. Of course, the credence of men, in an age which believed in the possibility of the supernatural, is more easy, and their testimony less cogent, than that of a jury of twentieth-century scientific skeptics. But the expectation of miracle had been dead for centuries when Christ came; and at first, at all events, no anticipation that He would work them made it easier to believe that He did.

It would have been a sure way of exploding His pretensions, if the officials could have shown that His miracles were tricks. Not without weight is the attestation from the foe that "this man casteth out demons." The preposterous explanation that He cast out demons by Beelzebub, is the very last resort of hatred so deep that it will father an absurdity rather than accept the truth. It witnesses to the inefficiency of explanations of Him which omit the supernatural. The scribes recognized that here was a man who was in touch with the unseen. They fell back upon "by Beelzebub," and thereby admitted that humanity, without seeing something more at the back of it, never made such a man as Jesus.

It is very easy to solve an insoluble problem, if you begin by taking the insoluble elements out of it. That is how a great many modern attempts to account for Christianity go to work. Knock out the miracles, waive Christ's own claims as mistaken reports, declare His resurrection to be entirely unhistorical, and the remainder will be easily accounted for, and not worth accounting for. But the whole life of the Christ of the Gospels is adequately explained by no explanation which leaves out His coming forth from the Father, and His exercise of powers above those of humanity and "nature."

This explanation is an instance of the credulity of unbelief. It is more difficult to believe the explanation than the alternative which it is framed to escape. If like produces like, Christ cannot be explained by anything but the admission of His divine nature. Serpents' eggs do not hatch out into doves. The difficulties of faith are "gnats" beside the "camels" which unbelief has to swallow.

2. The true explanation of Christ's power over *demoniacs*. Jesus has no difficulty in putting aside the absurd theory that, in destroying the kingdom of evil, He was a servant of evil and its dark ruler. Common sense says, If Satan cast out Satan, he is divided against himself, and his kingdom cannot stand. An old play is entitled, "The Devil is an Ass," but he is not such an ass as to fight against himself. As the proverb has it, "Hawks do not pick out hawks' eyes."

It would carry us too far to deal at length with the declarations of our Lord here, which throw a dim light into the dark world of supernatural evil. His words are far too solemn and didactic to be taken as accommodations to popular prejudice, or as mere metaphor. Is it not strange that people will believe in spiritual communications, when they are vouched for by a newspaper editor, more readily than when Christ asserts their reality? Is it not strange that scientists, who find difficulty in the importance which Christianity attaches to man in the plan of the universe, and will not believe that all its starry orbs were built for him (which Christianity does not allege), should be incredulous of teachings which reveal a crowd of higher intelligences?

Jesus not only tests the futile explanation by common sense, but goes on to suggest the true one. He accepts the belief that there is a "prince of the demons." He regards the souls of men who have not yielded themselves to God as His "goods." He declares that the lord of the house must be bound before his property can be taken from him. We cannot stay to enlarge on the solemn view of the condition of unredeemed men thus given. Let us not put it lightly away. But we must note how deep into the center of Christ's work this teaching leads us. Translated into plain language it just means that Christ by incarnation, life, death, resurrection, ascension, and present work from the throne, has broken the power of evil in its central hold. He has crushed the serpent's head, his heel is firmly planted on it, and, though the reptile may still "swinge the scaly horror of his folded tail," it is but the dying flurries of the creature. He was manifested "that He might destroy the works of the devil."

No trace of indignation can be detected in Christ's answer to the hideous charge. But His patient heart overflows in pity for the reckless slanderers, and He warns them that they are coming near the edge of a precipice. Their malicious blindness is hurrying them towards a sin which hath never forgiveness. Blasphemy is, in form, injurious speaking, and in essence, it is scorn or malignant antagonism. The Holy Spirit is the divine agent in revealing God's heart and will. To blaspheme Him is "the external symptom of a heart so radically and finally set against God that no power which God can consistently use will ever save it." "The sin, therefore, can only be the culmination of a long course of self-hardening and depraving." It is unforgivable, because the soul which can recognize God's revelation of Himself in all His goodness and moral perfection, and be stirred only to hatred thereby, has reached a dreadful climax of hardness, and has ceased to be capable of being influenced by His beseeching. It has passed beyond the possibility of penitence and acceptance of forgiveness. The sin is unforgiven, because the sinner is fixed in impenitence, and his stiffened will cannot bow to receive pardon.

The true reason why that sin has never forgiveness is suggested by the accurate rendering, "Is guilty of an eternal sin" (RV). Since the sin is eternal, the forgiveness is impossible. Practically, hardened and permanent unbelief, conjoined with malicious hatred of the only means of forgiveness, is the unforgivable sin. Much torture of heart would have been saved if it had been observed that the Scripture expression is not *sin,* but *blasphemy*. Fear that it has been committed is proof positive that it has not; for, if it have been, there will be no relenting in enmity, nor any wish for deliverance.

But let not the terrible picture of the depths of impenitence to which a soul may fall, obscure the blessed universality of the declaration from Christ's lips which preludes it, and declares that all sin but the sin of not desiring pardon is pardoned. No matter how deep the stain, no matter how inveterate the habit, whosoever will can come and be sure of pardon.

3. The attempt of Christ's relatives to withdraw Him from publicity, and His reply to it. Verse 21 tells us that His kindred sent out to lay hold on Him; for they thought Him beside Himself. He was to be shielded from the crowd of followers, and from the plots of scribes, by being kept at home and treated as a harmless lunatic. Think of Jesus defended from the imputation of being in league with Beelzebub by the excuse that He was mad! This visit of His mother and brethren must be connected with their plan to lay hold on Him, in order to apprehend rightly Christ's answer. If they did not mean to use violence, why should they have tried to get Him away from the crowd of followers, by a message, when they could have reached Him as easily as it did? He knew the snare laid for Him, and puts it aside without shaming its contrivers. With a wonderful blending of dignity and tenderness, He turns from kinsmen who were not akin, to draw closer to Himself, and pour His love over, those who do the will of God.

The test of relationship with Jesus is obedience to His Father. Christ is not laying down the means of becoming His kinsmen, but the tokens that we are such. He is sometimes misunderstood as saying, "Do God's will without My help, and ye will become My kindred." What He really says is, "If ye are My kindred, you will do God's will; and if you do, you will show that you are such." So the statement that we become His kindred by faith does not conflict with this great saying. The two take hold of the Christian life at different points: the one deals with the means of its origination, the other with the tokens of its reality. Faith is the root of obedience, obedience is the blossom of faith. Jesus does not stand like a stranger till we have hammered out obedience to His Father, and then reward us by welcoming us as His brethren, but He answers our faith by giving us a life kindred with, because derived from, His own, and then we can obey.

It is active submission to God's will, not orthodox creed or devout emotion, which shows that we are His blood relations. By such obedience, we draw His love more and more to us. Though it is not the means of attaining to kinship with Him, it *is* the condition of receiving love-tokens from Him, and of increasing affinity with Him.

That relationship includes and surpasses all earthly ones. Each obedient man is, as it were, all three —mother, sister, and brother. Of course the enumeration had reference to the members of the waiting group, but the remarkable expression has deep truth in it. Christ's relation to the soul covers all various sweetnesses of earthly bonds, and is spoken of in terms of many of them. He is the bridegroom, the brother, the companion, and friend. All the scattered fragrances of these are united and surpassed in the transcendent and ineffable union of the soul with Jesus. Every lonely heart may find in Him what it most needs, and perhaps is bleeding away its life for the loss or want of it. To many a weeping mother He has said, pointing to Himself, "Woman, behold thy son"; to many an orphan He has whispered, revealing His own love, "Son, behold thy mother."

All earthly bonds are honored most when they are woven into crowns for His head; all human love is then sweetest when it is as a tiny mirror in which the great Sun is reflected. Christ is husband, brother, sister, friend, lover, mother, and more than all which these sacred names designate,—even Saviour and life. If His blood is in our veins, and His spirit is the spirit of our lives, we shall do the will of His and our Father in heaven.

Christ's Kindred

> *There came then His brethren and His mother, and standing without, sent unto Him, calling Him. 32. And the multitude sat about Him; and they said unto Him, Behold, Thy mother and Thy brethren without seek for Thee. 33. And He answered them, saying, Who is My mother, or My brethren? 34. And He looked round about on them which sat about Him, and said, Behold My mother and My brethren! 35. For whosoever shall do the will of God, the same is My brother, and My sister, and mother.* MARK 3:31–35.

We learn from an earlier part of this chapter, and from it only, the significance of this visit of Christ's brethren and mother. It was prompted by the belief that "He was beside Himself," and they meant to lay hands on Him, possibly with a kindly wish to save Him from a worse fate, but certainly to stop His activity. We do not know whether Mary consented, in her mistaken maternal affection, to the scheme, or whether she was brought unwillingly to give a color to it, and influence our Lord. The sinister purpose of the visit betrays itself in the fact that the brethren did not present themselves before Christ, but sent a messenger; although they could as easily have had access to His presence as their messenger could. Apparently they wished to get Him by Himself, so as to avoid the necessity of using force against the force that His disciples would be likely to put forth. Jesus knew their purpose, though they thought it was hidden deep in the recesses of their breasts. And that falls in with a great many other incidents which indicate His superhuman knowledge of "the thoughts and intents of the heart."

But, however that may be, our Lord here, with a singular mixture of dignity, tenderness, and decisiveness, puts aside the insidious snare without shaming its contrivers, and turns from the kinsmen, with whom He had no real bond, to draw closer to Himself, and pour out His love over, those who do the will of His Father in heaven. His words go very deep; let us try to gather some, at any rate, of the surface lessons which they suggest.

1. First, then, the true token of blood relationship to Jesus Christ is obedience to God. "Whosoever shall do the will of God, the same is My brother, and My sister, and mother." Now I must not be betrayed into a digression from my main purpose by dwelling upon what yet is worthy of notice—viz., the consciousness, on the part of Jesus Christ, which here is evidently implied, that the doing of the will of God was the very inmost secret of His own being. He was conscious, only and always, of delighting to do the will of God. When, therefore, He found that delight in others, there He recognized a bond of union between Him and them.

We must carefully observe that these great words of our Lord are not intended to describe the means by which men become His kinsfolk, but the tokens that they are such. He is not saying—as superficial readers sometimes run away with the notion that He is saying—"If a man will, apart from Me, do the will of God, then he will become My true kinsman," but He is saying, "If you are My kinsman, you will do the will of God, and if you do it, you will show that you are related to Myself." In other words, He is not speaking about the means of originating this relationship, but about the signs of its reality. And, therefore, the words of my text need, for their full understanding, and for placing them in due relation to all the rest of Christ's teaching, to be laid side by side with other words of His, such as these: "Apart from Me ye can do nothing." For the deepest truth in regard to relationship to Jesus Christ and obedience is this, that the way by which men are made able to do the will of God is by receiving into themselves the very life-blood of Jesus Christ. The relationship must precede the obedience, and the obedience is the sign, because it is the sequel, of the relationship.

But far deeper down than mere affinity lies the true bond between us and Christ, and the true means of performing the commandments of God. There must be a passing over into us of His own life-spirit. By His inhabiting our hearts, and molding our wills, and being the life of our lives and the soul of our souls, are we made able to do the commandments of the Lord. And so, seeing that actual union with Jesus Christ, and the reception into ourselves of His life, is the precedent condition of all true obedience, then the more familiar form of presenting the bond between Him and us, which runs through the New Testament, falls into its proper place, and the faith, which is the condition of receiving the life of Christ into our hearts, is at once the affinity which makes us His kindred, and the means by which we appropriate to ourselves the power of obedient submission and conformity to the will of God. "This is the work of God, that ye believe on Him whom He hath sent."

So, then, my text does not in the slightest degree contradict or interfere with the great teaching that the one way by which we become Christ's brethren is by trusting in Him. For the text and the doctrine that faith unites us to Him take up the process at different stages: the one pointing to the means of origination, the other to the tokens of reality. Faith is the root, obedience is the flower and the fruit. He that doeth the will of God, does it, not in order that he may become, but because he already is, possessor of a blood-relationship to Jesus Christ.

Then, notice, again, with what emphatic decisiveness our Lord here takes simple, practical obedience in daily life, in little and in great things, as the manifestation of being akin to Himself. Orthodoxy is all very well; religious experiences, inward emotions, sweet, precious, secret feelings and sentiments cannot be overestimated. External forms, whether of the more simple or of the more ornate and sensuous kind, may be helps for the religious life; and are so in view of the weaknesses that are always associated with it. But all these, a true creed, a belief in the creed, the joyous and deep and secret emotions that follow thereupon, and the participation in outward services which may help to these, all these are but scaffolding: the building is character and conduct conformed to the will of God.

Evangelical preachers, and those who in the main hold that faith, are often charged with putting too little stress on practical homely righteousness. I would that the charge had less substance in it. But let me lay it upon your consciences, dear brethren, now, that no amount of right credence, no amount of trust, nor of love and hope and joy will avail to witness kindred to Christ. It must be the daily life, in its efforts after conformity to the known will of God, in great things and in small things, that attests the family resemblance. If Christ's blood be in our veins, if "the law of the spirit of life" in Him is the law of the spirit of our lives, then these lives will run parallel with His, in some visible measure, and we, too, shall be able to say, "Lo! I come. I delight to do Thy will; and Thy law is within my heart." Obedience is the test of relationship to Jesus.

Then, still further, note how, though we must emphatically dismiss the mistake that we make ourselves Christ's brethren and friends by independent efforts after keeping the commandments, it is true that, in the measure in which we do thus bend our wills to God's will, whether in the way of action or of endurance, we realize more blessedly and strongly the tie that binds us to the Lord, and as a matter of fact do receive, in the measure of our obedience, sweet tokens of union with Him, and of love in His heart to us. No man will fully feel living contact with Jesus Christ if between Christ and him there is a film of conscious and voluntary disobedience to the will of God. The smallest crumb that can come in between two polished plates will prevent their adherence. A trivial sin will slip your hand out of Christ's hand; and though His love will still come and linger about you, until the sin is put out it cannot enter in.

> It can but listen at the gate,
> And hear the household jar within.

''He that doeth the will of God, the same is''—and feels himself to be—''My brother, and sister, and mother.''

2. This relationship includes all others. That is a very singular form of expression which our Lord employs. ''Whosoever shall do the will of God, the same is My brother, and sister, and mother.'' We should have expected, seeing that He was speaking about three different relationships, that He would have used the plural verb, and said, ''The same *are* My brother, and sister, and mother.'' And I do not think that it is pedantic grammatical accuracy to point out this remarkable form of speech, and even to venture to draw a conclusion from it—viz., that what our Lord meant was, not that if there were three people, of different sexes, and of different ages, all doing the will of God, one of these sweet names of relationship would apply to A, another to B, and the other to C; but that to each who does the will of God, all the sweetnesses that are hived in all the names, and in any other analogous ones that can be uttered, belong. Of course the selection here of relationships specified has reference to the composition of that group outside the circle. But there is a great deal more than that in it. Whether you accept the grammatical remark that I have made or no, we shall, at least, I suppose, all agree in this, that, in fact, the bond of kindred that unites a trusting obedient soul with Jesus Christ does in itself include whatsoever of sweetness, of power, of protection, of clinging trust, and of any other blessed emotion that makes a shadow of Eden still upon earth, has ever been attached to human bonds.

Remember how many of these, Christ, and His servants for Him, have laid their hands upon, and claimed to be His. ''Thy Maker is thy husband''; ''He that hath the Bride is the bridegroom''; ''Go tell My brethren''; ''I have not called you servants, but friends.'' And if there be any other sweet names, they belong to Him, and in His one pure, all-sufficient love they are all enclosed. Fragmentary preciousnesses are strewed about us. There is ''one pearl of great price.'' Many fragrances come from the flowers that grow on the dunghill of the world, but they are all gathered in Him whose name is "as ointment poured forth," filling the house with its fragrance.

For Christ is to us all that all separated lovers and friends can be. And whatsoever our poor hearts may need most, of human affection and sympathy, and may see least possibility of finding now, among the incompletenesses and limitations of earth, that Christ is waiting to be. All solitary souls and mourning hearts may turn themselves to, and rest themselves on, these great words. And as they look at the empty places in their circle, in their homes, and feel the ache of the empty places in their hearts, they may hear His voice saying, "Behold My mother and My brethren." He comes to us all in the character that we need most. Just as the great ocean, when it flows in amongst the land, takes the shape imposed upon it by the containing banks of the inlet, so Christ pours Himself into our hearts, and there assumes the form that the outline of their emptiness tells we need most. To many, in all generations, who have been weeping over departed joys, He says again, though with a different application, turning not away from but to Himself mourning eyes and hearts, "Woman, behold thy Son"—not on the cross nor in the grave, but on the throne—"Son, behold Thy mother."

3. Lastly, this relationship requires always the subordination, and sometimes the sacrifice, of the lower ones. We have to think of Christ here as Himself putting away the lower claims, in order more fully to yield Himself to the higher. It was because it would have been impossible for Him to do the will of His Father if He had yielded to the purposes of His brethren and His mother, that He steeled His heart and made solemn His tone in refusing to go with them.

That group that had come for Him suggests to us the ways in which earthly ties may limit heavenly obedience. In regard to them, the situation was complicated, because Jesus Christ was their kinsman according to the flesh, and their Messiah, according to the spirit. But in them their earthly love, and familiarity with Him, hid from them His higher glory; and in them He found impediments to His true consecration, and would-be thwarters of His highest work. And, in like manner, all our earthly relationships may become means of obscuring to us the transcendent brightness and greatness of Jesus Christ as our Saviour. And, in like manner as to Him these, His brethren, became "stumbling blocks" that He had decisively to put behind Him, so in regard to us "a man's foes may be those of his own household"; and not least his foes when they are most his idols, his comforts, and his sweetnesses. If our earthly loves and relationships obscure to us the face of Christ; if we find enough in them for our hearts, and go not beyond them for our true love; if they make us negligent of duty; if they bind us to the present; if they make us careless of that loftier affection which alone can satisfy us; if they clog our steps in the divine life, then they are our foes. They need to be always subordinated, and, so subordinated, they are more precious than when they are placed mistakenly foremost. They are better second than first. They are full of sweetness when our hearts know a sweetness surpassing theirs; they are robbed of their possible power to harm when they are rigidly held in inferiority to the one absolute and supreme love. There need be no collision—there will be no collision—if the second is second and the first is first. But sometimes beggars get upon horseback, and the crew mutinies and would displace the commander, and then there is nothing for it but sacrifice. "If thy hand offend thee, cut it off and cast it from thee." "I communed not with flesh and blood," and we must not, if ever they conflict with our supreme devotion to Jesus Christ.

These other things and relationships are precious to us, but He is priceless. They are shadows, but He is the substance. They are brooks by the way; He is the boundless, bottomless ocean of delights and loves. Shall we not always subordinate—and sometimes, if needful, sacrifice—the less to the greater? If we do, we shall get the less back, greatened by its surrender. "He that loveth father or mother more than Me is not worthy of Me" commands the sacrifice. "There is no man that hath left brethren or sisters, or father or mother, or wife or children, for My sake and the Gospel's, but he shall receive a hundredfold *now,* in this time" promises the reward.

4

Stories and Storms

Four Soils for One Seed

And when He was alone, they that were about Him with the twelve
asked of Him the parable. 11. And He said unto them, Unto you it
is given to know the mystery of the kingdom of God: but unto them
that are without, all these things are done in parables: 12. That
seeing they may see, and not perceive; and hearing they may hear,
and not understand; lest at any time they should be converted, and
their sins should be forgiven them. 13. And He said unto them,
Know ye not this parable? and how then will ye know all parables?
14. The sower soweth the word. 15. And these are they by the way
side, where the word is sown; but when they have heard, Satan
cometh immediately, and taketh away the word that was sown in
their hearts. 16. And these are they likewise which are sown on
stony ground; who, when they have heard the word, immediately
receive it with gladness; 17. And have no root in themselves, and
so endure but for a time: afterward, when affliction or persecution
ariseth for the word's sake, immediately they are offended. 18. And
these are they which are sown among thorns; such as hear the word,
19. And the cares of this world, and the deceitfulness of riches, and
the lusts of other things entering in, choke the word, and it becometh
unfruitful. 20. And these are they which are sown on good ground;
such as hear the word, and receive it, and bring forth fruit, some
thirtyfold, some sixty, and some an hundred. MARK 4:10–20.

Dean Stanley and others have pointed out how the natural features of the land round the lake of Gennesaret are reflected in the parable of the sower. But we must go deeper than that to find its occasion. It was not because Jesus may have seen a sower in a field which had these three varieties of soil that He spoke, but because He saw the frivolous crowd gathered to hear His words. The sad, grave description of the threefold kinds of vainly sown ground is the transcript of His clear and sorrowful insight into the real worth of the enthusiasm of the eager listeners on the beach. He was under no illusions about it; and, in this parable, He seeks to warn His disciples against expecting much from it, and to bring its subjects to a soberer estimate of what His word required to them. The full force and pathos of the parable is felt only when it is regarded as the expression of our Lord's keen consciousness of His wasted words. This passage falls into two parts—Christ's explanation of the reasons for His use of parables, and His interpretation of the parable itself.

1. Christ was the center of three circles: the outermost consisting of the fluctuating masses of merely curious hearers; the second, the true but somewhat loosely attached disciples, whom Mark here calls "they that were about Him"; and the innermost, the twelve. The two latter appear, in our first verse, as asking further instruction as to "the parable," a phrase which includes both parts of Christ's answer. The statement of His reason for the use of parables is startling. It sounds as if those who needed light most were to get least of it, and as if the parabolic form was deliberately adopted for the express purpose of hiding the truth. No wonder that men have shrunk from such a thought, and tried to soften down the terrible words. Inasmuch as a parable is the presentation of some spiritual truth under the guise of an incident belonging to the material sphere, it follows, from its very nature, that it may either reveal or hide the truth, and that it will do the former to susceptible, and the latter to unsusceptible, souls. The eye may either dwell upon the colored glass or on the light that streams through it; and, as is the case with all revelations of spiritual realities through sensuous mediums, gross and earthly hearts will not rise above the medium, which to them, by their own fault, becomes a medium of obscuration, not of revelation. This double aspect belongs to all revelation, which is both a "savor of life unto life and of death unto death." It is most conspicuous in the parable, which careless listeners may take for a mere story, and which those who feel and see more deeply will apprehend in its depth. These twofold effects are certain, and must therefore be embraced in Christ's purpose; for we cannot suppose that issues of His teaching escaped His foresight; and all must be regarded as part of His design. But may we not draw a distinction between design and desire? The primary purpose of all revelation is to reveal. If the only intention were to hide, silence would secure that, and the parable were needless. But if the twofold operation is intended, we can understand how mercy and righteous retribution both preside over the use of parables; how the thin veil hides that it may reveal, and how the very obscurity may draw some grosser souls to a longer gaze, and so may lead to a perception of the truth, which, in its purer form, they are neither worthy nor capable of receiving. No doubt, our Lord here announces a very solemn law, which runs through all the divine dealings, "To him that hath shall be given; and from him that hath not, shall be taken away even which he hath.''

2. We turn to the exposition of the parable of the sower, or rather of the fourfold soils in which he sows the seed. A sentence at the beginning disposes of the personality of the sower, which in Mark's version does not refer exclusively to Christ, but includes all who carry the word to men. The likening of ''the word'' to seed needs no explanation. The tiny, living nucleus of force, which is thrown broadcast, and must sink underground in order to grow, which does grow, and comes to light again in a form which fills the whole field where it is sown, and nourishes life as well as supplies material for another sowing, is the truest symbol of the truth in its working on the spirit. The threefold causes of failure are arranged in progressive order. At every stage of growth there are enemies. The first sowing never gets into the ground at all; the second grows a little, but its greenness soon withers; the third has a longer life, and a yet sadder failure, because a nearer approach to fertility. The types of character represented are unreceptive carelessness, emotional facility of acceptance, and earthly-mindedness, scotched, but not killed, by the word. The dangers which assault, but too successfully, the seed are the personal activity of Satan, opposition from without, and conflicting desires within. On all the soils the seed has been sown by hand; for drills are modern inventions; and sowing broadcast is the only right husbandry in Christ's field with Christ's seed. He is a poor workman, and an unfaithful one, who wants to pick his ground. Sow everywhere; ''Thou canst not tell which shall prosper, whether this or that.'' The character of the soil is not irrevocably fixed; but the trodden path may be broken up to softness, and the stony heart changed, and the soul filled with cares and lusts be cleared, and any soil may become good ground. So the seed is to be flung out broadcast; and prayer for seed and soil will often turn the weeping sower into the joyous reaper.

The seed sown on the trodden footpath running across the field never sinks below the surface. It lies there, and has no real contact, nor any chance of growth. It must be in, not on, the ground, if its mysterious power is to be put forth. A pebble is as likely to grow as a seed, if both lie side by side, on the surface. Is not this the description of a mournfully large proportion of hearers of God's truth? It never gets deeper than their ears, or, at the most, effects a shallow lodgment on the surface of their minds. So many feet pass along the path, and beat it into hardness, that the truth has no chance to take root. Habitual indifference to the Gospel, masked by an utterly unmeaning and unreal acceptance of it, and by equally habitual decorous attendance on its preaching, is the condition of a dreadfully large proportion of church-goers. Their very familiarity with the truth robs it of all penetrating power. They know all about it, as they suppose; and so they listen to it as they would to the clank of a mill wheel to which they were accustomed, missing its noise if it stops, and liking to be sent to sleep by its hum. Familiar truth often lies ''bedridden in the dormitory of the soul, beside exploded errors.''

And what comes of this idle hearing, without acceptance or obedience? Truth which is common, and which a man supposes himself to believe, without having ever reflected on it, or let it influence conduct, is sure to die out. If we do not turn our beliefs into practice they will not long be our beliefs. Neglected impressions fade; the seed is only safe when it is buried. There are flocks of hungry, sharp-eyed, quick-flying thieves ready to pounce down on every exposed grain. So Mark uses here again his favorite ''straightway'' to express the swift disappearance of the seed. As soon as the preacher's voice is silent, or the book closed, the words are forgotten. The impression of a gliding keel on a smooth lake is not more evanescent.

The distinct reference to Satan as the agent in removing the seed is not to be passed by lightly. Christ's words about demons have been emptied of meaning by the allegation that He was only accommodating Himself to the superstition of the times, but no explanation of that sort will do in this case. He surely commits Himself here to the assertion of the existence and agency of Satan; and surely those who profess to receive His words as the truth ought not to make light of them, in reference to so solemn and awe-inspiring a revelation.

The seed gets rather farther on the road to fruit in the second case. A thin surface of mold above a shelf of rock is like a greenhouse in hot countries. The stone keeps the heat and stimulates growth. The very thing that prevents deep rooting facilitates rapid shooting. The green spikelets will be above ground there long before they show in deeper soil. There would be many such hearers in the ''very great multitude'' on the shore, who were attracted, they scarcely knew why, and were the more enthusiastic the less they understood the real scope of Christ's teaching. The disciple who pressed forward with his excited and unasked ''Master, I will follow Thee whithersoever Thou goest!'' was one of such—well-meaning, perfectly sincere, warmly affected, and completely unreliable. Lightly come is lightly go. When such people forsake their fervent purposes, and turn their backs on what they have been so eagerly pursuing, they are quite consistent; for they are obeying the uppermost impulse in both cases, and, as they were easily drawn to follow without consideration, they are easily driven back with as little. The first taste of supposed good secured their giddy-pated adhesion; the first taste of trouble ensures their desertion. They are the same men acting in the same fashion at both times. Two things are marked by our Lord as suspicious in such easily won discipleship—its suddenness and its joyfulness. Feelings which are so easily stirred are superficial. A puff of wind sets a shallow pond in wavelets. Quick maturity means brief life and swift decay, as every "revival" shows. The more earnestly we believe in the possibility of sudden conversions, the more we should remember this warning, and make sure that, if they are sudden, they shall be thorough, which they may be. The swiftness is not so suspicious if it be not accompanied with the other doubtful characteristic—namely, immediate joy. Joy is the result of true acceptance of the Gospel; but not the first result. Without consciousness of sin and apprehension of judgment there is no conversion. We lay down no rules as to depth or duration of the "godly sorrow" which precedes all well-grounded "joy in the Lord"; but the Christianity which has taken a flying leap over the valley of humiliation will scarcely reach a firm standing on the rock. He who "straightway with joy" receives the word, will straightway, with equal precipitation, cast it away when the difficulties and oppositions which meet all true discipleship begin to develop themselves. Fair-weather crews will desert when storms begin to blow.

The third sort of soil brings things still farther on before failure comes. The seed is not only covered and germinating, but has actually begun to be fruitful. The thorns are supposed to have been cut down, but their roots have been left, and they grow faster than the wheat. They take the "goodness" out of the ground, and block out sun and air; and so the stalks, which promised well, begin to get pale and droop, and the half-formed ear comes to nothing, or, as the other version of the parable has it, brings "forth no fruit to perfection." There are two crops fighting for the upper hand on the one ground, and the earlier possessor wins. The "struggle for existence" ends with the "survival of the fittest"; that is, of the worst, to which the natural bent of the desires and inclinations of the unrenewed man is more congenial. The "cares of this world" and the "deceitfulness of riches" are but two sides of one thing. The poor man has cares; the rich man has the illusions of his wealth. Both men agree in thinking that this world's good is most desirable. The one is anxious because he has not enough of it, or fears to lose what he has; the other man is full of foolish confidence because he has much. Eager desires after creatural goods are common to both; and, what with the anxiety lest they lose, and the self-satisfaction because they have, and the mouths watering for the world's good, there is no force of will, nor warmth of love, nor clearness of vision, left for better things. That is the history of the fall of many a professing Christian, who never apostatizes, and keeps up a reputable appearance of godliness to the end; but the old worldliness, which was cut down for a while, has sprung again in his heart, and, by slow degrees, the word is "choked"—a most expressive picture of the silent, gradual dying-out of its power for want of sun and air——and "he" or "it" "becometh unfruitful," relapsing from a previous condition of fruit-bearing into sterility. No heart can mature two crops. We must choose between God and Mammon—between the word and the world.

There is nothing fixed or necessary in the faults of these three classes, and they are not so much the characteristics of separate types of men as evils common to all hearers, against which all have to guard. They depend upon the will and affections much more than on anything in temperament fixed and not to be got rid of. So there is no reason why any one of the three should not become "good soil"; and it is to be noted that the characteristic of that soil is simply that it receives and grows the seed. Any heart that will, can do that; and that is all that is needed. But to do it, there will have to be diligent care, lest we fall into any of the evils pointed at in the preceding parts of the parable, which are ever waiting to entrap us. The true "accepting" of the word requires that we shall not let it lie on the surface of our minds, as in the case of the first; nor be satisfied with its penetrating a little deeper and striking root in our emotions, like the second, of whom it is said with such profound truth, that they "have no root in themselves," their roots being only in the superficial part of their being, and never going down to the true central self; nor let competing desires grow up unchecked, like the third; but cherish the "word of the truth of the gospel" in our deepest hearts, guard it against foes, let it rule there, and mold all our conduct in conformity with its blessed principles. The true Christian is he who can truly say, "Thy word have I hid in mine heart." If we do, *we* shall be fruitful, because *it* will bear fruit in us. No man is obliged, by temperament or circumstances, to be "wayside," or "stony," or "thorny" ground. Wherever a heart opens to receive the Gospel, and keeps it fast, there the increase will be realized—not in equal measure in all, but in each according to faithfulness and diligence. Mark arranges the various yields in ascending scale, as if to teach our hopes and aims a growing largeness, while Matthew orders them in the opposite fashion, as if to teach that, while the hundredfold, which is possible for all, is best, the smaller yield is accepted by the great Lord of the harvest, who Himself not only sows the seed, but gives it its vitality, blesses its springing, and rejoices to gather the wheat into His barn.

Lamps and Bushels

And Jesus said unto them, Is a candle brought to be put under a bushel; or under a bed? and not to be set on a candlestick? MARK 4:21.

The furniture of a very humble Eastern home is brought before us in this saying. In the original, each of the nouns has the definite article attached to it, and so suggests that in the house there was but one of each article; one lamp, a flat saucer with a wick swimming in oil; one measure for corn and the like; one bed, raised slightly, but sufficiently to admit of a flat vessel being put under it without danger, if for any reason it were desired to shade the light; and one lampstand.

The saying appeals to common sense. A man does not light a lamp and then smother it. The act of lighting implies the purpose of illumination, and, with everybody who acts logically, its sequel is to put the lamp on a stand, where it may be visible. All is part of the nightly routine of every Jewish household. Jesus had often watched it; and, commonplace as it is, it had mirrored to Him large truths. If our eyes were opened to the suggestions of common life, we should find in them many parables and reminders of high matters.

Now this saying is a favorite and familiar one of our Lord, occurring four times in the Gospels. It is interesting to notice that He, too, like other teachers, had His favorite maxims, which He turned round in all sorts of ways, and presented as reflecting light at different angles and suggesting different thoughts. The four occurrences of the saying are these. In my text, and in the parallel in Luke's Gospel, it is appended to the Parable of the Sower, and forms the basis of the exhortation, "Take heed how ye hear." In another place in Luke's Gospel it is appended to our Lord's words about "the sign of the prophet Jonah," which is explained to be the resurrection of Jesus Christ, and it forms the basis of the exhortation to cultivate the single eye which is receptive of the light. In the Sermon on the Mount it is appended to the declaration that the disciples are the lights of the world, and forms the basis of the exhortation, "Let your light so shine before men." I have thought that it may be interesting and instructive if in this sermon we throw together these three applications of this one saying, and try to study the threefold lessons which it yields, and the weighty duties which it enforces.

1. So, then, I have to ask you, first, to consider that we have a lesson as to the apparent obscurities of revelation and of our duty concerning them. That is the connection in which the words occur in our text, and in the other place in Luke's Gospel, to which I have referred. Our

Lord has just been speaking the Parable of the Sower. The disciples' curiosity has been excited as to its significance. They ask Him for an explanation, which He gives minutely point by point. Then He passes to this general lesson of the purpose of the apparent veil which He had cast round the truth, by throwing it into a parabolic form. In effect He says: "If I had meant to hide My teaching by the form into which I cast it, I should have been acting as absurdly and as contradictorily as a man would do who should light a lamp and immediately obscure it." True, there is the veil of parable, but the purpose of that relative concealment is not hiding, but revelation. "There is nothing covered but that it should be made known." The veil sharpens attention, stimulates curiosity, quickens effort, and so becomes positively subsidiary to the great purpose of revelation for which the parable is spoken. The existence of this veil of sensuous representation carries with it the obligation, "Take heed how ye hear."

Now all these thoughts have a far wider application than in reference to our Lord's parables. And I may suggest one or two of the considerations that flow from the wider reference of the words before us.

"Is a candle brought to be put under a bushel, or under a bed and not upon a candlestick?" There are no gratuitous and dark places in anything that God says to us. His revelation is absolutely clear. We may be sure of that if we consider the purpose for which He spoke at all. True, there are dark places; true, there are great gaps; true, we sometimes think, "Oh! it would have been so easy for Him to have said one word more; and the one word more would have been so infinitely precious to bleeding hearts or wounded consciences or puzzled understandings." But "is a candle brought to be set under a bushel?" Do you think that if He took the trouble to light it He would immediately smother it, or arbitrarily conceal anything that the very fact of the revelation declares His intention to make known? His own great word remains true, "I have never spoken in secret, in a dark place on the earth." If there be, as there are, obscurities, there are none there that would have been better away.

For the intention of all God's hiding—which hiding is an integral part of his revealing—is not to conceal, but to reveal. Sometimes the best way of making a thing known to men is to veil it in a measure, in order that the very obscurity, like the morning mists which prophesy a blazing sun in a clear sky by noonday, may demand search and quicken curiosity and spur to effort. He is not a wise teacher who makes things too easy. It is good that there should be difficulties; for difficulties are like the veins of quartz in the soil, which may turn the edge of the plowshare or the spade, but prophesy that there is gold there for the man who comes with fitting tools. Wherever, in the broad land of God's word to us, there lie dark places, there are assurances of future illumination. God's hiding is in order to revelation, even as the prophet of old, when he was describing the great Theophany which flashed in light from the one side of the heaven to the other, exclaimed, "There was the hiding of His power."

> He hides the purpose of His grace
> To make it better known.

And the end of all the concealments, and apparent and real obscurities, that hang about His word, is that for many of them patient and diligent attention and docile obedience should unfold them here, and for the rest, "the day shall declare them." The lamp is the light for the nighttime, and it leaves many a corner in dark shadow; but, when "night's candles are burnt out, and day sits jocund on the misty mountaintops," much will be plain that cannot be made plain now.

Therefore, for us the lesson from this assurance that God will not stultify Himself by giving to us a revelation that does not reveal, is, "Take heed how ye hear." The effort will not be in vain. Patient attention will ever be rewarded. The desire to learn will not be frustrated. In this school truth lightly won is truth loosely held; and only the attentive scholar is the receptive and retaining disciple. A great man once said, and said, too, presumptuously and proudly, that he had rather have the search after truth than truth. But yet there is a sense in which the saying may be modifiedly accepted; for, precious as is all the revelation of God, not the least precious effect that it is meant to produce upon us is the consciousness that in it there are unscaled heights above, and unplumbed depths beneath, and untraversed spaces all around it; and that for us that Word is like the pillar of cloud and fire that moved before Israel, blends light and darkness with the single office of guidance, and gleams ever before us to draw desires and feet after it. The lamp is set upon a stand. "Take heed how ye hear."

2. Secondly, the saying, in another application on our Lord's lips, gives us a lesson as to Himself and our attitude to Him. I have already pointed out the other instance in Luke's Gospel in which this saying occurs, in the 11th chapter, where it is brought into immediate connection with our Lord's declaration that the sign to be given to His generation was "the sign of the prophet Jonah," which sign He explains as being reproduced in His own case in His Resurrection. And then he adds the word of our text, and immediately passes on to speak about the light in us which perceives the lamp, and the need of cultivating the single eye.

So, then, we have, in the figure thus applied, the thought that the earthly life of Jesus Christ necessarily implies a subsequent elevation from which He shines down upon all the world. God lit that lamp, and it is not going to be quenched in the darkness of the grave. He is not going to stultify Himself by sending the Light of the World, and then letting the endless shades of death muffle and obscure it. But, just as the conclusion of the process which is begun in the kindling of the light is setting it on high on the stand, that it may beam over all the chamber, so the resurrection and ascension of Jesus Christ, His exaltation to the supremacy from which He shall draw all men unto Him, are the necessary and, if I may so say, the logical result of the facts of His incarnation and death.

Then from this there follows what our Lord dwells upon at greater length. Having declared that the beginning of His course involved the completion of it in His exaltation to glory, He then goes on to say to us, "You have an organ that corresponds to Me. I am the kindled lamp; you have the seeing eye." "If the eye were not sunlike," says the great German thinker, "how could it see the sun?" If there were not in me that which corresponds to Jesus Christ, He would be no Light of the World, and no light to me. My reason, my affection, my conscience, my will, the whole of my spiritual being, answer to Him, as the eye does to the light, and for everything that is in Christ there is in humanity something that is receptive of, and that needs, Him.

So, then, that being so, He being our light, just because He fits our needs, answers our desires, satisfies our cravings, fills the clefts of our hearts, and brings the response to all the questions of our understandings—that being the case, if the lamp is lit and blazing on the lampstand, and you and I have eyes to behold it, let us take heed that we cultivate the single eye which apprehends Christ. Concentration of purpose, simplicity and sincerity of aim, a heart centered upon Him, a mind drawn to contemplate unfalteringly and without distraction of crosslights His beauty, His supremacy, His completeness, and a soul utterly devoted to Him—these are the conditions to which that light will ever manifest itself, and illumine the whole man. But if we come with divided hearts, with distracted aims, giving Him fragments of ourselves, and seeking Him by spasms and at intervals, and having a dozen other deities in our Pantheon, beside the calm form of the Christ of Nazareth, what wonder is there that we see in Him "no beauty that we should desire Him"? "Unite my heart to fear Thy name." Oh! if that were our prayer, and if the effort to secure its answer were honestly the effort of our lives, all His loveliness, His sweetness, His adaptation to our whole being, would manifest themselves to us. The eye must be "single," directed to Him, if the heart is to rejoice in His light.

I need not do more than remind you of the blessed consequence which our Lord represents as flowing from this union of the seeing heart and the revealing light—viz., "Thy whole body shall be full of light." In every eye that beholds the flame of the lamp there is a little lamp-flame mirrored and manifested. And just as what we see makes its image on the seeing organ of the body, so the Christ beheld is a Christ embodied in us; and we, gazing upon Him, are "changed into the same image from glory to glory, even as by the Lord the Spirit." Light that remains without us does not illuminate; light that passes into us is the light by which we see, and the Christ beheld is the Christ ensphered in our hearts.

3. So, lastly, this great saying gives us a lesson as to the duties of Christian men as lights in the world. I pointed out that another instance of the occurrence of the saying is in the Sermon on the Mount, where it is transferred from the revelation of God to His written word, and in His Incarnate Word, to the relation of Christian men to the world in which they dwell. I need not remind you how frequently that same metaphor occurs in Scripture; how in the early Jewish ritual the great seven-branched lampstand which stood at first in the Tabernacle was the emblem of Israel's office in the whole world, as it rayed out its light through the curtains of the Tabernacle into the darkness of the desert. Nor need I remind you how our Lord bare witness to His forerunner by the praise that "He was a burning and a shining light," nor how He commanded His disciples to have their "loins girt and their lamps burning," nor how He spoke the Parable of the Ten Virgins with their lamps.

From all these there follows the same general thought that Christian men, not so much by specific effort, nor by words, nor by definite proclamation, as by the raying out from them in life and conduct of a Christlike spirit, are set for the illumination of the world. The bearing of our text in reference to that subject is just this—our obligation as Christians to show forth the glories of Him who hath "called us out of darkness into His marvelous light" is rested upon His very purpose in drawing us to Himself, and receiving us into the number of his people. If God in Christ, by communicating to us "the light of the knowledge of the glory of God, in the face of Jesus Christ," has made us lights of the world, it is not done in order that the light may be smothered incontinently, but His act of lighting indicates His purpose of illumination. What are you a Christian for? That you may go to Heaven? Certainly. That your sins may be forgiven? No doubt. But is that the only end? Are you such a very great being as that your happiness and well-being can legitimately be the ultimate purpose of God's dealings with you? Are you so isolated from all mankind as that any gift which He bestows on you is to be treated by you as a morsel that you can take into your corner and devour, like a grudging dog, by yourselves? By no means. ''God, who commanded the light to shine out of darkness, hath shined into our hearts in order that'' we might impart the light to others. Or, as Shakespeare has it, in words perhaps suggested by the Scripture metaphor:

> Heaven doth with us as we with torches do,
> Not light them for themselves.

He gave you His Son that you may give the Gospel to others, and you stultify His purpose in your salvation unless you become ministers of His grace and manifesters of His light.

Then take from this emblem, too, a homely suggestion as to the hindrances that stand in the way of our fulfilling the Divine intention in our salvation. It is, perhaps, a piece of fancy, but still it may point a lesson. The lamp is not hid ''under a bushel,'' which is the emblem of commerce or business, and is meant for the measurement of material wealth and sustenance, or ''under a bed''—the place where people take their ease and repose. These two loves—the undue love of the bushel and the corn that is in it, and the undue love of the bed and the leisurely ease that you may enjoy there—are large factors in preventing Christian men from fulfilling God's purpose in their salvation.

Then take a hint as to the means by which such a purpose can be fulfilled by Christian souls. They are suggested in two other uses of this emblem by our Lord Himself. The first is when He said, ''Let your loins be girded''—they are not so, when you are in bed—''and your lamps burning.'' Your light will not shine in a naughty world without your strenuous effort, and ungirt loins will very shortly lead to extinguished lamps. The other means to this manifestation of visible Christlikeness lies in that tragical story of the foolish virgins who took no oil in their vessels. If light expresses the outward Christian life, oil, in accordance with the whole tenor of Scripture symbolism, expresses the inward gift of the Divine Spirit. And where that gift is neglected, where it is not earnestly sought and carefully treasured, there may be a kind of smoky illuminations, which, in the dark, may pass for bright lights, but, when the Lord comes, shudder into extinction, and, to the astonishment of the witless five who carried them, are found to be ''going out.'' Brethren, only He who does not quench the smoking flax but tends it to a flame, will help us to keep our lamps bright.

First of all, then, let us gaze upon the light in Him, until we become ''light in the Lord.'' And then let us see to it that, by girt loins and continual reception of the illuminating principle of the Divine Spirit's oil, we fill our lamps with "deeds of odorous light, and hopes that breed not shame." Then,

> When the Bridegroom, with his feastful friends,
> Passes to bliss on the mid-hour of night,

we shall have "gained our entrance" among the "virgins wise and pure."

The Storm Stilled

And the same day, when the even was come, He saith unto them, Let us pass over unto the other side. 36. And when they had sent away the multitude, they took Him even as He was in the ship. And there were also with Him other little ships. 37. And there arose a great storm of wind, and the waves beat into the ship, so that it was now full. 38. And He was in the hinder part of the ship, asleep on a pillow: and they awake Him, and say unto Him, Master, carest Thou not that we perish? 39. And He arose, and rebuked the wind, and said unto the sea, Peace, be still. And the wind ceased, and there was a great calm. 40. And He said unto them, Why are ye so fearful? how is it that ye have no faith? 41. And they feared exceedingly, and said one to another, What manner of man is this, that even the wind and the sea obey Him? MARK 4:35–41.

Mark seldom dates his incidents, but he takes pains to tell us that this run across the lake closed a day of labor. Jesus was wearied, and felt the need of rest. He had been pressed on all day by "a very great multitude," and felt the need of solitude. He could not land from the boat which had been His pulpit, for that would have plunged Him into the thick of the crowd, and so the only way to get away from the throng was to cross the lake. But even there He was followed; "other boats were with Him."

1. The first point to note is the wearied sleeper. The disciples "take Him, . . . even as He was," without preparation or delay, the object being simply to get away as quickly as might be, so great was His fatigue and longing for quiet. We almost see the hurried starting and the intrusive followers scrambling into the little skiffs on the beach and making after Him. The "multitude" delights to push itself into the private hours of its heroes, and is devoured with rude curiosity. There was a leather, or perhaps wooden, movable seat in the stern for the steersman, on which a wearied-out man might lay his head, while his body was stretched in the bottom of the boat. A hard "pillow" indeed, which only exhaustion could make comfortable! But it was soft enough for the worn-out Christ, who had apparently flung Himself down in sheer tiredness as soon as they set sail. How real such a small detail makes the transcendent mystery of the Incarnation!

Jesus is our pattern in small common things as in great ones, and among the sublimities of character set forth in Him as our example, let us not forget that the homely virtue of hard work is also included. Jonah slept in a storm the sleep of a skulking sluggard, Jesus slept the sleep of a wearied laborer.

2. The next point is the terrified disciples. The evening was coming on, and, as often on a lake set among hills, the wind rose as the sun sank behind the high land on the western shore astern. The fishermen disciples were used to such squalls, and, at first, would probably let their sail down, and pull so as to keep the boat's head to the wind. But things grew worse, and when the crazy, undecked craft began to fill and get water-logged, they grew alarmed. The squall was fiercer than usual, and must have been pretty bad to have frightened such seasoned hands. They awoke Jesus, and there is a touch of petulant rebuke in their appeal, and of a sailor's impatience at a landsman lying sound asleep while the sweat is running down their faces with their hard pulling. It is to Mark that we owe our knowledge of that accent of complaint in their words, for he alone gives their ''Carest Thou not?''

But it is not for us to fling stones at them, seeing that we also often may catch ourselves thinking that Jesus has gone to sleep when storms come on the Church, or on ourselves, and that He is ignorant of, or indifferent to, our plight. But though the disciples were wrong in their fright, and not altogether right in the tone of their appeal to Jesus, they were supremely right in that they did appeal to Him. Fear which drives us to Jesus is not all wrong. The cry to Him, even though it is the cry of unnecessary terror, brings Him to His feet for our help.

3. The next point is the word of power. Again we have to thank Mark for the very words, so strangely, calmly authoritative. May we take ''Peace!'' as spoken to the howling wind, bidding it to silence; and ''Be still!'' as addressed to the tossing waves, smoothing them to a calm plain? At all events, the two things to lay to heart are that Jesus here exercises the divine prerogative of controlling matter by the bare expression of His will, and that this divine attribute was exercised by the wearied man, who, a moment before, had been sleeping the sleep of human exhaustion. The marvelous combination of apparent opposites, weakness, and divine omnipotence, which yet do not clash, nor produce an incredible monster of a being, but coalesce in perfect harmony, is a feat beyond the reach of the loftiest creative imagination. If the Evangelists are not simple biographers, telling what eyes have seen and hands have handled, they have beaten the greatest poets and dramatists at their own weapons, and have accomplished "things unattempted yet in prose or rhyme."

A word of loving rebuke and encouragement follows. Matthew puts it before the stilling of the storm, but Mark's order seems the more exact. How often we too are taught the folly of our fears by experiencing some swift, easy deliverance! Blessed be God! He does not rebuke us first and help us afterwards, but rebukes by helping. What *could* the disciples say, as they sat there in the great calm, in answer to Christ's question, "Why are ye fearful?" Fear can give no reasonable account of itself, if Christ is in the boat. If our faith unites us to Jesus, there is nothing that need shake our courage. If He is "our fear and our dread," we shall not need to "fear their fear," who have not the all-conquering Christ to fight for them.

Well roars the storm to them who hear
A deeper voice across the storm.

Jesus wondered at the slowness of the disciples to learn their lesson, and the wonder was reflected in the sad question, "Have ye not *yet* faith?"—not yet, after so many miracles, and living beside Me for so long? How much more keen the edge of that question is when addressed to us, who know Him so much better, and have centuries of His working for His servants to look back on. When, in the tempests that sweep over our own lives, we sometimes pass into a great calm as suddenly as if we had entered the center of a typhoon, we wonder unbelievingly instead of saying, out of a faith nourished by experience, "It is just like Him."

The Toiling Christ

They took Him even as He was in the ship. . . . And He was in the hinder part of the ship; asleep on a pillow. MARK 4:36, 38.

Among the many loftier characteristics belonging to Christ's life and work, there is a very homely one which is often lost sight of; and that is, the amount of hard physical exertion, prolonged even to fatigue and exhaustion, which He endured.

Christ is our pattern in a great many other things more impressive and more striking; and He is our pattern in this, that "in the sweat of His brow" He did His work, and knew not only what it was to suffer, but what it was to toil for man's salvation. And, perhaps, if we thought a little more than we do of such a prosaic characteristic of His life as that, it might invest it with some more reality for us, besides teaching us other large and important lessons.

I have thrown together these two clauses for our text now, simply for the sake of that one feature which they both portray so strikingly.

"They took Him even as He was in the ship." Now many expositors suppose that in the very form of that phrase there is suggested the extreme of weariness and exhaustion which He suffered, after the hard day's toil. Whether that be so or no, the swiftness of the move to the little boat, although there was nothing in the nature of danger or of imperative duty to hurry Him away, and His going on board without a moment's preparation, leaving the crowd on the beach, seem most naturally accounted for by supposing that He had come to the last point of physical endurance, and that His frame, worn out by the hard day's work, needed one thing—rest.

And so, the next that we see of Him is that, as soon as He gets into the ship He falls fast asleep on the wooden pillow—a hard bed for His head!—in the stern of the little fishing boat, and there He lies so tired—let us put it into plain prose and strip away the false veil of big words with which we invest that nature—so tired that the storm does not awaken Him; and they have to come to Him, and lay their hands upon Him, and say to Him, "Master, carest Thou not that we perish?" before compassion again beat back fatigue, and quickened Him for fresh exertions.

This, then, is the one lesson which I wish to consider now, and there are three points which I deal with in pursuance of my task. I wish to point out a little more in detail the signs that we have in the Gospels of this characteristic of Christ's work—the toilsomeness of His service; then to consider, secondly, the motives which He Himself tells us impelled to such service; and then, finally, the worth which that toil bears for us.

1. First, then, let me point out some of the significant hints which the Gospel records give us of the toilsomeness of Christ's service. Now we are principally indebted for these to this Gospel by Mark, which ancient tradition has set forth as being especially and eminently the "Gospel of the Servant of God," therein showing a very accurate conception of its distinguishing characteristics. Just as Matthew's Gospel is the Gospel of the King, regal in tone from the beginning to end; just as Luke's is the Gospel of the Man, human and universal in its tone; just as John's is the Gospel of the Eternal Word, so Mark's is the Gospel of the Servant. The inscription written over it all might be, "Lo, I come to do Thy will, O God." "Behold my Servant whom I uphold."

And if you will take this briefest of all the Gospels, and read it over from that point of view, you will be surprised to discover what a multitude of minute traits make up the general impression, and what a unity is thereby breathed into the narrative.

For instance, did you ever observe the peculiar beginning of this Gospel? There are here none of the references to the prophecies of the King, no tracing of His birth through the royal stock to the great progenitor of the nation, no adoration by the Eastern sages, which we find in Matthew, no miraculous birth nor growing childhood as in Luke, no profound unveiling of the union of the Word with God before the world was, as in John; but the narrative begins with His baptism, and passes at once to the story of His work. The same ruling idea accounts for the uniform omission of the title "Lord," which in Mark's Gospel is never applied to Christ until after the resurrection. There is only one apparent exception, and there good authorities pronounce the word to be spurious. Even in reports of conversations which are also given in the other Gospels, and where "Lord" occurs, Mark, of set purpose, omits it, as if its presence would disturb the unity of the impression which he desires to leave. You will find the investigation of the omissions in this Gospel full of interest, and remarkably tending to confirm the accuracy of the view which regards it as the Gospel of the Servant.

Notice then these traits of His service which it brings out:

The first of them I would suggest is—how distinctly it gives the impression of swift, strenuous work. The narrative is brief and condensed. We feel, all through these earlier chapters, at all events, the presence of the pressing crowd coming to Him and desiring to be healed, and but a word can be spared for each incident as the story hurries on, trying to keep pace with His rapid service of quick-springing compassion and undelaying help. There is one word which is reiterated over and over again in these earlier chapters, remarkably conveying this impression of haste and strenuous work; Mark's favorite word is "straightway," "immediately," "forthwith," "anon," which are all translations of one expression. You will find, if you glance over the first, second, or third chapters at your leisure, that it comes in at every turn. Take these instances which strike one's eye at the moment. "*Straightway* they forsook their nets"; "*Straightway* He entered into the synagogue"; "*Immediately* His fame spread abroad throughout all the region"; *Forthwith* they entered into the house of Simon's mother"; "*Anon,* they tell Him of her"; "*Immediately* the fever left her." And so it goes on through the whole story, a picture of a constant succession of rapid acts of mercy and love. The story seems, as it were, to pant with haste to keep up with Him as He moves among men, swift as a sunbeam, and continuous in the outflow of His love as are these unceasing rays.

Again, we see in Christ's service, toil prolonged to the point of actual physical exhaustion. The narrative before us is the most striking instance of that which we meet with. It had been a long wearying day of work. According to this chapter, the whole of the profound parables concerning the kingdom of God had immediately preceded the embarkation. But even these, with their explanation, had been but a part of that day's labors. For, in Matthew's account of them, we are told that they were spoken on the same day as that on which His mother and brethren came desiring to speak with Him,—or, as we elsewhere read, with hostile intentions to lay hold on Him as mad and needing restraint. And that event, which we may well believe touched deep and painful chords of feeling in His human heart, and excited emotions more exhausting than much physical effort, occurred in the midst of an earnest and prolonged debate with emissaries from Jerusalem, in the course of which He spoke the solemn words concerning blasphemy against the Holy Ghost, and Satan casting out Satan, and poured forth some of His most terrible warnings, and some of His most beseeching entreaties. No wonder that, after such a day, the hard pillow of the boat was a soft resting place for His wearied head; no wonder that, as the evening quiet settled down on the mountain-girdled lake, and the purple shadows of the hills stretched athwart the water, He slept; no wonder that the storm which followed the sunset did not wake Him; and beautiful, that wearied as He was, the disciples' cry at once rouses Him, and the fatigue which shows His manhood gives place to the divine energy which says unto the sea, "Peace! be still." The lips which, a moment before, had been parted in the soft breathing of wearied sleep, now open to utter the omnipotent word—so wonderfully does He blend the human and the divine, "the form of a servant" and the nature of God.

We see, in Christ, toil that puts aside the claims of physical wants. Twice in this Gospel we read of this "The multitude cometh together again, so that they could not so much as eat bread." "There were many coming, and they had no leisure so much as to eat."

We see in Christ's service a love which is at every man's beck and call, a toil cheerfully rendered at the most unreasonable and unseasonable times. As I said a moment or two ago, this Gospel makes one feel, as none other of these narratives do, the pressure of that ever-present multitude, the whirling excitement that eddied round the calm center. It tells us, for instance, more than once, how Christ, wearied with His toil, feeling in body and in spirit the need of rest and still communion, withdrew Himself from the crowd. He once departed alone that He might seek God in prayer; once He went with His wearied disciples apart into a desert place to rest awhile. On both occasions the retirement is broken in upon before it is well begun. The sigh of relief in the momentary rest is scarcely drawn, and the burden laid down for an instant, when it has to be lifted again. His solitary prayer is interrupted by the disciples, which "All men seek for Thee," and, without a murmur or a pause, He buckles to His work again, and says, "Let us go into the next towns that I may preach there also; for therefore am I sent."

When He would carry His wearied disciples with Him for a brief breathing time to the other side of the sea, and get away from the thronging crowd, "the people saw Him departing, and ran afoot out of all cities," and, making their way round the head of the lake, were all there at the landing place before Him. Instead of seclusion and repose He found the same throng and bustle. Here they were, most of them from mere curiosity, some of them no doubt with deeper feelings; here they were, with their diseased and their demoniacs, and as soon as His foot touches the shore He is in the midst of it all again. And He meets it, not with impatience at this rude intrusion on His privacy, not with refusals to help. Only one emotion fills His heart. He forgot all about weariness, and hunger, and retirement, and "He was moved with compassion towards them, because they were as sheep not having a shepherd, and He began to teach them many things." Such a picture may well shame our languid, self-indulgent service, may stir us to imitation and to grateful praise.

There is only one other point which I touch upon for a moment, as showing the toil of Christ, and that is drawn from another Gospel. Did you ever notice the large space occupied in Matthew's Gospel by the record of the last day of His public ministry, and how much of all that we know of His mission and message, and the future of the world and of all men, we owe to the teaching of these four-and-twenty hours? Let me put together, in a word, what happened on that day.

It included the conversation with the chief priests and elders about the baptism of John, the parable of the householder that planted a vineyard and digged a winepress, the parables of the kingdom of heaven, the controversy with the Herodians about the tribute money, the conversation with the Sadducees about the resurrection, with the Pharisee about the great commandment in the law, the silencing of the Pharisees by pointing to the 110th Psalm, the warning to the multitude against the scribes and Pharisees who were hypocrites, protracted and prolonged up to that wail of disappointed love, "Behold! your house is left unto you desolate." And, as though that had not been enough for one day, when He is going home from the Temple to find, for a night, in that quiet little home of Bethany, the rest that He wants, as He rests wearily on the slopes of Olivet, the disciples come to Him, "Tell us, when shall these things be? and what shall be the sign of Thy coming?" and there follows all that wonderful prophecy of the destruction of Jerusalem and the end of the world, the parable of the fig tree, the warning not to suffer the thief to come, and the promise of reward for the faithful and wise servant, the parable of the ten virgins, and in all probability the parable of the king with the five talents; and the words, that might be written in letters of fire, that tell us the final course of all things, and the judgment of life eternal and death everlasting! All this was the work of "one of the days of the Son of Man." Of Him it was prophesied long ago, "For Jerusalem's sake I will not rest"; and His life on earth, as well as His life in heaven, fulfills the prediction—the one by the toilsomeness of His service, the other by the unceasing energy of His exalted power. He toiled unwearied here; He works unresting there.

2. In the second place, let me ask you to notice how we get from our Lord's own words a glimpse into the springs of this wonderful activity. There are three points which distinctly come out in various places in the Gospels as His motives for such unresting sedulousness and continuance of toil. The first is conveyed by such words as these: "I must work the works of Him that sent Me." "Let us preach to other cities, also: for therefore am I sent." "Wist ye not that I must be about My Father's business?" "My meat is to do the will of Him that sent Me, and to finish His work." All these express one thought. Christ lived and toiled, and bore weariness and exhaustion, and counted every moment as worthy to be garnered up and precious, as to be filled with deeds of love and kindness, because wherever He went, and to whatsoever He set His hand, He had the one consciousness of a great task laid upon Him by a loving Father whom He loved, and whom, therefore, it was His joy and His blessedness to serve.

And, remember that this motive made the life homogeneous—of a piece. In all the variety of service, one spirit was expressed, and, therefore, the service was one. No matter whether He were speaking words of grace or of rebuke, or working works of power and love, or simply looking a look of kindness on some outcast, or taking a little child in His arms, or stilling with the same arms outstretched the wild uproar of the storm—it was all same. To Him life was all one. There was nothing great, nothing small; nothing so insignificant that it could be done negligently; nothing so hard that it surpassed His power. The one motive made all duties equal; obedience to the Father called forth His whole energy at every moment. To Him life was not divided into a set of tasks of varying importance, some of which could be accomplished with a finger's touch, and some of which demanded a dead lift and strain of all the muscles. But whatsoever His hand found to do He did with His might and that because He felt, be it great or little, that it all came, if I may so say, into the day's work, and all was equally great because the Father that sent Him had laid it upon Him.

There is one thing that makes life mighty in its veriest trifles, worthy in its smallest deeds, that delivers it from monotony, that delivers it from insignificance. All will be great, and nothing will be overpowering, when, living in communion with Jesus Christ, we say as He says, "My meat is to do the will of Him that sent Me."

And then, still further, another of the secret springs that move His unwearied activity, His heroism of toil, is the thought expressed in such words as these:—"While I am in the world I am the light of the world." "I must work the works of Him that sent Me while it is day; the night cometh when no man can work."

Jesus Christ manifested on earth performs indeed a work—the mightiest which He came to do—which was done precisely then when the night did come—namely, the work of His death, which is the atonement and "propitiation for the sins of the world." And, further, the "night, when no man can work," was not the end of His activity for us; for He carries on His work of intercession and rule, His work of bestowing the gifts purchased by His blood, amidst the glories of heaven; and that perpetual application and dispensing of the blessed issues of His death He has Himself represented as greater than the works, to which His death put a period, in which He healed the bodies and spoke to the hearts of those who heard, and lived a perfect life here upon this sinful earth. But yet even He recognized the brief hour of sunny life as being an hour that must be filled with service, and recognized the fact that there was a task that He could only do when He lived the life of a man upon earth. And so, if I might so say, He was a miser of the moments, and carefully husbanding and garnering up every capacity and every opportunity, He toiled with the toil of a man who has a task before him, that must be done before the clock strikes six, and who sees the hands move over the dial, and by every glance that he casts at it is stimulated to intenser service and to harder toil. Christ felt that impulse to service which we all ought to feel—"The night cometh; let me fill the day with work."

And then there is a final motive which I need barely touch. He was impelled to His sedulous service not only by loving, filial obedience to the divine law, and by the consciousness of a limited and defined period into which all the activity of one specific kind must be condensed, but also by the motive expressed in such words as these, in which this Gospel is remarkably rich, "And Jesus, moved with compassion, put forth His hand and touched him." Thus, along with that supreme consecration, along with that swift ardor that will fill the brief hours ere nightfall with service, there was the constant pity of that beating heart that moved the diligent hand. Christ, if I may so say, could not help working as hard as He did, so long as there were so many men round about Him that needed His sympathy and His aid.

3. So much then for the motives; and now a word finally as to the worth of this toil for us. I do not stay to elucidate one consideration that might be suggested, viz., how precious a proof it is of Christ's humanity. We find it easier to bring home His true manhood to our thoughts, when we remember that He, like us, knew the pressure of physical fatigue. Not only was it a human spirit that wept and rejoiced, that was moved with compassion, and sometimes with indignation, but it was a human body, bone of our bone, and flesh of our flesh, that, wearied with walking in the burning sun, sat on the margin of the well; that was worn out and needed to sleep; that knew hunger, as is testified by His sending the disciples to buy meat; that was thirsty, as is testified by His saying, "Give Me to drink." The true corporeal manhood of Jesus Christ, and the fact that that manhood is the tabernacle of God—without these two facts the morality and the teaching of Christianity swing loose *in vacuo,* and have no holdfast in history, nor any leverage by which they can move men's hearts! But, when we know that the common necessities of fatigue, and hunger, and thirst belonged to Him, then we gratefully and reverently say, "Forasmuch as the children were partakers of flesh and blood, he also Himself took part of the same."

This fact of Christ's toil is of worth to us in other ways.

Is not that hard work of Jesus Christ a lesson for us, brethren, in our daily tasks and toils—a lesson which, if it were learned and practiced, would make a difference not only on the intensity but upon the spirit with which we labor? A great deal of fine talk is indulged in about the dignity of labor and the like. Labor is a curse until communion with God in it, which is possible through Jesus Christ, makes it a blessing and a joy. Christ, in the sweat of His brow, won our salvation; and our work only becomes great when it is work done in, and for, and by Him.

And what do we learn from His example? We learn these things: the plain lesson, first—task all your capacity and use every minute in doing the duty that is plainly set before you to do. Christian virtues are sometimes thought to be unreal and unworldly things. I was going to say the root of them, certainly the indispensable accompaniment for them all, is the plain, prosaic, most unromantic virtue of hard work.

And beyond that, what do we learn? The lesson that most toilers in England want. There is no need to preach to the most of us to work any harder, in one department of work at any rate; but there is great need to remind us of what it was that at once stirred Jesus Christ into energy and kept Him calm in the midst of labor—and that was that everything was equally and directly referred to His Father's will. People talk nowadays about "missions." The only thing worth giving that name to is the "mission" which *He* gives us, who sends us into the world not to do our own will, but to do the will of Him that sent us. There is a fatal monotony in all our lives—a terrible amount of hard drudgery in them all. We have to set ourselves morning after morning to tasks that look to be utterly insignificant and disproportionate to the power that we bring to bear upon them, so that men are like elephants picking up pins with their trunks; and yet we may make all our commonplace drudgery great, and wondrous, and fair, and full of help and profit to our souls, if, over it all—our shops, our desks, our ledgers, our studies, our kitchens, and our nurseries—we write, "My meat is to do the will of Him that sent me." We may bring the greatest principles to bear upon the smallest duties.

What more do we learn from Christ's toil? The possible harmony of communion and service. His labor did not break His fellowship with God. He was ever in the "secret place of the Most High," even while He was in the midst of crowds. He has taught us that it is possible to be in the "house of the Lord" all the days of our lives, and by His example, as by His granted Spirit, encourages us to aim at so serving that we shall never cease to behold, and so beholding that we shall never cease to serve our Father. The life of contemplation and the life of practice, so hard to harmonize in our experience, perfectly meet in Christ.

What more do we learn from our Lord's toils? The cheerful constant postponement of our own ease, wishes, or pleasure to the call of the Father's voice, or to the echo of it in the sighing of such as be sorrowful. I have already referred to the instances of His putting aside His need for rest, and His desire for still fellowship with God, at the call of whoever needed Him. It was the same always. If a Nicodemus comes by night, if a despairing father forces his way into the house of feasting, if another suppliant finds Him in a house, where He would have remained hid, if they come running to Him in the way, or drop down their sick before Him through the very roof—it is all the same. He never thinks of Himself, but gladly addresses Himself to heal and bless. How such an example followed would change our lives and amaze and shake the world!—"I come, not to do Mine own will." "Even Christ pleased not Himself."

But that toil is not only a pattern for our lives; it is an appeal to our grateful hearts. Surely a toiling Christ is as marvelous as a dying Christ. And the immensity and the purity and the depth of His love are shown no less by this, that He labors to accomplish it, than by this, that He dies to complete it. He will not give blessings which depend upon mere will, and can be bestowed as a king might fling a largess to a beggar without effort, and with scarce a thought, but blessings which He Himself has to agonize and to energize, and to lead a life of obedience, and to die a death of shame, in order to procure. ''I will not offer burnt-offering to God of that which doth cost me nothing,'' says the grateful heart. But in so saying it is but following in the track of the loving Christ, who will not give unto man that which cost Him nothing, and who works, as well as dies, in order that we may be saved.

Think of the contrast between what Christ has done to save us, and what we do to secure and appropriate that salvation! He toiled all His days, buying our peace with His life, going down into the mine and bringing up the jewels at the cost of His own precious blood. And you and I stand with folded arms, too apathetic to take the rich treasures that are freely given to us of God! He has done everything, that we may have nothing to do, and we will not even put out our slack hands to clasp the grace purchased by His blood, and commended by His toil! ''Therefore we ought to give the more earnest heed to the things which we have heard, lest at any time we should let them slip.''

5

Dispelling the Darkness

The Lord of Demons

And they came over unto the other side of the sea, into the country of the Gadarenes. 2. And when He was come out of the ship, immediately there met Him out of the tombs a man with an unclean spirit, 3. Who had his dwelling among the tombs; and no man could bind him, no, not with chains: 4. Because that he had been often bound with fetters and chains, and the chains had been plucked asunder by him, and the fetters broken in pieces: neither could any man tame him. 5. And always, night and day, he was in the mountains, and in the tombs, crying, and cutting himself with stones. 6. But when he saw Jesus afar off, he ran and worshipped Him, 7. And cried with a loud voice, and said, What have I to do with Thee, Jesus, Thou Son of the most high God? I adjure Thee by God, that Thou torment me not. 8. For He said unto him, Come out of the man, thou unclean spirit. 9. And He asked him, What is thy name? And he answered, saying, My name is Legion: for we are many. 10. And he besought Him much that He would not send them away out of the country. 11. Now there was there nigh unto the mountains a great herd of swine feeding. 12. And all the devils besought Him, saying, Send us into the swine, that we may enter into them. 13. And forthwith Jesus gave them leave. And the unclean spirits went out, and entered into the swine: and the herd ran violently down a steep place into the sea, (they were about two thousand;) and were choked in the sea. 14. And they that fed the swine fled, and told it in the city, and in the country. And they went out to see what it was that was done. 15. And they come to Jesus, and see him that was possessed with the devil, and had the legion, sitting, and clothed, and in his right mind: and they were afraid. 16. And they that saw it told them how it befell to him that was possessed with the devil, and also concerning the swine. 17. And they began to pray Him to depart out of their coasts. 18. And when He was come into the ship, he that had been possessed with the devil prayed Him that he might be with Him. 19. Howbeit Jesus suffered him not, but saith unto him, Go home to thy friends, and tell them how great things the Lord hath done for thee, and hath had compassion on thee. 20. And he departed, and began to publish in Decapolis how great things Jesus had done for him: and all men did marvel. MARK 5:1–20.

The awful picture of this demoniac is either painted from life, or it is one of the most wonderful feats of the poetic imagination. Nothing more terrible, vivid, penetrating, and real was ever conceived by the greatest creative genius. If it is not simply a portrait, Aeschylus or Dante might own the artist for a brother. We see the quiet landing on the eastern shore, and almost hear the yells that broke the silence as the fierce, demon-ridden man hurried to meet them, perhaps with hostile purpose. The dreadful characteristics of his state are sharply and profoundly signalized. He lives up in the rock-hewn tombs which overhang the beach; for all that belongs to corruption and death is congenial to the subjects of that dark kingdom of evil. He has superhuman strength, and has known no gentle efforts to reclaim, but only savage attempts to "tame" by force, as if he were a beast. Fetters and manacles have been snapped like rushes by him. Restless, sleepless, hating men, he has made the night hideous with his wild shrieks, and fled, swift as the wind, from place to place among the lonely hills. Insensible to pain, and deriving some dreadful satisfaction from his own wounds, he has gashed himself with splinters of rock, and howled, in a delirium of pain and pleasure, at the sight of his own blood. His sharpened eyesight sees Jesus from afar, and, with the disordered haste and preternatural agility which marked all his movements, he runs towards Him. Such is the introduction to the narrative of the cure. It paints for us not merely a maniac, but a demoniac. He is not a man at war with himself, but a man at war with other beings, who have forced themselves into his house of life. At least, so says Mark, and so said Jesus; and if the story before us is true, its subsequent incidents compel the acceptance of that explanation. What went into the herd of swine?

The narrative of the restoration of the sufferer has a remarkable feature, which may help to mark off its stages. The word "besought" occurs four times in it, and we may group the details round each instance.

1. The demons beseeching Jesus through the man's voice. He was, in the exact sense of the word, *distracted*—drawn two ways. For it would seem to have been the self in him that ran to Jesus and fell at His feet, as if in some dim hope of rescue; but it is the demons in him that speak, though the voice be his. They force him to utter their wishes, their terrors, their loathing of Christ, though he says "I" and "me," as if these were his own. That horrible condition of a double, or, as in this case, a manifold personality, speaking through human organs, and overwhelming the proper self, mysterious as it is, is the very essence of the awful misery of the demoniacs. Unless we are resolved to force meanings of our own on Scripture, I do not see how we can avoid recognizing this. What black thoughts, seething with all rebellious agitation, the reluctant lips have to utter! The self-drawn picture of the demoniac nature is as vivid as, and more repellent than, the Evangelist's terrible portrait of the outward man. Whatever dumb yearning after Jesus may have been in the oppressed human consciousness, his words are a shriek of terror and recoil. The mere presence of Christ lashes the demons into paroxysms: but before the man spoke, Christ had spoken His stern command to come forth. He is answered by this howl of fear and hate. Clear recognition of Christ's person is in it, and not difficult to explain, if we believe that others than the sufferer looked through his wild eyes, and spoke in his loud cry. They know Him who had conquered their prince long ago; if the existence of fallen spirits be admitted, their knowledge is no difficulty.

The next element in the words is hatred, as fixed as the knowledge is clear. God's supremacy and loftiness, and Christ's nature, are recognized, but only the more abhorred. The name of God can be used as a spell to sway Jesus, but it has no power to touch this fierce hatred into submission. "The devils also believe and tremble." This, then, is a dark possibility, which has become actual for real living beings, that they should know God, and hate as heartily as they know clearly. That is the terminus towards which human spirits may be travelling. Christ's power, too, is recognized, and His mere presence makes the flock of obscene creatures nested in the man uneasy, like bats in a cave, who flutter against a light. They shrink from Him, and shudderingly renounce all connection with Him, as if their cries would alter facts, or make Him relax His grip. The very words of the question prove its folly. "What is there to me and thee?" implies that there were two parties to the answer; and the writhings of one of them could not break the bond. To all this is to be added that the "torment" deprecated was the expulsion from the man, as if there were some grim satisfaction and dreadful alleviation in being there, rather than "in the abyss"—as Luke gives it—which appears to be the alternative. If we put all these things together, we get an awful glimpse into the secrets of that dark realm, which it is better to ponder with awe than flippantly to deny or mock.

How striking is Christ's unmoved calm in the face of all this fury! He is always laconic in dealing with demoniacs; and, no doubt, His tranquil presence helped to calm the man, however it excited the demon. The distinct intention of the question, "What is thy name?" is to rouse the man's self-consciousness, and make him feel his separate existence, apart from the alien tyranny which had just been using his voice and usurping his personality. He had said "I" and "me." Christ meets him with, Who is the "I"? and the very effort to answer would facilitate the deliverance. But for the moment the foreign influence is still too strong, and the answer, than which there is nothing more weird and awful in the whole range of literature, comes: "My name is Legion; for we are many." Note the momentary gleam of the true self in the first word or two, fading away into the old confusion. He begins with "my," but he drops back to "we." Note the pathetic force of the name. This poor wretch had seen the solid mass of the Roman legion, the instrument by which foreign tyrants crushed the nations. He felt himself oppressed and conquered by their multitudinous array. The voice of the "legion" has a kind of cruel ring of triumph, as if spoken as much to terrify the victim as to answer the question.

Again the man's voice speaks, beseeching the direct opposite of what he really would have desired. He was not so much in love with his dreadful tenants as to pray against their expulsion, but their fell power coerces his lips, and he asks for what would be his ruin. That prayer, clean contrary to the man's only hope, is surely the climax of the horror. In a less degree, we also too often deprecate the stroke which delivers, and would fain keep the legion of evils which riot within.

2. The demons beseeching Jesus without disguise. There seems to be intended a distinction between "he besought," in verse 10, and "they besought," in verse 12. Whether we are to suppose that, in the latter case, the man's voice was used or no, the second request was more plainly not his, but theirs. It looks as if, somehow, the command was already beginning to take effect, and "he" and "they" were less closely intertwined. It is easy to ridicule this part of the incident, and as easy to say that it is incredible; but it is wiser to remember the narrow bounds of our knowledge of the unseen world of being, and to be cautious in asserting that there is nothing beyond the horizon but vacuity. If there be unclean spirits, we know too little about them to say what is possible. Only this is plain—that the difficulty of supposing them to inhabit swine is less, if there be any difference, than of supposing them to inhabit men, since the animal nature, especially of such an animal, would correspond to their impurity, and be open to their driving. The house and the tenant are well matched. But why should the expelled demons seek such an abode? It would appear that anywhere was better than "the abyss," and that unless they could find some creature to enter, thither they must go.

It would seem, too, that there was no other land open to them—for the prayer on the man's lips had been not to send them "out of the country," as if that was the only country on earth open to them. That makes for the opinion that demoniacal possession was the dark shadow which attended, for reasons not discoverable by us, the light of Christ's coming, and was limited in time and space by His earthly manifestation. But on such matters there is not ground enough for certainty.

Another difficulty has been raised as to Christ's right to destroy property. It was very questionable property, if the owners were Jews. Jesus owns all things, and has the right and the power to use them as He will; and if the purposes served by the destruction of animal life or property are beneficent and lofty, it leaves no blot on His goodness. He used His miraculous power twice for destruction—once on a fig tree, once on a herd of swine. In both cases, the good sought was worth the loss. Whether was it better, that the herd should live and fatten, or that a man should be delivered, and that he and they who saw should be assured of his deliverance and of Christ's power? "Is not a man much better than a sheep," and much more than a pig? They are born to be killed, and nobody cries out cruelty. Why should not Christ have sanctioned this slaughter, if it helped to steady the poor man's nerves, or to establish the reality of possession and of his deliverance? Notice that the drowning of the herd does not appear to have entered into the calculations of the unclean spirits. They desired houses to live in after their expulsion, and for them to plunge the swine into the lake would have defeated their purpose. The stampede was an unexpected effect of the commingling of the demonic with the animal nature, and outwitted the demons. "The devil is an ass." There is a lower depth than the animal nature; and even swine feel uncomfortable when the demon is in them, and in their panic rush anywhere to get rid of the incubus, and, before they know, find themselves struggling in the lake. "Which things are an allegory."

3. The terrified Gerasenes beseeching Jesus to leave them. They had rather have their swine than their Saviour, and so, though they saw the demoniac sitting, "clothed, and in his right mind," at the feet of Jesus, they in turn beseech that He should take Himself away. Fear and selfishness prompted the prayer. The communities on the eastern side of the lake were largely Gentile; and, no doubt, these people knew that they did many worse things than swinekeeping, and may have been afraid that some more of their wealth would have to go the same road as the herd. They did not want instruction, nor feel that they needed a healer. Were their prayers so very unlike the wishes of many of us? Is there nobody nowadays unwilling to let the thought of Christ into his life, because he feels an uneasy suspicion that, if Christ comes, a good deal will have to go? How many trades and schemes of life really beseech Jesus to go away and leave them in peace!

And He goes away. The tragedy of life is that we have the awful power of severing ourselves from His influence. Christ commands unclean spirits, but He can only plead with hearts. And if we bid Him depart, He is fain to leave us for the time to the indulgence of our foolish and wicked schemes. If any man open, He comes in—oh, how gladly! but if any man slam the door in His face, He can but tarry without and knock. Sometimes His withdrawing does more than His loudest knocking; and sometimes they who repelled Him as He stood on the beach call Him back, as He moves away to the boat. It is in the hope that they may, that He goes.

4. The restored man's beseeching to abide with Christ. No wonder that the spirit of this man, all tremulous with conflict, and scarcely able yet to realize his deliverance, clung to Christ, and besought Him to let him continue by His side. Conscious weakness, dread of some recurrence of the inward hell, and grateful love, prompted the prayer. The prayer itself was partly right and partly wrong. Right, in clinging to Jesus as the only refuge from the past misery; wrong, in clinging to His visible presence as the only way of keeping near Him. Therefore, He who had permitted the wish of the demons, and complied with the entreaties of the terrified mob, did *not* yield to the prayer, throbbing with love and conscious weakness. Strange that Jesus should put aside a hand that sought to grasp His in order to be safe; but His refusal was, as always, the gift of something better, and He ever disappoints the wish in order more truly to satisfy the need. The best defense against the return of the evil spirits was in occupation. It is the "empty" house which invites them back. Nothing was so likely to confirm and steady the convalescent mind as to dwell on the fact of his deliverance. Therefore he is sent to proclaim it to friends who had known his dreadful state, and amidst old associations which would help him to knit his new life to his old, and to treat his misery as a parenthesis. Jesus commanded silence or speech according to the need of the subjects of His miracles. For some, silence was best, to deepen the impression of blessing received; for others, speech was best, to engage and so to fortify the mind against relapse.

A Refused Request

He that had been possessed with the devil prayed Jesus that he might be with Him. 19. Howbeit Jesus suffered him not, but saith

> *unto him, Go home to thy friends, and tell them how great things the Lord hath done for thee.* MARK 5:18, 19.

There are three requests, singularly contrasted with each other, made to Christ in the course of this miracle of healing the Gadarene demoniac. The evil spirits ask to be permitted to go into the swine; the men of the country, caring more for their swine than their Saviour, beg Him to take Himself away, and relieve them of His unwelcome presence; the demoniac beseeches Him to be allowed to stop beside Him. Two of the requests are granted; one is refused. The one that was refused is the one that we might have expected to be granted.

Christ forces Himself upon no man, and so, when they besought Him to go, He went, and took salvation with Him in the boat. Christ withdraws Himself from no man who desires Him. "Howbeit Jesus suffered him not, and said, Go home to thy friends, and tell them how great things the Lord hath done for thee."

Now, do you not think that if we put these three petitions and their diverse answers together, and look especially at this last one, where the natural wish was refused, we ought to be able to learn some lessons?

1. The first thing I would notice is, the clinging of the healed man to his Healer. Think of him half an hour before, a raging maniac; now all at once conscious of a strange new sanity and calmness; instead of lashing himself about, and cutting himself with stones, and rendering his chains and fetters, "sitting clothed, and in his right mind," at the feet of Jesus. No wonder that he feared that when the Healer went the demons would come back—no wonder that he besought Him that he might still keep within that quiet sacred circle of light which streamed from His presence, across the border of which no evil thing could pass. Love bound him to his Benefactor; dread made him shudder at the thought of losing his sole Protector, and being again left, in that partly heathen land, solitary, to battle with the strong foes that had so long rioted in his house of life. And so "he begged that he might be with Him."

That poor heathen man—for you must remember that this miracle was not wrought on the sacred soil of Palestine—that poor heathen man, just having caught a glimpse of how calm and blessed life might be, is the type of us all. And there is something wrong with us if our love does not, like his, desire above all things the presence of Jesus Christ; and if our consciousness of impotence does not, in like manner, drive us to long that our sole Deliverer shall not be far away from us. Merchant ships in time of war, like a flock of timid birds, keep as near as they can to the armed convoy, for the only safety from the guns of the enemy's cruisers is in keeping close to their strong protector. The traveler upon some rough, unknown road, in the dark, holds on by his guide's skirts or hand, and feels that if he loses touch he loses the possibility of safety. A child clings to his parent when dangers are round him. The convalescent patient does not like to part with his doctor. And if we rightly learned who it is that has cured us, and what is the condition of our continuing whole and sound, like this man we shall pray that He may suffer us to be with Him. Fill the heart with Christ, and there is no room for the many evil spirits that make up the legion that torments it. The empty heart invites the devils, and they come back. Even if it is "swept and garnished," and brought into respectability, propriety, and morality, they come back. There is only one way to keep them out; when the ark is in the Temple, Dagon will be lying, like the brute form that he is, a stump upon the threshold. The condition of our security is close contact with Jesus Christ. If we know the facts of life, the temptations that ring us round, the weakness of these wayward wills of ours and the strength of this intrusive and masterful flesh and sense that we have to rule, we shall know and feel that our only safety is our Master's presence.

2. Further, note the strange refusal. Jesus Christ went through the world, or at least the little corner of it which His earthly career occupied, seeking for men that desired to have Him, and it is impossible that He should have put away any soul that desired to be present with Him. Yet, though His one aim was to draw men to Him, and the prospect that He should be able to exercise a stronger attraction over a wider area reconciled Him to the prospect of the Cross, so that He said in triumph, "I, when I am lifted up from the earth, will draw all men unto Me," he meets this heathen man, feeble in his crude and recent sanity, with a flat refusal. "He suffered him not." Most probably the reason for the strange and apparently anomalous dealing with such a desire was to be found in the man's temperament. Most likely it was the best thing for *him* that he should stop quietly in his own house, and have no continuance of the excitement and perpetual change which would have necessarily been his lot if he had been allowed to go with Jesus Christ. We may be quite sure that when the Lord with one hand seemed to put him away, He was really, with a stronger attraction, drawing him to Himself; and that the peculiarity of the method of treatment was determined with exclusive reference to the real necessities of the person who was subject to it.

But yet, underlying the special case, and capable of being stated in the most general terms, lies this thought, that Jesus Christ's presence, the substance of the demoniac's desire, may be as completely, and, in some cases, will be more completely, realized amongst the secularities of ordinary life than amidst the sanctities of outward communion and companionship with Him. Jesus was beginning here to wean the man from his sensuous dependence upon His localized and material presence. It was good for him, and it is good for us all, to "feel our feet," so to speak. Responsibility laid, and felt to be laid, upon us is a steadying and ennobling influence. And it was better that the demoniac should learn to stand calmly, when apparently alone, than that he should childishly be relying on the mere external presence of his Deliverer.

Be sure of this, that when the Lord went away across the lake, He left His heart and His thoughts, and His care and His power over there, on the heathen side of the sea; and that when "the people thronged Him" on the other side, and the poor woman pressed through the crowd, that virtue might come to her by her touch, virtue was at the same time raying out across the water to the solitary, newly healed demoniac, to sustain him too.

And so we may all learn that we may have, and it depends upon ourselves whether we do or do not have, all protection, all companionship, and all the sweetness of Christ's companionship and the security of Christ's protection just as completely when we are at home amongst our friends—that is to say, when we are about our daily work, and in the secularities of our calling or profession—as when we are in the "secret place of the Most High" and holding fellowship with a present Christ. Oh, to carry Him with us into every duty, to realize Him in all circumstances, to see the light of His face shine amidst the darkness of calamity, and the pointing of His directing finger showing us our road amidst all perplexities of life! Brethren, that is possible. When Jesus Christ "suffered him not to go with Him," Jesus Christ stayed behind with the man.

3. Lastly, we have here the duty enjoined. "Go home to thy friends, and tell them how great things the Lord hath done for thee." The man went home and translated the injunction into word and deed. As I said, the reason for the peculiarity of his treatment, in his request being refused, was probably his peculiar temperament. So again I would say the reason for the commandment laid upon him, which is also anomalous, was probably the peculiarity of his disposition. Usually our Lord was careful to enjoin silence upon those whom He benefited by His miraculous cures. That injunction of silence was largely owing to His desire not to create or fan the flame of popular excitement. But that risk was chiefly to be guarded against in the land of Israel, and here, where we have a miracle upon Gentile soil, there was not the same occasion for avoiding talk and notoriety.

But probably the main reason for the exceptional commandment to go and publish abroad what the Lord had done was to be found in the simple fact that this man's malady and his disposition were such that external work of some sort was the best thing to prevent him from relapsing into his former condition. His declaration to everybody of his cure would help to confirm his cure; and whilst he was speaking about being healed, he would more and more realize to himself that he was healed. Having work to do would take him out of himself, which no doubt was a great security against the recurrence of the evil from which he had been delivered. But however that may be, look at the plain lesson that lies here. Every healed man should be a witness to his Healer; and there is no better way of witnessing than by our lives, by the elevation manifested in our aims, by our aversion from all low, earthly, gross things, by the conspicuous—not made conspicuous by us, conspicuous because it cannot be hid—concentration and devotion, and unselfishness and Christlikeness of our daily lives to show that we are really healed. If we manifest these things in our conduct, then, when we say "it was Jesus Christ that healed me," people will be apt to believe us. But if this man had gone away into the mountains and amongst the tombs as he used to do, and had continued all the former characteristics of his devil-ridden life, who would have believed him when he talked about being healed? And who ought to believe you when you say, "Christ is my Saviour," if your lives are, to all outward seeming, exactly what they were before?

The sphere in which the healed man's witness was to be borne tested the reality of his healing. "Go home to thy friends, and tell *them*." I wonder how many Christian professors there are who would be least easily believed by those who live in the same house with them, if they said that Jesus had cast their devils out of them. It is a great mistake to take recent converts, especially if they have been very profligate beforehand, and to hawk them about the country as trophies of God's converting power. Let them stop at home, and bethink themselves, and get sober and confirmed, and let their changed lives prove the reality of Christ's healing power. They can speak to some purpose after that.

Further, remember that there is no better way for keeping out devils than working for Jesus Christ. Many a man finds that the true cure—say, for instance, of doubts that buzz about him and disturb him, is to go away and talk to some one about his Saviour. Work for Jesus amongst people that do not know Him is a wonderful sieve for sifting out the fundamental articles of the Christian faith. And when we go to other people, and tell them of that Lord, and see how the message is sometimes received, and what it sometimes does, we come away with confirmed faith.

But, in any case, it is better to work for Him than to sit alone, thinking about Him. The two things have to go together; and I know very well that there is a great danger, in the present day, of exaggeration, and insisting too exclusively upon the duty of Christian work while neglecting to insist upon the duty of Christian meditation. But, on the other hand, it blows the cobwebs out of a man's brain; it puts vigor into him, it releases him from himself, and gives him something better to think about, when he listens to the Master's voice, "Go home to thy friends, and tell them what great things the Lord hath done for thee."

"Master! it is good for us to be here. Let us make three tabernacles. Stay here; let us enjoy ourselves up in the clouds, with Moses and Elias; and never mind about what goes on below." But there was a demoniac boy down there that needed to be healed; and the father was at his wits' end, and the disciples were at theirs because they could not heal him. And so Jesus Christ turned His back upon the Mount of Transfiguration, and the company of the blessed two, and the Voice that said, "This is My beloved Son," and hurried down where human woes called Him, and found that He was as near God, and so did Peter and James and John, as when up there amid the glory.

"Go home to thy friends, and tell them," and you will find that to do that is the best way to realize the desire which seemed to be put aside, the desire for the presence of Christ. For be sure that wherever He may not be, He always is where a man, in obedience to Him, is doing His commandments. So when He said, "Go home to thy friends," He was answering the request that He seemed to reject, and when the Gadarene obeyed, he would find, to his astonishment and his grateful wonder, that the Lord had *not* gone away in the boat, but was with him still. "Go ye into all the world and preach the Gospel. Lo! I am with you always."

Talitha Cumi

And, behold, there cometh one of the rulers of the synagogue, Jairus by name; and when he saw Him, he fell at His feet, 23. And besought Him greatly, saying, My little daughter lieth at the point of death: I pray Thee, come and lay Thy hands on her, that she may be healed; and she shall live. 24. And Jesus went with him; and much people followed Him, and thronged Him. . . . 35. While He yet spake, there came from the ruler of the synagogue's house certain which said, Thy daughter is dead: why troublest thou the Master any further? 36. As soon as Jesus heard the word that was spoken, He saith unto the ruler of the synagogue, Be not afraid, only believe. 37. And He suffered no man to follow Him, save Peter, and James, and John the brother of James. 38. And He cometh to the house of the ruler of the synagogue, and seeth the tumult, and them that wept and wailed greatly. 39. And when He was come in, He saith unto them, Why make ye this ado, and weep? the damsel is not dead, but sleepeth. 40. And they laughed Him to scorn. But when He had put them all out, He taketh the father and the mother of the damsel, and them that were with Him, and entereth in where the damsel was lying. 41. And He took the damsel by the hand, and said unto her, Talitha cumi; which is, being interpreted, Damsel, I say unto thee, arise. 42. And straightway the damsel arose, and walked; for she was of the age of twelve years. And they were astonished with a great astonishment. 43. And He charged them straitly that no man should know it; and commanded that something should be given her to eat. MARK 5:22–24, 35–43.

The scene of this miracle was probably Capernaum; its time, according to Matthew, was the feast at his house after his call. Mark's date appears to be later, but he may have anticipated the feast in his narrative, in order to keep the whole of the incidents relating to Matthew's apostleship together. Jairus's knowledge of Jesus is implied in the story, and perhaps Jesus' acquaintance with him.

1. We note, first, the agonized appeal and the immediate answer. Desperation makes men bold. Conventionalities are burned up by the fire of agonized petitioning for help in extremity. Without apology or preliminary, Jairus bursts in, and his urgent need is sufficient excuse. Jesus never complains of scant respect when wrung hearts cry to Him. But this man was not only driven by despair, but drawn by trust. He was sure that, even though his little darling had been all but dead when he ran from his house, and was dead by this time, for all he knew, Jesus could give her life. Perhaps he had not faced the stern possibility that she might already be gone, nor defined precisely what he hoped for in that case. But he was sure of Jesus' power, and he says nothing to show that he doubted His willingness. A beautiful trust shines through his words, based, no doubt, on what he had known and seen of Jesus' miracles. *We* have more pressing and deeper needs, and we have fuller and deeper knowledge of Jesus, wherefore our approach to Him should be at least as earnest and confidential as Jairus's was. If our Lord was at the feast when this interruption took place, His gracious, immediate answer becomes more lovely, as a sign of His willingness to bring the swiftest help. "While they are yet speaking, I will hear." Jairus had not finished asking before Jesus was on His feet to go.

The father's impatience would be satisfied when they were on their way, but how he would chafe, and think every moment an age, while Jesus stayed, as if at entire leisure, to deal with another silent petitioner! But His help to one never interferes with His help to another, and no case is so pressing as that He cannot spare time to stay to bless someone else. The poor, sickly, shamefaced woman shall be healed, and the little girl shall not suffer.

2. We have next the extinction and rekindling of Jairus's glimmer of hope. Distances in Capernaum were short, and the messenger would soon find Jesus. There was little sympathy in the harsh, bald announcement of the death, or in the appended suggestion that the Rabbi need not be further troubled. The speaker evidently was thinking more of being polite to Jesus than of the poor father's stricken heart. Jairus would feel then what most of us have felt in like circumstances—that he had been more hopeful than he knew. Only when the last glimmer is quenched do we feel, by the blackness, how much light had lingered in our sky. But Jesus knew Jairus's need before Jairus himself knew it, and His strong word of cheer relit the torch ere the poor father had time to speak. That loving eye reads our hearts and anticipates our dreary hopelessness by His sweet comfortings. Faith is the only victorious antagonist of fear. Jairus had every reason for abandoning hope, and his only reason for clinging to it was faith. So it is with us all. It is vain to bid us not be afraid when real dangers and miseries stare us in the face; but it is not vain to bid us "believe," and if we do that, faith, cast into the one scale, will outweigh a hundred good reasons for dread and despair cast into the other.

3. We have next the tumult of grief and the word that calms. The hired mourners had lost no time, and in Eastern fashion were disturbing the solemnity of death with their professional shrieks and wailings. True grief is silent. Woe that weeps aloud is soon consoled.

What a contrast between the noise outside and the still death chamber and its occupant, and what a contrast between the agitation of the sham comforters and the calmness of the true Helper! Christ's great word was spoken for us all when our hearts are sore and our dear ones go. It dissolves the dim shape into nothingness, or, rather, it transfigures it into a gracious, soothing form. Sleep is rest, and bears in itself the pledge of waking. So Christ has changed the "shadow feared of man" into beauty, and in the strength of His great word we can meet the last enemy with "Welcome! friend." It is strange that anyone reading this narrative should have been so blind to its deepest beauty as to suppose that Jesus was here saying that the child had only swooned, and was really alive. He was not denying that she was what men call "dead," but He was, in the triumphant consciousness of His own power, and in the clear vision of the realities of spiritual being, of which bodily states are but shadows, denying that what men call death deserves the name. "Death" is the state of the soul separated from God, whether united to the body or no—not the separation of body and soul, which is only a visible symbol of the more dread reality.

4. We have finally the life-giving word and the life-preserving care. Probably Jesus first freed His progress from the jostling crowd, and then, when arrived, made the further selection of the three apostles —the first three of the mighty ones—and, as was becoming, of the father and mother.

With what hushed, tense expectation they would enter the chamber! Think of the mother's eyes watching Him. The very words that He spoke were like a caress. There was infinite tenderness in that "Damsel!" from His lips, and so deep an impression did it make on Peter that he repeated the very words to Mark, and used them, with the change of one letter ("Ta*b*itha" for "Ta*l*itha"), in raising Dorcas. The same tenderness is expressed by His taking her by the hand, as, no doubt, her mother had done, many a morning, on waking her. The father had asked Him to lay His hand on her, that she might be made whole and live. He did as He was asked —He always does—and His doing according to our desire brings larger blessings than we had thought of. Neither the touch of His hand nor the words He spoke were the real agents of the child's returning to life. It was His will which brought her back from whatever vasty dimness she had entered. The forthputting of Christ's will is sovereign, and His word runs with power through all regions of the universe. "The dull, cold ear of death" hears, and "they that hear shall live," whether they are, as men say, dead, or whether they are "dead in trespasses and sins." The resurrection of a soul is a mightier act—if we can speak of degrees of might in His acts—than that of a body.

It would be calming for the child of such strange experiences to see, for the first thing that met her eyes opening again on the old familiar home as on a strange land, the bending face of Jesus, and His touch would steady her spirit and assure of His love and help. The quiet command to give her food knits the wonder with common life, and teaches precious lessons as to His economy of miraculous power, like His bidding others loosen Lazarus's wrappings, and as to His devolution on us of duties towards those whom He raises from the death of sin. But it was given, not didactically, but lovingly. The girl was exhausted, and sustenance was necessary, and would be sweet. So He thought upon a small bodily need, and the love that gave life took care to provide what was required to support it. He gives the greatest; He will take care that we shall not lack the least.

The Power of Feeble Faith

And a certain woman . . . 27. When she had heard of Jesus, came in the press behind, and touched His garment. 28. For she said, If I may touch but His clothes, I shall be whole. MARK 5:25, 27, 28.

In all the narratives of this miracle, it is embedded in the story of Jairus's daughter, which it cuts in twain. I suppose that the Evangelists felt, and would have us feel, the impression of calm consciousness of power and of leisurely dignity produced by Christ's having time to pause even on such an errand, in order to heal by the way, as if parenthetically, this other poor sufferer. The child's father with impatient earnestness pleads the urgency of her case—"She lieth at the point of death"; and to him and to the group of disciples, it must have seemed that there was no time to be lost. But He who knows that His resources are infinite can afford to let her die, while He cures and saves this woman. She shall receive no harm, and her sister suppliant has as great a claim on Him. "The eyes of all wait" on His equal love; He has leisure of heart to feel for each, and fulness of power for all; and none can rob another of his share in the Healer's gifts, nor any in all that dependent crowd jostle his neighbor out of the notice of the Saviour's eye.

The main point of the story itself seems to be the illustration which it gives of the genuineness and power of an imperfect faith, and of Christ's merciful way of responding to and strengthening such a faith. Looked at from that point of view, the narrative is very striking and instructive.

The woman is a poor shrinking creature, broken down by long illness, made more timid still by many disappointed hopes of cure, depressed by poverty to which her many doctors had brought her. She does not venture to stop this new Rabbi-physician, as He goes with the rich church dignitary to heal his daughter, but lets Him pass before she can make up her mind to go near Him at all, and then comes creeping up in the crowd behind, puts out her wasted, trembling hand to His garment's hem—and she is whole. She would fain have stolen away with her new-found blessing, but Christ forces her to stand out before the throng, and there, with all their eyes upon her—cold, cruel eyes some of them—to conquer her diffidence and shame, and tell all the truth. Strange kindness that!—strangely contrasted with His ordinary care to avoid notoriety, and with His ordinary tender regard for shrinking weakness! What may have been the reason? Certainly it was not for His own sake at all, nor for others' chiefly, but for hers, that He did this. The reason lay in the incompleteness of her faith. It was very incomplete—although it was, Christ answered it. And then He sought to make the cure, and the discipline that followed it, the means of clearing and confirming her trust in Himself.

1. Following the order of the narrative thus understood, we have here first the great lesson, that very imperfect faith may be genuine faith. There was unquestionable confidence in Christ's healing power, and there was earnest desire for healing. Our Lord Himself recognizes her faith as adequate to be the condition of her receiving the cure which she desired. Of course, it was a very different thing from the faith which unites us to Christ, and is the condition of our receiving our soul's cure; and we shall never understand the relation of multitudes of the people in the Gospels to Jesus, if we insist upon supposing that the "faith to be healed," which many of them had, was a religious, or, as we call it, "saving faith." But still, the trust which was directed to Him, as the giver of miraculous temporal blessings, is akin to that higher trust into which it often passed, and the principles regulating the operation of the loftier are abundantly illustrated in the workings of the lower.

The imperfections, then, of this woman's faith were many. It was intensely *ignorant* trust. She dimly believes that, somehow or other, this miracle-working Rabbi will heal her, but the cure is to be a piece of magic, secured by material contact of her finger with His robe. She has no idea that Christ's will, or His knowledge, much less His pitying love, has anything to do with it. She thinks that she may get her desire furtively, and may carry it away out of the crowd, and He, the source of it, be none the wiser, and none the poorer, for the blessing which she has stolen from Him. What utter blank ignorance of Christ's character and way of working! What complete misconception of the relation between Himself and His gift! What low, gross, superstitious ideas! Yes, and with them all what a hunger of intense desire to be whole; what absolute assurance of confidence that one fingertip on His robe was enough! Therefore she had her desire, and her Lord recognized her faith as true, foolish and unworthy as were the thoughts which accompanied it!

Thank God! the same thing is true still, or what would become of any of us? There may be a real faith in Christ, though there be mixed with it many and grave errors concerning His work, and the manner of receiving the blessings which He bestows. A man may have a very hazy apprehension of the bearing and whole scope of even Scripture declarations concerning the profounder aspects of Christ's person and work, and yet be holding fast to Him by living confidence. I do not wish to underrate for one moment the absolute necessity of clear and true conceptions of revealed truth, in order to a vigorous and fully developed faith; but, while there can be no faith worth calling so, which is not based upon the intellectual reception of truth, there may be faith based upon the very imperfect intellectual reception of very partial truth. The power and vitality of faith are not measured by the comprehensiveness and clearness of belief. The richest soil may bear shrunken and barren ears; and on the arid sand, with the thinnest layer of earth, gorgeous cacti may bloom out, and fleshy aloes lift their sworded arms, with stores of moisture to help them through the heat. It is not for us to say what amount of ignorance is destructive of the possibility of real confidence in Jesus Christ. But for ourselves, feeling how short a distance our eyesight travels, and how little, after all our systems, the great bulk of men in Christian lands know lucidly and certainly of theological truth, and how wide are the differences of opinion amongst us, and how soon we come to towering barriers, beyond which our poor faculties can neither pass nor look, it ought to be a joy to us all, that a faith which is clouded with such ignorance may yet be a faith which Christ accepts. He that knows and trusts Him as Brother, Friend, Saviour, in whom he receives the pardon and cleansing which he needs and desires, may have very much misconception and error cleaving to him, but Christ accepts him. If at the beginning His disciples know but this much, that they are sick unto death, and have tried without success all other remedies, and this more, that Christ will heal them; and if their faith builds upon that knowledge, then they will receive according to their faith. By degrees they will be taught more; they will be brought to the higher benches in His school; but, for a beginning, the most cloudy apprehension that Christ is the Saviour of the world, and my Saviour, may become the foundation of a trust which will bind the heart to Him and knit Him to the heart in eternal union. This poor woman received her healing, although she said, "If I may touch but the hem of His garment, I shall be whole."

Her error was akin to one which is starting into new prominence again, and with which I need not say that I have no sort of sympathy—that of people who attach importance to externals as means and channels of grace, and in whose system the hem of the garment and the touch of the finger are apt to take the place which the heart of the wearer and the grasp of faith should hold. The more our circumstances call for resistance to this error, the more needful is it to remember that, along with it and uttering itself through it, may be a depth of devout trust in Christ, which should shame us. Many a poor soul that clasps the base of the crucifix clings to the cross; many a devout heart, kneeling before the altar, sees through the incense smoke the face of Christ. The faith that is tied to form, though it be no faith for a man, though in some respects it darken God's Gospel, and bring it down to the level of magical superstition, may yet be, and often is, accepted by Him whose merciful eye recognized, and whose swift power answered, the mistaken trust of her who believed that healing lay in the fringes of His robe, rather than in the pity of His heart.

Again, her trust was very *selfish*. She wanted health; she did not care about the Healer. She thought much of the blessing in itself, little or nothing of the blessing as a sign of His love. She would have been quite contented to have had nothing more to do with Christ if she could only have gone away cured. She felt but little glow of gratitude to Him whom she thought of as unconscious of the good which she had stolen from Him. All this is a parallel to what occurs in the early stages of many a Christian life. The first inducement to a serious contemplation of Christ is, ordinarily, the consciousness of one's own sore need. Most men are driven to Him as a refuge from self, from their own sin, and from the wages of sin. The soul, absorbed in its own misery, and groaning in a horror of great darkness, sees from afar a great light, and stumbles towards it. Its first desire is deliverance, forgiveness, escape; and the first motions of faith are impelled by consideration of personal consequences. Love comes after, born of the recognition of Christ's great love to which we owe our salvation; but faith precedes love in the natural order of things, however closely love may follow faith; and the predominant motive in the earlier stages of many men's faith is distinctly self-regard. Now, that is all right, and as it was meant to be. It is an overstrained and caricatured doctrine of self-abnegation, which condemns such a faith as wrong. The most purely self-absorbed wish to escape from the most rudely pictured hell may be, and often is, the beginning of a true trust in Christ. Some of our superfine modern teachers who are shocked at Christianity, because it lays the foundation of the loftiest, most self-denying morality in "selfishness" of that kind, would be all the wiser for going to school to this story, and laying to heart the lesson it contains, of how a desire no nobler than to get rid of a painful disease was the starting point of a moral transformation, which turned a life into a peaceful, thankful surrender of the cured self to the service and love of the mighty Healer.

But while this faith, for the sake of the blessing to be obtained, is genuine, it is undoubtedly imperfect. Quite legitimate and natural at first, it must grow into something nobler when it has once been answered. To think of the disease mainly is inevitable before the cure, but, after the cure, we should think most of the Physician. Self-love may impel to His feet; but Christ-love should be the moving spring of life thereafter. Ere we have received anything from Him, our whole soul may be a longing to have our gnawing emptiness filled; but when we have received His own great gift, our whole soul should be a thank-offering. The great reformation which Christ produces is, that He shifts the center for us from ourselves to Himself; and whilst He uses our sense of need and our fear of personal evil as the means towards this, He desires that the faith, which has been answered by deliverance, should thenceforward be a "faith which worketh by love." As long as we live, either here or yonder, we shall never get beyond the need for the exercise of the primary form of faith, for we shall ever be compassed by many needs, and dependent for all help and blessedness on Him; but as we grow in experience of His tender might, we should learn more and more that His gifts cannot be separated from Himself. We should prize them most for His sake, and love Him more than we do them. We should be drawn to Him as well as driven to Him. Faith may begin with desiring the blessing rather than the Christ. It must end with desiring Him more than all besides, and with losing self utterly in His great love. Its starting point may rightly be, "Save, Lord, or I perish." Its goal must be, "I live, yet not I, but Christ liveth in me."

Again, here is an instance of real faith weakened and interrupted by much *distrust*. There was not a full, calm reliance on Christ's power and love. She dare not appeal to His heart, she shrinks from meeting His eye. She will let Him pass, and then put forth a tremulous hand. Cross-currents of emotion agitate her soul. She doubts, yet she believes; she is afraid, yet emboldened by her very despair; too diffident to cast herself on His pity, she is too confident not to resort to His healing virtue.

And so is it ever with our faith. Its ideal perfection would be that it should be unbroken, undashed by any speck of doubt. But the reality is far different. It is no full-orbed completeness, but, at the best, a growing segment of reflected light, with many a rough place in its jagged outline, prophetic of increase; with many a deep pit of blackness on its silver surface; with many a stormcloud sweeping across its face; conscious of eclipse and subject to change. And yet it is the light which He has set to rule the night of life, and we may rejoice in its crescent beam. We are often tempted to question the reality of faith in ourselves and others, by reason of the unbelief and disbelief which co-exist with it. But why should we do so? May there not be an inner heart and center of true trust, with a nebulous environment of doubt, through which the nucleus shall gradually send its attracting and consolidating power, and turn it, too, into firm substance? May there not be a germ, infinitesimal, yet with a real life throbbing in its microscopic minuteness, and destined to be a great tree, with all the fowls of the air lodging in its branches? May there not be hid in a heart a principle of action, which is obviously marked out for supremacy, though it has not yet come to sovereign power and manifestation in either the inward or the outward being? Where do we learn that faith must be complete to be genuine? Our own weak hearts say it to us often enough; and our lingering unbelief is only too ready to hiss into our ears the serpent's whisper, "You are deceiving yourself; look at your doubts, your coldness, your forgetfulness: *you* have no faith at all.'' To all such morbid thoughts, which only sap the strength of the spirit, and come from beneath, not from above, we have a right to oppose the first great lesson of this story—the reality of an imperfect faith. And, turning from the profitless contemplation of the feebleness of our grasp of Christ's robe to look on Him, the fountain of all spiritual energy, let us cleave the more confidently to Him for every discovery of our own weakness, and cry to Him for help against ourselves, that He would not ''quench the smoking flax''; for the old prayer is never offered in vain, when offered, as at first, with tears, ''Lord, I believe; help Thou mine unbelief.''

2. The second stage of this story sets forth a truth involved in what I have already said, but still needing to be dealt with for a moment by itself—namely, that Christ answers the imperfect faith. There was no real connection between the touch of His robe and the cure, but the poor ignorant sufferer thought that there was; and, therefore, Christ stoops to her childish thought, and allows her to prescribe the path by which His gift shall reach her. That thin wasted hand stretched itself up beyond the height to which it could ordinarily reach, and, though that highest point fell far short of Him, He lets His blessing down to her level. He does not say, ''Understand Me, put away thy false notion of healing power residing in My garment's hem, or I heal thee not.'' But He says, ''Dost thou think that it is through thy finger on My robe? Then, through thy finger on My robe it shall be. According to thy faith, be it unto thee.''

And so it is ever. Christ's mercy, like water in a vase, takes the shape of the vessel that holds it. On the one hand, His grace is infinite, and ''is given to every one of us according to the measure of the gift of Christ''—with no limitation but His own unlimited fulness; on the other hand, the amount which we practically receive from that inexhaustible store is, at each successive moment, determined by the measure and the purity and the intensity of our faith. On His part there is no limit but infinity, on our sides the limit is our capacity, and our capacity is settled by our desires. His word to us ever is, ''Open thy mouth wide, and I will fill it.'' ''Be it unto thee even as thou wilt.''

A double lesson, therefore, lies in this thought for us all. First, let us labor that our faith may be enlightened, importunate, and firm: for every flaw in it will injuriously affect our possession of the grace of God. Errors in opinion will hinder the blessings that flow from the truths which we misconceive or reject. Languor of desire will diminish the sum and enfeeble the energy of the powers that work in us. Wavering confidence, crossed and broken, like the solar spectrum, by many a dark line of doubt, will make our conscious possession of Christ's gift fitful. We have a deep well to draw from. Let us take care that the vessel with which we draw is in size proportionate to *its* depth and *our* need, that the chain to which it hangs is strong, and that no leaks in it let the full supply run out, nor any stains on its inner surface taint and taste the bright treasure.

And the other lesson is this. There can be no faith so feeble that Christ does not respond to it. The most ignorant, self-regarding, timid trust may unite the soul to Jesus Christ. To desire is to have; and "whosoever will, may take of the water of life freely." If you only come to Him, though He have passed, He will stop. If you come trusting and yet doubting, He will forgive the doubt and answer the trust. If you come to Him, knowing but that your heart is full of evil which none save He can cure, and putting out a lame hand—or even a tremulous fingertip—to touch His garment, be sure that anything is possible rather than that He should turn away your prayer, or His mercy from you.

3. The last part of this miracle teaches us that Christ corrects and confirms an imperfect faith by the very act of answering it. Observe how the process of cure and the discipline which followed are, in Christ's loving wisdom, made to fit closely to all the faults and flaws in the suppliant's faith.

She had thought of the healing energy as independent of the Healer's knowledge and will. Therefore His very first word shows her that He is aware of her mute appeal, and conscious of the going forth from Him of the power that cures—"Who touched Me?" As was said long ago, "the multitudes thronged Him, but the woman touched." Amidst all the jostling of the unmannerly crowd that trod with rude feet on His skirts, and elbowed their way to see this new Rabbi, there was one touch unlike all the rest; and, though it was only that of the fingertip of a poor woman, wasted to skin and bone with twelve years' weakening disease, He knew it; and His will and love sent forth the "virtue" which healed. May we not fairly apply this lesson to ourselves? Christ is, as most of us, I suppose, believe, Lord of all creatures, administering the affairs of the universe; the steps of His throne and the precincts of His court are thronged with dependents whose eyes wait upon Him, and who are fed from His stores; and yet my poor voice may steal through that chorus shout of petition and praise, and His ear will detect its lowest note, and will separate the thin stream of my prayer from the great sea of supplication which rolls to His seat, and will answer *me*. My hand uplifted among the millions of empty and imploring palms that are raised towards the heaven will receive into its clasping fingers the special blessing for my special wants.

Again, she had been selfish in her faith, had not cared for any close personal relation with Him; and so she was taught that He was in all His gifts, and that He was more than all His gifts. He compels her to come to His feet that she may learn His heart, and may carry away a blessing not stolen, but bestowed.

With open love, not secret cure,
The Lord of hearts would bless.

And thus is laid the foundation for a personal bond between her and Christ, which shall be for the joy of her life, and shall make of that life a thankful sacrifice to Him, the Healer.

Thus it is with us all. We may go to Him, at first, with no thought but for ourselves. But we have not to carry away His gift hidden in our hands. We learn that it is a love token from Him. And so we find in His answer to faith the true and only cure for all self-regard; and moved by the mercies of Christ, are led to do what else were impossible—to yield ourselves as "living sacrifices" to Him.

Again, she had shrunk from publicity. Her womanly diffidence, her enfeebled health, the shame of her disease, all made her wish to hide herself and her want from His eye, and to hide herself and her treasure from men. She would fain steal away unnoticed, as she hoped she had come. But she is dragged out before all the thronging multitude, and has to tell the whole. The answer to her faith makes her bold. In a moment she is changed from timidity to courage; a tremulous invalid ready to creep into any corner to escape notice, she stretched out her hand—the instant after, she knelt at His feet in the spirit of a confessor. This is Christ's most merciful fashion of curing our cowardice—not by rebukes, but by giving us, fainthearted though we be, the gift which out of weakness makes us strong. He would have us testify to Him before men, and that for our own sakes, since faith unacknowledged, like a plant in the dark, is apt to become pale and sickly, and bear no bright blossoms nor sweet fruit. But, ere He bids us own His name, He pours into our hearts, in answer to our secret appeal, the health of His own life, and the blissful consciousness of that great gift which makes the tongue of the dumb sing. Faith at first may be very timid, but faith will grow bold to witness of Him and not be ashamed, in the exact proportion in which it is genuine, and receives from Christ of His fulness.

And then—with a final word to set forth still more clearly that she had received the blessing from His love, not from His magical power, and through her confidences not through her touch—"Daughter! thy faith"—not thy finger—"hath made thee whole; go in peace and be whole"—Jesus confirms by His own authoritative voice the furtive blessing, and sends her away, perhaps to see Him no more, but to live in tranquil security, and in her humble home to guard the gift which He had bestowed on her imperfect faith, and to perfect—we may hope—the faith which He had enlightened and strengthened by the over-abundance of His gift.

This poor woman represents us all. Like her, we are sick of a sore sickness, we have spent our substance in trying physicians of no value, and are "nothing the better, but rather the worse." Oh! is it not strange that you should need to be urged to go to the Healer to whom she went? Do not be afraid, my brother, of telling Him all your pain and pining—He knows it already. Do not be afraid that your hand may not reach Him for the crowd, or that your voice may fail to fall on His ear. Do not be afraid of your ignorance, do not be afraid of your wavering confidence and many doubts. All these cannot separate you from Him who "Himself took our infirmities and bare our sicknesses." Fear but one thing—that He pass on to carry life and health to other souls, ere you resolve to press to His feet. Fear but one thing—that whilst you delay, the hem of the garment may be swept beyond the reach of your slow hand. Imperfect faith may bring salvation to a soul: hesitation may ruin and wreck a life.

The Looks of Jesus

And He looked round about to see her that had done this thing. MARK 5:32.

This Gospel of Mark is full of little touches that speak an eyewitness who had the gift of noting and reproducing vividly small details which make a scene live before us. Sometimes it is a word of description: "There was much grass in the place." Sometimes it is a note of Christ's demeanor: "Looking up to heaven, He sighed." Sometimes it is the very Aramaic words He spoke: "Ephphatha." Very often the Evangelist tells us of our Lord's looks, the gleams of pity and melting tenderness, the grave rebukes, the lofty authority that shone in them. We may well believe that on earth as in heaven, "His eyes were as a flame of fire," burning with clear light of knowledge and pure flame of love. These looks had pierced the soul, and lived forever in the memory, of the eyewitness, whoever he was, who was the informant of Mark. Probably the old tradition is right, and it is Peter's loving quickness of observation that we have to thank for these precious minutiæ. But be that as it may, the record in this Gospel of the *looks* of Christ are very remarkable. My present purpose is to gather them together, and by their help to think of Him whose meek, patient ‘‘eye’’ is ‘‘still upon them that fear Him,’’ beholding our needs and our sins.

Taking the instances in the order of their occurrence, they are these—‘‘He looked round on the Pharisees with anger, being grieved for the hardness of their hearts’’ (3:5). He looked on His disciples and said, ‘‘Behold My mother and My brethren!’’ (3:32). He looked round about to see who had touched the hem of His garment (5:32). He turned and looked on His disciples before rebuking Peter (8:33). He looked lovingly on the young questioner, asking what he should do to obtain eternal life (10:21), and in the same context, He looked round about to His disciples after the youth had gone away sorrowful, and enforced the solemn lesson of His lips with the light of His eye (10:23, 27). Lastly, He looked round about on all things in the temple on the day of His triumphal entry into Jerusalem (11:11). These are the instances in this Gospel. One look of Christ’s is not mentioned in it, which we might have expected—namely, that which sent Peter out from the judgment hall to break into a passion of penitent tears. Perhaps the remembrance was too sacred to be told—at all events, the Evangelist who gives us so many similar notes is silent about that look, and we have to learn of it from another.

We may throw these instances into groups according to their objects, and so bring out the many-sided impression which they produce.

1. The welcoming look of love and pity to those who seek Him. Two of the recorded instances fall into their place here. The one is this of our text, of the woman who came behind Christ to touch His robe, and be healed: the other is that of the young ruler.

Take that first instance of the woman, wasted with disease, timid with the timidity of her sex, of her long sickness, of her many disappointments. She steals through the crowd that rudely presses on this miracle-working Rabbi, and manages somehow to stretch out a wasted arm through some gap in the barrier of people about Him, and with her pallid, trembling finger to touch the edge of His robe. The cure comes at once. It was all that she wanted, but not all that He would give her. Therefore He turns and lets His eye fall upon her. That draws her to Him. It told her that she had not been too bold. It told her that she had not surreptitiously stolen healing, but that He had knowingly given it, and that His loving pity went with it. So it confirmed the gift, and, what was far more, it revealed the Giver. She had thought to bear away a secret boon unknown to all but herself. She gets instead an open blessing, with the Giver’s heart in it.

The look that rested on her, like sunshine on some plant that had long pined and grown blanched in the shade, revealed Christ’s knowledge, sympathy, and loving power. And in all these respects it is a revelation of the Christ for all time, and for every seeking timid soul in all the crowd. Can my poor feeble hand find a cranny anywhere through which it may reach the robe? What am I, in all this great universe blazing with stars, and crowded with creatures who hang on Him, that I should be able to secure personal contact with Him? The multitude—innumerable companies from every corner of space—press upon Him and throng Him, and I—out here on the verge of the crowd—how can I get at Him?—how can my little thin cry live and be distinguishable amid that mighty storm of praise that thunders round His throne? We may silence all such hesitancies of faith, for He who knew the difference between the light touch of the hand that sought healing, and the jostling of the curious crowd, bends on us the same eye, a God's in its perfect knowledge, a man's in the dewy sympathy which shines in it. However imperfect may be our thoughts of His blessing, their incompleteness will not hinder our reception of His gift in the measure of our faith, and the very bestowment will teach us worthier conceptions of Him, and hearten us for bolder approaches to His grace. He still looks on trembling suppliants, though they may know their own sickness much better than they understand Him, and still His look draws us to His feet by its omniscience, pity, and assurance of help.

The other case is very different. Instead of the invalid woman, we see a young man in the full flush of his strength, rich, needing no material blessing. Pure in life, and righteous according to even a high standard of morality, he yet feels that he needs something. Having real and strong desires after "eternal life," he comes to Christ to try whether this new Teacher could say anything that would help him to the assured inward peace and spontaneous goodness for which he longed, and had not found in all the round of punctilious obedience to unloved commandments. As he kneels there before Jesus, in his eager haste, with sincere and high aspirations stamped on his young ingenuous face, Christ's eyes turn on him, and that wonderful word stands written, "Jesus, beholding him, loved him."

He reads him through and through, knowing all the imperfection of his desires after goodness and eternal life, and yet loving him with more than a brother's love. His sympathy does not blind Jesus to the limitations and shallowness of the young man's aspirations, but His clear knowledge of these does not harden the gaze into indifference, nor check the springing tenderness in the Saviour's heart. And the Master's words, though they might sound cold, and did embody a hard requirement, are beautifully represented in the story as the expression of that love. He cared for the youth too much to deceive him with smooth things. The truest kindness was to put all his eagerness to the test at once. If he accepted the conditions, the look told him what a welcome awaited him. If he started aside from them, it was best for him to find out that there were things which he loved more than eternal life. So with a gracious invitation shining in His look, Christ places the course of self-denial before him; and when he went away sorrowful, he left behind One more sorrowful than himself. We can reverently imagine with what a look Christ watched his retreating figure; and we may hope that, though he went away then, the memory of that glance of love, and of those kind, faithful words, sooner or later drew him back to his Saviour.

Is not all this too an everlasting revelation of our Lord's attitude? We may be sure that He looks on many a heart—on many a young heart—glowing with noble wishes and half-understood longings, and that His love reaches every one who, groping for the light, asks Him what to do to inherit eternal life. His great charity "hopeth all things," and does not turn away from longings because they are too weak to lift the soul above all the weights of sense and the world. Rather He would deepen them and strengthen them, and His eternal requirements addressed to feeble wills are not meant to "quench the smoking flax," but to kindle it to decisive consecration and self-surrender. The loving look interprets the severe words. If once we meet it full, and our hearts yield to the heart that is seen in it, the cords that bind us snap, and it is no more hard to "count all things but loss," and to give up ourselves, that we may follow Him. The sad and feeble and weary who may be half despairingly seeking for alleviation of outward ills, and the young and strong and ardent whose souls are fed with high desires, have but little comprehension of one another, but Christ knows them both, and loves them both, and would draw them both to Himself.

2. The Lord's looks of love and warning to those who have found Him. There are three instances of this class. The first is when He looked round on His disciples and said, "Behold My mother and My brethren!" (3:34). Perhaps no moment in all Christ's life had more of humiliation in it than that. There could be no deeper degradation than that His own family should believe Him insane. Not His brethren only, but His mother herself seems to have been shaken from her attitude of meek obedience so wonderfully expressed in her two recorded sayings, "Be it unto me according to Thy word," and "Whatsoever He saith unto you, do it." She too appears to be in the shameful conspiracy, and to have consented that her name should be used as a lure in the wily message meant to separate Him from His friends, that He might be seized and carried off as a madman. What depth of tenderness was in that slow circuit of His gaze upon the humble loving followers grouped round Him! It spoke the fullest trustfulness of them, and His rest in their sympathy, partial though it was. It went before His speech like the flash before the report, and looked what in a moment He said, "Behold My mother and My brethren!" It owned spiritual affinities as more real than family bonds, and proved that He required no more of us than He was willing to do Himself when He bid us "forsake father and mother, and wife and children" for Him. We follow Him when we tread that road, hard though it be. In Him every mother may behold her son, in Him we may find more than the reality of every sweet family relationship. That same love, which identified Him with these half-enlightened followers here, still binds Him to us, and He looks down on us from amid the glory, and owns us for His true kindred.

That look of unutterable love is strangely contrasted with the next instance. We read (8:32) that Peter "took Him"—apart a little way, I suppose—"and began to rebuke Him." He turns away from the rash Apostle, will say no word to him alone, but summons the others by a glance, and then, having made sure that all were within hearing, He solemnly rebukes Peter with the sharpest words that ever fell from His lips. That look calls them to listen, not that they may be witnesses of Peter's chastisement, but because the severe words concern them all. It bids them search themselves as they hear. They too may be "Satans." They too may shrink from the cross, and "mind the things that be of men."

We may take the remaining instance along with this. It occurs immediately after the story of the young seeker, to which we have already referred. Twice within five verses (10:23–27) we read that He "looked on His disciples," before He spoke the grave lessons and warnings arising from the incident. A sad gaze that would be!—full of regret and touched with warning. We may well believe that it added weight to the lesson He would teach, that surrender of all things was needed for discipleship. We see that it had been burned into the memory of one of the little group, who told long years after how He had looked upon them so solemnly, as seeming to read their hearts while He spoke. Not more searching was the light of the eyes which John in Patmos saw, "as a flame of fire." Still He looks on His disciples, and sees our inward hankerings after the things of men. All our shrinkings from the cross and cleaving to the world are known to Him. He comes to each of us with that sevenfold proclamation, "I know thy works," and from His loving lips falls on our ears the warning, emphasized by that sad, earnest gaze, "How hard is it for them that have riches to enter into the Kingdom of God!" But, blessed be His name, the stooping love which claims us for His brethren shines in His regard none the less tenderly, though He reads and warns us with His eye. So, we can venture to spread all our evil before Him, and ask that He would look on it, knowing that, as the sun bleaches cloth laid in its beams, He will purge away the evil which He sees, if only we let the light of His face shine full upon us.

3. The Lord's look of anger and pity on His opponents. That instance occurs in the account of the healing of a man with a withered arm, which took place in the synagogue of Capernaum (3:1–5). In the vivid narrative, we can see the scribes and Pharisees, who had already questioned Him with insolent airs of authority about His breach of the Rabbinical Sabbatic rules, sitting in the synagogue, with their gleaming eyes ''watching Him'' with hostile purpose. They hope that He will heal on the Sabbath day. Possibly they had even brought the powerless-handed man there, on the calculation that Christ could not refrain from helping him when He saw his condition. They are ready to traffic in human misery if only they can catch Him in a breach of law. The fact of a miracle is nothing. Pity for the poor man is not in them. They have neither reverence for the power of the miracle-worker, nor sympathy with His tenderness of heart. The only thing for which they have eyes is the breach of the complicated web of restrictions which they had spun across the Sabbath day. What a strange, awful power the pedantry of religious forms has of blinding the vision and hardening the heart as to the substance and spirit of religion! That Christ should heal neither made them glad nor believing, but that He should heal on the Sabbath day roused them to a deadly hatred. So there they sit, on the stretch of expectation, silently watching. He bids the man stand forth—a movement, and there the cripple stands alone in the midst of the seated congregation. Then comes the unanswerable question which cut so deep, and struck their consciences so hard that they could answer nothing, only sit and scowl at Him with a murderous light gleaming in their eyes. He fronts them with a steady gaze that travels over the whole group, and that showed to at least one who was present an unforgettable mingling of displeasure and pity. ''He looked round about on them with anger, being grieved for the hardness of their hearts.'' In Christ's perfect nature, anger and pity could blend in wondrous union, like the crystal and fire in the abyss before the throne.

The soul that has not the capacity for anger at evil wants something of its due perfection, and goes ''halting'' like Jacob after Peniel. In Christ's complete humanity, it could not but be present, but in pure and righteous form. His anger was no disorder of passion, or ''brief madness'' that discomposed the even motion of His spirit, nor was there in it any desire for the hurt of its objects, but, on the contrary, it lay side by side with the sorrow of pity, which was intertwined with it like a golden thread. Both these two emotions are fitting to a pure manhood in the presence of evil.

They heighten each other. The perfection of righteous anger is to be tempered by sympathy. The perfection of righteous pity for the evildoer is to be saved from immoral condoning of evil as if it were only calamity, by an infusion of some displeasure. We have to learn the lesson and take this look of Christ's as our pattern in our dealings with evildoers. Perhaps our day needs more especially to remember that a righteous severity and recoil of the whole nature from sin is part of a perfect Christian character. We are so accustomed to pity transgressors, and to hear sins spoken of as if they were misfortunes mainly due to "environment," or to inherited tendencies, that we are apt to forget the other truth, that they are the voluntary acts of a man who could have refrained if he had wished, and whose not having wished is worthy of blame. But we need to aim at just such a union of feeling as was revealed in that gaze of Christ's, and neither to let our wrath dry up our pity nor our pity put out the pure flame of our indignation at evil.

That look comes to us too with a message, when we are most conscious of the evil in our own hearts. Every man who has caught even a glimpse of Christ's great love, and has learned something of himself in the light thereof, must feel that wrath at evil sits ill on so sinful a judge as he feels himself to be. How can I fling stones at any poor creature when I am so full of sin myself? And how does that Lord look at me and all my wanderings from Him, my hardness of heart, my Pharisaism and deadness to His spiritual power and beauty? Can there be anything but displeasure in Him? The answer is not far to seek, but, familiar though it be, it often surprises a man anew with its sweetness, and meets recurring consciousness of unworthiness with a bright smile that scatters fears. In our deepest abasement we may take courage anew when we think of that wondrous blending of anger shot with pity.

4. The look of the Lord on the profaned Temple. On the day of Christ's triumphal entry into Jerusalem, apparently the Sunday before His crucifixion, we find (11:11) that He went direct to the Temple, and "looked round about on all things." The King has come to His palace, the Lord has "suddenly come to His Temple." How solemn that careful, all-comprehending scrutiny of all that He found there—the bustle of the crowds come up for the Passover, the trafficking and the fraud, the heartless worship! He seems to have gazed upon all, that evening in silence, and, as the shades of night began to fall, He went back to Bethany with the Twelve. Tomorrow will be time enough for the "whip of small cords," for today enough to have come as Lord to the temple, and with intent, all-comprehending gaze to have traversed its courts.

Apparently He passed through the crowds there unnoticed, and beheld all, while Himself unrecognized.

Is not that silent, unobserved Presence, with His keen searching eye that lights on all, a solemn parable of a perpetual truth? He "walks amidst the seven golden candlesticks" today, as in the temple of Jerusalem, and in the vision of Patmos. His eyes like a flame of fire regard and scrutinize us, too. "I know thy works" is still upon His lips. Silent and by many unseen, that calm, clear-eyed, loving but judging Christ walks amongst His churches today. Alas! what does He see there? If He came in visible form into any church congregation today, would He not find merchandise in the sanctuary, formalism and unreality standing to minister, and pretense and hypocrisy bowing to worship? How much of all our service could live in the light of His felt presence? And are we never going to stir ourselves up to a truer devotion and a purer service by remembering that He is here as really as He was in the Temple of old? Our drowsy prayers, and all our conventional repetitions of devout aspirations, not felt at the moment, but inherited from our fathers, our confessions which have no penitence, our praises without gratitude, our vows which we never mean to keep, and our creeds which in no operative fashion we believe—all the hollowness of profession with no reality below it, like a great cooled bubble on a lava stream, would crash in and go to powder if once we really believed what we so glibly say—that Jesus Christ was looking at us. He keeps silence today, but as surely as He knows us now, so surely will He come tomorrow with a whip of small cords and purge His Temple from hypocrisy and unreality, from traffic and thieves. All the churches need the sifting. Christ has done and suffered too much for the world, to let the power of His Gospel be neutralized by the sins of His professing followers, and Christ loves the imperfect friends that cleave to Him, though their service be often stained, and their consecration always incomplete, too well to suffer sin upon them. Therefore He will come to purify His Temple. Well for us, if we thankfully yield ourselves to His merciful chastisements, howsoever they may fall upon us, and believe that in them all He looks on us with love, and wishes only to separate us from that which separates us from Him!

On us all that eye rests with all these emotions fused and blended in one gaze of love that passeth knowledge—a look of love and welcome whenever we seek Him, either to help us in outward or inward blessings; a look of love and warning to us, owning us also for His brethren, and cautioning us lest we stray from His side; a look of love and displeasure at any sin that blinds us to His gracious beauty; a look of love and observance of our poor worship and spotted sacrifices.

Let us lay ourselves full in the sunshine of His gaze, and take for ours the old prayer, "Search me, O Christ, and know my heart!" It is heaven on earth to feel His eye resting upon us, and know that it is love. It will be the heaven of heaven to see Him "face to face," and "to know even as we are known."

6

Rejection

The Master Rejected: The Servants Sent Forth

And He went out from thence, and came into His own country; and
His disciples follow Him. 2. And when the Sabbath day was come,
He began to teach in the synagogue: and many hearing Him were
astonished, saying, From whence hath this man these things? and
what wisdom is this which is given unto Him, that even such mighty
works are wrought by His hands? 3. Is not this the carpenter, the
Son of Mary, the Brother of James, and Joses, and of Juda, and
Simon? and are not His sisters here with us? And they were offended
at Him. 4. But Jesus said unto them, A prophet is not without
honour, but in his own country, and among his own kin, and in his
own house. 5. And He could there do no mighty work, save that
He laid His hands upon a few sick folk, and healed them. 6. And
He marveled because of their unbelief. And He went round about the
villages, teaching. 7. And He called unto Him the twelve, and
began to send them forth by two and two; and gave them power over
unclean spirits; 8. And commanded them that they should take
nothing for their journey, save a staff only; no scrip, no bread, no
money in their purse: 9. But be shod with sandals; and not put on
two coats. 10. And He said unto them, In what place soever ye
enter into an house, there abide till ye depart from that
place. 11. And whosoever shall not receive you, nor hear you,
when ye depart thence, shake off the dust under your feet for a
testimony against them. Verily I say unto you, It shall be more
tolerable for Sodom and Gomorrah in the day of judgment, than for
that city. 12. And they went out, and preached that men should
repent. 13. And they cast out many devils, and anointed with oil
many that were sick, and healed them. MARK 6:1–13.

An easy day's journey would carry Jesus and His followers from Capernaum, on the lakeside, to Nazareth, among the hills. What took our Lord back there? When last He taught in the synagogue of Nazareth, His life had been in danger; and now He thrusts Himself into the wolf's den. Why? Mark seems to wish us to observe the connection between this visit and the great group of miracles which he has just recorded; and possibly the link may be our Lord's hope that the report of these might have preceded Him and prepared His way. In His patient long-suffering He will give His fellow-villagers another chance; and His heart yearns for "His own country," and "His own kin," and "His own house," of which He speaks so pathetically in the context.

1. We have here unbelief born of familiarity, and its effects on Christ (verses 1–6). Observe the characteristic avoidance of display, and the regard for existing means of worship, shown in His waiting till the Sabbath, and then resorting to the synagogue. He and His hearers would both remember His last appearance in it; and He and they would both remember many a time before that, when, as a youth, He had sat there. The rage which had exploded on His first sermon has given place to calmer, but not less bitter, opposition. Mark paints the scene, and represents the hearers as discussing Jesus while He spoke. The decorous silence of the synagogue was broken by a hubbub of mutual questions. "Many" spoke at once, and all had the same thing to say. The state of mind revealed is curious. They own Christ's wisdom in His teaching, and the reality of His miracles, of which they had evidently heard; but the fact that He was one of themselves made them angry that He should have such gifts, and suspicious of where He had got them. They seem to have had the same opinion as Nathanael—that no "good thing" could "come out of Nazareth." Their old companion could not be a prophet; that was certain. But He had wisdom and miraculous power; that was as certain. Where had they come from? There was only one other source; and so, with many headshakings, they were preparing to believe that the Jesus whom they had all known, living His quiet life of labor among them, was in league with the devil, rather than believe that He was a messenger from God.

We note in their questions, first, the glimpse of our Lord's early life. They bring before us the quiet, undistinguished home and the long years of monotonous labor. We owe to Mark alone the notice that Jesus actually wrought at Joseph's handicraft. Apparently the latter was dead, and, if so, Jesus would be the head of the house, and probably the "breadwinner." One of the fathers preserves the tradition that He "made plows and yokes, by which He taught the symbols of righteousness and an active life." That good father seems to think it needful to find symbolical meanings, in order to save Christ's dignity; but the prose fact that He toiled at the carpenter's bench, and handled hammer and saw, needs nothing to heighten its value as a sign of His true participation in man's lot, and as the hallowing of manual toil. How many weary arms have grasped their tools with new vigor and contentment when they thought of Him as their Pattern in their narrow toils!

The Nazarenes' difficulty was but one case of a universal tendency. Nobody finds it easy to believe that some village child, who had grown up beside him, and whose undistinguished outside life he knows, has turned out a genius or a great man. The last people to recognize a prophet are always his kindred and his countrymen. "Far-away birds have fine feathers." Men resent it as a kind of slight on themselves that the other, who was one of them but yesterday, should be so far above them today. They are mostly too blind to look below the surface, and they conclude that, because they saw so much of the external life, they knew the man that lived it. The elders of Nazareth had seen Jesus grow up, and to them He would be "the carpenter's son" still. The more important people had known the humbleness of His home, and could not adjust themselves to look up to Him, instead of down. His equals in age would find their boyish remembrances too strong for accepting Him as a prophet. All of them did just what the most of us would have done, when they took it for certain that the Man whom they had known so well, as they fancied, could not be a prophet, to say nothing of the Messiah so long looked for. It is easy to blame them; but it is better to learn the warning in their words, and to take care that we are not blind to some true messenger of God just because we have been blessed with close companionship with him. Many a household has had to wait for death to take away the prophet before they discern him. Some of us entertain "angels unawares," and have bitterly to feel, when too late, that our eyes were holden that we should not know them.

These questions bring out strongly what we too often forget in estimating Christ's contemporaries—namely, that His presence among them, in the simplicity of His human life, was a positive hindrance to their seeing His true character. We sometimes wish that we had seen Him, and heard His voice. We should have found it more difficult to believe in Him if we had. "His flesh" was a "veil" in other sense than the Epistle to the Hebrews means; for, by reason of men's difficulty in piercing beneath it, it hid from many what it was meant and fitted to reveal. Only eyes purged beheld the glory of "the Word" become flesh when it "dwelt among us"—and even they saw Him more clearly when they saw Him no more. Let us not be too hard on these simple Nazarenes, but recognize our kith and kin.

The facts on which the Nazarenes grounded their unbelief are really irrefragable proof of Christ's divinity. Whence had this man His wisdom and mighty works? Born in that humble home, reared in that secluded village, shut out from the world's culture, buried, as it were, among an exclusive and abhorred people, how came He to tower above all teachers, and to sway the world? "With whom took He counsel? and who instructed Him, and taught Him?" The character and work of Christ, compared with the circumstances of His origin and environment, are an insoluble riddle, except on one supposition—that He was the word and power of God.

The effects of this unbelief on our Lord were twofold. It limited His power. Matthew says that "He did not many mighty works." Mark goes deeper, and boldly says "He could not." It is mistaken jealousy for Christ's honor to seek to pare down the strong words. The atmosphere of chill unbelief froze the stream. The power was there, but it required for its exercise some measure of moral susceptibility. His miraculous energy followed, in general, the same law as His higher exercise of saving grace does; that is to say, it could not force itself upon unwilling men. Christ "cannot" save a man who does not trust Him. He was hampered in the outflow of His healing power by unsympathetic disparagement and unbelief. Man can thwart God. Faith opens the door, and unbelief shuts it in His face. He "would have gathered," but they "would not," and therefore He "could not."

The second effect of unbelief on Him was that He "marveled." He is twice recorded to have wondered—once at a Gentile's faith, once at His townsmen's unbelief. He wondered at the first because it showed so unusual a susceptibility; at the second, because it showed so unreasonable a blindness. All sin is a wonder to eyes that see into the realities of things and read the end; for it is all utterly unreasonable (though it is, alas! not unaccountable) and suicidal. "Be astonished, O ye heavens, at this." Unbelief in Christ is, by Himself, declared to be the very climax of sin, and its most flagrant evidence (John 16:9); and of all the instances of unbelief which saddened His heart, none struck more chill than that of these Nazarenes. They had known His pure youth; He might have reckoned on some touch of sympathy and predisposition to welcome Him. His wonder is the measure of His pain as well as of their sin.

Nor need we wonder that He wondered; for He was true man, and all human emotions were His. To one who lives ever in the Father's bosom, what can seem so strange as that men should prefer homeless exposedness and dreary loneliness? To one whose eyes ever behold unseen realities, what so marvelous as men's blindness? To one who knew so assuredly His own mission and rich freightage of blessing, how strange it must have been that He found so few to accept His gifts! Jesus knew that bitter wonder which all men who have a truth to proclaim which the world has not learned, have to experience—the amazement at finding it so hard to get any others to see what they see. In His manhood, He shared the fate of all teachers, who have, in their turn, to marvel at men's unbelief.

2. The new instrument which Christ fashions to cope with unbelief. What does Jesus do when thus "wounded in the house of His friends"? Give way to despondency? No; but meekly betake Himself to yet obscurer fields of service, and send out the Twelve to prepare His way, as if He thought that they might have success where He would fail. What a lesson for people who are always hankering after conspicuous "spheres," and lamenting that their gifts are wasted in some obscure corner, is that picture of Jesus, repulsed from Nazareth, patiently turning to the villages! The very summary account of the trial mission of the Twelve here given presents only the salient points of the charge to them, and in its condensation makes these the more emphatic. Note the interesting statement that they were sent out two-and-two. The other Evangelists do not tell us this, but their lists of the Apostles are arranged in pairs. Mark's list is not so arranged, but he supplies the reason for the arrangement, which he does not follow; and the other Gospels, by their arrangement, confirm his statement, which they do not give. Two-and-two is a wise rule for all Christian workers. It checks individual peculiarities of self-will, helps to keep off faults, wholesomely stimulates, strengthens faith by giving another to hear it and to speak it, brings companionship, and admits of division of labor. One-and-one are more than twice one.

The first point is the gift of power. Unclean spirits are specified, but the subsequent verses show that miracle-working power in its other forms was included. We may call that Christ's greatest miracle. That He could, by His mere will, endow a dozen men with such power, is more, if degree come into view at all, than that He Himself should exercise it. But there is a lesson in the fact for all ages—even those in which miracles have ceased. Christ gives before He commands, and sends no man into the field without filling his basket with seed corn. His gifts assimilate the receiver to Himself, and only in the measure in which His servants possess power which is like His own, and drawn from Him, can they proclaim His coming, or prepare hearts for it. The second step is their equipment. The special commands here given were repealed by Jesus when He gave His last commands. In their letter they apply only to that one journey, but in their spirit they are of universal and permanent obligation. The Twelve were to travel light. They might carry a staff to help them along, and wear sandals to save their feet on rough roads; but that was to be all. Food, luggage, and money, the three requisites of a traveler, were to be "conspicuous by their absence." That was repealed afterwards, and instructions given of an opposite character, because, after His ascension, the Church was to live more and more by ordinary means; but in this journey they were to learn to trust Him without means, that afterwards they might trust Him in the means. He showed them the purpose of these restrictions in the act of abrogating them. "When I sent you forth without purse . . . lacked ye anything?" But the spirit remains unabrogated, and the minimum of outward provision is likeliest to call out the maximum of faith. We are more in danger from having too much baggage than from having too little. And the one indispensable requirement is that, whatever the quantity, it should hinder neither our march nor our trust in Him who alone is wealth and food.

Next comes the disposition of the messengers. It is not to be self-indulgent. They are not to change quarters for the sake of greater comfort. They have not gone out to make a pleasure tour, but to preach, and so are to stay where they are welcomed, and to make the best of it. Delicate regard for kindly hospitality, if offered by ever so poor a house, and scrupulous abstinence from whatever might suggest interested motives, must mark the true servant. That rule is not out of date. If ever a herald of Christ falls under suspicion of caring more about life's comforts than about his work, goodbye to his usefulness! If ever he does so care, whether he be suspected of it or no, spiritual power will ebb from him.

The next step is the messengers' demeanor to the rejecters of their message. Shaking the dust off the sandals is an emblem of solemn renunciation of participation, and perhaps of disclaimer of responsibility. It means certainly, "We have no more to do with you," and possibly, "Your blood be on your own heads." This journey of the Twelve was meant to be of short duration, and to cover much ground, and therefore no time was to be spent unnecessarily. Their message was brief, and as well told quickly as slowly. The whole conditions of work now are different. Sometimes, perhaps, a Christian is warranted in solemnly declaring to those who receive not his message, that he will have no more to say to them. That may do more than all his other words. But such cases are rare; and the rule that it is safest to follow is rather that of love which despairs of none, and, though often repelled, returns with pleading, and, if it have told often in vain, now tells with tears, the story of the love that never abandons the most obstinate.

Such were the prominent points of this first Christian mission. They who carry Christ's banner in the world must be possessed of power, His gift, must be lightly weighted, must care less for comfort than for service, must solemnly warn of the consequences of rejecting the message; and so they will not fail to cast out devils, and to heal many that are sick.

Christ Thwarted

And He could there do no mighty work, save that He laid His hands upon a few sick folk, and healed them. And He marveled because of their unbelief. MARK 6:5, 6.

It is possible to live too near a man to see him. Familiarity with the small details blinds most people to the essential greatness of any life. So these fellow villagers of Jesus in Nazareth knew Him too well to know Him rightly as they talked Him over; they recognized His wisdom and His mighty works; but all the impression that these would have made was neutralized by their acquaintance with His former life, and they said, "Why, we have known Him ever since He was a boy. We used to take our plows and yokes to Him to mend in the carpenter's shop. His brothers and sisters are here with us. Where did *He* get His wisdom?" So *they* said; and so it has been ever since. "A prophet is not without honor, save in his own country."

Surrounded thus by unsympathetic carpers, Jesus Christ did not exercise His full miraculous power. Other Evangelists tell us of these limitations, but Mark is alone in the strength of his expression. The others say, "*did* no mighty works"; Mark says "*could* do no mighty works." Startling as the expression is, it is not to be weakened down because it is startling, and if it does not fit in with your conceptions of Christ's nature, so much the worse for the conceptions. Matthew states the reason for this limitation more directly than Mark does, for he says, "He did no mighty works because of their unbelief." But Mark suggests the reason clearly enough in his text clause, when he says; "He marveled because of their unbelief." There is another limitation of Christ's nature. He wondered as at an astonishing and unexpected thing. We read that He "marveled" twice: once at great faith, once at great unbelief. The centurion's faith was marvelous; the Nazarenes' unbelief was as marvelous. The "wild grapes" bore clusters more precious than the tended "vines" in the "vineyard." Faith and unbelief do not depend upon opportunity, but upon the bent of the will and the sense of need.

But I have chosen these words now because they put in its strongest shape a truth of large importance, and of manifold applications—viz., that man's unbelief hampers and hinders Christ's power. Now let me apply that principle in two or three directions.

1. Let us look at this principle in connection with the case before us in the text. You will find that, as a rule and in general, our Lord's miracles require faith, either on the part of the persons helped, or on the part of those who interceded for them. But while that is the rule there are distinct exceptions, as for instance, in the case of the feeding of the thousands, and in the case of the raising of the widow's son of Nain, as well as in other examples. And here we find that, though the prevalent unbelief hindered the flow of our Lord's miraculous power, it did not so hinder it as to stop some little trickle of the stream. "He laid His hands on a few sick folk, and healed them." The brook was shrunken as compared with the abundance of the flood recorded in the previous chapter.

Now, why was that? There is no such natural connection between faith and the working of a miracle as that the latter is only possible in conjunction with the former. And the exceptions show us that Jesus Christ was not so limited as that men's unbelief could wholly prevent the flow of His love and His power. But still there was a restriction. And what sort of a "could not" was it that thus hampered Him in His work? We know far too little about the conditions of miracle-working to entitle us to dogmatize on such a matter, but I suppose that we may venture to say this, that the working of the miracles was "impossible" in the absence of faith and the presence of its opposite, regard being had to the purposes of the miracle and of Christ's whole work. It was not congruous, it was not morally possible, that He should force His benefits upon unwilling recipients.

Now, I need not do more than just in a sentence call attention to the bearing of this fact upon the true notion of the purpose of Christ's miraculous works. A superficial, and, as I think, very vulgar, estimate, says that Christ's miracles were chiefly designed to produce faith in Him and in His mission. If that had been their purpose, the very place for the most abundant exhibition of them would have been the place where unbelief was most pronounced. The atmosphere of non-receptiveness and non-sympathy would have been the very one that ought to have evoked them most. Where the darkness was the deepest, there should the torch have flared. Where the stupor was most complete, there should the rousing shock have been administered. But the very opposite is the case. Where faith is present already, the miracle comes. Where faith is absent, miracles fail. Therefore, though a subsidiary purpose of our Lord's miracles was, no doubt, to evoke faith in His mission, their chief purpose is not to be found in that direction. It was a condescension to men's weakness and obstinacy when He said, "If ye believe not Me, believe the works." But the works were signs, symbols, manifestations on the lower material platform of what He would be and do for men in the higher, and they were the outcome of His own loving heart and ever-flowing compassion, and only secondarily were they taken, and have they ever been taken, when Christian faith has been robust and intelligent, as being evidences of His Messiahship and Divinity.

But there is another consideration that I would like to suggest in reference to this limitation of our Lord's power, by reason of the prevalence of an atmosphere of unbelief, and that is that it is a pathetic proof of His manhood's being influenced by all the emotions and circumstances that influence us. We all know how hearts expand in the warm atmosphere of affection and sympathy, and shut themelves up like tender flowerets when the cold east wind blows. And just as a great orator subtly feels the sympathy of his audience, and is buoyed up by it to higher flights, while in the presence of cold and indifferent and critical hearers his tongue stammers, and he falls beneath himself, so we may reverently say Jesus Christ *could* not put forth His mightiest and most abundant miraculous powers when the cold wind of unbelieving criticism blew in His face.

If that is true, what a glimpse it gives us of the conditions of His earthly life, and how wonderful it makes that love which, though it was hampered, was never stifled by the presence of scorn and malice and of hatred. He is our Brother, bone of our bone and flesh of our flesh; and even when the divinity within was in possession of the power of working the miracle, the humanity in which it dwelt felt the presence of the cold frost and closed its petals. "He could do no mighty works," and it was "because of their unbelief."

2. But now, secondly, let us apply this principle in regard to Christ's working on ourselves. I have said that there was no such natural connection between faith and miracle as that miracle was absolutely impossible in the absence of faith. But when we lift the thought into the higher region of our religious and spiritual life, we do come across an absolute impossibility. There, in regard to all that appertains to the inward life of a soul, Christ *can* do no mighty works, in the absence of our faith. By faith, I mean, of course, not the mere intellectual reception of the Christian narratives or of the Christian doctrines as true, but I mean what the Bible means by it always, a process subsequent to that intellectual reception—viz., the motion of the will and of the heart towards Christ. Faith is belief, but belief is not faith. Faith is belief *plus* trust. And it is that which is the condition of all Christ's gifts being received by any of us.

Now, a great many people seem to think that what Jesus Christ brings to the world, and offers to each of us, is simply the escape from the penal consequences of our past transgressions. If you conceive salvation to be nothing else than shutting the doors of an outward hell, and opening the doors of an outward Heaven, I can quite understand why you should boggle at the thought that faith is a condition of these. For if salvation is such a material, external, and forensic matter as that, then I do not see why God should not have given it to everybody, without any conditions at all. But if you will understand rightly what Christ's gifts are, you will see that they cannot be bestowed upon men irrespective of the condition of their wills, desires, and hearts.

For what is salvation? What are the blessings that Jesus Christ bestows? A new life, a new love, new desires, a new direction of the whole being, a new spirit within us. These are the gifts; and how can these be given to a man if he has not trust in the Giver? Salvation is at bottom that a man's will shall be harmonized with the will of God. But if a man has not faith, his will is discordant with the will of God, and how can it be harmonized and discordant at the same time? What are the powers by which Christ works upon men's hearts? His truth, His love, His Spirit. How can a truth operate if it is not believed? How can love bless and cherish if it is not trusted? How can the Spirit hallow and cleanse if it is not yielded to? The condition is inherent in the nature of God the Giver, of man the receiver, and of the gifts bestowed.

And so we understand the metaphors that put that inevitable connection in various forms. Faith is "a door." How can you enter if the door be fast closed? He knocks; if any man opens He comes in. If a man does not open,

> He can but listen at the gate,
> And hear the household jar within.

Faith is the connection between the fountain and the reservoir. If there is no such connection, how can the reservoir be filled? Faith is the hand with stretched-out empty palms, and widespread fingers for the reception of the gifts. How can the gifts be put into it if it hangs listless by the side, or is obstinately closed and pushed behind the back? He "can do no mighty works" on an unbelieving soul.

Now, brethren, let me insist, in one sentence, on this solemn truth; God would save every man if He could, faith or no faith. But the condition which brings faith into connection with salvation as its necessary prerequisite is no arbitrary condition. The love of God cannot alter it. In the nature of things it must be so. "He that believeth shall be saved; he that believeth not shall be condemned." That is no result of an artificial scheme, but of the necessities of the case.

Again, let me remind you that the measure of our faith is the measure of our possession of these gifts. Our Lord more than once put the whole doctrine of this matter, in regard, however, to the lower plane of miracle, when He said, "According to your faith be it unto you," "Open thy mouth wide, and I will fill it." We have an inheritance like that of men who get a piece of land in some mining district: so much as we peg out and claim is ours, and no more.

Let me narrate a parable of my own making. There was once a king who told all his people that on a given day the fountain in the market-place in the center of the city would flow with wine and other precious liquors, and that every man was free to bring his vessel and carry away as much as he would. The man that brought a tiny wineglass got a glassful; the man that brought a gallon pitcher got that full. The measure of your desires is the measure of your possessions of Christ's power. Our faith determines the amount of His cleansing, healing, vivifying energy which will reside in us. The width of the bore of the waterpipe that is laid down settles the amount of water that will come into your cistern. The water may be high outside the lock. If the lock gate be kept fast closed, the height of the water outside produces no raising of the low level of that within. If you open a chink of the gate a trickle will pass through, and if you fling the gates wide the levels will be the same on both sides. The only limit of our possession of God is our faith and desire. The true limit is His own boundlessness. It is possible that a man may be "filled with all the fullness of God"; but the real working limit for each of us is our own faith. So, brethren, endless progress is possible for us, on condition of continual trust.

3. Lastly, let us apply this principle in regard to Christ's working through His people. Jesus Christ cannot work mightily through a feebly believing Church. And here is the reason why Christianity has taken so long to do so little in this world of ours; and why nineteen centuries after the Cross and Pentecost there remaineth yet so much land to be possessed. "Ye are not straitened in Me, ye are straitened in your own selves." We hinder Christ from doing His work through us by reason of our own unbelief. The men that have done most for the Lord Jesus, and for their fellows in this world, have been of all sorts, of all conditions, of all grades of intellectual ability and acquirement; some of them scholars, some of them tinkers, some of them philosophers, some of them next door to fools. They have belonged to different communions and have held different ecclesiastical and theological dogmas, and sometimes, alas! they have not been able to discern each other's Christlike lineaments. But there is one thing in which they have all been alike, and that is that they have been men of faith, intense, operative, perpetual. And that is why they have succeeded. If we were what we might be, "full of faith," we should, as the Acts of the Apostles teaches us, by its collocation in the description of one of its characters, be "full of the Holy Spirit and of power."

Brethren, you hear a great deal today about new ways of Christian working, about the necessity of adapting the forms of setting forth Christ's truth to the spirit of the age, and new ideas. Adopt new methods if you like; methods are not sacred. Fashion new forms of presenting Christian truths if you please; our forms are only forms. But you may alter your methods and you may modify your dogmas as you like, and you will do nothing to move the world unless the Church is again baptized with the Divine Spirit, which will only be the case if the Church again puts forth a far mightier faith than it exercises today. If only we will trust Jesus Christ absolutely, and live near Him by our faith, His power will flow into us, and of us, too, it will be said, "through faith they wrought righteousness . . . subdued kingdoms . . . waxed valiant in fight, turned to flight the armies of the aliens." But if the low level of average Christian faith in all the churches is not elevated, then the attempts to conquer the world by half-believing Christians will meet with the old fate, and the man in whom the evil spirit was will leap upon them and overcome them, and say, "Jesus I know, and Paul I know, but who are ye?" "Why could we not cast him out?" And He answered and said unto them, "Because of your unbelief."

Brethren, we may starve in the midst of plenty, if we lock our lips. We can be like some obstinate black rock, washed over forever by the Atlantic surges, and yet so close-grained that only the surface is moistened, and, an inch within, it is dry. "Neither life, nor death, nor angels, nor principalities, nor powers, nor things present, nor things to come, nor height, nor depth, nor any other creature, is able to separate you from the love and power of God which are in Christ Jesus our Lord." But you can separate yourselves, and you do separate yourselves, by your unbelief. The all-sufficiency of Christ's redemption, and the yearning of His love to bless each of us individually, will be nothing to us if we lift up between Him and us the black barrier of unbelief, and so dam back the stream that was meant to give life to all the world and life to us. Christ infinitely desires to bless us, but He cannot unless we trust Him. I beseech you, do not let this be the epitaph on your tombstone:—"Christ could there do no mighty work because of *his* unbelief."

Herod—A Startled Conscience

But when Herod heard thereof, he said, It is John, whom I beheaded: he is risen from the dead. MARK 6:16.

The character of this Herod, surnamed Antipas, is a sufficiently common and a sufficiently despicable one. He was an Eastern despot; capricious and crafty, as the epithet which Christ applied to him, "That fox!" shows; cruel, as the story of the murder of John the Baptist proves; sensuous and lustful; and withal weak of fiber and infirm of purpose. He, Herodias, and John the Baptist make a triad singularly like the other triad in the Old Testament, of Ahab, Jezebel, and Elijah. In both cases we have the weak ruler, the beautiful she-devil at his side, inspiring him for all evil, and the stern prophet, the rebuker and the incarnate conscience for them both.

The words that I have read are the terrified exclamation of this weak and wicked man when he was brought in contact with the light and beauty of Jesus Christ. And if we think who it was that frightened him, and ponder the words in which his fear expressed itself, we get, as it seems to me, some lessons worth the drawing.

1. You have here the voice of a startled conscience. Herod killed John without much sense of doing wrong. He was sorry, no doubt, for he had a kind of respect for the man, and he was reluctant to put him to death. But though there was reluctance, there was no hesitation. His fantastic sense of honor came in the way. In the one scale there was the life of a poor enthusiast who had amused him for a while, but of whom he had got tired. In the other scale there were his word, the pleasure of Herodias, and the applause of the half-drunken boon companions that were sitting with them at the table. So, of course, the prophet was slain, and the pale head brought in to that wild revel; and, except for the malignant gloating of the woman over her gratified revenge, the event, no doubt, very quickly passed from the memories of all concerned.

But then there came stealing into the silken seclusion of the palace, where he was wallowing in his sensuality like a hog in the sty, the tidings of another peasant Teacher that had risen up among the people. Christ's name had been ringing through the land, and been sounded with blessings in poor men's huts long before it got within the gates of Herod's palace. That is the place where religious earnestness makes its mark last of all. But it finally ran thither also; and light gossip went round concerning this new sensation. "Who is He? Who is He?" Each man had his own theory about Him, but a sudden memory started up in the frivolous despot's soul, and it was with a trembling heart that he said to himself, "I know! I know! It is John, whom I beheaded! He is risen from the dead!" His conscience and his memory and his fears all awoke.

Now, my friends, I pray you to lay that simple lesson to heart. We all of us do evil things with regard to which it is not hard for us to bribe or to silence our memories and our consciences. The hurry and bustle of daily life, the very weakness of our characters, the rush of sensuous delights, may make us blind and deaf to the voice of conscience; and we think that all chance of the evil deed rising again to harm us is past. But some trifle touches the hidden spring by mere accident; as in the old story of the man groping along a wall till his finger happens to fall upon one inch of it, and immediately the concealed door flies open, and there is the skeleton. So with us, some merely fortuitous association may freshen faded memories and wake a dormant conscience. An apparently trivial circumstance, like some hooked pole pushed at random into the sea, may bring up by the locks some pale and drowned memory long plunged in an ocean of oblivion. Here, in Herod's case, a report reaches him of a new Rabbi who bears but a very faint resemblance to John, and that is enough to bring his crime back in its naked atrocity.

My friends, we all have these hibernating serpents in our consciences, and nobody knows when the needful warmth may come that will wake them and make them lift their forked heads to sting. The whole landscape of my past life lies there behind the mists of apparent forgetfulness, and any light of suggestion may sweep away the clouds and show it all. What have you laid up in these memories of yours to start into life some day: "at the last biting like a serpent and stinging like an adder"? "It is John! It is John, whom I beheaded!"

Take this other thought, how, as the story shows us, when once at the bidding of memory conscience begins to work, all illusions as to the nature of my action and as to my share in it are swept away.

When the evil deed was done, Herod scarcely felt as if *he* did it. There was his plighted troth, there was Herodias's pressure, there was the excitement of the moment. He seemed forced to do it, and scarcely responsible for doing it. And no doubt, if he ever thought about it afterwards, he shuffled off a large percentage of the responsibility of the guilt upon the shoulders of the others. But when,

> In the silent sessions of things past,

the image and remembrance of the deed come up to him, all the helpers and tempters have disappeared, and "it is John, whom *I* beheaded!" (There is emphasis in the Greek upon the "I".) "Yes, it was *I*. Herodias tempted me; Herodias' daughter titillated my lust; I fancied that my oath bound me; I could not help doing what would please those who sat at the table—I said all that *before* I did it. But now, when it is done, they have all disappeared, every one of them to his quarter; and I and the ugly thing are left together alone. It was I that did it, and nobody besides."

The blackness of the crime, too, presents itself to the startled conscience as it did not in the doing. There are many euphemisms and soft words in which, as in cotton wool, we wrap our evil deeds and so deceive ourselves as to their hardness and their edge; but when conscience gets hold of them, and they pass out of the realm of fact into the mystical region of remembrance, all the wrappings, and all the apologies, and all the soft phrases drop away; and the ugliest, briefest, plainest word is the one by which my conscience describes my own evil. "*I* beheaded him! *I*, and none else, was the murderer." Oh! dear brethren, do you see to it that what you store up in these caves and treasure cellars of memory which we all carry with us, are deeds that will bear being brought out again and looked at in the pure white light of conscience, and which you will neither be ashamed nor afraid to lay your hand upon and say: "It is mine; *I* planted and sowed and worked it, and I am ready to reap the fruit." "If thou be wise thou shalt be wise for thyself, if thou scornest thou alone shalt bear it." Take care of the storehouses of memory and of conscience, and mind what kind of things you lay up there.

2. Now, once more, I take these words as setting before us an example of a conscience awakened to the unseen world. Many commentators tell us that this Herod was a Sadducee; that is to say that theologically and theoretically he had given up the belief in a future state and in spiritual existence. I do not know that that can be sustained, but much more probably he was only a Sadducee in the way in which a great many of us are Sadducees: he never thought about these things, he did not think about them enough to know whether he believed in them or not. He was a practical, if not a theoretical Sadducee; that is to say, this present was his world, and as for the future, it did not come much into his mind. But now, notice that when conscience begins to stir, it at once sends his thoughts into that unseen world beyond.

There is a very close connection, as all history proves, between theoretical disbelief in a future life and in spiritual existence, and superstition. So strong is the bond which unites men with the unseen world, that if they do not link themselves with that world in the legitimate and true fashion, it is almost certain to avenge itself upon them by leading them to all manner of low and abject superstitions. Spiritualism is the disease of a generation that disbelieves in another life. The French Revolution, with its infidelities, was also the age of quacks and impostors such as Cagliostro and the like. The time when Christ lived presented precisely the same phenomena. If Herod was a Sadducee, Herod's Sadduceeism, like frost upon the windowpanes, was such a thin layer shutting out the invisible world, that the least warmth of conscience melted it, and the clear daylight glared in upon him. And I am afraid that there are a great many of us who may be half-inclined to reject the belief in another life, who would find precisely the same thing happening to us.

But be that as it may, it seems to me that whenever a man comes to think very seriously about his conduct as being wrong in the sight of God, there at once starts up before him the thought of a future life and a judgment bar. And I want to know why and how it is that the vigorous operation of conscience is always accompanied with a ''fearful looking for of judgment and fiery indignation.'' I think it is worth your while to reflect upon the fact, and to try and ascertain for yourselves the reason of it, that whenever a man's conscience begins to tell him of his wrong, its message is not only of transgressions but of judgment, and that beyond the grave.

And, moreover, notice here how the startled conscience, when it becomes aware of an unseen world beyond the grave, cannot but think that out of that world there will come evil for it. These words of my text are obviously the words of a frightened man. It was terror that made Herod say: ''It is John, whom I beheaded. He is risen from the dead!'' Who was it that frightened Herod? It was He who came from the bosom of the Father, with His hands full of blessings and His heart full of love: who came to quiet all fears, and to cleanse all consciences, and to satisfy all men's souls with His own sweet love and His perfect righteousness. And it was this genial and gracious and divine form, with all its actualities of gentleness and its possibilities of grace, which the evil conscience of the terrified tetrarch converted into a messenger of judgment come from the tomb to rebuke and to smite him for his evils.

That is to say, men may always make that future life and their relation to it what they will. Either the heavens may pour down their dewy influences of benediction and fruitfulness upon them, or may pour down fire and brimstone upon their spirits. Men have the choice which it shall be. The evil conscience drapes the future in darkness, and is right in doing it. The evil conscience forebodes chastisement, judgment, condemnation coming to it from out of the unseen world, and, with limitations, it is right in doing it. You can make Christ Himself the Messenger of condemnation and of death to you. My dear friends, do you choose whether, fronting eternity with an unforgiven burden of sin upon your shoulders and a conscience unsprinkled by the blood of Jesus Christ, you make of it one great fear; or whether you make it what it really is, a lustrous hope, a perfect joy. Is the Messenger that comes out of the unseen to come to you as a Judge of your buried evils started into life, or is He to come to you as the Christ that bears in His hand the price of your redemption, and with His blood ''sprinkles your conscience from dead works'' and from all its terrors?

3. And now, lastly, I see in this saying an illustration of a conscience which, partially stirred, soon went finally to sleep again. Strangely enough, if we pursue the story, this very terror and clear-eyed perception of the nature of his action led the frivolous king to nothing more than a curious wish to see this new Teacher. It was not gratified; and thus by degrees he came to hate Him and to wish to kill Him. And then, finally, on the eve of the Crucifixion Jesus was brought into his presence, and Herod was glad that his curiosity was satisfied at last. His conscience lay perfectly still. There was no trace of the old convictions or of the old tremor. He ''questioned Jesus many things, and Christ answered him nothing,'' because He knew it was of no use to speak to him. So ''Herod and his men of war mocked Him and set Him at nought''; and sent Him back to Pilate; and he let his last chance of salvation go, and never knew what he had done.

Now, *there* is a lesson for us all. Do not tamper with partially awakened consciences; do not rest satisfied till they are quieted in the legitimate way. There was a man who trembled when he heard Paul remonstrating with him about ''righteousness and temperance''—both of which the unjust judge had set at naught—''and judgment to come.'' And he ''sent for him often and communed with him gladly,'' but we never hear that Felix trembled any more. It is possible for you so to lull yourselves into indifference, and, as it were, so to waterproof your consciences that appeals, threatenings, pleadings, mercies, the words of men, the Gospel of God, and the beseechings of Christ Himself may all run off them and leave them dry and hard.

One very potent means of rendering consciences insensible is to neglect their voice. The convictions which you have not followed out, like the ruins of a bastion shattered by shell, protect your remaining fortifications against the impact of God's truth. I believe that there is no man, woman, or child listening to me at this moment but has had, some time or other in the course of his or her life, convictions which only needed to be followed out, gleams of guidance which only required to be faithfully pursued, to bring him or her into loving fellowship with, and true faith in, Jesus Christ. But some of you have neglected them; some of you have choked them with cares and studies and occupations of different kinds; and you are driving on to this result—I do not know that it is ever reached in this life, but a man may come indefinitely near it—that you shall stand, like Herod, face to face with Jesus Christ and feel nothing, and that all His love and grace shall be offered and not excite the faintest stirring in your hearts of a desire to accept it.

We have all of us evils enough in our memory to make us dread the awakening of conscience, to make us look with fear and apprehension beyond the veil to a judgment seat. And, blessed be God! we have all of us had, and some of us have now, drawings to which we need but to yield ourselves in order to find that He who comes from the heavens is no "John whom we beheaded," risen for judgment, but a mightier than he, that Son of God who came "not to condemn the world, but that the world through Him might be saved."

The Martyrdom of John

For Herod himself had sent forth and laid hold upon John, and bound him in prison for Herodias' sake, his brother Philip's wife: for he had married her. 18. For John had said unto Herod, It is not lawful for thee to have thy brother's wife. 19. Therefore Herodias had a quarrel against him, and would have killed him; but she could not: 20. For Herod feared John, knowing that he was a just man and an holy, and observed him; and when he heard him, he did many things, and heard him gladly. 21. And when a convenient day was come, that Herod on his birthday made a supper to his lords, high captains, and chief estates of Galilee; 22. And when the daughter of the said Herodias came in, and danced, and pleased Herod and them that sat with him, the king said unto the damsel, Ask of me whatsoever thou wilt, and I will give it thee. 23. And he sware unto her, Whatsoever thou shalt ask of me, I will give it thee, unto the half of my kingdom. 24. And she went forth, and said unto her mother, What shall I ask? And she said, The head of John the Baptist. 25. And she came in straightway with haste unto the king, and asked, saying, I will that thou give me by and by in a charger the head of John the Baptist. 26. And the king was exceeding sorry; yet for his oath's sake, and for their sakes which sat with him, he would not reject her. 27. And immediately the king sent an executioner, and commanded his head to be brought: and he went and beheaded him in the prison. 28. And brought his head in a charger, and gave it to the damsel: and the damsel gave it to her mother. MARK 6:17–22.

This Herod was a son of the grim old tiger who slew the infants of Bethlehem. He was a true cub of a bad litter, with his father's ferocity, but without his force. He was sensual, cruel, cunning, and infirm of purpose. Rome allowed him to play at being a king, but kept him well in hand. No doubt his anomalous position as a subject prince helped to make him the bad man he was. Herodias, the Jezebel to this Ahab, was his brother's wife, and niece to both her husband and Herod. Elijah was not far off; John's daring outspokenness, of course, made the indignant woman his implacable enemy.

1. This story gives an example of the waking of conscience. When Christ's name reached even the court, where such tidings would have no ready entrance, what was only an occasion of more or less languid gossip and curiosity to others stirred the sleeping accuser in Herod's breast. He had no doubt as to who this new Teacher, armed with mightier powers than John who "did no miracles" had ever possessed, was. His conviction that he was John, come back with increased power, was immediate, and was held fast, in spite of the buzz of other opinions.

Note the unusual order of the sentence in verse 16: "John whom I beheaded, he is," etc. The terrified king blurts out the name of his dread first, then tremblingly takes the guilt of the deed to himself, and last speaks the terrifying thought that he is risen. A man who has a sin in his memory can never be sure that its ghost will not suddenly start up. Trivial incidents will rouse the sleeping conscience. Some nothing, a chance word, a scent, a sound, the look on a face, the glow of an evening sky, may bring all the foul past up again. A puff of wind clears away the mist of oblivion, and the old sin starts into vividness as if done yesterday. You touch a secret spring, and there yawns in the floor a gap leading down to a dungeon.

Conscience thus wakened is free from all illusions as to guilt. "*I* beheaded." There are no excuses now about Herodias' urgency, or Salome's beauty, or the rash oath, or the need of keeping it, before his guests. The deed stands clear of all these, as his own act. It is ever so. When conscience speaks, sophistications about temptations or companions, or necessity, or the more learned excuses which philosophers make about environment and heredity as weakening responsibility and diminishing guilt, shrivel to nothing. The present operations of conscience distinctly predict future still more complete remembrance of, and sense of responsibility for, long past sins. There will be a resurrection of men's evil deeds, as well as of their bodies, and each of them will shake its gory locks at its author, and say, "Thou didst it."

There is no proof that Herod was a Sadducee, disbelieving in a resurrection; but, whether he was or not, the terrors of conscience made short work of the difficulties in the way of his supposition. He was right in believing that evil deeds are gifted with an awful immortality, and will certainly rise again to shake their doer's soul with terrors.

2. The narrative harks back to tell the story of John's martyrdom. It sets forth vividly the inner discord and misery of half-and-half convictions. Herodias was strong enough to get John put in prison, and apparently she tried with all the tenacity of malignant woman to have him assassinated, by contrived accident or open sentence; but *that* she could not manage.

Mark's analysis of the play of contending feeling in the weak king is barely intelligible in the Authorized Version, but is clearly shown in the Revised Version. He "feared John,"—the jailer afraid of his prisoner — "knowing that he was a righteous man and an holy." Goodness is awful. The worst men know it when they see it, and pay it the homage of dread, if not of love. "And kept him safe" (not *ob-* but *pre*-served him); that is, from Herodias' revenge. "And when he heard him, he was much perplexed." The reading thus translated differs from that in the Authorized Version by two letters only, and obviously is preferable. Herod was a weak-willed man, drawn by two stronger natures pulling in opposite directions.

So he alternated between lust and purity, between the foul kisses of the temptress at his side and the warnings of the prophet in his dungeon. But in all his vacillation he could not help listening to John, but "heard him gladly," and mind and conscience approved the nobler voice. Thus he staggered along, with religion enough to spoil some of his sinful delights, but not enough to make him give them up.

Such a state of partial conviction is not unusual. Many of us know quite well that, if we would drop some habit, which may not be very grave, we should be less encumbered in some effort which it is our interest or duty to make; but the conviction has not gone deeper than the understanding. Like a shot which has only got halfway through the armored skin of a man-of-war, it has done no execution, nor reached the engine room where the power that drives the life is. In more important matters such imperfect convictions are widespread. The majority of slaves to vice know perfectly well that they should give it up. And in regard to the salvation which is in Christ, there are multitudes who know in their inmost consciousness that they ought to be Christians.

Such a condition is one liable to unrest and frequent inner conflict. Truly, he is "much perplexed" whose conscience pulls him one way, and his inclinations another. There is no more miserable condition than that of the man whose will is cleft in twain, and who has a continual battle raging within. Conscience may be bound and thrust down into a dungeon, like John, and lust and pride may be carousing overhead, but their mirth is hollow, and every now and then the stern voice comes up through the gratings, and the noisy revelry is hushed, while *it* speaks doom.

Such a state of inner strife comes often from unwillingness to give up one special evil. If Herod could have plucked up resolve to pack Herodias about her business, other things might have come right. Many of us are ruined by being unwilling to let some dear delight go. "If thine eye causeth thee to stumble, pluck it out."

We do not make up for such cowardly shrinking from doing right by pleasure in the divine word which we are not obeying. Herod no doubt thought that his delight in listening to John went some way to atone for his refusal to get rid of Herodias. Some of us think ourselves good Christians because we assent to truth, and even like to hear it, provided the speaker suit our tastes. Glad hearing only aggravates the guilt of not doing. It is useless to admire John if you keep Herodias.

3. The end of the story gives an example of the final powerlessness of such half-convictions. One need not repeat the grim narrative of the murder. We all know it. One knows not which is the more repugnant—the degradation of the poor child Salome to the level of a dancing girl, the fell malignity of the mother who would shame her daughter for such an end, the maudlin generosity of Herod, flushed with wine and excited passion, the hideous request from lips so young, the ineffectual sorrow of Herod, his fantastic sense of obligation, which scrupled to break a wicked promise and did not scruple to murder a prophet, or the ghastly picture of the girl hurrying to her mother with the freshly severed head, dripping on to the platter and staining her fair young hands.

This was what all the convictions of John's righteousness had come to. So had ended the half yielding to his brave rebukes and the ineffectual aspirations after cleaner living. That chaos of lust and blood teaches that partial reformation is apt to end in a deeper plunge into fouler mire. If a man is false to his feeblest conviction, he makes himself a worse man all through. A partial thaw is generally followed by keener frost than before. A soul half-melted and cooled again is harder to melt than before. An abortive slave uprising rivets the chains.

The incident teaches that simple weakness may come to be the parent of great sin. In a world like this, where there are always more voices soliciting to wrong than to right, to be weak is in the long run to be wicked. Fatal facility of disposition ruins hundreds of unthinking men. Nothing is more needful than that young people should learn to say "No," and should cultivate a wholesome obstinacy which is afraid of nothing but of sinning against God.

If we look onwards to this Herod's last appearance in Scripture, we get further lessons. He desired to see Jesus that he might see a miracle done to amuse him, like a conjuring trick. Convictions and terrors had faded from his frivolous soul. He has forgotten that he once thought Jesus to be John come again. He sees Christ, and sees nothing in Him; and Christ says nothing to Herod, because He knew it would be useless.

It is an awful thing to put one's self beyond the hearing of that voice, which "all that are in the graves shall hear." The most effectual stopping for our ears is neglect of what we know to be His will. If we will not listen to Him, we shall gradually lose the power of hearing Him, and then He will lock His lips, and answer nothing. We dare not say that Jesus is dumb to any man while life lasts, but we dare not refrain from saying that that condition of utter insensibility to His voice may be indefinitely approached by us, and that neglected convictions bring us terribly far on the way towards it.

The World's Bread

And the apostles gathered themselves together unto Jesus, and
told Him all things, both what they had done, and what they had
taught. 31. And He said unto them, Come ye yourselves apart into
a desert place, and rest a while: for there were many coming and
going, and they had no leisure so much as to eat. 32. And they
departed into a desert place by ship privately. 33. And the people
saw them departing, and many knew Him, and ran afoot thither out
of all cities, and outwent them, and came together unto Him.
34. And Jesus, when He came out, saw much people, and was moved
with compassion toward them, because they were as sheep not hav-
ing a shepherd: and He began to teach them many things. 35. And
when the day was now far spent, His disciples came unto Him, and
said, This is a desert place, and now the time is far passed: 36.
Send them away, that they may go into the country round about, and
into the villages, and buy themselves bread: for they have nothing to
eat. 37. He answered and said unto them, Give ye them to eat. And
they say unto Him, Shall we go and buy two hundred penny-worth of
bread, and give them to eat? 38. He saith unto them, How many
loaves have ye? go and see. And when they knew, they say, Five, and
two fishes. 39. And He commanded them to make all sit down by
companies upon the green grass. 40. And they sat down in ranks,
by hundreds, and by fifties. 41. And when He had taken the five
loaves and the two fishes, He looked up to heaven, and blessed, and
brake the loaves, and gave them to His disciples to set before them;
and the two fishes divided He among them all. 42. And they did all
eat, and were filled. 43. And they took up twelve baskets full of the
fragments, and of the fishes. 44. And they that did eat of the loaves
were about five thousand men. MARK 6:30–44.

This is the only miracle recorded by all four Evangelists. Matthew brings it into immediate connection with John's martyrdom, while Mark links it with the Apostles' return from their first mission. His account is, as usual, full of graphic touches, while John shows more intimate knowledge of the parts played by the Apostles, and sets the whole incident in a clearer light.

1. Mark brings out the preceding events, and especially the seeking for solitude, which was balked by popular enthusiasm. The Apostles came back to Jesus full of wondering joy, and were eager to tell what they had done and taught. Note that order, which hints that they thought more of the miracles than of the message. They were flushed and excited by success, and needed calming down even more than physical rest. So Jesus, knowing their need, bids them come with Him into healing solitude, and rest awhile.

After any great effort, the body cries for repose, but still more does the soul's health demand quiet after exciting and successful work for Christ. Without much solitary communion with Jesus, effort for Him tends to become mechanical, and to lose the elevation of motive and the suppression of self which give it all its power. It is not wasted time which the busiest worker, confronted with the most imperative calls for service, gives to still fellowship in secret with God. There can never be too much activity in Christian work, but there is often disproportioned activity, which is too much for the amount of time given to meditation and communion. That is one reason why there is so much sowing and so little reaping in Christian work today.

But, on the other hand, we have sometimes to do as Jesus was driven to do in this incident; namely, to forgo cheerfully, after brief repose, the blessed and strengthening hour of quiet. The motives of the crowds that hurried round the head of the lake while the boat was pulled across, and so got to the other side before it, were not very pure. Curiosity drove them as much as any nobler impulse. But we must not be too particular about the reasons that induce men to resort to Jesus, and if we can give them more than they sought, so much the better. Let us be thankful if, for any reason, we can get them to listen.

Jesus ''came forth''; that is, probably from a short withdrawal with the Twelve. Brief repose snatched, He turned again to the work. The ''great multitude'' did not make Him impatient, though, no doubt, some of the Apostles were annoyed. But He saw deeply into their condition, and pity welled in His heart. If we looked on the crowds in our great cities with Christ's eyes, their spiritual state would be the most prominent thing in sight. And if we saw that as He saw it, disgust, condemnation, indifference, would not be uppermost, as they too often are, but some drop of His great compassion would trickle into our hearts. The masses are still "as sheep without a shepherd," ignorant of the way, and defenseless against their worst foes. Do we habitually try to cultivate as ours Christ's way of looking at men, and Christ's emotions towards men? If we do, we shall imitate Christ's actions for men, and shall recognize that, to reproduce as well as we can the "many things" which He taught them, is the best contribution which His disciples can make to healing the misery of a Christless world.

2. The difference between John and Mark in regard to the conversation of Jesus with the disciples about finding food for the crowd, is easily harmonized. John tells us what Jesus said at the first sight of the multitude; Mark takes up the narrative at the close of the day. We owe to John the knowledge that the exigency was not first pointed out by the disciples, but that His calm, loving prescience saw it, and determined to meet it, long before they spoke. No needs arise unforeseen by Christ, and He requires no prompting to help. Difficulties which seem insoluble to us, when we too late wake to peceive them, have long ago been taken into account and solved by Him.

The Apostles, according to Mark, came with a suggestion of helpless embarrassment. They could think of nothing but to disperse the crowd, and so get rid of responsibility. He answers with a paradox of conscious power, which commands a seeming impossibility, and therein prophesies endowment that will make it possible. Has not the Church ever since been but too often faithless enough to let the multitudes drift away to "the cities and villages round about," and there, amid human remedies for their sore needs, "buy themselves," with much expenditure, a scanty provision? Are we not all tempted to shuffle off responsibility for the world's hunger? Do we not often think that our resources are absurdly insufficient, and so, faintheartedly make them still less? Is not His command still, "Give ye them to eat"? Let us rise to the height of our duties and of our power, and be sure that whoever has Christ has enough for the world's hunger, and is bound to call men from "that which is not bread," and to feed them with Him who is.

Philip's morning calculation (curiously in keeping with his character) seems to have been repeated by the Apostles, as, no doubt, he had been saying the same thing all day at intervals. They had made a rough calculation of how much would be wanted. It was a sum far beyond their means—equal to eight month's wages. And where was such wealth as that in that company? But calculations which leave out Christ's power are not quite conclusive. The Apostles had reckoned up the requirement, but they had not taken stock of their resources. So they were sent to hunt up what they could, and John tells us that it was Andrew who found the boy with five barley loaves and two fishes. How came a boy to be so provident? Probably he had come to try a bit of trade on his own account. At all events, the Twelve seem to have been able to buy his little stock, which done, they went back to tell Jesus, no doubt thinking that such a meager supply would end all talk of their giving the crowd to eat. Jesus would have us count our own resources, not that we may fling up His work in despair, but that we may realize our dependence on Him, and that the consciousness of our own insufficiency may not diminish one jot our sense of obligation to feed the multitude. It is good to learn our own weakness if it drives us to lean on His strength. "Five loaves and two fishes," plus Jesus Christ, come to a good deal more than "two hundred pennyworth of bread."

3. The miracle is told with beautiful vividness and simplicity. Mark's picturesque words show the groups sitting by companies of hundreds or of fifties. He uses a word which means "the square garden plots in which herbs are grown." So they sat on the green grass, which at that Passover season would be fresh and abundant. What half-amused and more than half-incredulous wonder as to what would come next would be in the people! Many of them would be saying in their hearts, and perhaps some in words, "Can God furnish a table in the wilderness?" (Psalms 78:19). In that small matter Jesus shows that He is "not the Author of confusion," but of order. The rush of five thousand hungry men struggling to get a share of what seemed an insufficient supply would have been unseemly and dangerous to the women and children, but the seated groups become as companies of guests, and He the orderer of the feast. To get at the numbers would be easy, while the passage of the Apostles through the groups was facilitated, and none would be likely to remain unsupplied or passed over.

The point at which the miraculous element entered is not definitely stated, but if each portion passed through the hands of Christ to the servers, and from them to the partakers, the multiplication of the bread must have been effected while it lay in His hand; that is to say, the loaves were not diminished by His giving. That is true about all divine gifts. He bestows, and is none the poorer. The streams flow from the golden vase, and, after all outpouring, it is brimful.

Many irrelevant difficulties have been raised about the mode of the miracle, and many lame analogies have been suggested, as if it but hastened ordinary processes. But these need not detain us. Note rather the great lesson which John records that our Lord Himself drew from this miracle. It was a symbol, in the material region, of His work in the spiritual, as all His miracles were. He is the Bread of the world. He gives Himself still, and in a yet more wonderful sense He gave His flesh for the life of the world. He gives us Himself for our own nourishment, and also that we may give Him to others. It was an honor to the Twelve that they should be chosen to be His almoners. It should be felt an honor by all Christians that through them Christ wills to feed a hungry world.

A somewhat different application of the miracle reminds us that Jesus uses our resources, scanty and coarse as five barley loaves, for the basis of His wonders. He did not create the bread, but multiplied it. Our small abilities, humbly acknowledged to be small, and laid in His hands, will grow. There is power enough in the Church, if the power were consecrated, to feed the world.

All four Gospels tell the command to gather up the "broken pieces" (not the fragments left by the eaters, but the unused pieces broken by Christ). This union of economy with creative power could never have been invented. Unused resources are retained. The exercise of Christian powers multiplies them, and after the feeding of thousands more remains than was possessed before. "There is that scattereth, and yet increaseth."

7

The Master Serves

Children and Little Dogs

And from thence He arose, and went into the borders of Tyre and Sidon, and entered into an house, and would have no man know it: but He could not be hid. 25. For a certain woman, whose young daughter had an unclean spirit, heard of Him, and came and fell at His feet: 26. The woman was a Greek, a Syrophenician by nation; and she besought Him that He would cast forth the devil out of her daughter. 27. But Jesus said unto her, Let the children first be filled: for it is not meet to take the children's bread, and to cast it unto the dogs. 28. And she answered and said unto Him, Yes, Lord: yet the dogs under the table eat of the children's crumbs. 29. And He said unto her, For this saying go thy way; the devil is gone out of thy daughter. 30. And when she was come to her house, she found the devil gone out, and her daughter laid upon the bed. MARK 7:24–30.

Our Lord desired to withdraw from the excited crowds who were flocking after Him as a mere miracle-worker and from the hostile espionage of emissaries of the Pharisees, "which had come from Jerusalem." Therefore He sought seclusion in heathen territory. He, too, knew the need of quiet, and felt the longing to plunge into privacy, to escape for a time from the pressure of admirers and of foes, and to go where no man knew Him. How near to us that brings Him! And how the remembrance of it helps to explain His demeanor to the Syrophenician woman, so unlike His usual tone!

Naturally the presence of Jesus leaked out, and perhaps the very effort to avoid notice attracted it. Rumor would have carried His name across the border, and the tidings of His being among them would stir hope in some hearts that felt the need of His help. Of such was this woman, whom Mark describes first, generally, as a "Greek" (that is, a Gentile), and then particularly as "a Syrophenician by race"; that is, one of that branch of the Phenician race who inhabited maritime Syria, in contradistinction from the other branch inhabiting Northeastern Africa, Carthage, and its neighborhood. Her deep need made her bold and persistent, as we learn in detail from Matthew, who is in this narrative more graphic than Mark. He tells us that she attacked Jesus in the way, and followed Him, pouring out her loud petitions, to the annoyance of the disciples. They thought that they were carrying out His wish for privacy in suggesting that it would be best to "send her away" with her prayer granted, and so stop her "crying after us," which might raise a crowd, and defeat the wish. We owe to Matthew the further facts of the woman's recognition of Jesus as "the Son of David," and of the strange ignoring of her cries, and of His answer to the disciples' suggestion, in which He limited His mission to Israel, and so explained to them His silence to her. Mark omits all these points, and focuses all the light on the two things—Christ's strange and apparently harsh refusal, and the woman's answer, which won her cause.

Certainly our Lord's words are startlingly unlike Him, and as startlingly like the Jewish pride of race and contempt for Gentiles. But that the woman did not take them so is clear; and that was not due only to her faith, but to something in Him which gave her faith a foothold. We are surely not to suppose that she drew from His words an inference which He did not perceive in them, and that He was, as some commentators put it, "caught in His own words." Mark alone gives us the first clause of Christ's answer to the woman's petition: "Let the children first be filled." And that "first" distinctly says that their prerogative is priority, not monopoly. If there is a "first," there will follow a second. The very image of the great house in which the children sit at the table, and the "little dogs" are in the room, implies that children and dogs are part of one household; and Jesus meant by it just what the woman found in it,—the assurance that the mealtime for the dogs would come when the children had done. That is but a picturesque way of stating the method of divine revelation through the medium of the chosen people, and the objections to Christ's words come at last to be objections to the "committing" of the "oracles of God" to the Jewish race; that is to say, objections to the only possible way by which a historical revelation could be given. It must have personal mediums, a place and a sequence. It must prepare fit vehicles for itself and gradually grow in clearness and contents. And all this is just to say that revelation for the world must be first the possession of a race. The fire must have a hearth on which it can be kindled and burn, till it is sufficient to bear being carried thence.

Universalism was the goal of the necessary restriction. Pharisaism sought to make the restriction permanent. Jesus really threw open the gates to all in this very saying, which at first sounds so harsh. "First" implies second, children and little dogs are all parts of the one household. Christ's personal ministry was confined to Israel for obvious and weighty reasons. He felt, as Matthew tells us, that He said in this incident that He was not sent but to the lost sheep of that nation. But His worldwide mission was as clear to Him as its temporary limit, and in His first discourse in the synagogue at Nazareth He proclaimed it to a scowling crowd. We cannot doubt that His sympathetic heart yearned over this poor woman and His seemingly rough speech was meant partly to honor the law which ruled His mission even in the act of making an exception to it, and partly to test, and so to increase, her faith.

Her swift laying of her finger on the vulnerable point in the apparent refusal of her prayer may have been due to a woman's quick wit, but it was much more due to a mother's misery and to a suppliant's faith. There must have been something in Christ's look, or in the cadence of His voice, which helped to soften the surface harshness of His words, and emboldened her to confront Him with the plain implications of His own words. What a constellation of graces sparkles in her ready reply! There is humility in accepting the place He gives her; insight in seeing at once a new plea in what might have sent her away despairing; persistence in pleading; confidence that He can grant her request and that He would gladly do so. Our Lord's treatment of her was amply justified by its effects. His words were like the hard steel that strikes the flint and brings out a shower of sparks. Faith makes obstacles into helps, and stones of stumbling into "steppingstones to higher things." If we will take the place which He gives us, and hold fast our trust in Him even when He seems silent to us, and will so far penetrate His designs as to find the hidden purpose of good in apparent repulses, the honey secreted deep in the flower, we shall share in this woman's blessing in the measure in which we share in her faith.

Jesus obviously delighted in being at liberty to stretch His commission so as to include her in its scope. Joyful recognition of the ingenuity of her pleading, and of her faith's bringing her within the circle of the "children," are apparent in His word, "For this saying go thy way." He ever looks for the disposition in us which will let Him, in accordance with His great purpose, pour on us His full-flowing tide of blessing, and nothing gladdens Him more than that, by humble acceptance of our assigned place, and persistent pleading, and trust that will not be shaken, we should make it possible for Him to see in us recipients of His mercy and healing grace.

The Pattern of Service

He touched his tongue; and looking up to heaven, He sighed, and saith Ephphatha, that is, Be opened. MARK 7:33, 34.

For what reason was there this unwonted slowness in Christ's healing works? For what reason was there this unusual emotion ere He spoke the word which cleansed?

As to the former question, a partial answer may perhaps be that our Lord is here on half-heathen ground, where aids to faith were much needed, and His power had to be veiled that it might be beheld. Hence the miracle is a process rather than an act; and, advancing as it does by distinct stages, is conformed in appearance to men's works of mercy, which have to adapt means to ends, and creep to their goal by persevering toil. As to the latter, we know not why the sight of this one poor sufferer should have struck so strongly on the ever-tremulous chords of Christ's pitying heart; but we do know that it was the vision brought before His spirit by this single instance of the world's griefs and sicknesses—in which mass, however, the special case before Him was by no means lost—that raised His eyes to heaven in mute appeal, and forced the groan from His breast.

The "missionary spirit" is but one aspect of the Christian spirit. We shall only strengthen the former as we invigorate the latter. Harm has been done, both to ourselves and to that great cause, by seeking to stimulate compassion and efforts for heathen lands by the use of other excitements, which have tended to vitiate even the emotions they have aroused, and are apt to fail us when we need them most. It may therefore be profitable if we turn to Christ's own manner of working, and His own emotions in His merciful deeds, set forth in this remarkable narrative, as containing lessons for us in our missionary and evangelistic work. I must necessarily omit more than a passing reference to the slow process of healing which this miracle exhibits. But that, too, has its teaching for us, who are so often tempted to think ourselves badly used, unless the fruit of our toil grows up, like Jonah's gourd, before our eyes. If our Lord was content to reach His end of blessing step by step, we may well accept "patient continuance in well-doing" as the condition indispensable to reaping in due season.

But there are other thoughts still more needful which suggest themselves. Those minute details which this Evangelist ever delights to give of our Lord's gestures, words, looks, and emotions, not only add graphic form to the narrative but are precious glimpses into the very heart of Christ. That fixed gaze into heaven, that groan which neither the glories seen above nor the conscious power to heal could stifle, that most gentle touch, as if removing material obstacles from the deaf ears, and moistening the stiff tongue that it might move more freely in the parched mouth, that word of authority which could not be wanting even when His working seemed likest a servant's, do surely carry large lessons for us. The condition of all service, the cost of feeling at which our work must be done, the need that the helpers should identify themselves with the sufferers and the victorious power of Christ's word over all dead ears—these are the thoughts which I desire to connect with our text and to commend to your meditation now.

1. We have here set forth, in the Lord's heavenward look, the foundation and condition of all true work for God. The profound questions which are involved in the fact that, as man, Christ held communion with God in the exercise of faith and aspiration, the same in kind as ours, do not concern us here. I speak to those who believe that Jesus is for us the perfect example or complete manhood, and who therefore believe that He is "the leader of faith," the head of the long processions of those who in every age have trusted in God and been "lightened." But, perhaps, though that conviction holds its place in our creeds, it has not been as completely incorporated with our thoughts as it should have been. There has, no doubt, been a tendency, operating in much of our evangelical teaching, and in the common stream of orthodox opinion, to except, half unconsciously, the exercises of the religious life from the sphere of Christ's example, and we need to be reminded that Scripture presents His vow, "I will put my trust in Him," as the crowning proof of His brotherhood, and that the prints of His kneeling limbs have left their impressions where we kneel before the throne. True, the relation of the Son to the Father involves more than communion—namely, unity. But if we follow the teaching of the Bible, we shall not presume that the latter excludes the former, but understand that the unity is the foundation of perfect communion, and the communion the manifestation, so far as it can be manifested, of the unspeakable unity. The solemn words which shine like stars—starlike in that their height above us shrinks their magnitude and dims their brightness, and in that they are points of radiance partially disclosing, and separated by, abysses of unlighted infinitude—tell us that in the order of eternity, before creatures were, there was communion, for "the Word was with God," and there was unity, for "the Word was God." And in the records of the life manifested on earth the consciousness of unity loftily utters itself in the unfathomable declaration, "I and my Father are one"; whilst the consciousness of communion, dependent like ours on harmony of will and true obedience, breathes peacefully in the witness which He leaves to Himself: "The Father has not left Me alone, for I do always the things that please Him."

We are fully warranted, then, in supposing that that wistful gaze to heaven means, and may be taken to symbolize, our Lord's conscious direction of thought and spirit to God as He wrought His work of mercy. There are two distinctions to be noted between His communion with God and ours before we can apply the lesson to ourselves. His heavenward look was not the renewal of interrupted fellowship, but rather, as a man standing firmly on firm rock may yet lift his foot to plant it again where it was before, and settle himself in his attitude before he strikes with all his might; so we may say Christ fixes Himself where He always stood, and grasps anew the hand that He always held, before He does the deed of power. The communion that had never been broken was renewed; how much more the need that in *our* work for God the renewal of the—alas! too sadly sundered—fellowship should ever precede and always accompany our efforts! And again, Christ's fellowship was with the Father, while ours must be with the Father through the Son. The communion to which we are called is with Jesus Christ, in whom we find God.

The manner of that intercourse, and the various discipline of ourselves with a view to its perfecting which Christian prudence prescribes, need not concern us here. As for the latter, let us not forget that a wholesome and wide-reaching self-denial cannot be dispensed with. Hands that are full of gilded toys and glass beads cannot grasp durable riches, and eyes that have been accustomed to glaring lights see only darkness when they look up to the violet heaven with all its stars. As to the former, every part of our nature above the simply animal is capable of God, and the communion ought to include our whole being. Christ is truth for the understanding, authority for the will, love for the heart, certainty for the hope, fruition for all the desires, and for the conscience at once cleansing and law. Fellowship with Him is no indolent passiveness, nor the luxurious exercise of certain emotions, but the contact of the whole nature with its sole adequate object and rightful Lord.

Such intercourse, brethren, lies at the foundation of all work for God. It is the condition of all our power. It is the measure of all our success. Without it we may seem to realize the externals of prosperity, but it will be an illusion. With it we may perchance seem to "spend our strength for nought"; but heaven has its surprises; and those who toiled, nor left their hold of their Lord in all their work, will have to say at last with wonder, as they see the results of their poor efforts, "Who hath begotten me these? behold, I was left alone; these, where had they been?"

Consider in few words the manifold ways in which the indispensable prerequisite of all right effort for Christ may be shown to be communion with Christ.

The heavenward look is the renewal of our own vision of the calm verities in which we trust, the recourse for ourselves to the realities which we desire that others should see. And what is equal in persuasive power to the simple utterance of one's own intense conviction? He only will infuse his own religion into other minds, whose religion is not a set of hard dogmas, but is fused by the heat of personal experience into a river of living fire. It will flow then not otherwise. The only claim which the hearts of men will listen to, in those who would win them to spiritual beliefs, is that ancient one: "That which we have seen with our eyes, which we have looked upon, declare we unto you." Mightier than all arguments than all "proofs of the truth of the Christian religion," and penetrating into a sphere deeper than that of the understanding, is the simple proclamation, "We have found the Messias." If we would give sight to the blind, we must ourselves be gazing into heaven. Only when we testify of that which we see, as one might who, standing in a beleaguered city, discerned on the horizon the filmy dust cloud through which the spearheads of the deliverers flashed at intervals, shall we win any to gaze with us till they too behold and know themselves set free.

The heavenward look draws new strength from the source of all our might. In our work, dear brethren, contemplating as it ought to do exclusively spiritual results, what we do depends largely on what we are, and what we are depends on what we receive, and what we receive depends on the depth and constancy of our communion with God. "The help which is done upon earth He doeth it all Himself." We and our organizations are but the channels through which this might is poured; and if we choke the bed with turbid masses of drift and heavy rocks of earthly thoughts, or build from bank to bank thick dams of worldliness compact with slime of sin, how shall the full tide flow through us for the healing of the salt and barren places? Will it not leave its former course silted up with sand, and cut for itself new outlets, while the useless quays that once rang with busy life stand silent, and "the cities are solitary that were full of people"? We are

> The trumpet at Thy lips, the clarion
> Full of Thy cry, sonorous with Thy breath.

Let us see to it that by fellowship with Christ we keep the passage clear, and become recipients of the inspiration which shall thrill our else-silent spirits into the blast of loud alarm and the ringing proclamation of the true King.

The heavenward look will guard us from the temptations which surround all our service, and the distractions which lay waste our lives. It is habitual communion with Christ that alone will give the persistency that makes systematic, continuous efforts for Him possible, and yet will keep systematic work from degenerating, as it ever tends to do, into mechanical work. There is no greater virtue in irregular desultory service than in systematized labor. The one is not freer from besetting temptations than the other, only the temptations are of different sorts. Machinery saves manual toil, and multiplies force. But we may have too heavy machinery for what engineers call the boiler power—too many wheels and shafts for the steam we have to drive them with. What we want is not less organization, or other sorts of it, but more force. Any organization will do if we have God's Spirit breathing through it. None will be better than so much old iron if we have not.

We are ever apt to trust to our work, to do it without a distinct recurrence at each moment to the principles on which it rests and the motives by which it should be actuated—to become so absorbed in details that we forget the purpose which alone gives them meaning, to overestimate the external aspects of it, to lose sight of the solemn truths which make it so grand, and to think of it as commonplace because it is common, as ordinary because it is familiar. And from these most real dangers, which beset us all, there is no refuge but the frequent, the habitual, gaze into the open heavens, which will show us again the realities of things, and bring to our spirits, dwarfed even by habits of goodness, the renewal of former motives by the vision of Jesus Christ.

Such constant communion will further surround us with an atmosphere through which none of the many influences which threaten our Christian life and our Christian work can penetrate. As the diver in his bell sits dry at the bottom of the sea, and draws a pure air from the free heavens far above him, and is parted from that murderous waste of green death that clings so closely round the translucent crystal walls which keep him safe; so we, enclosed in God, shall repel from ourselves all that would overflow to destroy us and our work, and may by His grace lay deeper than the waters some courses in the great building that shall one day rise, stately and many-mansioned, from out of the conquered waves. For ourselves, and for all that we do for Him, living communion with God is the means of power and peace, of security and success.

It was never more needful than now. Feverish activity rules in all spheres of life. The iron wheels of the car which bears the modern idol of material progress whirl fast, and crush remorselessly all who cannot keep up the pace. Christian effort is multiplied and systematized beyond all precedent. And all these facts make calm fellowship with God hard to compass. The measure of the difficulty is the measure of the need. I, for my part, believe that there are few Christian duties more neglected than that of meditation, the very name of which has fallen of late into comparative disuse, that augurs ill for the frequency of the thing. We are so busy thinking, discussing, defending, inquiring; or preaching, and teaching, and working, that we have no time and no leisure of heart for quiet contemplation, without which the exercise of the intellect upon Christ's truth will not feed, and busy activity in Christ's cause may starve, the soul. There are few things which the Church of this day in all its parts needs more than to obey the invitation, "Come ye yourselves apart into a lonely place, and rest a while."

Christ has set us the example. Let our prayers ascend as His did, and in our measure the answers which came to Him will not fail us. For us, too, "praying, the heavens" shall be "opened," and the peace-bringing spirit fall dove-like on our meek hearts. For us, too, when the shadow of our cross lies black and gaunt upon our paths, and our souls are troubled, communion with heaven will bring the assurance, audible to our ears at least, that God will glorify Himself even in us. If, after many a weary day, we seek to hold fellowship with God as He sought it on the Mount of Olives, or among the solitudes of the midnight hills, or out in the morning freshness of the silent wilderness, like Him we shall have men gathering around us to hear us speak when we come forth from "the secret place of the Most High." If our prayer, like His, goes before our mighty deeds, the voice that first pierced the skies will penetrate the tomb, and make the dead stir in their graveclothes. If our longing, trustful look is turned to the heavens, we shall not speak in vain on earth when we say, "Be opened!"

Brethren, we cannot do without the communion which our Master needed. Do we delight in what strengthened Him? Does our work rest upon the basis of inward fellowship with God which underlay His? Alas! that our Pattern should be our rebuke, and that the readiest way to force home our faults on our consciences should be the contemplation of the life which we say that we try to copy!

2. We have here pity for the evils we would remove, set forth by the Lord's sigh. The frequency with which this Evangelist records our Lord's emotions on the sight of sin and sorrow has been often noticed. In his pages we read of Christ's grief at the hardness of men's hearts, of His marveling because of their unbelief, of His being moved with compassion for an outcast leper and a hungry multitude, of His sighing deeply in His spirit when prejudiced hostility, assuming the appearance of candid inquiry, asked of Him a sign from heaven. All these instances of true human feeling, like His tears at the grave of Lazarus, and His weariness as He sat on the well, and His tired sleep in the stern of the little fishing-boat, and His hunger and His thirst, are very precious as aids in realizing His perfect manhood; but they have a worth beyond even that. They show us how the manifold ills and evils of man's fate and conduct appealed to the only pure heart that ever beat, and how quickly and warmly it, by reason of its purity, throbbed in sympathy with all the woe. One might have thought that in the present case the consciousness that His help was so near would have been sufficient to repress the sigh. One might have thought that the heavenward look would have stayed the tears. But neither the happiness of active benevolence, nor the knowledge of immediate cure, nor the glories above flooding His vision, could lift the burden from His laboring breast. And surely in this too, we may discern a law for all our efforts, that their worth shall be in proportion to the expense of feeling at which they are done. Men predict the harvests in Egypt by the height, which the river marks on the gauge of the inundation. So many feet there represent so much fertility. Tell me the depth of a Christian man's compassion, and I will tell you the measure of his fruitfulness.

What was it that drew that sigh from the heart of Jesus? One poor man stood before him, by no means the most sorely afflicted of the many wretched ones whom He healed. But He saw in him more than a solitary instance of physical infirmities. Did there not roll darkly before His thoughts that whole weltering sea of sorrow that moans round the world of which here is but one drop that He could dry up? Did there not rise black and solid, against the clear blue to which He had been looking, the mass of man's sin, of which these bodily infirmities were but a poor symbol as well as a consequence? He saw, as none but He could bear to see, the miserable realities of human life. His knowledge of all that man might be, of all that the most of men were becoming, His power of contemplating in one awful aggregate the entire sum of sorrows and sins, laid upon His heart a burden which none but He has ever endured. His communion with heaven deepened the dark shadow on earth, and the eyes that looked up to God and saw Him, could not but see foulness where others suspected none, and murderous messengers of hell walking in darkness unpenetrated by mortal sight. And all that pain of clearer knowledge of the sorrowfulness of sorrow, and the sinfulness of sin, was laid upon a heart in which was no selfishness to blunt the sharp edge of the pain nor any sin to stagnate the pity that flowed from the wound. To Jesus Christ, life was a daily martyrdom before death had "made the sacrifice complete," and He "bore our griefs and carried our sorrows" through many a weary hour before He "bare them in His own body on the tree." Therefore, "Bear ye one another's burdens, and so fulfil the law" which

Christ obeyed, becomes a command for all who would draw men to Him. And true sorrow, a sharp and real sense of pain, becomes indispensable as preparation for, and accompaniment to, our work.

Mark how in us, as in our Lord, the sigh of compassion is to be connected with the look to heaven. It follows upon that gaze. The evils become more real, more terrible, by their startling contrast with the unshadowed light which lives above cloudracks and mists. It is a sharp shock to turn from the free sweep of the heavens, starry and radiant, to the sights that meet us in "this dim spot which men call earth." Thus habitual communion with God is the root of the truest and purest compassion. It does not withdraw us from our fellow feeling with our brethren, it cultivates no isolation for undisturbed beholding of God. It at once supplies a standard by which to measure the greatness of man's godlessness, and therefore of his gloom, and a motive for laying the pain of these upon our hearts, as if they were our own. He has looked into the heavens to little purpose who has not learned how bad and how sad the world now is, and how God bends over it in pitying love.

And that same fellowship which will clear our eyes and soften our hearts, is also the one consolation which we have when our sense of "all the ills that flesh is heir to" becomes deep nearly to despair. When one thinks of the real facts of human life, and tries to conceive of the frightful meanness and passion and hate and wretchedness that have been howling and shrieking and gibbering and groaning through dreary millenniums, one's brain reels, and hope seems to be absurdity, and joy a sin against our fellows, as a feast would be in a house next door to where was a funeral. I do not wonder at settled sorrow falling upon men of vivid imagination, keen moral sense, and ordinary sensitiveness, when they brood long on the world as it is. But I do wonder at the superficial optimism which goes on with its little prophecies about human progress, and its rose-colored pictures of human life, and sees nothing to strike it dumb for ever in men's writhing miseries, blank failures, and hopeless end. Ah! brethren, if it were not for the heavenward look, how could we bear the sight of earth? "We see not yet all things put under Him." No! God knows, far enough off from that. Man's folly, man's submission to the creatures he should rule, man's agonies, and man's transgression, are a grim contrast to the psalmist's vision. If we had only earth to look to, despair of the race, expressed in settled melancholy apathy or in fierce cynicism, were the wisest attitude. But there is more within our view than earth; "we see Jesus"; we look to the heaven, and as we behold the true Man, we see more than ever, indeed, how far from that Pattern we all are; but we can bear the thought of what men as yet have been, when we see that perfect Example of what men shall be. The root and the consolation of our sorrow for men's evils is communion with God.

Let me remind you, too, that still more dangerous than the pity which is not based upon, and corrected by, the look to heaven, is the pity which does not issue in strenuous work. It is easy to excite people's emotions; but it is perilous for both the operator and the subject, unless they be excited through the understanding, and pass on the impulse to the will and the practical powers. The surest way to petrify a heart is to stimulate the feelings, and give them nothing to do. They will never recover their original elasticity if they have been wantonly drawn forth thus. Coldness, hypocrisy, spurious sentimentalism, and a whole train of affectations and falsehoods follow the steps of an emotional religion, which divorces itself from active work. Pity is meant to impel to help. Let us not be content with painting sad and true pictures of men's woes,—of the gloomy hopelessness of idolatry, for instance—but let us remember that every time our compassion is stirred, and no action ensues, our hearts are in some measure indurated, and the sincerity of our religion in some degree impaired. White-robed Pity is meant to guide the strong powers of practical help to their work. She is to them as eyes to go before them and point their tasks. They are to her as hands to execute her gentle will. Let us see to it that we rend them not apart; for idle pity is unblessed and fruitless as a sigh cast into the fragrant air, and unpitying work is more unblessed and fruitless still. Let us remember, too, that Christlike and indispensable as Pity is, she is second, and not first. Let us take heed that we preserve that order in our own minds, and in our endeavors to stimulate one another. For if we reverse it, we shall surely find the fountains of compassion drying up long before the wide stretches of thirsty land are watered, and the enterprises which we have sought to carry on by appealing to a secondary motive, languishing when there is most need for vigor. Here is the true sequence which must be observed in our missionary and evangelistic work, "Looking up to heaven, He sighed."

Dear brethren! must we not all acknowledge woeful failures in this regard? How much of our service, our giving, our preaching, our planning, has been carried on without one thought of the ills and godlessness we profess to be seeking to cure! If some angel's touch could annihilate all that portion of our activity, what gaps would be left in all our subscription lists, our sermons, and our labors both at home and abroad! Annihilate, do I say? It is done already. Such work is nothing, and comes to nothing. "Yea, it shall not be planted; yea, it shall not be sown; and He shall also blow upon it, and it shall wither."

The hindrances to such abiding consciousness of and pity for the world's woes all run down to the one taproot of all sin, selfishness. The remedies all run up to the common form of all goodness, the self-absorbing communion with Jesus Christ. And besides that mother-tincture of everything wrong, subsidiary impediments may be found in the small amount of time and effort which any of us give to bring the facts of the world's condition vividly before our minds. The destruction of all emotion is the indolent acquiescence in general statements which we are too lazy or busy to break up into individual cases. To talk about hundreds of millions of idolaters leaves the heart untouched. But take one soul out of all that mass, and try to feel what his life is in its pitchy darkness, broken only by lurid lights of fear and sickly gleams of hope, in its passions ungoverned by love, its remorse uncalmed by pardon, its affections feeling like the tendrils of some climbing plant for the stay they cannot find, and in the cruel blackness that swallows it up irrevocably at last. Follow it from the childhood that knows no discipline to the grave that knows no waking, and will not the solitary instance come nearer our hearts than the millions?

But however that may be, the sluggishness of our imaginations, the very familiarity with the awful facts, our own feeble hold on Christ, our absorption in personal interests, the incompleteness and desultoriness of our communion with our Lord, do all concur with our natural selfishness to make a sadly large proportion of our apparent labors for God and men utterly cold and unfeeling, and therefore utterly worthless. Has the benighted world ever caused us as much pain as some trivial pecuniary loss has done? Have we ever felt the smart of the gaping wounds through which our brothers' blood is pouring forth as much as we do the tiniest scratch on our own fingers? Does it sound to us like exaggerated rhetoric when a prophet breaks out, "Oh that my head were waters, and mine eyes a fountain of tears, that I might weep night and day!" or when an Apostle in calmer tones declares, "I have great heaviness and continual sorrow of heart"? Some seeds are put to steep and swell in water, that they may be tested before sowing. The seed which we sow will not germinate unless it be saturated with our tears. And yet the sorrow must be blended with joy; for it is glad labor which is ordinarily productive labor—just as the growing time is the changeful April, and one knows not whether the promise of harvest is most sure in the clouds that drop fatness, or in the sunshine that makes their depths throb with whitest light, and touches the moist-springing blades into emeralds and diamonds. The gladness comes from the heavenward look, the pain is breathed in the deep-drawn sigh; both must be united in us if we would "approve ourselves as the servants of God—as sorrowful, yet always rejoicing."

3. We have here loving contact with those whom we would help set forth in the Lord's touch. The reasons for the variety observable in

Christ's method of communicating supernatural blessing were, probably, too closely connected with unrecorded differences in the spiritual conditions of the recipients to be distinctly traceable by us. But though we cannot tell why a particular method was employed in a given case, why now a word, and now a symbolic action, now the touch of His hand, and now the hem of His garment, appeared to be the vehicles of His power, we can discern the significance of these divers ways, and learn great lessons from them all.

His touch was sometimes obviously the result of what one may venture to call instinctive tenderness, as when He lifted the little children in His arms and laid His hands upon their heads. It was, I suppose, always the spontaneous expression of love and compassion, even when it was something more. The touch of His hand on the ghastly glossiness of the leper's skin was, no doubt, His assertion of priestly functions, and of elevation above all laws of defilement; but what was it to the poor outcast, who for years had never felt the warm contact of flesh and blood? It always indicated that He Himself was the source of healing and life. It always expressed His identification of Himself with sorrow and sickness. So that it is in principle analogous to, and may be taken as illustrative of, that transcendent act whereby He "became flesh, and dwelt among us." Indeed, the very word by which our Lord's taking the blind man by the hand is described in the chapter following our text, is that employed in the Epistle to the Hebrews when, dealing with the true brotherhood of Jesus, the writer says, "He took not hold of angels, but of the seed of Abraham He taketh hold." Christ's touch is His willing contact with man's infirmities and sins, that He may strengthen and hallow.

And the lesson is one of universal application. Wherever men would help their fellows, this is a prime requisite, that the would-be helper should come down to the level of those whom he desires to aid. If we wish to teach, we must stoop to think the scholar's thoughts. The master who has forgotten his boyhood will have poor success. If we would lead to purer emotions, we must try to enter into the lower feelings which we labor to elevate. It is of no use to stand at the mouth of the alleys we wish to cleanse, with our skirts daintily gathered about us, and smelling-bottle in hand, to preach homilies on the virtues of cleanliness. We must go in among the filth, and handle it, if we want to have it cleared away. The degraded must feel that we do not shrink from them, or we shall do them no good. The leper, shunned by all, and ashamed of himself because everybody loathes him, hungers in his hovel for the grasp of a hand that does not care for defilement, if it can bring cleansing. Even in regard to common material helps the principle holds good. We are too apt to cast our doles to the poor like bones to a dog, and then to wonder at what we are pleased to think men's ingratitude. A benefit may be so conferred as to hurt more than a blow; and we cannot be surprised if so-called charity which is given with contempt and a sense of superiority, should be received with a scowl, and chafe a man's spirit like a fetter. Such gifts bless neither him who gives nor him who takes. We must put our hearts into them, if we would win hearts by them. We must be ready, like our Master, to take blind beggars by the hand, if we would bless or help them. The despair and opprobrium of our modern civilization; the mournful failure of legalized help, and of delegated efforts to bridge it over, the darkening ignorance, the animal sensuousness, the utter heathenism that lives within a stone's throw of Christian houses, and near enough to hear the sound of public worship—will yield to nothing but that sadly forgotten law which enjoins personal contact with the sinful and the suffering, as one chief condition of raising them from the black mire in which they welter.

But the same law has its special application in regard to the enterprise of Christian missions.

It defines the spirit in which Christian men should proclaim the Gospel. The effect of much well-meant Christian effort is simply to irritate. People are very quick to catch delicate intonations which reveal a secret sense, "how much better, wiser, more devout I am than these people!" and wherever a trace of that appears in our work, the good of it is apt to be marred. We all know how hackneyed the charge of spiritual pride and Pharisaic self-complacency is, and, thank God, how unjust it often is. But averse as men may be to the truths which humble, and willing as they may be to assume that the very effort on our parts to present these to others implies a claim which they resent, we may at least learn from the threadbare calumny, what strikes men about our position, and what rouses their antagonism to us. It is allowable to be taught by our enemies, especially when it is such a lesson as this, that we must carefully divest our evangelistic work of apparent pretensions to superiority, and take our stand by the side of those to whom we speak. We cannot lecture men into the love of Christ. We can win them to it only by showing Christ's love to them; and not the least important element in that process is the exhibition of our own love. We have a Gospel to speak of which the very heart is that the Son of God stooped to become one with the lowliest and most sinful; and how can that Gospel be spoken with power unless we too stoop like Him? We have to echo the invitation, "Learn of Me, for I am lowly in heart"; and how can such divine words flow from lips into which like grace has not been poured? Our theme is a Saviour who shrank from no sinner, who gladly consorted with publicans and harlots, who laid His hand on pollution, and His heart, full of God and of love, on hearts reeking with sin; and how can our message correspond with our theme if, even in delivering it, we are saying to ourselves, ''The Temple of the Lord are we: this people which knoweth not the law is cursed''? Let us beware of the very real danger which besets us in this matter, and earnestly seek to make ourselves one with those whom we would gather into Christ, by actual familiarity with their condition, and by identification of ourselves in feeling with them, after the example of that greatest of Christian teachers who became ''all things to all men, that by all means he might gain some''; after the higher example, which Paul followed, of that dear Lord who, being Highest, descended to the lowest, and in the days of His humiliation was not content with speaking words of power from afar, nor abhorred the contact of morality and disease and loathsome corruption; but laid His hands upon death, and it lived; upon sickness, and it was whole; on rotting leprosy, and it was sweet as the flesh of a little child.

The same principle might be further applied to our Christian work, as affecting the form in which we should present the truth. The sympathetic identification of ourselves with those to whom we try to carry the Gospel will certainly make us wise to know how to shape our message. Seeing with their eyes, we shall be able to graduate the light. Thinking their thoughts, and having in some measure succeeded, by force of sheer community of feeling, in having, as it were, got inside their minds, we shall unconsciously, and without effort, be led to such aspects of Christ's all-comprehensive truth as they most need. There will be no shooting over people's heads, if we love them well enough to understand them. There will be no toothless generalities, when our interest in men keeps their actual condition and temptations clear before us. There will be no flinging fossil doctrines at them from a height, as if Christ's blessed Gospel were, in another than the literal sense, ''a stone of offense,'' if we have taken our place on their level. And without such sympathy, these and a thousand other weaknesses and faults will certainly vitiate much of our Christian effort.

Let me not be misunderstood when I speak of adapting our presentation of the Gospel to the wants of those to whom we carry it. That general statement may express the plainest dictate of Christian prudence or the most dangerous practical error. The one great truth of the Gospel wants no adaptation, by our handling, to any soul of man. It is fitted for all, and demands only plain, loving, earnest statement. There must be no tampering with central verities, nor any diplomatic reserve on the plea of consulting the needs of the men whom we address. Every sinful spirit needs the simple Gospel of salvation by Jesus Christ more than it needs anything else. Nor does adaptation mean deferential stretching a point to meet man's wishes in our presentation of the truth. Their wishes have to be contravened, that their wants may be met. The truth which a man or a generation requires most is the truth which he or it likes least; and the true Christian teacher's adaptation of his message will consist quite as much in opposing the desires and contradicting the lies, as in seeking to meet the felt wants, of the world. Nauseous medicines or sharp lancets are adapted to the sick man, quite as truly as pleasant food and soothing ointment.

But remembering all this, we still have a wide field for the operation of practical wisdom and loving common sense, in determining the form of our message and the manner of our action. And not the least important of qualifications for solving the problems connected therewith is cheerful identification of ourselves with the thoughts and feelings of those whom we would fain draw to the love of God. Such contact with men will win their hearts, as well as soften ours. It will make them willing to hear, as well as us wise to speak. It will enrich our own lives with wide experience and multiplied interests. It will lift us out of the enchanted circle which selfishness draws around us. It will silently proclaim the Lord from whom we have learnt it. The clasp of the hand will be precious, even apart from the virtue that may flow from it, and may be to many a soul burdened with a consciousness of corruption, the dawning of belief in a love that does not shrink even from its foulness. Let us preach the Lord's touch as the source of all cleansing. Let us imitate it in our lives, that "if any will not hear the word, they may without the word be won.

4. We have here the true healing power and the consciousness of wielding it set forth in the Lord's authoritative word. All the rest of His action was either the spontaneous expression of His true participation in human sorrow, or a merciful veiling of His glory that sense-bound eyes might see it the better. But the word was the utterance of His will, and that was omnipotent. The hand laid on the sick, the blind or the deaf was not even the channel of His power. The bare putting forth of His energy was all-sufficient. In these we see the loving, pitying man. In this blazes forth, yet more loving, yet more compassionate, the effulgence of manifest God. Therefore so often do we read the very syllables with which His "voice then shook the earth," vibrating through all the framework of the material universe. Therefore do the Gospels bid us listen when He rebukes the fever, and it departs; when He says to the demons "Go," and they go; when one word louder in its human articulation than the howling wind hushes the surges; when "Talitha cumi" brings back the fair young spirit from dreary wanderings among the shades of death. Therefore was it a height of faith not found in Israel when the Gentile soldier, whose training had taught him the power of absolute authority, as heathenism had driven him to long for a man who should speak with the imperial sway of a god, recognized in His voice an all-commanding power. From of old, the very signature of divinity has been declared to be, "He spake, and it was done"; and He, the breath of whose lips could set in motion material changes, is that Eternal Word, by whom all things were made.

What unlimited consciousness of sovereign dominion sounds in that imperative from His autocratic lips! It is spoken in deaf ears, but He knows that it will be heard. He speaks as the fontal source, not as the recipient channel, of healing. He anticipates no delay, no resistance. There is neither effort nor uncertainty in the curt command. He is sure that He has power, and He is sure that the power is His own.

There is no analogy here between us and Him. Alone, fronting the whole race of man, He stands—utterer of a word which none can say after Him, possessor of unshared might, "and of His fulness do all we receive." But even from that divine authority and solitary sovereign consciousness we may gather lessons of infinite value for all Christian workers. Of His fulness we *have* received, and the power of the word on His lips may teach us that of His word even on ours, as the victorious certainty with which He spake His will of healing may remind us of the confidence with which it becomes us to proclaim His name.

His will was almighty then. Is it less mighty or less loving now? Does it not gather all the world in the sweep of its mighty purpose of mercy? His voice pierced then into the dull, cold ear of death, and has it become weaker since? His word spoken *by* Him was enough to banish the foul spirits that run riot, swine-like, in the garden of God in man's soul, trampling down and eating up its flowers and fruitage; is the word spoken *of* Him less potent to cast them out? Were not all the mighty deeds which He wrought by the breath of His lips on men's bodies prophecies of the yet mightier ones which His Will of love, and the utterance of that Will by stammering lips, may work on men's souls? Let us not in our faint-heartedness number up our failures, the deaf that will not hear, the dumb that will not speak His praise, nor unbelievingly say, "Christ's own word was mighty, but the word concerning Christ is weak on our lips." Not so; our lips are unclean, and our words are weak, but His word—the utterance of His loving Will that men should be saved—is what it always was and always will be. We have it, brethren, to proclaim. Did our Master countenance the faithless contrast between the living force of His word when He dwelt on earth, and the feebleness of it as He speaks through His servant? If He did, what did He mean when He said, "He that believeth on Me, the works that I do shall he do also, and greater works than these shall he do, because I go unto the Father"?

And the reflection of Christ's triumphant consciousness of power should irradiate our spirits as we do His work, like the gleam from gazing on God's glory which shone on the lawgiver's stern face while he talked with men. We have everything to assure us that we cannot fail. The manifest fitness of the Gospel to be the food of all souls; the victories of nineteen centuries, which at least prove that all conditions of society, all classes of civilization, all varities of race, all peculiarities of individual temperament, all depths of degradation and distances of alienation, are capable of receiving the word, which, like corn, can grow in every latitude, and, though it be an exotic everywhere, can anywhere be naturalized; the firm promises of unchanging faithfulness, the universal aspect of Christ's work, the prevalence of His continual intercession, the indwelling of His abiding Spirit, and, not least, the unerring voice of our own experience of the power of the truth to bless and save—all these are ours. In view of these, what should make us doubt? Unwavering confidence is the only attitude that corresponds to such certainties. We have a rock to build on; let us build on it *with* rock. Putting fear and hesitancy far from us, let us gird ourselves with the joyful strength of assured victory, striking as those who know that conquest is bound to their standard, and who through all the dust of the field see the fair vision of the final triumph. The work is done before we begin it. "It is finished" was a clarion blast proclaiming that all was won when all seemed lost. Weary ages have indeed to roll away before the great voice from heaven shall declare, "It is done"; but all that lies between the two is but the gradual unfolding and appropriating of the results which are already secured. The "strong man" is bound; what remains is but the "spoiling of his house." The head is bruised; what remains is but the dying lashing of the snaky horror's powerless coils. "I send you to reap that whereon ye bestowed no labor." The tearful sowing in the stormy winter's day has been done by the Son of Man. For us there remains the joy of harvest—hot and hard work, indeed, but gladsome too.

Then, however languor and despondency may sometimes tempt us, thinking of slow advancement and of dying men who fade from the place of the living before the gradual light has reached their eyes, our duty is plain—to be sure that the word we carry cannot fail. You remember the old story how, when Jerusalem was in her hour of direst need, and the army of Babylon lay around her battered walls, the prophet was bid to buy "the field that is in Anathoth, in the country of Benjamin," for a sign that the transient fury of the invader would be beaten back, that Israel might again dwell safely in the land. So with us, the host of our King's enemies comes up like a river strong and mighty; but all this world, held though it be by the usurper is still "Thy land, O Immanuel," and over it all Thy peaceful rule shall be established!

Many things in this day tempt the witnesses of God to speak with doubting voice. Angry opposition, contemptuous denial, complacent assumption that a belief in old-fashioned evangelical truth is, *ipso facto,* a proof of mental weakness, abound. Let them not rob us of our confidence. Shame on us if we let ourselves be frightened from it by a sarcasm or a laugh! Do you fall back on all these grounds for assured reliance to which I have referred, and make the good old answer yours, "Why, herein is a marvelous thing, that ye know not whence He is, and yet—He hath opened mine eyes"!

Trust the word which you have to speak. Speak it and work for its diffusion as if you did trust it. Do not preach it as if it were a notion of your own. In so far as it is, it will share the fate of all human conceptions of divine realities—"will have its day, and cease to be." Do not speak it as if it were some new nostrum for curing the ills of humanity, which might answer or might not. Speak it as if it were what it is—"the word of God which liveth and abideth for ever." Speak it as if you were what you are, neither its inventors nor its discoverers, but only its messengers, who have but to "preach the preaching which He bids" you. And to all the widespread questionings of this day, filmy and air-filling as the gossamers of an autumn evening, to all the theories of speculation, and all the panaceas of unbelieving philanthropy, present the solid certainties of your inmost experience, and the yet more solid certainty of that all-loving name and all-sufficient work on which these repose. "*We know* that we are of God, and the whole world lieth in wickedness. And we know that the Son of God is come." Then our proclamation, "This is the true God and eternal life," will not be in vain; and our loving entreaty, "Keep yourselves from idols,' will be heard and yielded to in many a land.

The sum of the whole matter is briefly this. The root of all our efficiency in this great task to which we, unworthy, have been called, is in fellowship with Jesus Christ. "The branch cannot bear fruit of itself; without Me ye can do nothing." Living near Him, and growing like Him by gazing upon Him, His beauty will pass into our faces, His tender pity into our hearts, His loving identification of Himself with men's pains and sins will fashion our lives; and the word which He spoke with authority and assured confidence will be strong when we speak it with like calm certainty of victory. If the Church of Christ will but draw close to her Lord till the fulness of His life and the gentleness of His pity flow into her heart and limbs, she will then be able to breathe the life which she has received into the prostrate bulk of a dead world. Only she must do as the meekest of the prophets did in a like miracle. She must not shrink from the touch of the cold clay nor the odor of incipient corruption, but lip to lip and heart to heart must lay herself upon the dead and he will live.

The pattern for our work, dear brethren, is before us in the Lord's look, His sigh, His touch, His word. If we take Him for the example, and Him for the motive, Him for the strength, Him for the theme, Him for the reward, of our service, we may venture to look to Him as the prophecy of our success, and to be sure that when our own faint hearts or an unbelieving world question the wisdom of our enterprise or the worth of our efforts, we may answer as He did, "Go and show again those things which ye do hear and see; the blind receive their sight, and the lame walk, the lepers are cleansed, and the deaf hear, the dead are raised up, and the poor have the Gospel preached unto them."

8

Teaching Slow Learners

The Patient Teacher, and the Slow Scholars

And when Jesus knew it, He saith unto them, Why reason ye, because ye have no bread? perceive ye not yet, neither understand? have ye your heart yet hardened? 18. Having eyes, see ye not? having ears, hear ye not? and do ye not remember? MARK 8:17, 18.

How different were the thoughts of Christ and of His disciples, as they sat together in the boat, making their way across the lake! He was pursuing a train of sad reflections which, the moment before their embarkation, had caused Him to sigh deeply in His spirit and say, ''Why doth this generation seek after a sign?' Absorbed in thought, He spoke, ''Beware of the leaven of the Pharisees,'' who had been asking that question.

So meditated and spoke Jesus in the stern, and amidships the disciples' thoughts were only concerned about the negligent omission, very excusable in the hurry of embarkation, by which they had forgotten to lay in a fresh supply of provisions, and had set sail with but one loaf left in the boat. So taken up were they with this petty trouble that they twisted the Master's words as they fell from His lips, and thought that He was rebuking them for what they were rebuking themselves for. So apt are we to interpret others' sayings by the thoughts uppermost in our own minds.

And then our Lord poured out this altogether unusual—perhaps I may say unique—hail of questions which indicate how deeply moved from His ordinary calm He was by this strange slowness of apprehension on the part of His disciples. There is no other instance that I can recall in the whole Gospels, with the exception of Gethsemane, where our Lord's words seem to indicate such agitation of the windless sea of His spirit as this rapid succession of rebuking interrogations. They give a glimpse into the depths of His mind, showing us what He generally kept sacredly shut up, and let us see how deeply He was touched and pained by the slowness of apprehension of His servants.

Let us look at these questions as suggesting to us two things—the grieved Teacher and the slow scholars.

1. The Grieved Teacher. I have said that the revelation of the depths of our Lord's experience here is unexampled. We can understand the mood of which it is the utterance; the feeling of despair that sometimes comes over the most patient instructor when he finds that all his efforts to hammer some truth into, or to print some impression on, the brain or heart of man or boy, have been foiled, and that years, it may be, of patient work have scarcely left more traces on unretentive minds than remain on the ocean of the passage through it of a keel.

Christ felt that; and I do not think we half enough realize how large an element in the sorrows of the Man of Sorrows, and of the grief with which He was acquainted, was His necessary association with people who, He felt, did not in the least degree understand Him, however truly, blindly, and almost animally, they might love Him. It was His disciples' misconception that stung him most. If I might so say, He *calculated* upon being misunderstood by Pharisees and outsiders, but that these followers who had been gathered round about Him all these months, and had been the subjects of His sedulous toil, should blurt out such words as these which precede the question of my text, cut deep into that loving heart. It was not only the pain of being misunderstood, but also the pain of feeling that the people who cared most for Him did not understand Him, and were so hard to drag up to the level where they could even catch a glimpse of His meaning, that struck His heart with almost a kind of despair; and, as I said, made Him pour out this rain of questions.

And what do the questions suggest? Not only emotion very unusual in Him, yet truly human, and showing Him to be our Brother; but they suggest three distinct types of emotion, all of them dashed with pain.

"Why reason ye? Having eyes, see ye not? Do ye not remember?" That speaks of His astonishment. Do not start at the word, or suppose that it in any degree contradicts the lofty beliefs that I suppose most of us have with regard to the Deity of our Lord and Saviour. We find in another place in the Gospels, not by inference as here, but in plain words, the ascription to Him of wonder; "He marveled at their unbelief." And we read of a more blessed kind of surprise as having once been His, when He wondered at the faith of the heathen centurion. But here His astonishment is that after all these years of toil, and of sympathy, and of discipleship, and of listening and trying to get hold of His meaning, His disciples were so far away from any understanding of what He was driving at. He had to learn by experience the depths of men's stupidity and ignorance. And although He was the Word of God made flesh, we recognize here the token of a true brother in that He was capable not only of the physical feelings of weariness, and hunger, and thirst, and pain, but that He, too, had the emotion which only a limited understanding can have—the emotion of wonder. And it was drawn out by His disciples' denseness and inertness.

Ah! dear friends, does He not wonder at us? One of the prophets says, "Be astonished, O heavens!" And be sure of this, that the manhood of Jesus Christ is not now so lifted up above what it was upon earth as that the same sensation—twin sister to yours and mine—of surprise, does not sometimes visit Him when He looks down upon us; and has to say to us—as, alas! He has to say—what He once said to one of the Twelve, "Have I been so long time with you, and yet hast thou not known me, Philip?" Is not the same question coming to us? Why is it that we do not understand?

Wonder, then, is the first emotion that is expressed in this question. There is another one: Pain. And there again I fall back not upon inference, but upon plain words of another part of the Gospels. "He looked round upon them with anger, being *grieved* at the hardness of their hearts." It seems daring to venture to say that the exalted and glorified humanity of Jesus Christ today is, in any measure, capable of feeling analogous to that; but it will not seem so daring if you remember the solemn charge of one of the Apostles, "Grieve not the Holy Spirit of God." It is Christ's disciples that pain Him most. "They vexed His Holy Spirit, therefore He fought against them." Brethren, let us look into our own hearts and our own lives, and ask ourselves if there is not something there that gives a pang even to the heart of the glorified Master, and makes Him sigh deeply within Himself?

May I add one more emotion which seems to me to be unmistakably expressed by this rapid fusillade of questions? That is indignation. Again I fall back upon plain words: "He looked round about upon them with anger, being grieved." The two things were braided together in His heart, and did not conflict with each other. There were infinite sorrow, infinite pity, and real displeasure. You must take all notions of passion and of malignity, and of desire to do harm to the subject, out of the conception of anger as applied to God or Christ who is the revelation of God. But it seems to me that it is a maimed Christ that we put before the world unless we say that in the Love there lie the possibilities of Wrath. "Behold the Lion of the tribe of Judah, and I beheld, and lo! a Lamb!" Wrath and gentleness are in Him inseparably united, neither of them limiting nor making impossible the other.

So here we have a self-revelation, as by one glimpse into a great chamber, of the deep heart of Christ, the great Teacher, moved to astonishment, grief, and indignation.

2. Now let me say a word about the slow scholars. I have spoken of these questions as being rapid and repeated, and as a rain of what we may almost call fiery interrogation. But they are by no means tautology or useless and aimless repetition. If we look at them closely, I think we shall see that they open out to use several different sides and phases of the fault in His disciples that moves these emotions.

There is, first, His scholars' stolid insensibility, which moves Him to anger, to astonishment, and to grief. ''Are your hearts yet hardened?'' by which is meant, not hardened in the sense of being suddenly and stiffly set in antagonism to Him, but simply in the sense of being—may I use the word?—so pachydermatous, so thick-skinned, that nothing can go through them. They showed it is a dull, stolid insensibility, and it marks some of us professing Christians, on whom promises and invitations and revelations of truth all fall with equal ineffectiveness, and from whom they glide off with equal rapidity. You may rain upon a black basalt rock to all eternity, and nothing will grow upon it. All the drops will run down the polished sides, and a quarter of an inch below the surface it will be as dry as it was before the first drop fell. And here are we Christian ministers, talk-talk-talking, week in and week out; and here is Christ, by His providences and by His word, speaking far more loudly than any of us; and it all falls with absolute impotence on hosts of people that call themselves Christians. Ah! brethren, it is not only unbelievers who have their hearts hardened. Orthodox professors are often guilty of the same. If I might alter the metaphor, many of us have waterproofed our minds, and the ingredients of the mixture by which we have waterproofed them are our knowledge of ''the plan of salvation,'' our connection with a Christian community, our membership in a church, our obedience to the formalisms of the devout life. All these have only made a non-transmitting medium interposed between ourselves and the concentrated electric energy that ever flashes from Jesus Christ. Our hardened hearts, with their stolid insensibility, amaze our Master, and no wonder that they do.

But that is not all. There is not only what I have ventured to call stolid insensibility, but, as a result of it, there is the not using the capacities that we have. ''Having eyes, see ye not? Having ears, hear ye not?'' We are not like children that cannot, but like careless, untrained schoolboys that will not, learn. We have the capacity, and it is our own fault that we are dunces in the school, and at the bottom of the class. Use the power that you have, and ''unto him that hath shall be given, and he shall have in abundance.'' There are fishes in the caverns of North America that have lived so long in the dark, underground channels, that the present generation of them has no eyes. We are doing our best to deprive ourselves of our capacities of beholding by refusing to use them. ''Having eyes, see ye not?'' Our non-use of the powers we have amazes and grieves our Master.

Further, the reason why there are this stolid insensibility and this non-use of capacity lies here: ''Ye reason about the bread.'' The absorption of our minds and efforts and time with material things, that perish with the using, come in between us and our apprehension of Christ's teaching. Ah! brethren, it is not only the rich man that is swallowed up with the present world; the poor man may be so as really. All of us, by reason of the absolute necessities of our lives, are in danger of getting our hearts so filled and crowded with the things that are ''seen and temporal'' that we have no time, nor room, for the things that are ''unseen and eternal.'' I do not need to elaborate that point. We all know that it is there that our danger, in various forms, lies. If you in the bows of the ship are reasoning about bread, you will misunderstand Christ in the stern warning against ''the leaven of the Pharisees.''

The last suggestion from these questions is that the cure for all that stolid insensibility, and its resulting misuse of capacity, and the absorption in daily visible things, is remembrance of His and our past—''Do ye not remember?'' It was only that same morning, or the day before at the furthest, that one of the miracles of feeding the thousands had been performed. Christ wonders, as well He might, at the short memories of the disciples who, with the basketfuls of fragments scarcely eaten yet, could worry themselvs because there was only one loaf in the locker. ''Do ye not remember, when I broke the loaves among the thousands, how many baskets took ye up? And they said, seven. And He said, How is it that ye do not understand?'' Yes, Memory is the one wing and Hope the other, that lift our heaviness from earth towards heaven. And any man who will bethink himself of what Jesus Christ has been for him, did for him on earth, and has done for him during his life, will not be so absorbed in worldly cares as that he will have no eyes to see the things unseen and eternal; and the hard, dead insensibility of his heart will melt into thankful consecration, and so he will rise nearer and nearer to intelligent apprehension of the lofty and deep things that the Incarnate Word says to him. We are here in Christ's school, and it depends upon the place in the class that we take here where we shall be put at what schoolboys call the ''next remove.'' If here we have indeed ''learned of Him the truth as it is in Jesus,'' we shall be put up into the top classes yonder, and get larger and more blessed lessons in the Father's house above.

The Religious Uses of Memory

Do ye not remember! MARK 8:18.

The disciples had misunderstood our Lord's warning "against the leaven of the Pharisees," which they supposd to have been occasioned by their neglect to bring with them bread. Their blunder was like many others which they committed, but it seems to have singularly moved our Lord, who was usually so patient with His slow scholars. The swift rain of questions, like bullets rattling against a cuirass, of which my text is one, shows how much He was moved, if not to impatience or anger, at least to wonder.

But what I wish particularly to notice is that He traces the disciples' slowness of perception and distrust mainly to forgetfulness. There was a special reason for that, of course, in that the two miracles of the feeding the multitude, one of which had just before occurred, ought to have delivered them from any uneasiness, and to have led them to apprehend His higher meaning.

But there is a wider reason for the collocation of questions than this. There is no better armor against distrust, nor any surer purge of our spiritual sight, than religious remembrance. So my text falls in with what I hope are, or at any rate should be, thoughts which are busy in many of our hearts now. Every Sunday is the last Sunday of a year. But we are influenced by the calendar, even though there is nothing in reality to correspond with the apparent break, and though time runs on in a continuous course. I would fain say a word or two now which may fit in with thoughts that are wholesome for us always, but, I suppose, come with most force to most of us at such a date as this. And, if you will let me, I will put my observations in the form of exhortations.

1. First of all, then, remember and be thankful. There are few of us who have much time for retrospection, and there is a very deep sense in which it is wise to "forget the things that are behind," for the remembrance of them may burden us with a miserable entail of failure; may weaken us by vain regrets, may unfit us for energetic action in the living and available present. But oblivion is foolish, if it is continual, and a remembered past has treasures in it which we can little afford to lose.

Chiefest of these is the power of memory, when applied to our own past lives, to bring out, more clearly than was possible while that past was being lived, the perception of the ever-present care and working of our Father, God. It is hard to recognize Him in the bustle and hurry of our daily lives, and the meaning of each event can only be seen when it is seen in its relation to the rest of a life. Just as a landscape, which we may look at without the smallest perception of its beauty, becomes another thing when the genius of a painter puts it on canvas, and its symmetry and proportion become more manifest, and an ethereal clearness broods over it, and its colors are seen to be deeper than our eyes had discerned, so the common events of life, trivial and insignificant while they are passing, become, when painted on the canvas of memory, nobler and greater, and we understand them more completely than we can do whilst we are living in them.

We need to be at the goal in order to judge of the road. The parts are only explicable when we see the whole. The full interpretation of today is reserved for eternity. But, by combining and massing and presenting the consequences of the apparently insignificant and isolated events of the past, memory helps us to a clearer perception of God, and a better understanding of our own lives. On the mountain summit a man can look down all along the valley by which he has wearily plodded, and understand the meaning of the divergences in the road, and the rough places do not look quite so rough when their proportion to the whole is a little more clearly in his view.

Only, brethren, if we are wisely to exercise remembrance, and to discover God in the lives which, whilst they are passing, had little perception of Him, we must take into account what the meaning of all life is—that is, to make men of us after the pattern of His will.

> Not enjoyment, and not sorrow,
> Is our destined end or way.

But the growth of Christlike and God-pleasing character is the divine purpose, and should be the human aim, of all lives. Our tasks, our joys, our sorrows, our gains, our losses—these are all but the scaffolding, and the scaffolding is only there in order that, course upon course, there may rise the temple-palace of a spirit, devoted to, shaped and inhabited by, our Father, God.

So I venture to say that thankful remembrance should exclude no single incident, however bitter, however painful, of any life. There is a remembrance of vanished hands, of voices forever stilled, which is altogether wrong and weakening. There is a regret, a vain regret which comes with memory for some of us, that interferes with thankfulness.

But it is possible—and, if we understand that the meaning of all is to make us Godlike, it is not hard—to remember vanished joys, and to confer upon them by remembrance a kind of gentle immortality. And, thus remembered, they are ennobled; for all the gross material body of them, as it were, is got rid of, and only the fine spirit is left. The roses bloom, and overbloom, and drop, but a poignant perfume is distilled from the fallen petals. The departed are greatened by distance; when they are gone we recognize the "angels" that we "entertained unawares": and that recognition is no illusion, but it is the disclosure of their real character, to which they were sometimes untrue, and we were often blind. Therefore I say, "Thou shalt remember all the way by which the Lord thy God hath led thee," and in the thankfulness include departed joys, vanished hands, present sorrows, the rough places as well as the smooth, the crooked things as well as the straight.

2. Secondly, let me say, remember and repent. Memory is not wise unless it is, so to speak, the sergeant-at-arms of Conscience, and brings our past before the bar of that judge within, and puts into the hands of that judge the law of the Lord by which to estimate our deeds. We all have been making up our accounts to the 31st of December—or are going to do it tomorrow. And what I plead for is that we should take stock of our own characters and aims, and sum up our accounts with duty and with God.

We look back upon a past, of which God gave us the warp and we had to put in the woof. The warp is all bright and pure. The threads that have crossed it from our shuttles are many of them very dark, and all of them stained in some part. So, dear brethren, let us take the year that has gone, and spread them out by the agency of this servant of the court, Memory, before the supreme judge, Conscience.

Let us remember that we may be warned and directed. We shall understand the true moral character of our actions a great deal better when we look back upon them calmly, and when all the rush of temptation and the reducing whispers of our own weak wills are silenced. There is nothing more terrible, in one aspect, there is nothing more salutary and blessed in another, than the difference between the front and the back view of any temptation to which we yield—all radiant and beautiful on the hither side, and when we get past it and look back at it, all hideous. Like some of those painted canvases upon the theater stage: seen from this side, with the delusive brilliancy of the footlights thrown upon them, they are beautiful works of art; seen at the back, dirty and cobwebbed canvas, all splashes and spots and uglinesses. Let us be thankful if memory can show us the reverse side of the temptations that on the near side were so seductive.

It is when you see your life in retrospect that you understand the significance of the single deeds in it. We are so apt to isolate our actions that we are startled—and it is a wholesome shock—when we see how, without knowing it, we have dropped into a habit. When each temptation comes, as the moments are passing, we say, "Oh, just this once, just this once." And the *"onces"* come nearer and nearer together; and what seem to be distinctly separated points, coalesce into a line; and the acts that we thought isolated we find out to our horror—our wholesome horror—have become a chain that binds and holds us. Look back over the year, and drag its events to the bar of Conscience, and I shall be surprised if you do not discover that you haven fallen into wrong habits that you never dreamed had dominion over you. So, I say, remember and repent.

Brethren, I do not wish to exaggerate, I do not wish to urge upon you one-sided views of your character or conduct. I give all credit to many excellences, many acts of sacrifice, many acts of service; and yet I say that the main reason why any of us have a good opinion of ourselves is because we have no knowlege of ourselves; and that the safest attitude for all of us, in looking back over what we have made of life, is, hands on mouths, and mouths in dust, and the cry coming from them, "Unclean! Unclean!' A little mud in a stream may not be perceptible when you take a wineglassful of it and look at it, but if you saw a riverful or a lakeful you would soon discover the taint. Summon up the past year to the sessions of silent thought, and let the light of God's will pour in upon it, and you will find how dark has been the flow of the river of your lives.

The best use which the memory can serve for us is that it should drive us closer to Jesus Christ, and make us cling more closely to Him. That past can be cancelled, these multitudinous sins can be forgiven. Memory should be one of the strongest strands in the cord that binds our helplessness to the all-forgiving and all-cleansing Christ.

3. Lastly, let me say, remember and hope. Memory and Hope are twins. The latter can only work with the materials supplied by the former. Hope could paint nothing on the blank canvas of the future unless its palette were charged by Memory. Memory brings the yarn which Hope weaves.

Our thankful remembrance of a past which was filled and molded by God's perpetual presence and care ought to make us sure of a future which will in like manner be molded. "Thou hast been my help"—if we can say that, then we may confidently pray, and be sure of the answer, "Leave me not nor forsake me, O God of my salvation." And if we feel, as memory teaches us to feel, that God has been working for us, and with us, we can say with another psalmist: "Thy mercy, O Lord, endureth for ever. Forsake not the work of Thine own hands"; and we can rise to his confidence, "The Lord will perfect that which concerneth me."

Our remembrance, even of our imperfections and our losses and our sorrows, may minister to our hope. For surely the life of every man on earth, but most eminently the life of a Christian man, is utterly unintelligible, a mockery and a delusion and an incredibility, if there be a God at all, unless it prophesies of a region in which imperfection will be ended, aspirations will be fulfilled, desires will be satisfied. We have so much, that unless we are to have a great deal more, we had better have had nothing. We have so much, that if there be a God at all, we must have a great deal more. The new moon, with a ragged edge, "even in its imperfection beautiful," is a prophet of the complete resplendent orb. "On earth the broken arc, in heaven the perfect round."

Further, the memory of defeat may be the parent of the hope of victory. The stone Ebenezer, "Hitherto hath the Lord helped us," was set up to commemorate a victory that had been won on the very site where Israel, fighting the same foes, had once been beaten. There is no remembrance of failure so mistaken as that which takes the past failure as certain to be repeated in the future. Surely, though we have fallen seventy times seven—that is 490, is it not?—at the 491st attempt we may, and if we trust in God we shall, succeed.

So, brethren, let us set our faces to a new year with thankful remembrance of the God who has shaped the past, and will mold the future. Let us remember our failures, and learn wisdom and humility and trust in Christ from our sins. Let us set our "hope on God, and not forget the works of God, but Keep His commandments."

The Gradual Healing of the Blind Man

And Jesus cometh to Bethsaida; and they bring a blind man unto Him, and besought Him to touch him. 23. And He took the blind man by the hand, and led him out of the town; and when He had spit on his eyes, and put His hands upon Him, He asked him if he saw ought. 24. And he looked up, and said, I see men as trees, walking. 25. After that He put His hands again upon his eyes, and made him look up: and he was restored, and saw every man clearly. MARK 8:22–25.

This miracle, which is only recorded by the Evangelist Mark, has about it several very peculiar features. Some of these it shares with one other of our Lord's miracles, which also is found only in this Gospel, and which occurred nearly about the same time—that miracle of healing the deaf and dumb man recorded in the previous chapter. Both of them have these points in common: that our Lord takes the sufferer apart and works His miracle in privacy; that in both there is an abundant use of the same singular means—our Lord's touch and the saliva upon His finger; and that in both there is the urgent injunction of entire secrecy laid upon the recipient of the benefit.

But this miracle had another peculiarity in which it stands absolutely alone, and that is that the work is done in stages; that the power which at other times has but to speak and it is done, here seems to labor and the cure comes slowly; that in the middle Christ pauses, and, like a physician trying the experiment of a drug, asks the patient if any effect is produced, and, getting the answer that some mitigation is realized, repeats the application, and perfect recovery is the result.

Now, how unlike that is to all the rest of Christ's miraculous working we do not need to point out; but the question may arise, What is the meaning, and what the reason, and what the lessons of this unique and anomalous form of miraculous working? It is to that question that I wish to turn now; for I think that the answer will open up to us some very precious things in regard to that great Lord, the revelation of whose heart and character is the inmost and the loftiest meaning of both His words and His works.

I take these three points of peculiarity to which I have referred: the privacy, the strange and abundant use of means veiling the miraculous power, and the gradual, slow nature of the cure. I see in them these three things: Christ isolating the man that He would heal; Christ stooping to the sense-bound nature by using outward means; and Christ making His power work slowly to keep abreast of the man's slow faith.

1. First, then, here we have Christ isolating the man whom he wanted to heal. Now, there may have been something about our Lord's circumstances and purposes at the time of this miracle which accounted for the great urgency with which at this point He impressed secrecy upon all around Him. What that was it is not necessary for us to inquire here, but this is worth noticing, that in obedience to this wish, on His own part, for privacy at the time, He covers over with a veil His miraculous working, and does it quietly, as one might almost say, in a corner. He never sought to display His miraculous working; here He absolutely tries to hide it. That fact of Christ's taking pains to conceal His miracle carries in it two great truths—first, about the purpose and nature of miracles in general, and second, about His character—as to each of which a few words may be said.

This fact, of a miracle done in intended secrecy, and shrouded in deep darkness, suggests to us the true point of view from which to look at the whole subject of miracles.

People say they were meant to be attestations of His divine mission. Yes, no doubt that is true partially; but that was never the sole nor even the main purpose for which they were wrought; and when anyone asked Jesus Christ to work a miracle for that purpose only, He rebuked the desire and refused to gratify it. He wrought His miracles, not coldly, in order to witness to His mission, but every one of them was the token, because it was the outcome, of His own sympathetic heart brought into contact with human need. And instead of the miracles of Jesus Christ being cold, logical proofs of His mission, they were all glowing with the earnestness of a loving sympathy, and came from Him at sight of sorrow as naturally as rays beam out from the sun.

Then, on the other hand, the same fact carries with it, too, a lesson about His character. Is not He here doing what He tells us to do: "Let not thy left hand know what thy right hand doeth'? He dares not wrap His talent in a napkin, He would be unfaithful to His mission if He hid His light under a bushel. All goodness "does good by stealth," even if it does not "blush to find it fame"—and that universal mark of true benevolence marked His. He had to solve in His human life what we have to solve, the problem of keeping the narrow path between ostentation of powers and selfish concealmeant of faculty; and He solved it thus, "leaving us an example that we should follow in His steps."

But that is somewhat aside from the main purpose to which I intended to turn in these first remarks. Christ did not invest the miracle with any of its peculiarities for His own sake only. All that is singular about it, will, I think, find its best explanation in the condition and character of the subject, the man on whom it was wrought. What sort of a man was he? Well, the narrative does not tell us much, but if we use our historical imagination and our eyes we may learn something about him. First, he was a Gentile; the land in which the miracle was wrought was the half-heathen country on the east side of the Sea of Galilee. In the second place, it was other people that brought him; he did not come of his own accord. Then again, it is their prayer that is mentioned, not his—he asked nothing.

You see him standing there hopeless, listless; not believing that this Jewish stranger is going to do anything for him; with his impassive blind face glowing with no entreaty to reinforce his companions' prayers. And suppose he was a man of that sort, with no expectation of anything from this Rabbi, how was Christ to get at him? It is of no use to speak to him. His eyes are shut, so cannot see the sympathy beaming in His face. There is one thing possible—to lay hold of Him by the hand; and the touch, gentle, loving, firm, says this at least: "Here is a man that has some interest in me, and whether He can do anything or not for me, He is going to try something." Would not that kindle an expectation in him? And is it not in parable just exactly what Jesus Christ does for the whole world?

Is not that act of His by which He put out His hand and seized the unbelieving, limp hand of the blind man that hung by his side, the very same in principle as that by which He ''taketh hold of the seed of Abraham,'' and is made like to His brethren? Are not the mystery of the Incarnation and the meaning of it wrapped up as in a germ in that little simple incident ''He put out His hand and touched him''?

Is there not in it, too, a lesson for all you goodhearted Christian men and women, in all your work? If you want to do anything for your afflicted brethren, there is only one way to do it—to come down to their level and get hold of their hands, and then there is some chance of doing them good. We must be content to take the hands of beggars if we are to make the blind to see.

And then, having thus drawn near to the man, and established in his heart some dim expectation of something coming, He gently led him away out of the little village. I wonder no painter has ever painted that, instead of repeating *ad nauseam* two or three scenes out of the Gospels. I wonder none of them has ever seen what a parable it is—the Christ leading the blind man out into solitude before He can say to him ''Behold!'' How, as they went, step by step, the poor blind eyes not telling the man where they were going, or how far away he was being taken from his friends, his conscious dependence upon this stranger would grow! How he would feel more and more at each step, ''I am at His mercy; what *is* He going to do with me?'' And how thus there would be kindled in his heart some beginnings of an expectation, as well as some surrendering of himself to Christ's guidance! These two things, the expectation and the surrender, have in them, at all events, some faint beginnings and rude germs of the highest faith, to lead up to which is the purpose of all that Christ here does.

And is not that what He does for us all? Sometime by sorrows, sometimes by sickbeds, sometimes by shutting us out from chosen spheres of activity, sometimes by striking down the dear ones at our sides, and leaving us lonely in the desert—is He not saying to us in a thousand ways, ''Come ye yourselves apart into a desert place''? As Israel was led into the wilderness that God might ''speak to her heart,'' so often Christ draws us aside, if not by outward providences such as these, yet by awaking in us the solemn sense of personal responsibility and making us feel our solitude, that He may lead us to feel His all-sufficient companionship.

Ah! brethren, here is a lesson from all this—if you wish Jesus Christ to give you His highest gifts and to reveal to you His fairest beauty, you must be alone with Him. He loves to deal with single souls. Our lives, many of them, can never be outwardly alone. We are jammed up against one another in such a fashion, and the hurry and pressure of city life is so great with us all, that it is often impossible for us to secure outward secrecy and solitude. But a man may be alone in a crowd; the heart may be gathered up into itself, and there may be a still atmosphere round about us in the shop and in the market and amongst the busy ways of men, in which we and Christ shall be alone together. Unless there be, I do not think any of us will see the King in His beauty or the far-off land. "I was left alone, and I saw this great vision," is the law for all true beholding.

So, dear brethren, try to feel how awful this earthly life of ours is in its necessary solitude; that each of us by himself must shape out his own destiny, and make his own character; that every unit of the swarms upon our streets is a unit that has to face the solemn facts of life for and by itself; that alone we live, that alone we shall die; that alone we shall have to give account of ourselves before God, and in that solitude let the hand of your heart feel for His hand that is stretched out to grasp yours, and listen to Him saying, "Lo! I am with you always, even to the end of the world." There was no dreariness in the solitude when it was *Christ* that "took the blind man by the hand and led him out of the city."

2. We have Christ stooping to a sense-bound nature by the use of material helps. No doubt there was something in the man, as I have said, which made it advisable that these methods should be adopted. If he were the sort of person that I have described, slow of faith, not much caring about the possibility of cure, and not having much hope that any cure would come to pass—then we can see the fitness of the means adopted: the hand laid upon the eyes, the finger, possibly moistened with saliva, touching the ball, the pausing to question, the repeated application. These make a ladder by which his hope and confidence might climb to the apprehension of the blessing. And that points to a general principle of the divine dealings. God stoops to a feeble faith, and gives to it outward things by which it may rise to an apprehension of spiritual realities.

Is not that the meaning of the whole complicated system of Old Testament revelation? Is not that the meaning of the altars, and priests, and sacrifices, and the old cumbrous apparatus of the Mosaic law? Was it not all a picturebook in which the infant eyes of the race might see in a material form deep spiritual realities? Was not that the meaning and explanation of our Lord's parabolic teaching? He veils spiritual truth in common things that He may reveal it by common things—taking fishermen's boats, their nets, a sower's basket, a baker's dough, and many another homely article, and finding in them the emblems of the loftiest truth.

Is not that the meaning of His own Incarnation? It is of no use to talk to men about God—let them see Him; no use to preach about principles—give them the facts of His life. Revelation does not consist in the setting forth of certain propositions about God, but in the exhibition of the acts of God in a human life.

> And so the Word had breath, and wrought
> With human hands the creed of creeds.

And still further, may we not say that this is the inmost meaning and purpose of the whole frame of the material universe? It exists in order that, as a parable and a symbol, it may proclaim the things that are unseen and eternal. Its depths and heights, its splendors and its energies are all in order that through them spirits may climb to the apprehension of the "King, eternal, immortal, invisible," and the realities of His spiritual kingdom.

So in regard to all the externals of Christianity, forms of worship, ordinances, and so on—all these, in like manner, are provided in condescension to our weakness, in order that by them we may be lifted above themselves; for the purpose of the Temple is to prepare for the time and the place where the seer "saw no temple therein." They are but the cups that carry the wine, the flowers whose chalices bear the honey, the ladders by which the soul may climb to God Himself, the rafts upon which the precious treasure may be floated into our hearts.

If Christ's touch and Christ's saliva healed, it was not because of anything in them, but because He willed it so; and He Himself is the source of all the healing energy. Therefore, let us keep these externals in their proper place of subordination, and remember that in Him, not in them, lies the healing power; and that even Christ's touch may become the object of superstitious regard, as it was when the poor woman came through the crowd to lay her finger on the hem of His garment, thinking that she could bear away a surreptitious blessing without the conscious outgoing of His power. He healed her because there was a spark of faith in her superstition, but she had to learn that it was not the hem of the garment but the loving will of Christ that cured, in order that the dross of superstitious reliance on the outward vehicle might be melted away, and the pure gold of faith in His love and power might remain.

3. Last, we have Christ accommodating the pace of His power to the slowness of the man's faith. The whole story, as I have said, is unique, and especially this part of it—"He put His hands upon him, and asked him if he saw aught." One might have expected an answer with a little more gratitude in it, with a little more wonder in it, with a little more emotion in it. Instead of these, it is almost surly, or at any rate strangely reticent—a matter-of-fact answer to the question, and there an end. As our Revised Version reads it better: "I see men, for I behold them as trees walking." Curiously accurate! A dim glimmer had come into the eye, but there is not yet distinctness of outline nor sense of magnitude, which must be acquired by practice. The eye has not yet been educated, and it was only because these blurred figures were in motion that he knew they were not trees. "After that He put His hands upon his eyes and made him look up," or, as the Revised Version has it with a better reading, "and he looked steadfastly," with an eager straining of the new faculty to make sure that he had got it, and to test its limit and its perfection. "And he was restored and saw all things clearly."

Now I take it that the worthiest view of that strangely protracted process, broken up into two halves by the question that is dropped into the middle, is this, that it was determined by the man's faith, and was meant to increase it. He was healed slowly because he believed slowly. His faith was a condition of his cure, and the measure of it determined the measure of the restoration; and the rate of the growth of his faith settled the rate of the perfecting of Christ's work on him. As a rule, faith in His power to heal was a condition of Christ's healing, and that mainly because our Lord would rather make men believing than sound of body. They often wanted only the outward miracle, but He wanted to make it the means of insinuating a better healing into their spirits. And so, not that there was any necessary connection between their faith and the exercise of His miraculous power, but in order that He might bless them with His best gifts, He usually worked on the principle "According to your faith be it unto you." And here, as a nurse or a mother with her child might do, He keeps step with the little steps, and goes slowly because the man goes slowly.

Now, both the gradual process of illumination and the rate of that process as determined by faith, are true for us. How dim and partial a glimmer of light comes to many a soul at the outset of the Christian life! How little a new convert knows about God and self and the starry truths of His great revelation! Christian progress does not consist in seeing new things, but in seeing the old things more clearly: the same Christ, the same Cross, only more distinctly and deeply apprehended, and more closely incorporated into my very being. We do not grow away from Him, but we grow into knowledge of Him. The first lesson that we get is the last lesson that we shall learn, and He is the "Alpha" at the beginning, and the "Omega" at the end of that alphabet, the letters of which make up our knowledge for earth and heaven.

But then let me remind you that just in the measure in which you expect blessing of any kind, illumination and purifying and help of all sorts from Jesus Christ, just in that measure will you get it. You can limit the working of Almighty power, and can determine the rate of which it shall work on you. God fills the waterpots "to the brim," but not beyond the brim; and if, like the woman in the Old Testament story, we stop bringing vessels, the oil will stop flowing. It is an awful thing to think that we have the power, as it were, to turn a stopcock, and so increase or diminish, or cut off altogether, the supply of God's mercy and Christ's healing and cleansing love in our hearts. You will get as much of God as you want and no more. The measure of your desire is the measure of your capacity, and the measure of your capacity is the measure of God's gift. "Open thy mouth wide and I will fill it!" And if your faith is heavily shod and steps slowly, His power and His grace will step slowly along with it, keeping rank and step. "According to your faith shall it be unto you."

Ah! dear friends, "Ye are not straitened in Me, ye are straitened in yourselves." Desire Him to help and bless you, and He will do it. Expect Him to do it, and He will do it. Go to Him like the other blind man and say to Him—"Jesus, Thou Son of David, have mercy on me, that I may receive my sight," and He will lay His hand upon you, and at any rate a glimmer will come, which will grow in the measure of your humble, confident desire, until at last He takes you by the hand and leads you out of this poor little village of a world and lays His finger for a brief moment of blindness upon your eyes and asks you if you see aught. Then you will look up, and the first face that you will behold will be His, whom you saw "as through a glass darkly" with your dim eyes in this twilight world.

May that be your experience and mine, through His mercy!

Christ's Cross, and Ours

And Jesus went out, and His disciples, into the towns of Caesarea Phillippi: and by the way He asked His disciples, saying unto them, Whom do men say that I am? 28. And they answered, John the Baptist: but some say, Elias; and others, One of the prophets. 29. And He saith unto them, But whom say ye that I am? And Peter answereth and saith unto Him, Thou art the Christ. 30. And He charged them that they should tell no man of Him. 31. And He began to teach them, that the Son of Man must suffer many things, and be rejected of the elders, and of the chief priests, and scribes, and be killed, and after three days rise again. 32. And He spake that saying openly. And Peter took him, and began to rebuke Him. 33. But when He had turned about and looked on His disci-

ples, He rebuked Peter, saying, Get thee behind me, Satan: for thou savorest not the things that be of God, but the things that be of men. 34. And when He had called the people unto Him with His disciples also, He said unto them, Whosoever will come after Me, let him deny himself, and take up his cross, and follow Me. 35. For whosoever will save his life shall lose it; but whosoever shall lose his life for My sake and the gospel's, the same shall save it. 36. For what shall it profit a man, if he shall gain the whole world, and lose his own soul? 37. Or what shall a man give in exchange for his soul? 38. Whosoever therefore shall be ashamed of Me and of My words in this adulterous and sinful generation: of him also shall the Son of Man be ashamed, when He cometh in the glory of His Father with the holy angels. 9:1. And He said unto them, Verily I say unto you, That there be some of them that stand here, which shall not taste of death, till they have seen the kingdom of God come with power. MARK 8:27–9:1.

Our Lord led His disciples away from familiar ground into the comparative seclusion of the country round Caesarea Philippi, in order to tell them plainly of His death. He knew how terrible the announcement would be, and He desired to make it in some quiet spot, where there would be collectedness and leisure to let it sink into their minds. His consummate wisdom and perfect tenderness are equally and beautifully shown in His manner of disclosing the truth which would try their faithfulness and fortitude. From the beginning He had given hints, gradually increasing in clearness; and now the time had come for full disclosure. What a journey that was! He, with the heavy secret filling His thoughts; they, dimly aware of something absorbing Him, in which they had no part. And at last, "in the way," as if moved by some sudden impulse—like that which we all know, leading us to speak out abruptly what we have long waited to say—He gives them a share in the burden of His thought. But, even then, note how He leads up to it by degrees. This passage has the announcement of the Cross as its center, prepared for, on the one hand, by a question, and followed, on the other, by a warning that His followers must travel the same road.

1. Note the preparation for the announcement of the Cross (verses 27–30). Why did Christ begin by asking about the popular judgment of His personality? Apparently in order to bring clearly home to the disciples that, as far as the masses were concerned, His work and theirs had failed, and had, for net result, total misconception. Who that had the faintest glimmer of what He was could suppose that the stern, fiery spirits of Elijah or John had come to life again in Him? The second question, "But whom say ye that I am?'' with it sharp transition, is meant to force home the conviction of the gulf between His disciples and the whole nation. He would have them feel their isolation, and face the fact that they stood alone in their faith; and He would test them whether, knowing that they did stand alone, they had courage and tenacity to reassert it. The unpopularity of a belief drives away cowards, and draws the brave and true. If none else believed in Him, that was an additional reason for loving hearts to cleave to Him; and those only truly know and love Him who are ready to stand by Him, if they stand alone—*Athanasius contra mundum*. Note, too, that this is the all-important question for every man. Our own individual ''thought'' of Him determines our whole worth and fate.

Mark gives Peter's confession in a lower key, as it were, than Matthew does, omitting the full-toned clause, ''the Son of the Living God.'' This is not because Mark has a lower conception than his brother Evangelist, for the first words of this Gospel announce that it is ''the Gospel of Jesus, the Messiah, the Son of God.'' And, as he has identified the two conceptions at the outset, he must, in all fairness, be supposed to consider that the one implies the other, and to include both here. But possibly there is truth in the observation that the omission is one of a number of instances in which this Gospel passes lightly over the exalted side of Christ's nature, in accordance with its purpose of setting Him forth rather as the Servant than as the Lord. It is not meant that that exalted side was absent from Mark's thoughts, but that his design led him rather to emphasize the other. Matthew's is the Gospel of the King; Mark's, of the Worker.

The omission of Christ's eulogium on Peter has often been pointed out as an interesting corroboration of the tradition that he was Mark's source; and perhaps the failure to record the praise, and the carefulness to tell the subsequent rebuke, reveal the humblehearted ''elder'' into whom the self-confident young Apostle had grown. Flesh delights to recall praise; faith and self-knowledge find more profit in remembering errors forgiven and rebukes deserved, and in their severity, most loving. How did these questions and their answers serve as introduction to the announcement of the Cross? In several ways. They brought clearly before the disciples the hard fact of Christ's rejection by the popular voice, and defined their own position as sharply antagonistic. If His claims were thus unanimously tossed aside, a collision must come. A rejected Messiah could not fail to be, sooner or later, a slain Messiah. Then clear, firm faith in His Messiahship was needed to enable them to stand the ordeal to which the announcement, and, still more, its fulfilment, would subject them. A suffering Messiah might be a rude shock to all their dreams; but a suffering Jesus, who was not Messiah, would have been the end of their discipleship. Again, the significance and worth of the Cross could only be understood when seen in the light of that great confession. Even as now, we must believe that He who died was the Son of the living God before we can see what that Death was and did. An imperfect conception of who Jesus is takes the meaning and the power out of all His life, but, most of all, impoverishes the infinite preciousness of His Death.

The charge of silence contrasts singularly with the former employment of the Apostles as heralds of Jesus. The silence was partly punitive and partly prudential. It was punitive, inasmuch as the people had already had abundantly the proclamation of His Gospel, and had cast it away. It was in accordance with the solemn law of God's retributive justice that offers rejected should be withdrawn; and from them that had not, even that which they had should be taken away. Christ never bids His servants be silent until men have refused to hear their speech. The silence enjoined was also prudential, in order to avoid hastening on the inevitable collision; not because Christ desired escape, but because He would first fulfill His day.

2. We have here the announcement of the Cross. (verses 31–33). There had been many hints before this; for Christ saw the end from the beginning, however far back in the depths of time or eternity we place that beginning. We do not sufficiently realize that His Death was before Him, all through His days, as the great purpose for which He had come. If the anticipation of sorrow is the multiplication of sorrow, even when there is hope of escaping it, how much must His have been multiplied, and bitterness been diffused through all His life, by that foresight, so clear and constant, of the certain end! How much more gracious and wonderful His quick sympathy, His patient self forgetfulness, His unwearied toil, show against that dark background!

Mark here the solemn necessity. Why "must" He suffer? Not because of the enmity of the three sets of rejecters. He recognizes no necessity which is imposed by hostile human power. The cords which bind this sacrifice to the horns of the altar were not spun by men's hands. The great "must" which ruled His life was a cable of two strands—obedience to the Father, and love to men. These haled Him to the Cross, and fastened Him there. He would save, therefore He "must" die. The same "must" stretches beyond death. Resurrection is a part of His whole work; and, without it, His Death has no power, but falls into the undistinguished mass of human mortality. Bewildered as the disciples were, that assurance of resurrection had little present force, but even then would faintly hint at some comfort and blessed mystery. What was to them a nebulous hope is to us a sun of certitude and cheer. "Christ that died" is no Gospel until you go on to say, "Yea, rather, that is risen again."

Peter's rash "rebuke," like most of his appearances in the Gospel, is strangely compounded of warmhearted, impulsive love and presumptuous self-confidence. No doubt, the praise which he had just received had turned his head, not very steady in these early days at it best, and the dignity which had been promised him would seem to him to be sadly overclouded by the prospect opened in Christ's forecast. But he was not thinking of himself; and when he said, "This shall not be unto Thee," probably he meant to suggest that they would all draw the sword to defend their Master. Mark's use of the word "rebuke," which is also Matthew's, seems to imply that he found fault with Christ. For what? Probably for not trusting to His followers' arms, or for letting Himself become a victim to the "must," which Peter thought of as depending only on the power of the ecclesiastics in Jerusalem. He blames Christ for not hoisting the flag of a revolt.

This blind love was the nearest approach to sympathy which Christ received; and it was repugnant to Him, so as to draw the sharpest words from Him that He ever spoke to a loving heart. In his eagerness, Peter had taken Jesus on one side to whisper his suggestion; but Christ will have all hear His rejection of the counsel. Therefore He "turned about," facing the rest of the group, and by the act putting Peter behind Him, and spoke aloud the stern words. Not thus was he wont to repel ignorant love, nor to tell out faults in public; but the act witnessed to the recoil of His fixed spirit from the temptation which addressed His natural human shrinking from death, as well as to His desire that once for all, every dream of resistance by force should be shattered. He hears in Peter's voice the tone of that other voice, which, in the wilderness, had suggested the same temptation to escape the Cross and win the crown by worshipping the Devil; and he puts the meaning of His instinctive gesture into the same words in which he had rejected that earlier seducing suggestion. Jesus was a man, and "the things that be of men" found a response in His sinless nature. It shrank from pain and the Cross with innocent and inevitable shrinking. Does not the very severity of the rebuke testify to its having set some chords vibrating in His soul? Note that it may be the work of "Satan" to appeal to "the things that be of men," however innocent, if by so doing obedience to God's will is hindered. Note, too, that a Simon may be "Peter" at one moment, and "Satan" at the next.

3. We have here the announcement of the Cross as the law for the disciples, too (verses 34–38). Christ's followers must follow, but men can choose whether they will be His followers or not. So the "must" is changed into "let him," and the "if any man will" is put in the forefront. The conditions are fixed, but the choice as to accepting the position is free. A wider circle hears the terms of discipleship than heard the announcement of Christ's own sufferings. The terms are for all and for us. The law is stated in verse 34, and then a series of reasons for it, and motives for accepting it, follow.

The law for every disciple is self-denial and taking up his cross. How present His own Cross must have been to Christ's vision, since the thought is introduced here, though He had not spoken of it, in foretelling His own death! It is not Christ's Cross that we have to take up. His sufferings stand alone, incapable of repetition and needing none; but each follower has his own. To slay the life of self is always pain, and there is no discipleship without crucifying "the old man." Taking up my cross does not merely mean meekly accepting God-sent or man-inflicted sorrows, but persistently carrying on the special form of self-denial which my special type of character requires. It will include these other meanings, but it goes deeper than they. Such self-immolation is the same thing as following Christ; for, with all the infinite difference between His Cross and ours, they are both crosses, and on the one hand there is no real discipleship without self-denial, on the other there is no full self-denial without discipleship.

The first of the reasons for the law, in verse 35, is a paradox, and a truth with two sides. To wish to save life is to lose it; to lose it for Christ's sake is to save it. Both are true, even without taking the future into account. The life of self is death; the death of the lower self is the life of the true self. The man who lives absorbed in the miserable care for his own well-being is dead to all which makes life noble, sweet, and real. Flagrant vice is not needed to kill the real life. Clean, respectable selfishness does the work effectually. The deadly gas is invisible, and has no smell. But while all selfishness is fatal, it is self-surrender and sacrifice, "for My sake and the gospel's," which is life-giving. Heroism, generous self-devotion without love to Christ, is noble, but falls short of discipleship, and may even aggravate the sin of the man who exhibits it, because it shows what treasures he could lay at Christ's feet, if he would. It is only self-denial made sweet by reference to Him that leads to life. Who is this who thus demands that He should be the motive for which men shall "hate" their own lives, and calmly assumes power to reward such sacrifice with a better life? The paradox is true, if we include a reference to the future, which is usually taken to be its only meaning; but on that familiar thought we need not enlarge.

The "for" of verse 36 seems to refer back to the law in verse 34, and the verse enforces the command by an appeal to self-interest, which, in the highest sense of the word, dictates self-sacrifice. The men who live for self are dead, as Christ has been saying. Suppose their self-living had been "successful" to the highest point, what would be the good of all the world to a dead man? "Shrouds have no pockets." He makes a poor bargain who sells his soul for the world. A man gets rich, and in the process drops generous impulses, affections, interest in noble things, perhaps principle and religion. He has shrivelled and hardened into a mere fragment of himself; and so, when success comes, he cannot much enjoy it, and was happier, poor and sympathetic and enthusiastic and generous, than he is now, rich and dwindled. He who loses himself in gaining the world does not win it, but is mastered by it. This motive, too, like the preceding, has a double application—to the facts of life here, when they are seen in their deepest reality, and to the solemn future.

To that future our Lord passes, as His last reason for the command and motive for obeying it, in verse 38. One great hindrance to out-and-out discipleship is fear of what the world will say. Hence come compromises and weak compliance on the part of disciples too timid to stand alone, or too sensitive to face a sarcasm and a smile. A wholesome contempt for the world's cackle is needed for following Christ. The geese on the common hiss at the passerby who goes steadily through the flock. How grave and awful is that irony, if we may call it so, which casts the retribution in the mold of the sin! The judge shall be "ashamed" of such unworthy disciples—shall blush to own such as His. May we venture to put stress on the fact that He does not say that He will reject them? They who were ashamed of Him were secret and imperfect disciples. Perhaps, though He be ashamed of them, though they have brought Him no credit, He will not wholly turn from them.

How marvelous the transition from the prediction of the Cross to this of the Throne! The Son of Man must suffer many things, and the same Son of Man shall come, attended by hosts of spirits who own Him for their King, and surrounded by the uncreated blaze of the glory of God in which He sits throned as His active abode. We do not know Jesus unless we know Him as the crucified Sacrifice for the world's sins, and as the exalted Judge of the world's deeds.

He adds a weighty word of enigmatical meaning, lest any should think that He was speaking only of some far-off judgment. The destruction of Jerusalem seems to be the event intended, which was, in fact, the beginning of retribution for Israel, and the starting point of a more conspicuous manifestation of the kingdom of God. It was, therefore, a kind of rehearsal, or picture in little, of that coming and ultimate great day of the Lord, and was meant to be a "sign" that it should surely come.

9

Mountains and Valleys

The Transfiguration

And after six days Jesus taketh with Him Peter, and James, and
John, and leadeth them up into an high mountain apart by them-
selves: and He was transfigured before them. 3. And His raiment
became shining, exceeding white as snow; so as no fuller on earth
can white them. 4. And there appeared unto them Elias with Moses:
and they were talking with Jesus. 5. And Peter answered and said
to Jesus, Master, it is good for us to be here: and let us make three
tabernacles; one for Thee, and one for Moses, and one for Elias. 6.
For he wist not what to say; for they were sore afraid. 7. And there
was a cloud that overshadowed them: and a voice came out of the
cloud, saying, This is My beloved Son: hear Him. 8. And suddenly,
when they had looked round about, they saw no man any more, save
Jesus only with themselves. 9. And as they came down from the
mountain, He charged them that they should tell no man what things
they had seen, till the Son of Man were risen from the dead. 10.
And they kept that saying with themselves, questioning one with
another what the rising from the dead should mean. 11. And they
asked Him, saying, Why say the scribes that bliss must first
come? 12. And He answered and told them, Elias verily cometh
first, and restoreth all things; and how it is written of the Son of Man,
that He must suffer many things, and be set at nought. 13. But I say
unto you, That Elias is indeed come, and they have done unto him
whatsoever they listed, as it is written of him. MARK 9:2–13.

All three Evangelists are careful to date the Transfiguration by a reference to the solemn new teaching at Caesarea, and Mark's "six days" plainly cover the same time as Luke's "eight"—the former reckoning excluding in the count, and the latter including, the days on which the two incidents occurred. If we would understand the Transfiguration, then, we must look at it as the sequel to Jesus' open announcement of His death. His seeking the seclusion of the hills, attended only by the innermost group of the faithful three, is a touching token of the strain to which that week had subjected Him. How Peter's heart must have filled with thankfulness that, notwithstanding the stern rebuke, he was taken with the other two! There were three stages in the complex incident which we call the Transfiguration—the change in Jesus' appearance, the colloquy with Moses and Elijah, and the voice from the cloud.

Luke, who has frequent references to Jesus' prayers, tells us that the change in our Lord's countenance and raiment took place "as He prayed"; and probably we are reverently following his lead if we think of Jesus' prayer as, in some sense, the occasion of the glorious change. So far as we know, this was the only time when mortal eyes saw Him absorbed in communion with the Father. It was only "when He ceased praying" in a certain place that "they came to Him" asking to be taught to pray (Luke 11:1); and in Gethsemane the disciples slept while He prayed beneath the olives quivering in the moonlight. It may be that what the three then saw did not occur then only. "In such an hour of high communion with" His Father the elevated spirit may have more than ordinarily illuminated the pure body, and the pure body may have been more than ordinarily transparent. The brighter the light, fed by fragrant oil within an alabaster lamp, the more the alabaster will glow. Faint foreshadowings of the spirit's power to light up the face with unearthly beauty of holiness are not unknown among us. It may be that the glory which always shone in the depths of His perfectly holy manhood rose, as it were, to the surface for that one time, a witness of what He really was, a prophecy of what humanity may become.

Did Jesus will His transfiguration, or did it come about without His volition, or perhaps even without His consciousness? Did it continue during all the time on the mountain, or did it pass when the second stage of the incident began? We cannot tell. Matthew and Mark both say that Jesus was transfigured "before" the three, as if the making visible of the glory had special regard to them. It may be that Jesus, like Moses, "knew not that the skin of His face shone"; at all events, it was the second stage of the incident, the conversation with Elijah and Moses, that had a special message of strength for Him. The first and third stages were, apparently, intended for the three and for us all; and the first is a revelation, not only of the veiled glory that dwelt in Jesus, but of the beauty that may pass into a holy face, and of the possibilities of a bodily frame becoming a "spiritual body," the adequate organ and manifestation of a perfect spirit. Paul teaches the prophetic aspect of the Transfiguration when he says that Jesus "shall *change* the body of our humiliation that it may be fashioned like unto the body of His glory."

Luke adds two very significant points to the accounts by Matthew and Mark—namely, the disciples' sleep, and the subject on which Moses and Elijah talked with Jesus. Mark lays the main stress on the fact that the two great persons of the old economy, its founder and its restorer, the legislator and the chief of the prophets, came from the dim region to which one of them had passed in a chariot of fire, and stood by the transfigured Christ, as if witnessing to Him as the greater, to whom their ministries were subordinate, and in whom their teachings centered. Jesus is the goal of all previous revelation, mightier than the mightiest who are honored by being His attendants. He is the Lord both of the dead and of the living, and the "spirits of just men made perfect" bow before Him, and reverently watch His work on earth.

So much did that appearance proclaim to the mortal three, but their slumber showed that they were not principally concerned, and that the other three had things to speak which they were not fit to hear. The theme was the same which had been, a week before, spoken to them, and had doubtless been the subject of all Jesus' teachings for these "six days." No doubt, their horror at the thought, and His necessary insistence on it, had brought Him to need strengthening. And these two came, as did the angel in Gethsemane, and, like him, in answer to Christ's prayer, to bring the sought-for strength. How different it would be to speak to them "of the decease which He should accomplish at Jerusalem," from speaking to the reluctant, protesting Twelve! And how different to listen to them speaking of that miracle of divine love expressed in human death from the point of view of the "principalities and powers in heavenly places," as over against the remonstrances and misunderstandings with which He had been struggling for a whole week! The appearance of Moses and Elijah teaches us the relation of Jesus to all former revelation, the interest of the dwellers in heavenly light in the Cross, and the need which Jesus felt for strengthening to endure it.

Peter's foolish words, half excused by his being scarcely awake, may be passed by with the one remark that it was like him to say something, though he did not know what to say, and that it would therefore have been wise to say nothing.

The third part of this incident, the appearance of the cloud and the voice from it, was for the disciples. Luke tells us that it was a "bright" cloud, and yet it "overshadowed them." That sets us on the right track and indicates that we are to think of the cloud of glory, which was the visible token of the divine presence, the cloud which shone lambent between the cherubim, the cloud which at last "received Him out of their sight." Luke tells, too, that "they entered into it." Who entered? Moses and Elijah had previously "departed from Him." Jesus and the disciples remained, and we cannot suppose that the three could have passed into that solemn glory, if He had not led them in. In that sacred moment He was "the way," and keeping close to Him, mortal feet could pass into the glory which even a Moses had not been fit to behold. The spiritual significance of the incident seems to require the supposition that, led by Jesus, they entered the cloud. They were men, therefore they were afraid; Jesus was with them, therefore they stood within the circle of that light and lived.

The voice repeated the attestation of Jesus as the "beloved Son" of the Father, which had been given at the baptism, but with the addition, "Hear Him," which shows that it was now meant for the disciples, not, as at the baptism, for Jesus Himself. While the command to listen to His voice as to the voice from the cloud is perfectly general, and lays all His words on us as all God's words, it had special reference to the disciples, and that in regard to the new teaching which had so disturbed them—the teaching of the necessity for His death. "The offense of the Cross" began with the first dear statement of it, and in the hearts that loved Him best and came most near to understanding Him. To fail in accepting His teaching that it "behooved the Son of Man to suffer," is to fail in accepting it in the most important matter. There are sounds in nature too low-pitched to be audible to untrained ears, and the message of the Cross is unheard unless the ears of the deaf are unstopped. If we do not hear Jesus when He speaks of His passion, we may almost as well not hear Him at all.

Moses and Elijah had vanished, having borne their last testimony to Jesus. Peter had wished to keep them beside Jesus, but that could not be. Their highest glory was to fade in His light. They came, they disappeared; He remained—and remains. "They saw no man any more, save Jesus only with themselves." So should it be for us in life. So may it be with us in death! "Hear Him," for all other voices are but for a time, and die into silence, but Jesus speaks for eternity, and "His words shall not pass away." When time is ended, and the world's history is all gathered up into its final issue, His name shall stand out alone as Author and End of all.

"This Is My Beloved Son: Hear Him"

> *And there was a cloud that overshadowed them: and a voice came out of the cloud, saying, This is My beloved Son: hear Him.* MARK 9:7.

With regard to the first part of these words spoken at the Transfiguration, they open far too large and wonderful a subject for me to do more than just touch with the tip of my finger, as it were, in passing, because the utterance of the divine words, "This is My beloved Son,' in all the depth of their meaning and loftiness, is laid as the foundation of the two words that come after, which, for us, are the all-important things there. And so I would rather dwell upon them than upon the mysteries of the first part, but a sentence must be spared. If we accept this story before us as the divine attestation of the mystery of the person and nature of Jesus Christ, we must take the words to mean—as these disciples, no doubt, took them to mean—something pointing to a unique and solitary revelation which He bore to the Divine Majesty. We have to see in them the confirmation of the great truth that the manhood of Jesus Christ was the supernatural creation of a direct divine power. "Conceived of the Holy Ghost, born of the Virgin Mary"; therefore, "that Holy Thing which shall be born of thee shall be called the Son of God." And we have to go, as I take it, farther back than the earthly birth, and to say, "No man hath seen God at any time—the only begotten Son which is in the bosom of the Father." He was the Son here by human birth, and was in the bosom of the Father all through that human life. "He hath declared Him," and so not only is there here the testimony to the miraculous incarnation, and to the true and proper Divinity and Deity of Jesus Christ, but there is also the witness to the perfectness of His character in the great word, "This is My beloved Son,' which points us to an unbroken communion of love between Him and the Father, which tells us that in the depths of that divine nature there has been a constant play of mutual love, which reveals to us that in His humanity there never was anything that came as the faintest film of separation between His will and the will of the Father, between His heart and the heart of God.

But this revelation of the mysterious personality of the divine Son, the perfect harmony between Him and God, is here given as the ground of the command that follows: "Hear Him." God's voice bids you listen to Christ's voice—God's voice bids you listen to Christ's voice as His voice. Listen to Him when He speaks to you about God—do not trust your own fancy, do not trust your own fear, do not trust the dictates of your conscience, do not consult man, do not listen to others, do not speculate about the mysteries of the earth and the heavens, but go to Him, and listen to the only begotten Son in the bosom of the Father. He declares unto us God; in Him alone we have certain knowledge of a loving Father in heaven. Hear Him when He tells us of God's tenderness and patience and love. Hear Him above all when He says to us, "As Moses lifted up the serpent in the wilderness, even so must the Son of Man be lifted up." Hear Him when He says, "The Son of Man came to give His life a ransom for many." Hear Him when He speaks of Himself as Judge of you and me and all the world, and when He says, "The Son of Man shall come in His glory, and before Him shall be gathered all nations.'' Hear Him then. Hear Him when He calls you to Himself. Hear Him when He says to you, ''Come unto Me all ye that labor and are heavy laden.'' Hear Him when He says, ''If any man come unto Me he shall never thirst.'' Hear Him when He says, ''Cast your burden upon Me, and I will sustain you.'' Hear Him when He commands. Hear Him when He says, ''If ye love Me keep My commandments,'' and when He says, ''Abide in Me and I in you,'' hear Him then. ''In all time of our tribulation, in all time of our well-being, in the hour of death, and in the day of judgment,'' let us listen to Him.

Dear friends, there is no rest anywhere else; there is no peace, no pleasure, no satisfaction—except close at His side. ''Speak Lord! for Thy servant heareth.'' ''To whom shall we go but unto Thee? Thou hast the words of eternal life.'' Look how these disciples, groveling there on their faces, were raised by the gentle hand laid upon their shoulder, and the blessed voice that brought them back to consciousness, and how, as they looked about them with dazed eyes, all was gone. The vision, the cloud, Moses and Elias—the luster and radiance and the dread voice were past, and everything was as it used to be. Christ stood alone there like some solitary figure relieved against a clear daffodil sky upon some extended plain, and there was nothing else to meet the eye but He. Christ is there, and in Him is all.

That is a summing up of all Divine revelation. ''God, who at sundry times and in divers manners spake in time past unto the fathers by the prophets, hath, in these last days, spoken unto us by His Son.'' Moses dies, Elijah fades, clouds and symbols and voices and all mortal things vanish, but Jesus Christ stands before us, the manifest God, forever and ever, the sole illumination of the world. It is also a summing up of all earthly history. All other people go. The beach of time is strewed with wrecked reputations and forgotten glories. And I am not ashamed to say that I believe that, as the ages grow, and the world gets further away in time from the Cross upon Calvary, more and more everything else will sink beneath the horizon, and Christ alone be left to fill the past as He fills the present and the future.

We may make that scene the picture of our lives. Distractions and temptations that lie all round us are ever seeking to drag us away. There is no peace anywhere but in having Christ only—my only pattern, my only hope, my only salvation, my only guide, my only aim, my only Friend. The solitary Christ is the sufficient Christ, and that forever. Take Him for your only friend, and you need none other. Then at death there may be a brief spasm of darkness, a momentary fear, perchance, but then the touch of a Brother's hand will be upon us as we lie there prone in the dust, and we shall lift up our eyes, and lo! life's illusions are gone, and life's noises are fallen dumb, and we "see no man any more, save Jesus only," with ourselves.

Jesus Only!

They saw no man any more, save Jesus only with themselves. MARK 9:8.

The Transfiguration was the solemn inauguration of Jesus for His sufferings and death.

Moses, the founder, and Elijah, the restorer, of the Jewish polity, the great Lawgiver and the great Prophet, were present. The former had died and been mysteriously buried, the latter had been translated without "seeing death." So both are visitors from the unseen world, appearing to own that Jesus is the Lord of that dim land, and that there they draw their life from Him. The conversation is about Christ's "decease," the wonderful event which was to constitute Him Lord of the living and of the death. The divine voice of command, "Hear Him!" gives the meaning of their disappearance. At that voice they depart and Jesus is left alone. The scene is typical of the ultimate issue of the world's history. The King's name only will at last be found inscribed on the pyramid. Typical, too, is it not, of a Christian's blessed death? When the "cloud" is past no man is seen any more but "Jesus only."

I. The solitary Saviour.

The disciples are left alone with the divine Saviour.

1. He is alone in His nature, "Son of God."

2. He is alone in the sinlessness of His manhood. "My Beloved Son!"

3. He is alone as God's Voice to men. "Hear Him!" the solitary Saviour, because sufficient. "Thou, O Christ, art all I want."

Sufficient, too, forever.

His life is eternal.

His love is eternal.

The power of His Cross is eternal.

II. The vanishing witnesses.

1. The connection of the past with Christ. The authority of the two representatives of the Old Covenant was only *(a)* derived and subordinate; *(b)* prophetic; *(c)* transient.

2. The thought may be widened into that of the relation of all teachers and guides to Jesus Christ.

3. The two witness to the relation of the unseen world to Jesus Christ.

(a) Its inhabitants are undying, and

(b) Are subject to the sway of Jesus, and

(c) Are expectantly waiting a glorious future.

4. They witness to the central point of Christ's work—"His decease." This great event is the key to the world's history.

III. The waiting disciples.

1. What Christian life should be. Giving Him our sole trust and allegiance.

(a) Seeing Him in all things.

(b) Constant communion. "Abide in Me."

(c) Using everything as helps to Him.

2. What Christian death may become.

Christ's Lament Over Our Faithlessness

He answereth him and saith, O faithless generation, how long shall I be with you! how long shall I suffer you! MARK 9:19.

There is a very evident, and, I think, intentional contrast between the two scenes, of the Transfiguration, and of this healing of the maniac boy. And in nothing is the contrast more marked than in the demeanor of these enfeebled and unbelieving Apostles, as contrasted with the rapture of devotion of the other three, and with the lowly submission and faith of Moses and Elias. Perhaps, too, the difference between the calm serenity of the mountain, and the hell-tortured misery of the plain—between the converse with the sainted perfected dead, and the converse with their unworthy successors—made Christ feel more sharply and poignantly than He ordinarily did His disciples' slowness of apprehension and want of faith. At any rate, it does strike one as remarkable that the only occasion on which there came from His lips anything that sounded like impatience and a momentary flash of indignation was, when in sharpest contrast with "This is my beloved Son: hear Him," He had to come down from the mountain to meet the devil-possessed boy, the useless agony of the father, the sneering faces of the scribes, and the impotence of the disciples. Looking on all this, He turns to His followers—for it is to the Apostles that the text is spoken, and not to the crowd outside—with this most remarkable exclamation: "O faithless generation! how long shall I be with you? how long shall I suffer you?"

Now, I said that these words at first sight looked almost like a momentary flash of indignation, as if for once a spot had come on His pallid cheek—a spot of anger—but I do not think that we shall find it so if we look a little more closely.

The first thing that seems to be in the words is not anger, indeed, but a very distinct and very pathetic expression of Christ's infinite pain, because of man's faithlessness. The element of personal sorrow is most obvious here. It is not only that He is sad for their sakes that they are so unreceptive, and He can do so little for them—I shall have something to say about that presently—but that He feels for Himself, just as we do in our poor humble measure, the chilling effect of an atmosphere where there is no sympathy. All that ever the teachers and guides and leaders of the world have in this respect had to bear—all the misery of opening out their hearts in the frosty air of unbelief and rejection—Christ endured. All that men have ever felt of how hard it is to keep on working when not a soul understands them, when not a single creature believes in them, when there is no one that will accept their message, none that will give them credit for pure motives—Jesus Christ had to feel, and that in an altogether singular degree. There never was such a lovely soul on this earth as His, just because there never was one so pure and loving. "The little hills rejoice *together,*" as the Psalm says, "on every side," but the great Alpine peak is alone there, away up amongst the cold and the snows. Thus lived the solitary Christ, the uncomprehended Christ, the unaccepted Christ. Let us see in this exclamation of His how humanly, and yet how divinely, He felt the loneliness to which His love and purity condemned Him.

The plain felt soul-chilling after the blessed communion of the mountain. There was such a difference between Moses and Elias and the voice that said, "This is My beloved Son: hear Him," and the disbelief and slowness of spiritual apprehension of the people down below there, that no wonder that for once the pain that He generally kept absolutely down and silent, broke the bounds even of His restraint, and shaped for itself this pathetic utterance: "How long shall I be with you? how long shall I suffer you?"

Dear friends, here is "a little window through which we may see a great matter" if we will only think of how all that solitude, and all that sorrow of uncomprehended aims, was borne lovingly and patiently, right away on to the very end, for every one of us. I know that there are many of the aspects of Christ's life in which Christ's griefs tell more on the popular apprehension; but I do not know that there is one in which the title of "The Man of Sorrows" is to all deeper thinking more pathetically vindicated than in this—the solitude of the uncomprehended and the unaccepted Christ and His pain at His disciples' faithlessness.

And then do not let us forget that in this short sharp cry of anguish—for it is that—there may be detected by the listening ear not only the tone of personal hurt, but the tone of disappointed and thwarted love. Because of their unbelief He knew that they would not receive what He desired to give them. We find Him more than once in His life, hemmed in, hindered, balked of His purpose, thwarted, as I may, in His design, simply because there was no one with a heart open to receive the rich treasure that He was ready to pour out. He had to keep it locked up in His own spirit, else it would have been wasted and spilled upon the ground. "He could do no mighty works there because of their unbelief"; and here He is standing in the midst of the men that knew Him best, that understood Him most, that were nearest to Him in sympathy; but even they were not ready for all this wealth of affection, all this infinitude of blessing, with which His heart is charged. They offered no place to put it. They shut up the narrow cranny through which it might have come, and so He has to turn from them, bearing it away unbestowed, like some man who goes out in the morning with his seed basket full, and finds the whole field where he would fain have sown covered already with springing weeds or encumbered with hard rock, and has to bring back the germs of possible life to bless and fertilize some other soil. "He that goeth forth weeping, bearing precious seed, shall doubtless come again with joy"; but He that comes back weeping, bearing the precious seed that He found no field to sow in, knows a deeper sadness, which has in it no prophecy of joy. It is wonderfully pathetic and beautiful, I think, to see how Jesus Christ knew the pains of wounded love that cannot get expressed because there is no heart to receive it.

Here I would remark, too, before I go to another point, that these two elements—that of personal sorrow and that of disappointed love and balked purposes—continue still, and are represented as in some measure felt by Him now. It was to disciples that He said, "O faithless generation!" He did not mean to charge them with the entire absence of all confidence, but He did mean to declare that their poor, feeble faith, such as it was, was not worth naming in comparison with the abounding mass of their unbelief. There was one spark of light in them, and there was also a great heap of green wood that had not caught the flame and only smoked instead of blazing. And so He said to them, "O *faithless* generation!"

Ay, and if He came down here amongst us now, and went through the professing Christians in this land, to how many of us—regard being had to the feebleness of our confidence and the strength of our unbelief—He would have to say the same thing. "O faithless generation!"

The version of that clause in Matthew and Luke adds a significant word —"faithless and *perverse* generation." The addition carries a grave lesson, as teaching us that the two characteristics are inseparably united; that the want of faith is morally a crime and sin; that unbelief is at once the most tragic manifestation of man's perverse will, and also in its turn the source of still more obstinate and wide-spreading evil. Blindness to His light and rejected of His love, He treats as the very head and crown of sin. Like intertwining snakes, the loathly heads are separate; but the slimy convolutions are twisted indistinguishably together, and all unbelief has in it the nature of perversity, as all perversity has in it the nature of unbelief. "He will convince the world of sin, because they believe not on Me."

May we venture to say, as we have already hinted, that all this pain is in some mysterious way still inflicted on His loving heart? Can it be that every time we are guilty of unbelieving, unsympathetic rejection of His love, we send a pang of real pain and sorrow into the heart of Christ? It is a strange, solemn thought. There are many difficulties which start up, if we at all accept it. But still it does appear as if we could scarcely believe in His perpetual manhood, or think of His love as being in any real sense a human love, without believing that He sorrows when we sin; and that we can grieve, and wound, and cause to recoil upon itself, as it were, and close up that loving and gracious Spirit that delights in being met with answering love. If we may venture to take our love as in any measure analogous to His—and unless we do, His love is to us a word without meaning—we may believe that it is so. Do not we know that the purer our love, and the more it has purified us, the more sensitive it becomes, even while the less suspicious it becomes? Is not the purest, most unselfish, highest love, that by which the least failure in response is felt most painfully? Though there be no anger, and no change in the love, still there is a pang where there is an inadequate perception, or an unworthy reception, of it. And Scripture seems to countenance the belief that Divine Love, too, may know something, in some mysterious fashion, like that feeling, when it warns us, "Grieve not the Holy Spirit of God, whereby ye are sealed unto the day of redemption." So *we* may venture to say, Grieve not the Christ of God, who redeems us; and remember that we grieve Him most when we will not let Him pour His love upon us, but turn a sullen, unresponsive unbelief towards His pleading grace, as some glacier shuts out the sunshine from the mountainside with its thick-ribbed ice.

Another thought, which seems to me to be expressed in this wonderful exclamation of our Lord's, is—that this faithlessness bound Christ to earth, and kept Him here. As there is not anger, but only pain, so there is also I think, not exactly impatience, but a desire to depart coupled with the feeling that He cannot leave them till they have grown stronger in faith. And that feeling is increased by the experience of their utter helplessness and shameful discomfiture during His brief absence. They had shown that they were not fit to be trusted alone. He had been away for a day up in the mountain there, and though they did not build an altar to any golden calf, like their ancestors, when their leader was absent, still when

He comes back He finds things all gone wrong because of the few hours of His absence. What would they do if He were to go away from them altogether? They would never be able to stand it at all. It is impossible that He should leave them thus—raw, immature. The plant has not yet grown sufficiently strong to take away the prop round which it climbed. ''How long must I be with you? says the loving Teacher, who is prepared ungrudgingly to give His slow scholars as much time as they need to learn their lesson. He is not impatient, but He desires to finish the task; and yet He is ready to let the scholars' dullness determine the duration of His stay. Surely that is wondrous and heart-touching love, that Christ should let their slowness measure the time during which He should linger here, and refrain from the glory which He desired. We do not know all the reasons which determined the length of our Lord's life upon earth, but this was one of them —that He could not go away until He had left these men strong enough to stand by themselves, and to lay the foundations of the Church. Therefore He yielded to the plea of their faithlessness and backwardness, and with this wonderful word of condescension and appeal bade them say for how many more days He must abide in the plain, and turn His back on the glories that had gleamed for a moment on the mountain of transfiguration.

In this connection, too, is it not striking to notice how long His short life and ministry appeared to our Lord Himself? There is to me something very pathetic in that question He addressed to one of His Apostles near the end of His pilgrimage: ''Have I been so long time with you, and yet hast thou not known Me?'' It was not so very long—three years, perhaps, at the outside—and much less, if we take the shortest computation; and yet to Him it had been long. The days had seemed to go tardily. He longed that the ''fire'' which He came to fling on earth were already ''kindled,'' and the moment seemed to drop so slowly from the urn of time. But neither the holy longing to consummate His work by the mystery of His passion, to which more than one of His words bear witness, nor the not less holy longing to be glorified with ''the glory which He had with the Father before the world was,'' which we may reverently venture to suppose in Him, could be satisfied till his slow scholars were wiser, and His feeble followers stronger.

And then again, here we get a glimpse into the depth of Christ's patient forbearance. We might read these other words of our text, ''How long shall I suffer you?'' with such an intonation as to make them almost a threat that the limits of forbearance would soon be reached, and that He was not going to ''suffer them much longer. Some commentators speak of them expressing ''holy indignation,'' and I quite believe that there is such a thing, and that on other occasions it was plainly spoken in Christ's words. But I fail to catch the tone of it here. To me this plaintive question has the very opposite of indignation in its ring. It sounds rather like a pledge that as long as they need forbearance they will get it; but, at the same time, a question of "how long" that is to be. It implies the inexhaustible riches and resources of His patient mercy. And Oh, dear brethren! that endless forbearance is the only refuge and ground of hope we have. *His* perfect charity "is not soon angry; beareth all things," and "never faileth." To it we have all to make the appeal—

Though I have most unthankful been
Of all that e'er Thy grace received;
Ten thousand times Thy goodness seen,
Ten thousand times Thy goodness grieved;
Yet, Lord, the chief of sinners spare.

And, thank God! we do not make our appeal in vain.

There is rebuke in His question, but how tender a rebuke it is! He rebukes without anger. He names the fault plainly. He shows distinctly His sorrow, and does not hide the strain on His forbearance. That is His way of cure for His servants' faithlessness. It was His way on earth; it is His way in heaven. To us, too, comes the loving rebuke of this question, "How long shall I suffer you?"

Thank God that our answer may be cast into the words of His own promise: "I say not unto thee, until seven times; but until seventy times seven." "Bear with me till Thou hast perfected me; and then bear me to Thyself, that I may be with Thee forever, and grieve Thy love no more." So may it be, for "with Him is plenteous redemption," and His forbearing "mercy endureth for ever."

The Omnipotence of Faith

Jesus said unto him, If thou canst believe, all things are possible to him that believeth. MARK 9:23.

The necessity and power of faith is the prominent lesson of this narrative of the healing of a demoniac boy, especially as it is told by the Evangelist Mark. The lesson is enforced by the actions of all the persons in the group, except the central figure, Christ. The disciples could not cast out the demon, and incur Christ's plaintive rebuke, which is quite as much sorrow as blame: "O faithless generation! how long shall I be with you? how long shall I suffer you?" And then, in the second part of the story, the poor father, heartsick with hope deferred, comes into the foreground. The whole interest is shifted to him, and more prominence is given to the process by which his doubting spirit is led to trust, than to that by which his son is healed.

There is something very beautiful and tender in Christ's way of dealing with him, so as to draw him to faith. He begins with the question, "How long is it ago since this came unto him?" and so induces him to tell all the story of the long sorrow, that his burdened heart might get some ease in speaking, and also that the feeling of the extremity of the necessity, deepened by the very dwelling on all his boy's cruel sufferings, might help him to the exercise of faith. Truly "He knew what was in man," and with tenderness born of perfect knowledge and perfect love, He dealt with sore and sorrowful hearts. This loving artifice of consolation, which drew all the story from willing lips, is one more little token of His gentle mode of healing. And it is profoundly wise, as well as most tender. Get a man thoroughly to know his need, and vividly to feel his helpless misery, and you have carried him a long way towards laying hold of the refuge from it.

How wise and how tender the question is, is proved by the long circumstantial answer, in which the pent-up trouble of a father's heart pours itself out at the tiny opening which Christ has made for it. He does not content himself with the simple answer, "Of a child," but with the garrulousness of sorrow that has found a listener that sympathizes, goes on to tell all the misery, partly that he may move his hearer's pity, but more in sheer absorption with the bitterness that had poisoned the happiness of his home all these years. And then his graphic picture of his child's state leads him to the plaintive cry, in which his love makes common cause with his son, and unites both in one wretchedness. "If thou canst do anything, have compassion on *us* and help *us*."

Our Lord answers that appeal in the words of our text. There are some difficulties in the rendering and exact force of these words with which I do not mean to trouble you. We may accept the rendering as in our Bible, with a slight variation in the punctuation. If we take the first clause as an incomplete sentence, and put a break between it and the last words, the meaning will stand out more clearly. "If thou canst believe—all things are possible to him that believeth." We might paraphrase it somewhat thus: Did you say "If thou canst do anything"? That is the wrong "if." There is no doubt about that. That only "if" in the question is another one, not about me, but about you. "if *thou* canst believe—" and then the incomplete sentence might be supposed to be ended with some such phrase as "That is the only question. If thou canst believe—all depends on that. If thou canst believe, thy son will be healed," or the like. Then, in order to explain and establish what He had meant in the half-finished saying, He adds the grand, broad statement, on which the demand for the man's faith as the only condition of his wish being answered reposes: "All things are possible to him that believeth."

That wide statement is meant, I suppose, for the disciples as well as for the father. "All things are possible" both in reference to benefits to be received, and in reference to power to be exercised. "If thou canst believe, poor suppliant father, thou shalt have thy desire. If thou canst believe, poor devil-ridden son, thou shalt be set free. If ye can believe, poor baffled disciples, you will be masters of the powers of evil."

Do you remember another "if" with which Christ was once besought? "There came a leper to Him, beseeching Him, and kneeling down to Him, and saying unto Him, If Thou wilt, Thou canst make me clean." In some respects that man had advanced beyond the father in our story, for he had no doubt at all about Christ's power, and he spoke to Him as "Lord." But he was somehow not quite sure about Christ's heart of pity. On the other hand, the man in our narrative has no doubt about Christ's compassion. He may have seen something of His previous miracles, or there may still have been lying on our Lord's countenance some of the lingering glory of the Transfiguration—as indeed the narrative seems to hint, in its emphatic statement of the astonishment and reverential salutations of the crowd when He approached—or the tenderness of our Lord's listening sympathy may have made him feel sure of His willingness to help. At any rate, the leper's "if" has answered itself for him. His own lingering doubt, Christ waives aside as settled. His "if" is answered forever. So these two "ifs" in reference to Christ are beyond all controversy; His power is certain, and His love. The third "if" remains, the one that refers to us—"If thou canst believe"; all things on that, for "all things are possible to him that believeth."

Here, then, we have our Lord telling us that faith is omnipotent. That is a bold word; He puts no limitations; "all things are possible." I think that to get the true force of these words we should put alongside of them the other saying of our Lord's, "With God all things are possible." That is the foundation of the grand prerogative in our text. The power of faith is the consequence of the power of God. All things are possible to Him; therefore, all things are possible to me, believing in Him. If we translate that into more abstract words, it just comes to the principle that the power of faith consists in its taking hold of the power of God. It is omnipotent because it knits us to Omnipotence. Faith is nothing in itself, but it is that which attaches us to God, and then His power flows into us. Screw a pipe on to a water main and turn a handle, and out flows the water through the pipe and fills the empty vessel. Faith is as impotent in itself as the hollow water pipe is, only it is the way by which the connection is established between the fullness of God and the emptiness of man. By it divinity flows into humanity, and we have a share even in the divine Omnipotence. "My strength is made perfect in weakness." In itself nothing, it yet grasps God, and therefore by it we are strong, because by it we lay hold of His strength. Great and wonderful is the grace thus given to us, poor, struggling, sinful men, that, looking up to the solemn throne, where He sits in His power, we have a right to be sure that a true participation in His greatness is granted to us, if once our hearts are fastened to Him.

And there is nothing arbitrary nor mysterious in this flowing of divine power into our hearts on condition of our faith. It is the condition of possessing Christ, and in Christ, salvation, righteousness, and strength, not by any artificial appointment, but in the very nature of things. There is no other way possible by which God could give men what they receive through their faith, except only their faith.

In all trust in God there are two elements: a sense of need and of evil and weakness, and a confidence more or less unshaken and strong in Him, His love and power and all-sufficiency; and unless both of these two be in the heart, it is, in the nature of things, impossible, and will be impossible to all eternity, that purity and strength and peace and joy, and all the blessings which Christ delights to give to faith, should ever be ours.

Unbelief, distrust of Him, which separates us from Him and closes the heart fast against His grace, must cut us off from that which it does not feel that it needs, nor cares to receive; and must interpose a non-conducting medium between us and the electric influences of His might. When Christ was on earth, man's want of faith dammed back His miracle-working power, and paralyzed His healing energy. How strange that paradox sounds at first hearing, which brings together Omnipotence and impotence, and makes men able to counter-work the loving power of Christ. "He could there do no mighty work." The Evangelist intends a paradox, for he uses two kindred words to express the inability and the mighty work; and we might paraphrase the saying so as to bring out the seeming contradiction: "He there had no power to do any work of power." The same awful, and in some sense mysterious, power of limiting and restraining the influx of His love belongs to unbelief still, whether it take the shape of active rejection, or only of careless, passive non-reception. For faith makes us partakers of divine power by the very necessity of the case, and that power can attach itself to nothing else. So, "if thou canst believe, all things are possible to him that believeth."

Still further, we may observe that there is involved here the principle that our faith determines the amount of our power. That is true in reference to our own individual religious life, and it is true in reference to special capacities for Christ's service. Let me say a word or two about each of these. They run into each other, of course, for the truest power of service is found in the depth and purity of our own personal religion, and on the other hand our individual Christian character will never be deep or pure unless we are working for the Master. Still, for our present purpose, these two inseparable aspects of the one Christian life may be separated in thought.

As to the former, then, the measure of my trust in Christ in the measure of all the rest of my Christian character. I shall have just as much purity, just a much peace, just as much wisdom or gentleness or love or courage or hope, as my faith is capable of taking up, and, so to speak, holding in solution. The "point of saturation" in a man's soul, the quantity of God's grace which he is capable of absorbing, is accurately measured by his faith. How much do I trust God? That will settle how much I can take in of God.

So much as we believe, so much can we contain. So much as we can contain, so much shall we receive. And in the very act of receiving the "portion of our Father's goods that falleth" to us, we shall feel that there is a boundless additional portion ready to come as soon as we are ready for it, and thereby we shall be driven to larger desires and a wider opening of the lap of faith, which will ever be answered by "good measure, pressed together and running over, measured into our bosoms." But there will be no waste by the bestowment of what we cannot take. "According to your faith, be it unto you." That is the accurate thermometer which measures the temperature of our spiritual state. It is like the steam gauge outside the boiler, which tells to a fraction the pressure of steam within, and so the power which can at the moment be exerted.

May I make a very simple, close personal application of this thought? We have as much religious life as we desire; that is, we have as much as our faith can take. There is the reason why such hosts of so-called Christians have such poor, feeble Christianity. We dare not say of any, "They have a name to live, and are dead." There is only one Eye who can tell when the heart has ceased to beat. But we may say that there are a mournful number of people who call themselves Christians, who look so like dead that no eye but Christ's can tell the difference. They are in a syncope that will be death soon, unless some mighty power rouse them.

And then, how many more of us there are, not as bad as that, but still feeble and languid, whose Christian history is a history of weakness, while God's power is open before us, of starving in the midst of abundance, broken only by moments of firmer faith, and so of larger, happier possession, that make the poverty-stricken ordinary days appear ten times more poverty-stricken. The channel lies dry, a waste chaos of white stones and driftwood for long months, and only for an hour or two after the clouds have burst on the mountains does the stream fill it from bank to bank. Do not many of us remember moments of a far deeper and more earnest trust in Christ than marks our ordinary days? If such moments were continuous, should not we be the happy possessors of beauties of character and spiritual power, such as would put our present selves utterly to shame? And why are they not continuous? Why are our possessions in God so small, our power so weak? Dear friends! "ye are not straitened in yourselves." The only reason for defective spiritual progress and character is defective faith.

Then look at this same principle as it affects our faculties for Christian service. There, too, it is true that all things are possible to him that believeth. The saying had an application to the disciples who stood by, half-ashamed and half-surprised at their failure to cast out the demon, as well as to the father in his agony of desire and doubt. For them it meant that the measure of Christian service was mainly determined by the measure of their faith. It would scarcely be an exaggeration to say that in Christ's service a man can do pretty nearly what he believes he can do, if his confidence is built, not on himself, but on Christ.

If those nine Apostles, waiting there for their Master, had thought they could cast out the devil from the boy, do you not think that they could have done it? I do not mean to say that rash presumption, undertaking in levity and self-confidence unsuitable kinds of work, will be honored with success. But I do mean to say that, in the line of our manifest duty, the extent to which we can do Christ's work is very much the extent to which we believe, in dependence on Him, that we can do it. If we once make up our minds that we shall do a certain thing by Christ's help and for His sake, in ninety cases out of a hundred the expectation will fulfill itself, and we shall do it. "Why could not we cast him out?" They need not have asked the question. "Why could not you cast him out? Why, because you did not think you could, and with your timid attempt, making an experiment which you were not sure would succeed, provoked the failure which you feared." The Church has never believed enough in its Christ-given power to cast out demons. We have never been confident enough that the victory was in our hands if we knew how to use our powers.

The same thing is true of each one of us. Audacity and presumption are humility and moderation, if only we feel that "our sufficiency is of God." "I can do all things" is the language of simple soberness, if we go on to say "through Christ which strengtheneth me."

There is one more point, drawn from these words, viz., our faith can only take hold on the divine promises. Such language as this of my text and other kindred sayings of our Lord's has often been extended beyond its real force, and pressed into the service of a mistaken enthusiasm, for want of observing that very plain principle. The principle of our text has reference to outward things as well as to the spiritual life. But there are great exaggerations and misconceptions as to the province of faith in reference to these temporal things, and consequently there are misconceptions and exaggerations on the part of many very good people as to the province of prayer in regard to them.

It seems to me that we shall be saved from these, if we distinctly recognize a very obvious principle, namely, that ''faith'' can never go further than God's clear promises, and that whatever goes beyond God's word is not faith, but something else assuming its appearance.

For instance, suppose a father nowadays were to say: ''My child is sore vexed with sickness. I long for his recovery. I believe that Christ can heal him. I believe that He will. I pray in faith, and I know that I shall be answered.'' Such a prayer goes beyond the record. Has Christ told you that it is His will that your child shall be healed? If not, how can you pray in faith that it is? You may pray in confidence that he will be healed, but such confident persuasion is not faith. Faith lays hold of Christ's distinct declaration of His will, but such confidence is only grasping a shadow, your own wishes. The father in this story was entitled to trust, because Christ told him that his trust was the condition of his son's being healed. So in response to the great word of our text, the man's faith leaped up and grasped our Lord's promise, with ''Lord, I believe.'' But before Christ spoke, his desires, his wistful longing, his imploring cry for help, had no warrant to pass into faith, and did not so pass.

Christ's word must go before our faith, and must supply the object for our faith, and where Christ has not spoken, there is no room for the exercise of any faith, except the faith, ''It is the Lord; let Him do what seemeth to Him good.'' That is the true prayer of faith in regard to all matters of outward providence where we have no distinct word of God's which gives unmistakable indication of His will. The ''if'' of the leper, which has no place in the spiritual region, where we know that ''this is the will of God, even our sanctification,'' has full force in the temporal region, where we do not know before the event what the will of the Lord is, ''If Thou wilt, thou canst,'' is there our best prayer.

Wherever a distinct and unmistakable promise of God's goes, it is safe for faith to follow; but to outrun His word is not faith, but self-will, and meets the deserved rebuke, ''Should it be according to thy mind?'' There *are* unmistakable promises about outward things on which we may safely build. Let us confine our expectations within the limits of these, and turn them into the prayer of faith, so shooting back whence they came His winged words, "This is the confidence that we have, that if we ask anything according to His will He heareth us." Thus coming to Him, submitting all our wishes in regard to this world to His most loving will, and widening our confidence to the breadth of His great and loving purpose in regard to our own inward life, as well as in regard to our practical service, His answer will ever be, "Great is thy faith; be it unto thee even as thou wilt."

Unbelieving Belief

And straightway the father of the child cried out, and said with tears, Lord, I believe; help Thou mine unbelief. MARK 9:24.

We owe to Mark's Gospel the fullest account of the pathetic incident of the healing of the demoniac boy. He alone gives us this part of the conversation between our Lord and the afflicted child's father. The poor man had brought his child to the disciples, and found them unable to do anything with him. A torrent of appeal breaks from his lips as soon as the Lord gives him an opportunity of speaking. He dwells upon all the piteous details with that fondness for repetition which sorrow knows so well. Jesus gives him back his doubts. The father said, "If thou canst do anything, have compassion on us and help us." Christ's answer, according to the true reading, is not as it stands in our Authorized Version, "If thou canst *believe*"—throwing, as it were, the responsibility on the man—but it is a quotation of the father's own word, "If Thou *canst,*" as if He waves it aside with superb recognition of its utter unfitness to the present case. "Say not, If Thou canst. *That* is certain. All things are possible to thee" (not to *do,* but to *get*) *"if"*—which is the only "if" in the case—"thou believest. I can, and if thy faith lays hold on My Omnipotence, all is done."

That majestic word is like the blow of steel upon flint; it strikes a little spark of faith which lights up the soul and turns the smoky pillar of doubt into clear flame of confidence. "Lord, I believe; help Thou mine unbelief."

I think in these wonderful words we have four things—the birth, the infancy, the cry, and the education, of faith. And to these four I turn now.

1. First, then, note here the birth of faith. There are many ways to the temple, and it matters little by which of them a man travels, if so be he gets there. There is no royal road to the Christian faith which saves the soul. And yet, though identity of experience is not to be expected, men are like each other in the depths, and only unlike on the surfaces, of their being. Therefore one man's experience carefully analyzed is very apt to give, at least, the rudiments of the experience of all others who have been in similar circumstances. So I think we can see here, without insisting on any pedantic repetition of the same details in every case, in broad outline, a sketched map of the road. There are three elements here: eager desire, the sense of utter helplessness, and the acceptance of Christ's calm assurances. Look at these three.

This man knew what he wanted, and he wanted it very sorely. Whosoever has any intensity and reality of desire for the great gifts which Jesus Christ comes to bestow, has taken at least one step on the way to faith. Conversely, the hindrances which block the path of a great many of us are simply that we do not care to possess the blessings which Jesus Christ in His Gospel offers. I am not talking now about the so-called intellectual hindrances to belief, though I think that a great many of these, if carefully examined, would be found, in the ultimate analysis, to repose upon this same stolid indifference to the blessings which Christianity offers. But what I wish to insist upon is that for large numbers of us, and no doubt for many men and women whom I address now, the real reason why they have not trust in Jesus Christ is because they do not care to possess the blessings which Jesus Christ brings. Do you desire to have your sins forgiven? Has purity any attraction for you? Do you care at all about the calm and pure blessings of communion with God? Would you like to live always in the light of His face? Do you want to be the masters of your own lusts and passions? I do not ask you, Do you want to go to Heaven or to escape Hell, when you die? but I ask, Has that future in any of its aspects any such power over you as that it stirs you to any earnestness and persistency of desire, or is it all shadowy and vain, ineffectual and dim?

What we Christian teachers have to fight against is that we are charged to offer to men a blessing that they do not want, and have to create a demand before there can be any acceptance of the supply. "Give us the leeks and garlics of Egypt," said the Hebrews in the wilderness; "our soul loatheth this light bread." So it is with many of us; we do not want God, goodness, quietness of conscience, purity of life, self-consecration to a lofty ideal, one-thousandth part as much as we want success in our daily occupations, or some one or other of the delights that the world gives. I remember Luther, in his rough way, has a story—I think it is in his *Table-talk*—about a herd of swine to whom their keeper offered some rich dainties, and the pigs said, "Give us grains." That is what so many men do when Jesus Christ comes with His gifts and His blessings. They turn away, but if they were offered some poor earthly good, all their desires would go out towards it, and their eager hands would be scrambling who should first possess it.

Oh brethren, if we saw things as they are, and our needs as they are, nothing would kindle such intensity of longing in our hears as that rejected or neglected promise of life eternal and divine which Jesus Christ brings. If I could only once wake in some indifferent heart this longing, that heart would have taken at least the initial step to a life of Christian godliness.

Further, we have here the other element of a sense of utter helplessness. How often this poor father had looked at his boy in the grip of the fiend, and had wrung his hands in despair that he could not do anything for him! That same sense of absolute impotence is one which we all, if we rightly understand what we need, must cherish. Can you forgive your own sins? Can you cleanse your own nature? Can you make yourselves other than you are by any effort of volition, or by any painfulness of discipline? To a certain small extent you can. In regard to superficial culture and eradication, your careful husbandry of your own wills may do much, but you cannot deal with your deepest needs. If we understand what is required, in order to bring one soul into harmony and fellowship with God, we shall recognize that we ourselves can do nothing to save, and little to help ourselves. "Every man his own redeemer," which is the motto of some people nowadays, may do very well for fine weather and for superficial experience, but when the storm comes it proves a poor refuge, like the gay pavilions that they put up for festivals, which are all right whilst the sun is shining and the flags are fluttering, but are wretched shelters when the rain beats and the wind howls. We can do nothing for ourselves. The recognition of our own helplessness is the obverse, so to speak, and underside, of confidence in the divine help. The coin, as it were, has its two faces. On the one is written, "Trust in the Lord;" on the other is written, "Nothing is myself." A drowning man, if he tries to help himself, only encumbers his would-be rescuer, and may drown him too. The truest help he can give is to let the strong arm that has cleft the waters for his sake fling itself around him and bear him safe to land. So, eager desire after offered blessings and consciousness of my own impotence to secure them—these are the initial steps of faith.

And the last of the elements here is, listening to the calm assurance of Jesus Christ: "If Thou canst! Do not say that to Me; I can, and because I can, all things are possible for thee to receive." In like manner He stands at the door of each of our hearts and speaks to each of our needs, and says: "I can satisfy it. Rest for thy soul, cleansing for thy sins, satisfaction for thy desires, guidance for thy pilgrimage, power for thy duties, patience in thy sufferings—all these will come to thee, if thou layest hold of My hand.'' His assurance helps trembling confidence to be born, and out of doubt the great calm word of the Master smites the fire of trust. And we, dear brethren, if we will listen to Him, shall surely find in Him all that we need. Think how marvelous it is that this Jewish peasant should plant Himself in the front of humanity, over against the burdened, sinful race of men, and pledge Himself to forgive and to cleanse their sins, to bear all their sicknesses, to be their strength in weakness, their comfort in sorrow, the rest of their hearts, their heaven upon earth, their life in death, their glory in heaven, and their all in all; and not only should pledge Himself, but in the blessed experience of millions should have more than fulfilled all that. He promised. ''They trusted in Him, and were lightened, and their faces were not ashamed.'' Will you not answer His sovereign word of promise with your ''Lord, I believe''?

2. Then, secondly, we have here the infancy of faith. As soon as the consciousness of belief dawned upon the father, and the effort to exercise it was put forth, there sprang up the consciousness of its imperfection. He would never have known that he did not believe unless he had tried to believe. So it is in regard to all excellences and graces of character. The desire of possessing some feeble degree of any virtue or excellence, and the effort to put it forth, is the surest way of discovering how little of it we have. On the other side, sorrow for the lack of some form of goodness is itself a proof of the partial possession, in some rudimentary and incipient form, of that goodness. The utterly lazy man never mourns over his idleness; it is only the one that would fain work harder than he does, and already works tolerably hard, who does so. So the little spark of faith in this man's heart, like a taper in a cavern, showed the abysses of darkness that lay unillumined round about it.

Thus, then, in its infancy, faith may and does coexist with much unfaith and doubt. The same state of mind, looked at from its two opposite ends, as it were, may be designated faith or unbelief; just as a piece of shot silk, according to the angle at which you hold it, may show you only the bright colors of its warp or the dark ones of its weft. When you are traveling in a railway train with the sun streaming in at the windows, if you look out on the one hand you will see the illumined face of every tree and blade of grass and house; and if you look out on the other, you will see their shadowed side. And so the same landscape may seem to be all lit up by the sunshine of belief, or to be darkened by the gloom of distrust. If we consider how great and how perfect ought to be our confidence, to bear any due proportion to the firmness of that upon which it is built, we shall not be slow to believe that through life there will always be the presence in us, more or less, of these two elements. There will be all degrees of progress between the two extremes of infantile and mature faith.

There follows from that thought this practical lesson, that the discovery of much unbelief should never make a man doubt the reality or genuineness of his little faith. We are all apt to write needlessly bitter things against ourselves when we get a glimpse of the incompleteness of our Christian life and character. But there is no reason why a man should fancy that he is a hypocrite because he finds out that he is not a perfect believer. But, on the other hand, let us remember that the main thing is not the maturity, but the progressive character, of faith. It was most natural that this man in our text, at the very first moment when he began to put his confidence in Jesus Christ as able to heal his child, should be aware of much tremulousness mingling with it. But is it not most unnatural that there should be the same relative proportion of faith and unbelief in the heart and experience of men who have long professed to be Christians? You do not expect the infant to have adult limbs, but you do expect it to grow. True, faith at its beginning may be like a grain of mustard seed, but if the grain of mustard seed be alive it will grow to a great tree, where all the fowls of the air can lodge in the branches. Oh! it is a crying shame and sin that in all Christian communities there should be so many grayheaded babies, men who have for years and years been professing to be Christ's followers, and whose faith is but little, if at all, stronger—nay! perhaps is even obviously weaker—than it was in the first days of their profession. "Ye have need of milk, and not of strong meat," very many of you. And the vitality of your faith is made suspicious, not because it is feeble, but because it is not growing stronger.

3. Notice the cry of infant faith. "Help thou mine unbelief" may have either of two meanings. The man's desire was either that his faith should be increased and his unbelief "helped" by being removed by Christ's operation upon his spirit, or that Christ would "help" him and his boy by healing the child, though the faith which asked the blessing was so feeble that it might be called unbelief. There is nothing in the language or in the context to determine which of these two meanings is intended; we must settle it by our own sense of what would be most likely under the circumstances. To me it seems extremely improbable that, when the father's whole soul was absorbed in the healing of his son, he should turn aside to ask for the inward and spiritual process of having his faith strengthened. Rather he said, "Heal my child, though it is unbelief as much as faith that asks Thee to do it."

The lesson is that, even when we are conscious of much tremulousness in our faith, we have a right to ask and expect that it shall be answered. Weak faith *is* faith. The tremulous hand *does* touch. The cord may be slender as a spider's web that binds a heart to Jesus but it *does* bind. The poor woman in the other miracle who put out her wasted fingertip, coming behind Him in the crowd, and stealthily touching the hem of His garment, though it was only the end of her fingernail that was laid on the robe, carried away with her the blessing. And so the feeblest faith joins the soul, in the measure of its strength, to Jesus Christ.

But let us remember that, whilst thus the cry of infant faith is heard, the stronger voice of stronger faith is more abundantly heard. Jesus Christ once for all laid down the law when He said to one of the suppliants at His feet, "According to your faith be it unto you." The measure of our belief is the measure of our blessing. The wider you open the door, the more angels will crowd into it, with their white wings and their calm faces. The bore of the pipe determines the amount of water that flows into the cistern. Every man gets, in the measure in which he desires. Though a tremulous hand may hold out a cup into which Jesus Christ will not refuse to pour the wine of the kingdom, yet the tremulous hand will spill much of the blessing; and he that would have the full enjoyment of the mercies promised, and possible, must "ask in faith, nothing wavering." The sensitive paper which records the hours of sunshine in a day has great gaps upon its line of light answering to the times when clouds have obscured the sun; and the communication of blessings from God is intermittent, if there be intermittency of faith. If you desire an unbroken line of mercy, joy, and peace, keep up an unbroken continuity of trustful confidence.

4. Lastly, we have here the education of faith. Christ paid no heed in words to the man's confession of unbelief, but proceeded to do the work which answered his prayer in both its possible meanings. He responded to imperfect confidence by His perfect work of cure, and, by that perfect work of cure, He strengthened the imperfect confidence which it had answered.

Thus He educates us by His answers—His over-answers—to our poor desires; and the abundance of His gifts rebukes the poverty of our petitions more emphatically than any words of remonstrance beforehand could have done. He does not lecture us into faith, but He blesses us into it. When the Apostle was sinking in the flood, Jesus Christ said no word of reproach until He had grasped him with His strong hand and held him safe. And then, when the sustaining touch thrilled through all the frame, then, and not till then, He said—as we may fancy, with a smile on His face that the moonlight showed—as knowing how unanswerable His question was, "O thou of little faith, *wherefore* didst thou doubt?" That is how He will deal with us if we will; over-answering our tremulous petitions, and so teaching us to hope more abundantly that "we shall praise Him more and more."

The disappointments, the weaknesses, the shameful defeats which come when our confidence fails, are another page of His lessonbook. The same Apostle of whom I have been speaking got that lesson when, standing on the billows, and, instead of looking at Christ, looking at their wrath and foam, his heart failed him, and because his heart failed him he began to sink. If we turn away from Jesus Christ, and interrupt the continuity of our faith by calculating the height of the breakers and the weight of the water that is in them, and what will become of us when they topple over with their white crests upon our heads, then gravity will begin to work, and we shall begin to sink. And well for us if, when we have sunk as far as our knees, we look back again to the Master and say, "Lord, save me; I perish!" The weakness which is our own when faith sleeps, and the rejoicing power which is ours because it is His, when faith wakes, are God's education of it to fuller and ampler degrees and depth. We shall lose the meaning of life, and the best lesson that joy and sorrow, calm and storm, victory and defeat, can give us, unless all these make us "rooted and grounded in faith."

Dear friend, do you desire your truest good? Do you know that you cannot win it, or fight for it to gain it, or do anything to obtain it, in your own strength? Have you heard Jesus Christ saying to you, "Come . . . and I will give you rest"? Oh! I beseech you, do not turn away from Him, but like this agonized father in our story, fall at His feet with "Lord, I believe; help Thou mine unbelief," and He will confirm your feeble faith by His rich response.

Receiving And Forbidding

And He came to Capernaum: and being in the house He asked
them, What was it that ye disputed among yourselves by the way! 34.
But they held their peace: for by the way they had disputed among
themselves, who should be the greatest, 35. And He sat down, and
called the Twelve, and saith unto them, If any man desire to be first,
the same shall be last for all, and servant of all. 36. And He took
a child, and set him in the midst of them: and when He had taken him
in His arms, He said unto them, 37. Whosoever shall receive one
of such children in My name, receiveth Me: and whosoever shall
receive Me, receiveth not Me, but Him that sent Me. 38. And John
answered Him, saying, Master, we saw one casting out devils in Thy

name, and he followeth not us: and we forbade him, because he followeth not us. 39. But Jesus said, Forbid him not: for there is no man which shall do a miracle in My name, that can lightly speak evil of Me. 40. For he that is not against us is on our part. 41. For whosoever shall give you a cup of water to drink in My name, because ye belong to Christ, verily I say unto you, he shall not lose his reward. 42. And whosoever shall offend one of these little ones that believe in Me, it is better for him that a millstone were hanged about his neck, and he were cast into the sea. MARK 9:33–42.

Surely the disciples might have found something better to talk about on the road from Caesarea, where they had heard from Jesus of His sufferings, than this miserable wrangle about rank! Singularly enough, each announcement of the Cross seems to have provoked something of the sort. Probably they understood little of His meaning, but hazily thought that the crisis was at hand when He should establish the kingdom; and so their ambition, rather than their affection, was stirred. Perhaps, too, the dignity bestowed on Peter after his confession, and the favor shown to the three witnesses of the Transfiguration, may have created jealousy. Matthew makes the quarrel to have been about future precedence; Mark about present. The one was striven for with a view to the other. How chill it must have struck on Christ's heart, that those who loved Him best cared so much more for their own petty superiority than for His sorrows!

1. Note the law of service as the true greatness (verses 33–35). "When He was in the house, He asked them." He had let them talk as they would on the road, walking alone in front, and they keeping, as they thought, out of earshot; but, when at rest together in the house (perhaps Peter's) where He lived in Capernaum, He lets them see, by the question and still more by the following teaching, that He knew what He asked, and needed no answer. The tongues that had been so loud on the road were dumb in the house—silenced by conscience. His servants still do and say many things on the road which they would not do if they saw Him close beside them, and they sometimes fancy that these escape Him. But when they are "in the house" with Him, they will find that He knew all that was going on; and when He asks the account of it, they, too, will be speechless. "A thing which does not appear wrong by itself shows its true character when brought to the judgment of God and the knowledge of Jesus Christ" *(Bengel)*.

Christ deals with the fault with much solemnity, seating Himself, as Teacher and Superior, and summoning the whole Twelve to hear. We do not enter on the difficult question of the relation of Mark's report of our Lord's words to those of the other Evangelists, but rather try to bring out the significance of their form and connection here. Note, then, that here we have not so much the nature of true greatness, as the road to it. "If any man would be first," he is to be least and servant, and thereby he will reach his aim. Of course, that involves the conception of the nature of true greatness as service, but still the distinction is to be kept in view. Further, "last of all" is not the same as "servant of all." The one phrase expresses humility; the other, ministry. An indolent humility, so very humble that it does nothing for others, and a service which is not humble, are equally incomplete, and neither leads to or is the greatness at which alone a Christian ought to aim. There are two paradoxes here. The lowest is the highest, the servant is the chief; and they may be turned round with equal truth—the highest is the lowest, and the chief is the servant. The former tells us how things really are, and what they look like, when seen from the center by His eye. The latter prescribes the duties and responsibilities of high position. In fact and truth, to sink is the way to rise, and to serve is the way to rule—only the rise and the rule are of another sort than contents worldly ambition, and the Christian must rectify his notions of what loftiness and greatness are. On the other hand, distinguishing gifts of mind, heart, leisure, position, possessions, or anything else, are given us for others, and bind us to serve. Both things follow from the nature of Christ's kingdom, which is a kingdom of love; for in love the vulgar distinctions of higher and lower are abolished, and service is delight. This is no mere pretty sentiment, but a law which grips hard and cuts deep. Christ's servants have not learned it yet, and the world heeds it not; but, till it governs all human society, and pulls up ambition, domination, and pride of place by the roots, society will groan under ills which increase with the increase of wealth and culture in the hands of a selfish few.

2. Not the exhibition of the law in a life. Children are quick at finding out who loves them, and there would always be some hovering near for a smile from Christ. With what eyes of innocent wonder the child would look up at Him, as He gently set him there, in the open space in front of Himself! Mark does not record any accompanying words, and none were needed. The unconsciousness of rank, the spontaneous acceptance of inferiority, the absence of claims to consideration and respect, which naturally belong to childhood as it ought to be, and give it winningness and grace, are the marks of a true disciple, and are the more winning in such because they are not of nature, but regained by self-abnegation. What the child is we have to become. This child was the example of one-half of the law, being "least of all," and perfectly contented to be so; but the other half was not shown in him, for his little hands could do but small service. Was there, then, no example in this scene of that other requirement? Surely there was; for the child was not left standing, shy, in the midst, but, before embarrasssment became weeping, was caught up in Christ's arms, and folded to His heart. He had been taken as the instance of humility, and he then became the subject of tender ministry. Christ and he divided the illustration of the whole law between them, and the very inmost nature of true service was shown in our Lord's loving clasp and soothing pressure to His heart. It is as if He had said, "Look! this is how you must serve; for you cannot help the weak unless you open your arms and hearts to them." Jesus, with the child held to His bosom, is the living law of service, and the child nestling close to him, because sure of His love, is the type of the trustful affection which we must evoke if we are to serve or help. This picture has gone straight to the hearts of men; and who can count the streams of tenderness and practical kindliness of which it has been the source?

Christ goes on to speak of the child, not as the example of service, but of being served. The deep words carry us into blessed mysteries which will recompense the lowly servants, and lift them high in the kingdom. Observe the precision of the language, both as regards the persons received and the motive of reception. "One of such little children" means those who are thus lowly, unambitious, and unexacting. "In My name" defines the motive as not being simple humanity or benevolence, but the distinct recognition of Christ's command and loving obedience to His revealed character. No doubt, natural benevolence has its blessings for those who exercise it; but that which is here spoken of is something much deeper than nature, and wins a far higher reward.

That reward is held forth in unfathomable words, of which we can but skim the surface. They mean more than that such little ones are so closely identified with Him that, in His love, He reckons good done to them as done to Him. That is most blessedly true. Nor is it true only because He lovingly reckons the deed as done to Him, though it really is not; but, by reason of the derived life which all His children possess from Him, they are really parts of Himself; and in that most real though mystic unity, what is done to them is, in fact, done to Him. Further, if the service be done in His name, then, on whomsoever it may be done, it is done to Him. This great saying unveils the true sacredness and real recipient of all Christian service. But more than that is in the words. When we "receive" Christ's little ones by help and loving ministry, we receive Him, and in Him God, for joy and strength. Unselfish deeds in His name open the heart for more of Christ and God, and bring on the doer the blessing of fuller insight, closer communion, more complete assimilation to his Lord. Therefore such service is the road to the true superiority in His kingdom, which depends altogether on the measure of His own nature which has flowed into our emptiness.

3. The Apostles' conscience-stricken confession of their breach of the law (verses 38–40). Peter is not spokesman this time, but John, whose conscience was more quickly pricked. At first sight, the connection of his interruption with the theme of the discourse seems to be merely the recurrence of the phrase, "in Thy name"; but, besides that, there is an obvious contrast between "receiving" and "forbidding." The Apostle is uneasy when he remembers what they had done, and, like an honest man, he states the case to Christ, half-confession, and half-asking for a decision. He begins to think that perhaps the man whom they had silenced was "one such little child," and had deserved more sympathetic treatment. How he came to be so true a disciple as to share in the power of casting out devils, and yet not to belong to the closer followers of Jesus, we do not know, and need not guess. So it was; and John feels, as he tells the story, that perhaps their motives had not been so much their Master's honor as their own. "He followeth not us," and yet he is trenching on our prerogatives. The greater fact that he and they followed Christ was overshadowed by the lesser that he did not follow them. There spoke the fiery spirit which craved the commission to burn up a whole village, because of its inhospitality. There spoke the spirit of ecclesiastical intolerance, which in all ages has masqueraded as zeal for Christ, and taken "following us" and "following Him" to be the same thing. But there spoke, too, a glimmering consciousness that gagging men was not precisely "receiving" them, and that if "in Thy name" so sanctified deeds, perhaps the unattached exorcist, who could cast out demons by it, was "a little one" to be taken to their hearts, and not an enemy to be silenced. Pity that so many listen to the law, and do not, like John, feel it prick them!

Chirst forbids such "forbidding," and thereby sanctions "irregularities" and "unattached" work, which have always been the bugbears of sticklers for ecclesiastical uniformity, and have not seldom been the life of Christianity. That authoritative, unconditional "forbid him not" ought, long ago, to have rung the funeral knell of intolerance, and to have ended the temptation to idolize "conformity," and to confound union to organized forms of the Christian community with union to Chirst. But bigotry dies hard. The reasons appended serve to explain the position of the man in question. If he had wrought miracles in Christ's name, he must have had some faith in it; and his experience of its power would deepen that. So there was no danger of his contradicting himself by speaking against Jesus. The power of "faith in the Name" to hallow deeds, the certainty that rudimentary faith will, when exercised, increase, the guarantee of experience as such to lead to blessing from Jesus, are all involved in this saying. But its special importance is as a reason for the disciples' action. Because the man's action gives guarantees for his future, they are not to silence him. That implies that they are only to forbid those who do speak evil of Christ; and that to all others, even if they have not reached the full perception of truth, they are to extend patient forbearance and guidance. "The mouth of them that speak lies shall be stopped"; but the mouth that begins to stammer His name is to be taught and cherished.

Christ's second reason still more plainly claims the man for an ally. Commentators have given themselves a great deal of trouble to reconcile this saying with the other—"He that is not with Me is against Me." If by reconciling is meant twisting both to mean the same thing, it cannot be done. If preventing the appearance of contradiction is meant, it does not seem necessary. The two sayings do not contradict, but they complete, each other. They apply to different classes of persons, and common sense has to determine their application. This man did, in some sense, believe in Jesus, and worked deeds that proved the power of the Name. Plainly, such work was in the same direction as the Lord's and the disciples'. Such a case is one for the application of tolerance. But the principle must be limited by the other, else it degenerates into lazy indifference. "He that is not against us is for us," if it stood alone, would dissolve the Church, and destroy distinctions in belief and practice which it would be fatal to lose. "He that is not with Me is against Me," if it stood alone, would narrow sympathies, and cramp the free development of life. We need both to understand and get the good of either.

4. We have the reward of receiving Christ's little ones set over against the retribution that seizes those who cause them to stumble (verses 41, 42). These verses seem to resume the broken thread of verse 37, whilst they also link on to the great principle laid down in verse 40. He that is "not against" is "for," even if he only gives a "cup of water" to Christ's disciple because he is Christ's. That shows that there is regard for Jesus in him. It is a germ which may grow. Such a one shall certainly have his reward. That does not mean that he will receive it in a future life, but that here his deed shall bring after it blessed consequences to himself. Of these, none will be more blessed than the growing regard for the Name, which already is, in some degree, precious to him. The faintest perception of Christ's beauty, honestly lived out, will be increased. Every act strengthens its motive. The reward of living our convictions is firmer and more enlightened conviction. Note, too, that the person spoken of belongs to the same class as the silenced exorcist, and that this reads the disciples a further lesson. Jesus will look with love on the acts which even a John wished to forbid. Note, also, that the disciples here are the recipients of the kindness. They are no longer being taught to receive the "little ones," but are taught that they themselves belong to that class, and need kindly succor from these outsiders, whom they had proudly thought to silence.

The awful, reticent words, which shadow forth and yet hide the fate of those who cause the feeblest disciple to stumble, are not for us to dilate upon. Jesus saw the realities of future retribution, and deliberately declares that death is a lesser evil than such an act. The "little ones" are sacred because they are His. The same relation to Him which made kindness to them so worthy of reward, makes harm to them so worthy of punishment. Under the one lies an incipient love to Him; under the other, a covert and perhaps scarcely conscious opposition. It is devil's work to seduce simple souls from allegiance to Christ. There are busy hands today laying stumbling blocks in the way, especially of young Christians—stumbling blocks of doubt, of frivolity, of slackened morality, and the like. It were better, says One who saw clearly into that awful realm beyond, if a heavy millstone were knotted about their necks, and they were flung into the deepest place of the lake that lay before Him as he spoke. He does not speak exaggerated words; and if a solemn strain of vehemence, unlike His ordinary calm, is audible here, it is because what He knew, and did not tell, gave solemn earnestness to His veiled and awe-inspiring prophecy of doom. What imagination shall fill out the details of the "worse than" which lurks behind that "better"?

Salted with Fire

Every one shall be salted with fire. MARK 9:49.

Our Lord has just been uttering some of the most solemn words that ever came from His gracious lips. He has been enjoining the severest self-suppression, extending even to mutilation and excision of the eye, the hand, or the foot, that might cause us to stumble. He has been giving that sharp lesson on the ground of plain common sense and enlightened self-regard. It *is* better, obviously, to live maimed than to die whole. The man who elects to keep a mortified limb, and thereby to lose life, is a suicide and a fool. It is a solemn thought that a similar mad choice is possible in the moral and spiritual region.

To these stern injunctions, accompanied by the awful sanctions of that consideration, our Lord appends the words of my text. They are obscure and have often been misunderstood. This is not the place to enter on a discussion of the various explanations that have been proposed of them. A word or two is all that is needful to put us in possession of the point of view from which I wish to lay them on your hearts at this time.

I take the "every one" of my text to mean not mankind generally, but every individual of the class whom our Lord is addressing—that is to say, His disciples. He is laying down the law for all Christians. I take the paradox which brings together "salting" and "fire," to refer, not to salt as a means of communicating savor to food, but as a means of preserving from putrefaction. And I take the "fire" here to refer, not to the same process which is hinted at in the awful preceding words, "the fire is not quenched," but to be set in opposition to that fire, and to mean something entirely different. There is a fire that destroys, and there is a fire that preserves; and the alternative for every man is to choose between the destructive and the conserving influences. Christian disciples have to submit to be "salted with fire," lest a worse thing befall them.

1. And so the first point that I would ask you to notice here is—that fiery cleansing to which every Christian must yield. Now I have already referred to the relation between the words of my text and those immediately preceding, as being in some sense one of opposition and contrast. I think we are put on the right track for understanding the solemn words of this text if we remember the great saying of John the Baptist, where, in precisely similar fashion, there are set side by side the two conceptions of the chaff being cast into the unquenchable fire (the same expression as in our text), and "He shall baptize you with the Holy Ghost and with fire."

The salting fire, then, which cleanses and preserves, and to which every Christian soul must submit itself, to be purged thereby, is, as I take it, primarily and fundamentally the fire of that Divine Spirit which Christ Himself told us that He had come to cast upon the earth, and yearned, in a passion of desire, to see kindled. The very frequent use of the emblem in this same signification throughout Scripture, I suppose I need not recall to you. It seems to me that the only worthy interpretation of the words before us, which goes down into their depths and harmonizes with the whole of the rest of the teaching of Scripture, is that which recognizes these words of my text as no unwelcome threat, as no bitter necessity, but as a joyful promise bringing to men, laden and burdened with their sins, the Good News that it is possible for them to be purged from them entirely by the fiery ministration of that Divine Spirit. Just as we take a piece of foul clay and put into the furnace, and can see, as it gets red-hot, the stains melt away, as a cloud does in the blue, from its surface, so if we will plunge ourselves into the influences of that divine power which

Christ has come to communicate to the world, our sin and all our impurities will melt from off us, and we shall be clean. No amount of scrubbing with soap and water will do it. The stain is a great deal too deep for that, and a mightier solvent than any that we can apply, if unaided and unsupplied from above, is needed to make us clean. ''Who can bring a clean thing out of an unclean,'' especially when the would-be bringer is himself the unclean thing? Surely not one. Unless there be a power *ab extra,* unparticipant of man's evils, and yet capable of mingling with the evil man's inmost nature, and dealing with it, then I believe that universal experience and our individual experience tell us that there is no hope that we shall ever get rid of our transgressions.

Brethren, for a man by his own unaided effort, however powerful, continuous, and wisely directed it may be, to cleanse himself utterly from his iniquity, is as hopeless as it would be for him to sit down with a hammer and a chisel and try by mechanical means to get all the iron out of a piece of ironstone. The union is chemical, not mechanical. And so hammers and chisels will only get a very little of the metal out. The one solvent is fire. Put the obstinate crude ore into your furnace, and get the temperature up, and the molten metal will run clear. There should be mountains of scoriae, the dross and relics of our abandoned sins, around us all.

If we desire to be delivered, let us go into the fire. It will burn up all our evil, and it will burn up nothing else. Keep close to Christ. Lay your hearts open to the hallowing influences of the motives and the examples that lie in the story of His life and death. Seek for the fiery touch of that transforming Spirit, and be sure that you quench Him not, nor grieve Him. And then your weakness will be reinvigorated by celestial powers, and the live coal upon your lips will burn up all your iniquity.

But, subordinately to this deepest meaning, as I take it, of the great symbol of our text, let me remind you of another possible application of it, which follows from the preceding. God's Spirit cleanses men mainly by raising their spirits to a higher temperature. For coldness is akin to sin, and heavenly warmth is akin to righteousness. Enthusiasm always ennobles, delivers men, even on the lower reaches of life and conduct from many a meanness and many a sin. And when it becomes a warmth of spirit kindled by the reception of the fire of God, then it becomes the solvent which breaks the connection between me and my evil. It is the cold Christian who makes no progress in conquering his sin. The one who is filled with the love of God, and has the ardent convictions, and the burning enthusiasm which that love ought to produce in our hearts, is the man who will conquer and eject his evils.

Nor must we forget that there is still another possible application of the words. For whilst, on the one hand, the Divine Spirit's method of delivering us is very largely that of imparting to us the warmth of ardent, devout emotion; on the other hand, a part of this method is the passing of us through the fiery trials and outward disciplines of life. "Every one shall be salted with fire" in that sense. And we have learned, dear brethren, but little of the loving kindness of the Lord if we are not able to say, "I have grown more in likeness to Jesus Christ by rightly accepted sorrows than by anything besides." Be not afraid of calamities; be not stumbled by disaster. Take the fiery trial which is sent to you as being intended to bring about, at the last, the discovery "unto praise and honor and glory" of your faith, that is "much more precious than gold that perisheth, though it be tried with fire." "Every one shall be salted with fire," the Christian law of life is, Submit to the fiery cleansing. Alas! alas! for the many thousands of professing Christians who are wrapping themselves in such thick folds of non-conducting material that that fiery energy can only play on the surface of their lives, instead of searching them to the depths. Do you see to it, dear brethren, that you lay open your whole natures, down to the very inmost roots, to the penetrating, searching, cleansing power of that Spirit. And let us all go and say to Him, "Search me, O God! and try me, and see if there be any wicked way in me."

2. Notice the painfulness of this fiery cleansing. The same ideas substantially are conveyed in my text as are expressed, in different imagery, by the solemn words that precede it. The "salting with fire" comes substantially to the same thing as the amputation of the hand and foot, and the plucking out of the eye, that cause to stumble. The metaphor expresses a painful process. It is no pleasant thing to submit the bleeding stump to the actual cautery, and to press it, all sensitive, upon the hot plate that will stop the flow of blood. But such pain of shrinking nerves is to be borne, and to be courted, if we are wise, rather than to carry the hand or the eye that led astray unmutilated into total destruction. Surely that is common sense.

The process is painful because we are weak. The highest ideal of Christian progress would be realized if one of the metaphors with which our Lord expresses it were adequate to cover the whole ground, and we grew as the wheat grows, "first the blade, then the ear, after that the full corn in the ear." But the tranquility of vegetable growth, and the peaceful progress which it symbolizes, are not all that you and I have to expect. Emblems of a very different kind have to be associated with that of the quiet serenity of the growing corn, in order to describe all that a Christian man has to experience in the work of becoming like his Master. It is a fight as well as a growth; it is a building requiring our continuity of effort, as well as a growth. There is something to be got rid of as well as much to be appropriated. We do not only need to become better, we need to become less bad. Squatters have camped on the land, and cling to it and hold it *vi et armis;* and these have to be ejected before peaceful settlement is possible.

One might go on multiplying metaphors *ad libitum,* in order to bring out the one thought that it needs huge courage to bear being sanctified, or, if you do not like the theological word, to bear being made better. It is no holiday task, and unless we are willing to have a great deal that is against the grain done to us, and in us, and by us, we shall never achieve it. We have to accept the pain. Desires have to be thwarted, and that is not pleasant. Self has to be suppressed, and that is not delightsome. A growing conviction of the depth of one's own evil has to be cherished, and that is not a grateful thought for any of us. Pains external, which are felt by reason of disciplinary sorrows, are not worthy to be named in the same day as those more recondite and inward agonies. But, brother, they are all "light" as compared with the exceeding weight of "glory," coming from conformity to the example of our Master, which they prepare for us.

And so I bring you Christ's message: He will have no man to enlist in His army under false pretenses. He will not deceive any of us by telling us that it is all easy work and plain sailing. Salting by fire can never be other than to the worse self an agony, just because it is to the better self a rapture. And so let us make up our minds that no man is taken to heaven in his sleep, and that the road is a rough one, judging from the point of view of flesh and sense; but though rough, narrow, often studded with sharp edges, like the plow colters that they used to lay in the path in the old rude ordeals, it still leads straight to the goal, and bleeding feet are little to pay for a seat at Christ's right hand.

3. Lastly, notice the preservative result of this painful cleansing. Our Lord brings together, in our text, as is often His wont, two apparently contradictory ideas, in order, by the paradox, to fix our attention the more vividly upon His words. Fire destroys; salt preserves. They are opposites. But yet the opposites may be united in one mighty reality, a fire which preserves and does not destroy. The deepest truth is that the cleansing fire which the Christ will give us preserves us, because it destroys that which is destroying us. If you kill the germs of putrefaction in a bit of dead flesh, you preserve the flesh; and if you bring to bear upon a man the power which will kill the thing that is killing him, its destructive influence is the condition of its conserving one.

And so it is, in regard to that great spiritual influence which Jesus Christ is ready to give to every one of us. It slays that which is slaying us, for our sins destroy in us the true life of a man, and make us but parables of walking death. When the three Hebrews were cast into the fiery furnace in Babylon, the flames burned nothing but their bonds, and they walked at liberty in the fire. And so it will be with us. We shall be preserved by that which slays the sins that would otherwise slay us.

Let me lay on your hearts before I close the solemn alternative to which I have already referred, and which is suggested by the connection of my text with the preceding words. There is a fire that destroys and is not quenched. Christ's previous words are much too metaphorical for us to build dogmatic definitions upon. But Jesus Christ did not exaggerate. If here and now sin has so destructive an effect upon a man, O, who will venture to say that he knows the limits of its murderous power in that future life, when retribution shall begin with new energy, and under new conditions? Brethren, whilst I dare not enlarge, I still less dare to suppress; and I ask you to remember that not I, or any man, but Jesus Christ Himself, has put before each of us this alternative—either the fire unquenchable, which destroys a man, or the merciful fire which slays his sins and saves him alive.

Social reformers, philanthropists, you that have tried and failed to overcome your evil, and who feel the loathly thing so intertwisted with your being that to pluck it from your heart is to tear away the very heart's walls themselves, here is a hope for you. Closely as our evil is twisted in with the fibers of our character, there is a hand that can untwine the coils, and cast away the sin, and preserve the soul. And although we sometimes feel as if our sinfulness and our sin were so incorporated with ourselves that it made oneself, with a man's head and a serpent's tail, let us take the joyful assurance that if we trust ourselves to Christ, and open our hearts to His power, we can shake off the venomous beast into the fire and live a fuller life, because the fire has consumed that which would otherwise have consumed us.

"Salt in Yourselves"

Have salt in yourselves, and have peace one with another. MARK 9:50.

In the context "salt is employed to express the preserving, purifying, divine energy which is otherwise spoken of as "fire." The two emblems produce the same result. They both salt—that is, they cleanse and keep. And if in the one we recognize the quick energy of the Divine Spirit as the central idea, no less are we to see the same typified under a slightly different aspect in the other. The fire transforms into its own substance and burns away all the grosser particles. The salt arrests corruption, keeps off destruction, and diffuses its sanative influence through all the particles of the substance with which it comes in contact. And in both metaphors it is the operation of God's cleansing Spirit, in its most general form, that is set forth, including all the manifold ways by which God deals with us to purge us from our iniquity, to free us from the death which treads close on the heels of wrongdoing, the decomposition and dissolution which surely follow on corruption.

This the disciples are exhorted to have in themselves that they may be at peace one with another. Perhaps we shall best discover the whole force of this saying by dealing—

1. With the symbol itself and the ideas derived from it. The salt cleanses, arrests corruption which impends over the dead masses, sweetens and purifies, and so preserves from decay and dissolution. It works by contact, and within the mass. It thus stands as an emblem of the cleansing which God brings, both in respect to that on which it operates, to the purpose of its application, and to the manner in which it produces its effects.

(*a*) That on which it operates.

There is implied here a view of human nature, not flattering but true. It is compared with a dead thing, in which the causes that bring about corruption are already at work, with the sure issue of destruction. This in its individual application comes to the assertion of sinful tendency and actual sin as having its seat and root in all our souls, so that the present condition is corruption, and the future issue is destruction. The consequent ideas are that any power which is to cleanse must come from without, not from within; that purity is not to be won by our own efforts, and that there is no disposition in human nature to make these efforts. There is no recuperative power in human nature. True, there may be outward reformation of habits, etc., but, if we grasp the thought that the taproot of sin is selfishness, this impotence becomes clearer, and it is seen that sin affects all our being, and that therefore the healing must come from beyond us.

(*b*) The purpose—namely, cleansing.

In salt we may include the whole divine energy; the Word, the Christ, the Spirit. So the intention of the Gospel is mainly to make clean. Preservation is a consequence of that.

(*c*) The manner of its application.

Inward, penetrating, by contact; but mainly the great peculiarity of

Christian ethics is that the inner life is dealt with first, the will and the heart, and afterwards the outward conduct.

2. The part which we have to take in this cleansing process. "Have salt" is a command; and this implies that while all the cleansing energy comes from God, the working of it on our souls depends on ourselves

(*a*) Its original reception depends on our faith.

The "salt" is here, but our contact with it is established by our acceptance of it. There is no magical cleansing; but it must be received within if we would share in its operation.

(*b*) Its continuous energy is not secured without our effort.

Let us just recall the principle already referred to, that the "salt" implies the whole cleansing divine energies, and ask what are these? The Bible variously speaks of men as being cleansed by the "blood of Christ," by the "truth," by the "Spirit." Now, it is not difficult to bring all these into one focus, viz., that the Spirit of God cleanses us by bringing the truth concerning Christ to bear on our understandings and hearts.

We are sanctified in proportion as we are coming under the influence of Christian truth, which, believed by our understandings and our hearts, supplies motives to our wills which lead us to holiness by copying the example of Christ.

Hence the main principle is that the cleansing energy operates on us in proportion as we are influenced by the truths of the Gospel.

Again, it works in proportion as we seek for, and submit to, the guidance of God's Holy Spirit.

In proportion as we are living in communion with Christ.

In proportion as we seek to deny ourselves and put away those evil things which "quench the Spirit."

This great grace, then, is not ours without our own effort. No original endowment is enough to keep us right. There must be the daily contact with, and constant renewing of the Holy Ghost. Hence arises a solemn appeal to all Christians.

Note the independence of the Christian character.

"In yourselves." "The water that I shall give him shall be in him a fountain," etc. Not, therefore, derived from the world, nor at second-hand from other men, but you have access to it for yourselves. See that you use the gift. "Hold fast that which thou hast," for there are enemies to withstand—carelessness, slothfulness, and self-confidence, etc.

3. The relation to one another of those who possess this energy. In proportion as Christians have salt in themselves, they will be at peace with one another. Remember that all sin is selfishness; therefore if we are cleansed from it, that which leads to war, alienation, and coldness will be removed. Even in this world there will be an anticipatory picture of the perfect peace which will abound when all are holy. Even now this great hope should make our mutual Christian relations very sweet and helpful.

Thus emerges the great principle that the foundation of the only real love among men must be laid in holiness of heart and life. Where the Spirit of God is working on a heart, there the seeds of evil passions are stricken out. The causes of enmity and disturbance are being removed. Men quarrel with each other because their pride is offended, or because their passionate desires after earthly things are crossed by a successful rival, or because they deem themselves not sufficiently respected by others. The root of all strife is self-love. It is the root of all sin. The cleansing which takes away the root removes in the same proportion the strife which grows from it. We should not be so ready to stand on our rights if we remembered how we come to have any hopes at all. We should not be so ready to take offense if we thought more of Him who is not soon angry. All the train of alienations, suspicions, earthly passions, which exist in our minds and are sure to issue in quarrels or bad blood, will be put down if we have "salt in ourselves."

This makes a very solemn appeal to Christian men. The Church is the garden where this peace should flourish. The disgrace of the Church is its envyings, jealousies, ill-natured scandal, idle gossip, love of preeminence, willingness to impute the worst possible motives to one another, sharp eyes for our brother's failings and none for our own. I am not pleading for any mawkish sentimentality, but for a manly peacefulness which comes from holiness. The holiest natures are always the most generous.

What a contrast the Church ought to present to the prevailing tone in the world! Does it? Why not? Because we do not possess the "salt." The dove flees from the cawing of rooks and squabbling of kites and hawks.

The same principle applies to all our human affections. Our loves of all sorts are safe only when they are pure. Contrast the society based on common possession of the one Spirit with the companionships which repose on sin, or only on custom or neighborhood. In all these there are possibilities of moral peril.

The same principle intensified gives us a picture of heaven and of hell. In the one are the "solemn troops and sweet societies"; in the other, no peace, no confidence, no bonds, only isolation, because sin which is selfishness lies at the foundation of the awful condition.

Friends, without that salt our souls are dead and rotting. Here is the great cure. Make it your own. So purified, you will be preserved, but, on the other hand, unchecked sin leads to quick destruction.

The dead, putrefying carcass—what a picture of a soul abandoned to evil and fit only for Gehenna!

10

Real Children and Pseudo-Disciples

Children and Childlike Men

And they brought young children to Him, that He should touch them: and His disciples rebuked those that brought them. 14. But when Jesus saw it, He was much displeased, and said unto them, Suffer the little children to come unto Me, and forbid them not: for of such is the kingdom of God. 15. Verily I say unto you, Whosoever shall not receive the kingdom of God as a little child, he shall not enter therein. MARK 10:13–15.

It was natural that the parents should have wanted Christ's blessing, so that they might tell their children in later days that His hand had been laid on their heads, and that He had prayed for them. And Christ did not think of it as a mere superstition. The disciples were not so akin to the children as He was, and they were a great deal more tender of His dignity than He. They thought of this as an interruption disturbing their high intercourse with Christ. "These children are always in the way, this is tiresome," etc.

1. Christ blessing children. It is a beautiful picture: the great Messiah with a child in His arms. We could not think of Moses or of Paul in such an attitude. Without it, we should have wanted one of the sweetest, gentlest, most human traits in His character; and how worldwide in its effect that act has been! How many a mother has bent over her child with deeper love; how many a parent has felt the sacredness of the trust more vividly; how many a mother has been drawn nearer to Christ; and how many a little child has had childlike love to Him awakened by it; how much of practical benevolence and of noble sacrifice for children's welfare, how many great institutions, have really sprung from this one deed!

And, if we turn from its effects to its meaning, it reveals Christ's love for children:—in its human side, as part of His character as man; in its deeper aspect as a revelation of the divine nature. It corrects dogmatic errors by making plain that, prior to all ceremonies or to repentance and faith, little children are loved and blessed by Him. Unconscious infants as these were folded in His arms and love. It puts away all gloomy and horrible thoughts which men have had about the standing of little children.

This is an act of Christ to infants expressive of His love to them, His care over them, their share in His salvation. Baptism is an act of man's, a symbol of his repentance and dying to sin and rising to a new life in Christ, a profession of his faith, an act of obedience to his Lord. It teaches nothing as to the relation of infants to the love of Jesus or to salvation. It does not follow that because that love is most sure and precious, baptism must needs be a sign of it. The question, what does baptism mean, must be determined by examination of texts which speak about baptism; not by a sidelight from a text which speaks about something else. There is no more reason for making baptism proclaim that Jesus Christ loves children than for making it proclaim that two and two make four.

2. The child's nearness to Christ. "Of such is the kingdom." "Except ye be converted and become like little children," etc. Now this does not refer to innocence; for, as a matter of fact, children are not innocent, as all schoolmasters and nurses know, whatever sentimental poets may say. Innocence is not a qualification for admission to the kingdom. And yet it is true that "heaven lies about us in our infancy," and that we are further off from it than when we were children. Nor does it mean that children are naturally the subjects of the kingdom, but only that the characteristics of the child are those which the man must have, in order to enter the kingdom; that their natural disposition is such as Christ requires to be directed to Him; or, in other words, that childhood has a special adaptation to Christianity. For instance, take dependence, trust, simplicity, unconsciousness, and docility.

These are the very characteristics of childhood, and these are the very emotions of mind and heart which Christianity requires. Add the child's strong faculty of imagination and its implicit belief; making the form of Christianity as the story of a life so easy to them. And we may add too: the absence of intellectual pride; the absence of the habit of dallying with moral truth. Everybody is to the child either a "good" man or a "bad." They have an intense realization of the unseen; an absence of developed vices and hard worldliness; a faculty of living in the present, free from anxious care and worldly hearts. But while thus they have special adaptation for receiving, they too need to come to Christ. These characteristics do not make Christians. They are to be directed to Christ. "Suffer them to come unto Me," the youngest child needs to, can, ought to, come to Christ. And how beautiful their piety is, ''Out of the mouths of babes and sucklings Thou hast perfected praise.'' Their fresh, unworn trebles struck on Christ's ear. Children ought to grow up in Christian households, ''innocent from much transgression.'' We ought to expect them to grow up Christian.

3. The child and the church. The child is a pattern to us men. We are to learn of them as well as teach them; what they are naturally, we are to strive to become, not childish but childlike. ''Even as a weaned child'' (see Psalm 131). The child-spirit is glorified in manhood. It is possible for us to retain it, and lose none of the manhood. ''In malice be ye children, but in understanding be men.'' The spirit of the kingdom is that of immortal youth.

The children are committed to our care.

The end of all training and care is that they should by voluntary act draw near to Him. This should be the aim in Sunday schools, for instance, and in families, and in all that we do for the poor around us.

See that we do not hinder their coming. This is a wide principle, viz., not to do anything which may interfere with those who are weaker and lower than we are finding their way to Jesus. The Church, and we as individual Christians, too often hinder this ''coming.''

Do not hinder by the presentation of the Gospel in a repellent form, either harshly dogmatic or sour.

Do not hinder by the requirement of such piety as is unnatural to a child.

Do not hinder by inconsistencies. This is a warning for Christian parents in particular.

Do not hinder by neglect. ''*Despise* not one of these little ones.''

Almost a Disciple

And when He was gone forth into the way, there came one running, and kneeled to Him, and asked Him, Good Master, what shall I do that I may inherit eternal life? 18. And Jesus said unto him, Why callest thou Me good? there is none good but one, that is, God. 19. Thou knowest the commandments, Do not commit adultery, Do not kill, Do not steal, Do not bear false witness, Defraud not, Honor thy father and mother. 20. And he answered and said unto Him, Master, all these have I observed from my youth. 21. Then Jesus beholding him loved him, and said unto him, One thing thou lackest: go thy way, sell whatsoever thou hast, and give to the poor, and thou shalt have treasure in heaven: and come, take up the cross, and follow Me. 22. And he was sad at that saying, and went away grieved: for he had great possessions. 23. And Jesus looked round about and saith unto His disciples, How hardly shall they that have riches enter into the kingdom of God! 24. And the disciples were astonished at His words. But Jesus answereth again, and saith unto them, Children, how hard is it for them that trust in riches to enter into the kingdom of God! 25. It is easier for a camel to go through the eye of a needle, than for a rich man to enter into the kingdom of God. 26. And they were astonished out of measure, saying among themselves, Who then can be saved? 27. And Jesus looking upon them saith, With men it is impossible, but not with God: for with God all things are possible. MARK 10:17–27.

There were courage, earnestness, and humility in this young ruler's impulsive casting of himself at Christ's feet in the way, with such a question. He was not afraid to recognize a teacher in Him whom his class scorned and hated; he was deeply sincere in his wish to possess eternal life, and in his belief that he was ready to do whatever was necessary for that end; he bowed himself as truly as he bent his knees before Jesus, and the noble enthusiasm of youth breathed in his desires, his words, and his gesture.

But his question betrayed the defect which poisoned the much that was right and lovable in him. He had but a shallow notion of what was "good," as is indicated by his careless ascription of goodness to one of whom he knew so little as he did of Jesus, and by his conception that it was a matter of deeds. He is too sure of himself; for he thinks that he is ready and able to do all good deeds, if only they are pointed out to him.

How little he understood the resistance of "the mind of the flesh" to discerned duty! Probably he had had no very strong inclinations to contend against, in living the respectable life that had been his. It is only when we row against the stream that we find out how fast it runs. He was wrong about the connection of good deeds and eternal life, for he thought of them as done by himself, and so of buying it by his own efforts. Fatal errors could not have been condensed in briefer compass, or presented in conjunction with more that is admirable, than in his eager question, asked so modestly and yet so presumptuously.

Our Lord answers with a coldness which startles; but it was meant to rouse, like a dash of icy water flung in the face. "Why callest thou Me good?" is more than a waving aside of a compliment, or a lesson in accuracy of speech. It rebukes the young man's shallow conception of goodness, as shown by the facility with which he bestowed the epithet. "None is good save one, even God," cuts up by the roots his notion of the possibility of self-achieved goodness, since it traces all human goodness to its source in God. If He is the only good, then we cannot perform good acts by our own power, but must receive power from Him. How, then, can any man ''inherit eternal life'' by good deeds, which he is only able to do because God has poured some of His own goodness into him? Jesus shatters the young man's whole theory, as expressed in his question, at one stroke.

But while His reply bears directly on the errors in the question, it has a wider significance. Either Jesus is here repudiating the notion of His own sinlessness, and acknowledging, in contradition to every other disclosure of His self-consciousness, that He too was not through and through good, or else He is claiming to be filled with God, the source of all goodness, in a wholly unique manner. It is a tremendous alternative, but one which has to be faced. While one is thankful if men even imperfectly apprehend the character and nature of Jesus, one cannot but feel that the question may fairly be put to the many who extol the beauty of His life, and deny His divinity, ''Why callest thou Me good?'' Either He is ''God manifest in the flesh,'' or He is not ''good.''

The remainder of Christ's answer tends to deepen the dawning conviction of the impossibility of meriting eternal life by acts of goodness, apart from dependence on God. He refers to the second half of the Decalogue only, not as if the first were less important, but because the breaches of the second are more easily brought to consciousness. In thus answering, Jesus takes the standpoint of the law, but for the purpose of bringing to the very opposite conviction from that which the young ruler expresses in reply. He declares that he has kept them all from his youth. Jesus would have had him confess that in them was a code too high to be fully obeyed. ''By the law is the knowledge of sin,'' but it had not done its work in this young man. His shallow notion of goodness besets and blinds him still. He is evidently thinking about external deeds, and is an utter stranger to the depths of his own heart. It was an answer betraying great shallowness in his conception of duty and in his self-knowledge.

It is one which is often repeated still. How many of us are there who, if ever we cast a careless glance over our lives, are quite satisfied with their external respectability! As long as the chambers that look to the street are fairly clean, many think that all is right. But what is there rotting and festering down in the cellars? Do we ever go down there with the ''candle of the Lord'' in our hands? If we do, the ruler's boast, ''All these have I kept,'' will falter into ''All these have I broken.''

But let us be thankful for the love that shone in Christ's eyes as He looked on him. We may blame; He Loved. Jesus saw the fault, but He saw the longing to be better. The dim sense of insufficiency which had driven this questioner to Him was clear to that all-knowing and all-loving heart. Do not let us harshly judge the mistakes of those who would fain be taught, nor regard the professions of innocence, which come from defective perception, as if they were the proud utterances of a Pharisee.

But Christ's love is firm, and can be severe. It never pares down His requirements to make discipleship easier. Rather it attracts by heightening them, and insisting most strenuously on the most difficult surrender. That is the explanation of the stringent demand next made by Him. He touched the poisonous swelling as with a sharp lancet when He called for surrender of wealth. We may be sure that it was this man's money which stood between him and eternal life. If something else had been his chief temptation, that something would have been signalized as needful to be given up. There is no general principle of conduct laid down here, but a specific injunction determined by the individual's character. All diseases are not treated with the same medicines. The command is but Christ's application of His broad requirement, "If thine eye causeth thee to stumble, pluck it out." The principle involved is, surrender what hinders entire following of Jesus. When that sacrifice is made, we shall be in contact with the fountain of goodness, and have eternal life, not as payment, but as a gift.

"His countenance fell," or, according to Mark's picturesque word, "became lowering," like a summer sky when thunderclouds gather. The hope went out of his heart, and the light faded from his eager face. The prick of the sharp spear had burst the bubble of his superficial earnestness. He had probably never had anything like so repugnant a duty forced upon him, and he cannot bring himself to yield. Like so many of us, he says, "I desire eternal life," but when it comes to giving up the dearest thing, he recoils. "Anything else, Lord, thou shalt have, and welcome, but not that." And Christ says, "That, and nothing else, I must have, if thou art to have Me." So this man "went away sorrowful." His earnestness evaporated; he kept his possessions, and he lost Christ. A prudent bargain! But we may hope that, since "he went away sorrowful," he felt the ache of something lacking, that the old longings came back, and that he screwed up his resolution to make "the great surrender," and counted his wealth "but dung, that he might win Christ."

What a world of sad and disappointed love there would be in the look of Jesus to the disciples, as the young ruler went away with bowed head! How graciously He anticipates their probable censure, and turns their thoughts rather on themselves, by the acknowledgment that the failure was intelligible, since the condition was hard! How pityingly His thoughts go after the retreating figure! How universal the application of His words! Riches may become a hindrance to entering the kingdom. They do so when they take the first place in the affections and in the estimates of good. That danger besets those who have them and those who have them not. Many a poor man is as much caught in the toils of the love of money as the rich are. Jesus modifies the form of His saying when He repeats it in the shape of "How hardly shall they that trust in riches," etc. It is difficult to have, and not to trust in them. Rich men's disadvantages as to living a self-sacrificing Christian life are great. To Christ's eyes, their position was one to be dreaded rather than to be envied.

So opposed to current ideas was such a thought, that the disciples, accustomed to think that wealth meant happiness, were amazed. If the same doctrine were proclaimed in any great commercial center today, it would excite no less astonishment. At least, many Christians and others live as if the opposite were true. Wealth possessed, and not trusted in, but used aright, may become a help towards eternal life; but wealth as commonly regarded and employed by its possessors, and as looked longingly after by others, is a real, and in many cases an insuperable, obstacle to entering the strait gate. As soon drive a camel, humps and load and all, through "a needle's eye," as get a man who trusts in the uncertainty of riches squeezed through that portal. No communities need this lesson more than our great cities.

No wonder that the disciples thought that, if the road was so difficult for rich men, it must be hard indeed. Christ goes even farther. He declares that it is not only hard, but "impossible," for a man by his own power to tread it. That was exactly what the young man had thought that he could do, if only he were directed.

So our Lord's closing words in this context apply, not only to the immediately preceding question by the disciples, but may be taken as the great truth conveyed by the whole incident. Man's efforts can never put him in possession of eternal life. He must have God's power flowing into him if he is to be such as can enter the kingdom. It is the germ of the subsequent teaching of Paul; "The gift of God is eternal life." What we cannot do, Christ has done for us, and does in us. We must yield ourselves to Him, and surrender ourselves, and abandon what stands between us and Him, and then eternal life will enter into us here, and we shall enter into its perfect possession hereafter.

Christ on the Road to the Cross

And they were in the way going up to Jerusalem; and Jesus went before them: and they were amazed; and as they followed they were afraid. MARK 10:32.

We learn from John's Gospel that the resurrection of Lazarus precipitated the determination of the Jewish authorities to put Christ to death; and that immediately thereafter there was held the council at which, by the advice of Caiaphas, the former decision was come to. Thereupon our Lord withdrew Himself into the wilderness which stretches south and east of Jerusalem; and remained there for an unknown period, preparing Himself for the Cross. Then, full of calm resolve, He came forth to die. This is the crisis in our Lord's history to which my text refers. The graphic narrative of this Evangelist sets before us the little company on the steep rocky mountain road that leads up from Jericho to Jerusalem; our Lord, far in advance of His followers, with a fixed purpose stamped upon His face, and something of haste in His stride, and that in His whole demeanor which shed a strange astonishment and awe over the group of silent and uncomprehending disciples.

That picture has not attracted the attention that it deserves. I think if we ponder it with sympathetic imagination helping us, we may get from it some very great lessons and glimpses of our Lord's inmost heart in the prospect of His Cross. And I desire simply to set forth two or three of the aspects of Christ's character which these words seem to me to suggest.

1. We have here, then, first, what, for want of a better name, I would call the heroic Christ. I use the word to express simply strength of will brought to bear in the resistance to antagonism; and although that is a side of the Lord's character which is not often made prominent, it is there, and ought to have its due importance.

We speak of Him and delight to think of Him, as the embodiment of all loving, gracious, gentle virtues, but Jesus Christ as the ideal man unites in Himself what men are in the habit, somewhat superciliously, of calling the masculine virtues, as well as those which they somewhat contemptuously designate the feminine. I doubt very much whether that is a correct distinction. I think that the heroism of endurance, at all events, is far more an attribute of a woman than of a man. But be that as it may, we are to look to Jesus Christ as presenting before us the very type of all which men call heroism in the sense that I have explained, of an iron will, incapable of deflection by any antagonism, and which coerces the whole nature to obedience to its behests.

There is nothing to be done in life without such a will. "To be weak is to be miserable, doing or suffering." And our Master has set us the example of this; that unless there run through a man's life, like the iron framework on the top of the spire of Antwerp Cathedral, on which graceful fancies are strung in stone, the rigid bar of an iron purpose that nothing can bend, the life will be nought and the man will be a failure.

Christ is the pattern of heroic endurance, and reads to us the lesson to *resist* and *persist,* whatever stands between us and our goal.

So here, the Cross before Him flung out no repelling influence towards Him, but rather drew Him to itself. There is no reason that I can find for believing the modern theory of the rationalists' school that our Lord, in the course of His mission, altered His plan, or gradually had dawning upon His mind the conviction that to carry out His purposes He must be a martyr. That seems to me to be an entire misreading of the Gospel narrative which sets before us much rather this, that from the beginning of our Lord's public career there stood unmistakably before Him the Cross as the goal. He entertained no illusions as to His reception. He did not come to do certain work, and, finding that He could not do it, accepted the martyr's role; but He came for the twofold purpose of serving by His life, and of redeeming by His death. ''He came not to be ministered unto, but to minister, and to give His life a ransom for the many.'' And this purpose stood clear before Him, drawing Him to itself all through His career.

But, further, Christ's character teaches us what is the highest form of such strength and tenacity, viz., gentleness. There is no need to be brusque, obstinate, angular, self-absorbed, harsh, because we are fixed and determined in our course. These things are the caricatures and the diminutions, not the true forms nor the increase, of strength. The most tenacious steel is the most flexible, and he that has the most fixed and definite resolve may be the man that has his heart most open to all human sympathies, and is strong with the almightiness of gentleness, and not with the less closeknit strength of roughness and of hardness. Christ, because He is perfect love, is perfect power, and His will is fixed because it is love that fixes it. So let us take the lesson that the highest type of strength is strength in meekness, and that the Master who, I was going to say, kept His strength of will under, but I more correctly say, manifested His strength of will through, His gentleness, is the pattern for us.

2. Then again, we see here not only the heroic, but what I may call the self-sacrificing Christ. We have not only to consider the fixed will which this incident reveals, but to remember the purpose on which it was fixed, and that He was hastening to His Cross. The very fact of our Lord's going back to Jerusalem, with that decree of the Sanhedrin still in force, was tantamount to His surrender of Himself to death. It was as if, in the old days, some excommunicated man with the decree of the Inquistion pronounced against him had gone into Rome and planted himself in the front of the piazza before the buildings of the Holy Office, and lifted up his testimony there. So Christ, knowing that this council has been held, that this decree stands, goes back, investing of set purpose His return with all the publicity that He can bring to bear upon it. For this once He seems to determine that He will "cause His voice to be heard in the streets"; He makes as much of a demonstration as the circumstances will allow, and so acts in a manner opposite to all the rest of His life. Why? Because He had determined to bring the controversy to an end. Why? Was he flinging away His life in mere despair? Was He sinfully neglecting precautions? Was the same fanaticism of martyrdom which has often told upon men, acting upon Him? Were these His reasons? No, but He recognized that now that "hour" of which He spoke so much had come, and of His own loving will offered Himself as our Sacrifice.

It is all-important to keep in view that Christ's death was His own voluntary act. Whatever external forces were brought to bear in the accomplishment of it, He died because He chose to die. The "cords" which bound this sacrifice to the horns of the altar were cords woven by Himself.

So I point to the incident of my text, as linking in along with the whole series of incidents marking the last days of our Lord's life, in order to stamp on His death unmistakably this signature, that it was His own act. Therefore the publicity that was given to His entry; therefore His appearance in the Temple; therefore the increased sharpness and unmistakableness of His denunications of the ruling classes, the Pharisees and the scribes. Therefore the whole history of the Passion, all culminating in leaving this one conviction, that He had "power to lay down His life," that neither Caiaphas nor Annas, nor Judas, nor the band, nor priests, nor the Council, nor Pilate, nor Herod, nor soldiers, nor nails, nor cross, nor all together, killed Jesus, but that Jesus died because He would. The self-sacrifice of the Lord was not the flinging away of the life that He ought to have preserved, nor carelessness, nor the fanaticism of a martyr, nor the enthusiasm of a hero and a champion, but it was the voluntary death of Him who of His own will became in His death the "oblation and satisfaction of the sins of the whole world." Love to us, and obedience to the Father whose will He made His own, were the cords that bound Christ to the Cross on which He died. His sacrifice was voluntary; witness this fact that when He saw the Cross at hand He strode before His followers to reach that, the goal of His mission.

3. I venture to regard the incident as giving us a little glimpse of what I may call the shrinking Christ. Do we not see here a trace of something that we all know? May not part of the reason for Christ's haste have been that desire which we all have, when some inevitable grief or pain lies before us, to get it over soon, and to abbreviate the moments that lie between us and it? Was there not something of that feeling in our Lord's sensitive nature when He said, for instance, "I have a baptism to be baptized with, and how am I straitened until it be accomplished"? "I am come to send fire upon the earth, and O! how I wish that it were already kindled!" Was there not something of the same feeling, which we cannot call impatient, but which we may call shrinking from the Cross, and therefore seeking to draw the Cross nearer, and have done with it, in the words which He addressed to the betrayer, "That thou doest, do quickly," as if He were making a last appeal to the man's humanity, and in effect saying to him, "If you have a heart at all, shorten these painful hours, and let us have it over"?

And may we not see, in that swift advance in front of the lagging disciples, some trace of the same feeling which we recognize to be so truly human?

Christ *did* shrink from His Cross. Let us never forget that He recoiled from it, with the simple, instinctive, human shrinking from pain and death which is a matter of the physical nervous system, and has nothing to do with the will at all. If there had been no shrinking from it there had been no fixed will. If there had been no natural instinctive drawing back of the physical nature and its connections from the prospect of pain and death, there had been none of the heroism of which I am speaking. Though it does not become us to dogmatize about matters of which we know so little, I think we may fairly say that that shrinking never rose up into the regions of Christ's will; never became a desire; never became a purpose. Howsoever the ship might be tossed by the waves, the will always kept its level equilibrium. Howsoever the physical nature might incline to this side or to that, the will always kept parallel with the great underlying divine will, the Father's purpose which He had come to effect. There was shrinking which was instinctive and human, but it never disturbed the fixed purpose to die. It had so much power over Him as to make Him march a little faster to the Cross, but it never made Him turn from it. And so He stands before us as the Conqueror in a real conflict, as having yielded Himself up by a real surrender, as having overcome a real difficulty, "for the joy that was set before Him, having endured the Cross, despising the shame."

4. So, lastly, I would see here the lonely Christ. In front of His followers, absorbed in the thought of what was drawing so near, gathering together His powers in order to be ready for the struggle, with His heart full of the love and the pity which impelled Him, He is surrounded as with a cloud which shuts Him "out from their sight," as afterwards the cloud of glory "received Him."

What a gulf there was between them and Him, between their thoughts and His, as He passed up that rocky way! What were they thinking about? "By the way they had disputed amongst themselves which of them should be the greatest." So far did they sympathize with the Master! So far did they understand Him! Talk about men with unappreciated aims, heroes that have lived through a lifetime of misunderstanding and never have had anyone to sympathize with them! There never was such a lonely man in the world as Jesus Christ. Never was there one that carried deep in His heart so great a purpose and so great a love, which none cared a rush about. And those that were nearest Him, and loved Him best, loved Him so blunderingly and so blindly that their love must often have been quite as much of a pain as of a joy.

In His passion that solitude reached the point of agony. How touching in its unconscious pathos is His pleading request, "Tarry ye here, and watch with Me!" How touching in their revelation of a subsidiary but yet very real addition to His pains are His words, "All ye shall be offended because of Me this night." Oh, dear brethren! every human soul has to go down into the darkness alone, however close may be the clasping love which accompanies us to the portal; but the loneliness of death was realized by Jesus Christ in a very unique and solemn manner. For round Him there gathered the clouds of a mysterious agony, only faintly typified by the darkness of eclipse which hid the material sun in the universe, what time He died.

And all this solitude, the solitude of unappreciated aims, and unshared purposes, and misunderstood sorrow during life, and the solitude of death with its elements ineffable of atonement;—all this solitude was borne that no human soul, living or dying, might ever be lonely any more. "Lo! I," whom you all left alone "am with you," who left Me alone, "even till the end of the world."

So, dear brethren, ponder that picture that I have been trying very feebly to set before you, of the heroic, self-sacrificing, shrinking, solitary Saviour. Take Him as your Saviour, your Sacrifice, your Pattern; and hear Him saying, "If any man serve Me, let him follow Me, and where I am there shall also My servant be."

An old ecclesiastical legend comes into my mind at the moment, which tells how an emperor won the true Cross in battle from a pagan king, and brought it back, with great pomp, to Jerusalem; but found the gate walled up, and an angel standing before it, who said, "Thou bringest back the Cross with pomp and splendor. He that died upon it had shame for His companion; and carried it on His back, barefooted, to Calvary." Then, says the chronicler, the emperor dismounted from his steed, cast off his robes, lifted the sacred Rood on his shoulders, and with bare feet advanced to the gate, which opened of itself, and he entered in.

We have to go up the steep rocky road that leads from the plain where the Dead Sea is, to Jerusalem. Let us follow the Master, as He strides before us, the Forerunner and the Captain of our salvation.

Dignity and Service

And James and John, the sons of Zebedee, come unto Him, saying, Master, we would that Thou shouldest do for us whatsoever we shall desire.
36. And He said unto them, What would ye that I should do for you?
37. They said unto Him, Grant unto us that we may sit, one on Thy right hand, and the other on Thy left hand, in Thy glory.
38. But Jesus said unto them, Ye know not what ye ask: can ye drink of the cup that I drink of? and be baptized with the baptism that I am baptized with?
39. And they said unto Him, We can. And Jesus said unto them, Ye shall indeed drink of the cup that I drink of; and with the baptism that I am baptized withal shall ye be baptized:
40. But to sit on My right hand and on My left hand is not Mine to give; but it shall be given to them for whom it is prepared.
41. And when the Ten heard it, they began to be much displeased with James and John.
42. But Jesus called them to Him, and saith unto them, Ye know that they which are accounted to rule over the Gentiles exercise lordship over them; and their great ones exercise authority upon them.
43. But so shall it not be among you: but whosoever will be great among you, shall be your minister:
44. And whosoever of you will be the chiefest, shall be servant of all.
45. For even the Son of Man came not to be ministered unto, but to minister, and to give His life a ransom for many. MARK 10:34–45.

How lonely Jesus was! While He strode before the Twelve, absorbed in thoughts of the Cross to which He was pressing, they, as they followed, "amazed" and "afraid," were thinking not of what He would suffer, but of what they might gain. He saw the Cross. They understood little of it, but supposed that somehow it would bring in the kingdom, and they dimly saw thrones for themselves. Hence James and John try to secure the foremost places, and hence the others' anger at what they thought an unfair attempt to push in front of them. What a contrast between Jesus, striding on ahead with "set" face, and the Twelve unsympathetic and self-seeking, lagging behind to squabble about preeminence! We have in this incident two parts: the request and its answer, the indignation of the Ten and its rebuke. The one sets forth the qualifications for the highest place in the kingdom; the other, the paradox that preeminence there is service.

James and John were members of the group of original disciples who stood nearest to Jesus, and of the group of three whom He kept specially at His side. Their present place might well lead them to expect preeminence in the kingdom, but their trick was mean, as being an underhand attempt to forestall Peter, the remaining one of the three, as putting forward their mother as spokeswoman, and as endeavoring to entrap Jesus into promising before the disclosure of what was desired. Matthew tells that the mother was brought in order to make the request, and that Jesus brushed her aside by directing His answer to her sons ("Ye know not what *ye* ask"). The attempt to get Jesus' promise without telling what was desired betrayed the consciousness that the wish was wrong. His guarded counter-question would chill them and make their disclosure somewhat hesitating.

Note the strangely blended good and evil of the request. The gold was mingled with clay; selfishness and love delighting in being near Him had both place in it. We may well recognize our own likenesses in these two with their love spotted with self-regard, and be grateful for the gentle answer which did not blame the desire for preeminence, but sought to test the love. It was not only to teach them, that He brought them back to think of the Cross which must precede the glory, but because His own mind was so filled with it that He saw that glory only as through the darkness which had to be traversed to reach it. But for us all the question is solemn and heart-searching.

Was not the answer, "We are able," too bold? They knew neither what they asked nor what they promised; but just as their ignorant question was partly redeemed by its love, their ignorant vow was ennobled by its very rashness, as well as by the unfaltering love in it. They did not know what they were promising, but they knew that they loved Him so well that to share anything with Him would be blessed. So it was not in their own strength that the swift answer rushed to their lips, but in the strength of a love that makes heroes out of cowards. And they nobly redeemed their pledge. We, too, if we are Christ's, have the same question put to us, and, weak and timid as we are, may venture to give the same answer, trusting to His strength.

The full declaration of what had been only implied in the previous question follows. Jesus tells the two, and us all, that there are degrees in nearness to Him and in dignity in that future, but that the highest places are not given by favoritism, but attained by fitness. He does not deny that He gives, but only that He gives without regard to qualification. Paul expected the crown from "the righteous Judge," and one of these two brethren was chosen to record His promise of giving a seat on His throne to all that overcome. "Those for whom it is prepared" are those who are prepared for it, and the preparation lies in "being made conformable to His death," and being so joined to Him that in spirit and mind we are partakers of His sufferings, whether we are called to partake of them in outward form or not.

The two had had their lesson, and next the Ten were to have theirs. The conversation with the former had been private, for it was hearing of it that made the others so angry. We can imagine the hot words among them as they marched behind Jesus, and how they felt ashamed already when "He called them." What they were to be now taught was not so much the qualifications for pre-eminence in the kingdom, whether here or hereafter, as the meaning of pre-eminence and the service to which it binds. In the world, the higher men are, the more they are served; in Christ's kingdom, both in its imperfect earthly and in its perfect heavenly form, the higher men are, the more they serve. So-called "Christian" nations are organized on the former un-Christian basis still. But wherever pre-eminence is not used for the general good, there authority rests on slippery foundations, and there will never be social wellbeing or national tranquility until Christ's law of dignity for service and dignity by service shapes and sweetens society. "But it is not so among you" laid down the constitution for earth, and not only for some remote heaven; and every infraction of it, sooner or later, brings a Nemesis.

The highest is to be the lowest; for He who is "higher than the highest" has shown that such is the law which He obeys. The point in the heaven that is highest above our heads is in twelve hours deepest beneath our feet. Fellowship in Christ's sufferings was declared to be the qualification for our sharing in His dignity. His lowly service and sacrificial death are now declared to be the pattern for our use of dignity. Still the thought of the Cross looms large before Jesus, and He is not content with presenting Himself as the pattern of service only, but calls on His disciples to take Him as the pattern of utter self-surrender also. We cannot enter on the great teaching of these words, but can only beseech all who hear them to note how Jesus sets forth His death as the climax of His work, without which even that life of ministering were incomplete; how He ascribes to it the power of ransoming men from bondage and buying them back to God; and of how He presents even these unparalleled sufferings, which bear or need no repetition as long as the world lasts, as yet being the example to which our lives must be conformed. So His lesson to the angry Ten merges into that to the self-seeking two, and declares to each of us that, if we are ever to win a place at His right hand in His glory, we must here take a place with Him in imitating His life of service and His death of self-surrender for men's good. "If we endure, we shall also reign with Him."

Bartimeus

Blind Bartimeus, the son of Timeus, sat by the highway side begging. MARK 10:46.

The narrative of this miracle is contained in all the Synoptical Gospels, but the accounts differ in two respects—as to the number of men restored to sight, and as to the scene of the miracle. Matthew tells us that there were two men healed, and agrees with Mark in placing the miracle as Jesus was leaving Jericho. Mark says that there was one, and that the place was outside the gate in departing. Luke on the other hand, agrees with Matthew as to the number, and differs from him and Mark as to the place, which he sets at the entrance into the city. The first of these two discrepancies may very easily be put aside. The greater includes the less; silence is not contradiction. To say that there was one does not deny that there were two. And if Bartimeus was a Christian, and known to Mark's readers, as is probable from the mention of his name, it is easily intelligible how he, being also the chief actor and spokesman, should have had Mark's attention concentrated on him. As to the other discrepancy, many attempts have been made to remove it. None of them are altogether satisfactory. But what does it matter? The apparent contradiction may affect theories as to the characteristics of inspired books, but it has nothing to do with the credibility of the narratives, or with their value for us.

Mark's account is evidently that of an eyewitness. It is full of little particulars which testify thereto. Whether Bartimeus had a companion or not, he was obviously the chief actor and spokesman. And the whole story seems to me to lend itself to the enforcement of some very important lessons, which I will try to draw from it.

1. Notice the beggar's petition and the attempts to silence it. Remember that Jesus was now on His last journey to Jerusalem. That night He would sleep at Bethany; Calvary was but a week off. He had paused to win Zaccheus, and now He has resumed His march to His Cross. Popular enthusiasm is surging round Him, and for the first time He does not try to repress it. A shouting multitude are escorting Him out of the city. They have just passed the gates, and are in the act of turning towards the mountain gorge through which runs the Jerusalem road. A long file of beggars is sitting, as beggars do still in Eastern cities, outside the gate, well accustomed to lift their monotonous wail at the sound of passing footsteps. Bartimeus is amongst them. He asks according to Luke, what is the cause of the bustle, and is told that "Jesus of Nazareth is passing by." The name wakes strange hopes in him, which can only be accounted for by his knowledge of Christ's miracles done elsewhere. It is a witness to their notoriety that they had filtered down to be the talk of beggars at city gates. And so, true to his trade, he cries, "Jesus . . . have mercy upon me!"

Now, note two or three things about that cry. The first is the clear insight into Christ's place and dignity. The multitude said to him, "Jesus *of Nazareth* passeth by." That was all they cared for or knew. He cried, "Jesus, thou *Son of David,*" distinctly recognizing our Lord's Messianic character, His power and authority, and on that power and authority he built a confidence; for he says not as some other suppliants had done, either "If Thou wilt Thou canst," or "If Thou canst do anything, have compassion on us." He is sure of both the power and the will.

Now, it is interesting to notice that this same clear insight other blind men in the Evangelist's story are also represented as having had. Blindness has its compensations. It leads to a certain steadfast brooding upon thoughts, free from disturbing influences. Seeing Jesus did not produce faith; not seeing Him seems to have helped it. It left imagination to work undisturbed, and He was all the loftier to these blind men, because the conceptions of their minds were not limited by the vision of their eyes. At all events, here is a distinct piece of insight into Christ's dignity, power, and will, to which the seeing multitudes were blind.

Note, further, how in the cry there throbs the sense of need, deep and urgent. And note how in it there is also the realization of the possibility that the widely flowing blessings of which Bartimeus had heard might be concentrated and poured, in their full flood, upon himself. He individualizes himself, *his* need, Christ's power and willingness to help *him*. And because he has heard of so many who have, in like manner, received His healing touch, he comes with the cry, "Have mercy upon *me*."

All this is upon the low level of physical blessings needed and desired. But let us lift it higher. It is a mirror in which we may see ourselves, our necessities, and the example of what our desire ought to be. Ah! brethren, the deep consciousness of impotence, need, emptiness, blindness, lies at the bottom of all true crying to Jesus Christ. If you have never gone to Him, knowing yourself to be a sinful man, in peril, present and future, from your sin, and stained and marred by reason of it, you never have gone to Him in any deep and adequate sense at all. Only when I thus know myself am I driven to cry, "Jesus! have mercy on me." And I ask you not to answer to me, but to press the question on your own consciences—"Have I any experience of such a sense of need; or am I groping in the darkness and saying, I see? am I weak as water, and saying I am strong?'' ''Thou knowest not that thou art poor, and naked, and blind''; and so that Jesus of Nazareth should be passing by has never moved thy tongue to call, ''Son of David, have mercy upon me!''

Again, this man's cry expressed a clear insight into something at least of our Lord's unique character and power. Brethren, unless we know Him to be all that is involved in that august title, ''the Son of David,'' I do not think our cries to Him will ever be very earnest. It seems to me that they will only be so when, on the one hand, we recognize our need of a Saviour, and, on the other hand, behold in Him the Saviour whom we need. I can quite understand—and we may see plenty of illustrations of it all round us—a kind of Christianity real as far as it goes, but in my judgment very superficial, which has no adequate conception of what sin means, in its depth, in its power upon the victim of it, or in its consequences here and hereafter; and, that sense being lacking, the whole scale of Christianity, as it were, is lowered, and Christ comes to be, not, as I think the New Testament tells us that He is, the Incarnate Word of God, who for us men and for our salvation ''bare our sins in His own body on the tree,'' and ''was made sin for us, that we might be made the righteousness of God in Him,'' but an Example, a Teacher, or a pure Model, or a social Reformer, or the like. If men think of Him only as such, they will never cry to Him, ''Have mercy upon me!''

Dear friends, I pray you, whether you begin with looking into your own hearts and recognizing the crawling evils that have made their home there, and thence pass to the thought of the sort of Redeemer that you need and find in Christ—or whether you begin at the other side, and, looking upon the revealed Christ in all the fulness in which He is represented to us in the Gospels, from thence go back to ask yourselves the question, ''What sort of man must I be, if that is the kind of Saviour that I need?''—I pray you ever to blend these two things together, the consciousness of your own need of redemption in His blood and the assurance that by His death we are redeemed, and then to cry, ''Lord! have mercy upon *me,*'' and claim your individual share in the wide-flowing blessing. Turn all the generalities of His grace into the particularity of your own possession of it. We have to go one by one to His cross, and one by one to pass through the wicket gate. We have not cried to Him as we ought, if our cry is only ''Christ, have mercy upon us. Lord, have mercy upon us. Christ, have mercy upon us.'' We must be alone with Him, that into our own hearts we may receive all the fulness of His blessing; and our petition must be ''Thou Son of David! have mercy upon *me.*'' Have you cried that?

Notice, further, the attempts to stifle the cry. No doubt it was in defense of the Master's dignity, as they construed it, that the people sought to silence the persistent, strident voice piercing through their hosannas.

Ah! they did not know that the cry of wretchedness was far sweeter to Him than their shallow hallelujahs. Christian people of all churches, and of some stiffened churches very especially, have been a great deal more careful of Christ's dignity than He is, and have felt that their formal worship was indecorously disturbed when by chance some earnest voice forced its way through it with the cry of need and desire. But his man had been accustomed for many a day, sitting outside the gate, to reiterate his petition when it was unattended to, and to make it heard amidst the noise of passersby. So he was persistently bold and importunate and shameless, as the shallow critics thought, in this crying. The more they silenced him, the more a great deal he cried. Would God that we had more crying like that; and that Christ's servants did not so often seek to suppress it, as some of them do! If there are any of you who, by reason of companions, or cares, or habits, or sorrows, or a feeble conception of your own need or a doubtful recognition of Christ's power and mercy, have been tempted to stop your supplications, do like Bartimeus, and the more these, your enemies, seek to silence the deepest voice that is you, the more let it speak.

2. So, notice Christ's call and the suppliant's response. "He stood still, and commanded him to be called." Remember that He was on His road to His Cross, and that the tension of spirit which the Evangelists notice as attaching to Him then, and which filled the disciples with awe as they followed Him, absorbed Him, no doubt, at that hour, so that He heard but little of the people's shouts. But He did hear the blind beggar's cry, and He arrested His march in order to attend to it.

Now, dear friends, I am not merely twisting a biblical incident round to an interpretation which it does not bear, but am stating a plain unrhetorical truth when I say that it is so still. Jesus Christ is no dead Christ who is to be remembered only. He is a living Christ who, at this moment, is all that He ever was, and is doing in loftier fashion all the gracious things that He did upon earth. That pause of the King is repeated now, and the quick ear which discerned the difference between the unreal shouts of the crowd, and the agony of sincerity in the cry of the beggar, is still open. He is in the heavens, surrounded by its glories, and, as I think Scripture teaches us, wielding providence and administering the affairs to the universe. He does not need to pause in order to hear you and me. If He did, He would—if I may venture upon such an impossible supposition—bid the hallelujahs of heaven hush themselves, and suspend the operations of His providence if need were, rather than that you or I, or any poor man who cries to Him, should be unheard and unhelped. The living Christ is as tender a friend, has as quick an ear, is as ready to help at once, today, as He was when outside the gate of Jericho; and every one of us may lift his or her poor, thin voice, and it will go straight up to the throne, and not be lost in the clamor of the hallelujahs that echo round His seat. Christ still hears and answers the cry of need. Send you it up, and you will find that true.

Notice the suppliant's response. That is a very characteristic right-about-face of the crowd, who one moment were saying, "Hold your tongue and do not disturb Him," and the next moment were all eager to encumber him with help, and to say, "Rise up, be of good cheer; He calleth thee." No thanks to them that He did. And what did the man do? Sprang to his feet—as the word rightly rendered would be—and flung away the frowsy rags that he had wrapped round him for warmth and softness of seat, as he waited at the gate; "and he came to Jesus." Brethren, "casting aside every weight and the sin that doth so easily beset us, let us run" to the same Refuge. You have to abandon something if you are to go to Christ to be healed. I dare say you know well enough what it is. I do not; but certainly there is something that entangles your legs and keeps you from finding your way to Him. If there is nothing else, there is yourself and your trust in self, and that is to be put away. Cast away the "garment spotted with the flesh" and go to Christ, and you will receive succor.

3. Notice the question of all-granting love, and the answer of conscious need. "What wilt Thou that I should do unto thee?" A very few hours before He had put the same question with an entirely different significance, when the sons of Zebedee came to Him, and tried to get Him to walk blindfold into a promise. He upset their scheme with the simple question, "What is it that you want?" which meant, "I must know and judge before I commit Myself." But when He said the same thing to Bartimeus He meant exactly the opposite. It was putting the key of the treasurehouse into the beggar's hand. It was the implicit pledge that whatever he desired he should receive. He knew that the thing this man wanted was the thing that He delighted to give.

But the tenderness of these words, and the gracious promise that is hived in them, must not make us forget the singular authority that speaks in them. Think of a man doing as Jesus Christ did—standing before another and saying, "I will give you anything that you want." He must be either a madman or a blasphemer, or "God manifest in the flesh"; Almighty power guided by infinite love.

And what said the man? He had no doubt what he wanted most—the opening of these blind eyes of his. And, dear brother, if we knew ourselves as well as Bartimeus knew his blindness, we should have as little doubt what it is that we need most. Suppose you had this wishing cap that Christ put on Bartimeus's head put on yours: what would you ask? It is a penetrating question if men will answer it honestly. Think what you consider to be your chief need. Suppose Jesus Christ stood where I stand, and spoke to you: ''What wilt thou that I should do for you?'' If you are a wise man, if you know yourself and Him, your answer will come as swiftly as the beggar's—''Lord! heal me of my blindness, and take away my sin, and give me Thy salvation.'' There is no doubt about what it is that every one of us needs most. And there should be no doubt as to what each of us would ask first.

The supposition that I have been making is realized. That gracious Lord is here, and is ready to give you the satisfaction of your deepest need, if you know what it is, and will go to Him for it. ''Ask! and ye shall receive.''

4. Lastly, notice, sight given, and the giver followed. Bartimeus had scarcely ended speaking when Christ began. He was blind at the beginning of Christ's little sentence; he saw at the end of it. ''Go thy way; thy faith hath saved thee.'' The answer came instantly, and the cure was as immediate as the movement of Christ's heart in answer.

I am here to proclaim the possibility of an immediate passage from darkness to light. Some folk look askance at us when we talk about sudden conversions, but these are perfectly reasonable; and the experience of thousands asserts that they are actual. As soon as we desire, we have, and as soon as we have, we see. Whenever the lungs are opened the air rushes in; sometimes the air opens the lungs that it may. The desire is all but contemporaneous with the fulfilment, in Christ's dealing with men. The message is flashed along the wire from earth to heaven, in an incalculably brief space of time, and the answer comes, swift as thought and swifter than light. So, dear friends, there is no reason whatever why a similar instantaneous change should not pass over any man who hears the Good News. He may be unsaved when his hearing of it begins, and saved when his hearing of it ends. It is for himself to settle whether it shall be so or not.

Here we have a clear statement of the path by which Christ's mercy rushes into a man's soul. ''Thy faith hath saved thee.'' But it was Christ's power that saved him. Yes, it was; but it was faith that made it possible for Christ's power to make whole. Physical miracles indeed did not always require trust in Christ, as a preceding condition, but the possession of Christ's salvation does, and cannot but do so. There must be trust in Him, in order that we may partake of the salvation which is owing solely to His power, His love, His work upon the Cross. The condition is for us; the power comes from Him. My faith is the hand that grasps His; it is His hand, not mine, that holds me up. My faith lays hold of the rope; it is the rope and the Person above who holds it, that lift me out of the "horrible pit and the miry clay." My faith flees for refuge to the city; it is the city that keeps me safe from the avenger of blood. Brother! exercise that faith, and you will receive a better sight than was poured into Bartimeus's eyes.

Now, all this story should be the story of each one of us. One modification we have to make upon it, for we do not need to cry persistently for mercy, but to trust in, and to take, the mercy that is offered. One other difference there is between Bartimeus and many of my hearers. He knew what he needed, and some of you do not. But Christ is calling us all, and my business now is to say to each of you what the crowd said to the beggar, "Rise! be of good cheer; He calleth thee." If you will fling away your hindrances, and grope your path to His feet, and fall down before Him, knowing your deep necessity, and trusting to Him to supply it, He will save you. Your new sight will gaze upon your Redeemer, and you will follow Him in the way of loving trust and glad obedience.

Jesus Christ was passing by. He was never to be in Jericho any more. If Bartimeus did not get His sight then, he would be blind all his days. Christ and His salvation are offered to thee, my brother, now. Perhaps if you let Him pass, you will never hear Him call again, and may abide in the darkness for ever. Do not run the risk of such a fate.

An Eager Coming

And he, casting away his garment, rose, and came to Jesus. MARK 10:50.

Mark's vivid picture—long wail of the man, crowd silencing him, but wheeling round when Christ calls him—and the quick energy of the beggar, flinging away his cloak, springing to his feet—and blind as he was, groping his way.

1. What we mean by coming to Jesus: —faith, communion, occupation of mind, heart, and will.

2. How eagerly we shall come when we are conscious of need. This man wanted his eyesight; do we not want, too?

3. We must throw off our hindrances if we would come to Him. Impediments of various kinds. "Lay aside every weight"—not only sins, but even right things that hinder. Occupations, pursuits, affections, possessions, sometimes have to be put away altogether; sometimes but to be minimized and kept in restraint. There is no virtue in self-denial except as it helps us to come nearer Him.

4. We must do it with quick, glad energy. Bartimeus springs to his feet at once with a bound. So we should leap to meet Jesus, our sight-giver. How slothful and languid we often are. We do not put half as much heart into our Christian life as people do into common things. Far more pains are taken by a ballet dancer to learn her posturing than by most Christians to keep near Christ.

Love's Question

> *What wilt thou that I should do unto thee?* MARK 10:51.
> *What wilt Thou have me to do?* ACTS 9:6.

Christ asks the first question of a petitioner, and the answer is a prayer for sight. Saul asks the second question of Jesus, and the answer is a command. Different as they are, we may bring them together. The one is the voice of love, desiring to be besought in order that it may bestow; the other is the voice of love, desiring to be commanded in order that it may obey.

Love delights in knowing, expressing, and fulfilling the beloved's wishes.

1. The communion of love delights on both sides in knowing the beloved's wishes. Christ delights in knowing ours. He encourages us to speak though He knows, because it is pleasant to Him to hear, and good for us to tell. His children delight in knowing His will.

2. It delights in expressing wishes—His commandments are the utterance of His love: His Providences are His loving ways of telling us what He desires of us, and if we love Him as we ought, both commandments and providences will be received by us as lovers do gifts that have "with my love" written on them.

On the other hand, our love will delight in telling Him what we wish, and to speak all our hearts to Jesus will be our instinct in the measure of our love to Him.

3. It delights in fulfilling wishes—puts key of treasurehouse into our hands. He refused John and James. Be sure that He does still delight to give us our desires, and so be sure that when any of these are not granted there must be some loving reason for refusal.

Our delight should be in obedience, and only when our wills are submitted to His does He say to us, ''What wilt thou?'' ''If ye abide in Me and My words abide in you, ye shall ask what we will and it shall be done unto you.''

11

Needs of the Master

A Royal Progress

. . . Go your way into the village over against you: and as soon as ye be entered into it, ye shall find a colt tied, whereon never man sat; loose him, and bring him. MARK 11:2.

Two considerations help us to appreciate this remarkable incident of our Lord's triumphal entry into Jerusalem. The first of these is its date. It apparently occurred on the Sunday of the Passion Week. The Friday saw the crosses on Calvary. The night before, Jesus had sat at the modest feast that was prepared in Bethany, where Lazarus was one of the guests, Martha was the busy servant, and Mary poured out the lavish treasures of her love upon His feet. The resurrection of Lazarus had created great popular excitement; and that excitement is the second consideration which throws light upon this incident. The people had rallied round Christ, and, consequently, the hatred of the official and ecclesiastical class had been raised to boiling point. It was at that time that our Lord deliberately presented Himself before the nation as the Messiah, and stirred up still more this popular enthusiasm. Now, if we keep these two things in view, I think we shall be at the right point from which to consider the whole incident. To it, and not merely to the words which I have chosen as our starting point I wish to draw attention now. I am mistaken if there are not in it very important and practical lessons for ourselves.

1. First, note that deliberate assumption by Christ of royal authority. I shall have a good deal to say presently about the main fact which bears upon that, but in the meantime I would note, in passing, a subsidiary illustration of it, in the errand on which He sent these messengers to the little "village over against" them; and in the words which He put into their mouths. They were to go, and, without a word, to loose and bring away the colt fastened at a door, where it was evidently waiting the convenience of its owner to mount it. If, as was natural, any objection or question was raised, they were to answer exactly as servants of a king would do, if he sent them to make requisition on the property of his subjects, "The Lord hath need of him."

I do not dwell on our Lord's supernatural knowledge as coming out here; nor on the fact that the owner of the colt was probably a partial disciple, perhaps a secret one—ready to recognize the claim that was made. But I ask you to notice here the assertion, in act and word, of absolute authority, to which all private convenience and rights of possession are to give way unconditionally. The Sovereign's need is a sovereign reason. What He requires He has a right to take. Well for us, brethren, if we yield as glad, as swift, and as unquestioning obedience to His claims upon us, and upon our possessions, as that poor peasant of Bethphage gave in the incident before us!

But there is not only the assertion, here, of absolute authority, but note how, side by side with this royal style, there goes the acknowledgment of poverty. Here is a pauper King, who having nothing yet possesses all things. "The Lord"—that is a great title—"hath need of him"—that is a strange verb to go with such a nominative. But this little sentence, in its two halves of authority and of dependence, puts into four words the whole blessed paradox of the life of Jesus Christ upon earth. "Though He was rich, yet for our sakes He became poor"; and being Lord and Owner of all things, yet owed His daily bread to ministering women, borrowed a boat to preach from, a house wherein to lay His head, a shroud and a winding sheet to enfold His corpse, a grave in which to lie, and from which to rise, "the Lord of the dead and of the living."

Not only so, but there is another thought suggested by these words. The accurate, or, at least, the probable reading, of one part of the third verse is given in the Revised Version, "Say ye that the Lord hath need of him, and straightway he will send him *back* hither." That is to say, these last words are not Christ's assurance to His two messengers that their embassy would succeed, but part of the message which He sends by them to the owner of the colt, telling him that it was only a loan which was to be returned. Jesus Christ is debtor to no man. Anything given to Him comes back again. Possessions yielded to that Lord are recompensed a hundredfold in this life, if in nothing else in that there is a far greater sweetness in that which still remains. "What I gave I have," said the wise old epitaph. It is always true. Do you not think that the owner of the patient beast, on which Christ placidly paced into Jerusalem on His peaceful triumph, would be proud all his days of the use to which his animal had been put, and would count it as a treasure for the rest of its life? If you and I will yield our gifts to Him, and lay them upon His altar, be sure of this, that the altar will ennoble and will sanctify all that is laid upon it. All that we have rendered to Him gains fragrance from His touch, and comes back to us tenfold more precious because He has condescended to use it.

So, brethren, He still moves amongst us, asking for our surrender of ourselves and of our possessions to Him, and pledging Himself that we shall lose nothing by what we give to Him, but shall be infinitely gainers by our surrender. He still needs us. Ah! If He is ever to march in triumph through the world, and be hailed by the hosannas of all the tribes of the earth, it is requisite for that triumph that His children should surrender first themselves, and then all that they are, and all that they have, to Him. To us there comes the message, "The Lord hath need of you." Let us see that we answer as becomes us.

But then, more important is the other instance here of this assertion of royal authority. I have already said that we shall not rightly understand it unless we take into full account the state of popular feeling at the time. We find in John's Gospel great stress laid on the movement of curiosity and half-belief which followed on the resurrection of Lazarus. He tells us that crowds came out from Jerusalem the night before to gaze upon the Lifebringer and the quickened man. He also tells us that another enthusiastic crowd flocked out of Jerusalem before Jesus sent for the colt to the neighboring village. We are to keep in mind, therefore, that what He did here was done in the midst of a great outburst of popular enthusiasm. We are to keep in mind, too, the season of Passover, when religion and patriotism, which were so closely intertwined in the life of the Jews, were in full vigorous exercise. It was always a time of anxiety to the Roman authorities, lest this fiery people should break out into insurrection. Jerusalem at the Passover was like a great magazine of combustibles, and into it Jesus flung a lighted brand amongst the inflammable substances that were gathered there. We have to remember, too, that all His life long He had gone exactly on the opposite tack. Remember how He betook Himself to the mountain solitudes when they wanted to make Him a king. Remember how He was always damping down Messianic enthusiasm. But here, all at once, He reverses His whole conduct, and deliberately sets Himself to make the most public and the most exciting possible demonstration that He was "King of Israel."

For what was it that He did? Our Evangelist here does not quote the prophecy from Zechariah, but two other Evangelists do. Our Lord then deliberately dressed Himself by the mirror of prophecy, and assumed the very characteristics which the prophet had given long ago as the mark of the coming King of Zion. If He had wanted to excite a popular commotion, that is what He would have done.

Why did He act thus? He was under no illusion as to what would follow. For the night before He had said: "She hath come beforehand to anoint My body for the burial.' He knew what was close before Him in the future. And, because He knew that the end was at hand, He felt that, once at least, it was needful that He should present Himself solemnly, publicly, I may almost say ostentatiously, before the gathered nation, as being of a truth the Fulfiller and the fulfillment of all the prophecies and the hopes built upon them that had burned in Israel, with a smoky flame indeed, but for so many ages. He also wanted to bring the rulers to a point. I dare not say that He precipitated His death, or provoked a conflict, but I do say that deliberately, and with a clear understanding of what He was doing, He took a step which forced them to show their hand. For after such a public avowal of who He was, and such public hosannas surging round His meek feet as He rode into the city, there were but two courses open for the official class: either to acknowledge Him, or to murder Him. Therefore He reversed His usual action, and deliberately posed, by His own act, as claiming to be the Messiah long prophesied and long expected.

Now, what do you think of the man that did that? *If* He did it, then either He is what the rulers called Him, a "deceiver," swollen with inordinate vanity and unfit to be a teacher, or else we must fall at His feet and say "Rabbi! Thou art the Son of God; Thou art the King of Israel." I venture to believe that to extol Him and to deny the validity of His claims is in flagrant contradiction to the facts of His life, and is an unreasonable and untenable position.

2. Notice the revelation of a new kind of King and Kingdom. Our Evangelist, from whom my text is taken, has nothing to say about Zechariah's prophecy which our Lord set Himself to fulfill. He only dwells on the pathetic poverty of the pomp of the procession. But other Evangelists bring into view the deeper meaning of the incident. The center-point of the prophecy, and of Christ's intentional fulfilment of it, lies in the symbol of the meek and patient animal which He bestrode. The ass was, indeed, used sometimes in old days by rulers and judges in Israel, but the symbol was chosen by the prophet simply to bring out the peacefulness and the gentleness inherent in the Kingdom, and the King who thus advanced into His city. If you want to understand the meaning of the prophet's emblem, you have only to remember the sculptured slabs of Assyria and Babylon, or the paintings on the walls of Egyptian temples and tombs, where Sennacherib or Rameses ride hurtling in triumph in their chariots, over the bodies of prostrate foes; and then to set by the side of these, "Rejoice! O daughter of Zion; thy King cometh unto thee riding upon an ass, and upon a colt the foal of an ass." If we want to understand the significance of this sweet emblem, we need only, further, remember the psalm that, with poetic fervor, invokes the King: ''Gird Thy sword upon Thy thigh, O Most Mighty, and in Thy majesty ride prosperously . . . and Thy right hand shall teach thee terrible things. Thine arrows are sharp in the heart of the King's enemies; the people fall under Thee.'' That is all that that ancient singer could conceive of the triumphant King of the world, the Messiah; a conqueror, enthroned in His chariot, and the twanging bowstring, drawn by His strong hand, impelling the arrow that lodged in the heart of His foes. And here is the fulfilment. ''Go ye into the village over against you, and ye shall find a colt tied. . . . And they set Him thereon.'' Christ's kingdom, like its King, has no power but gentleness and the omnipotence of patient love.

If ''Christian'' nations, as they are called, and Churches had kept the significance of that emblem in mind, do you think that their hosannas would have gone up so often for conquerors on the battlefields; or that Christian communities would have been in complicity with war and the glorifying thereof, as they have been? And, if Christian churches had remembered and laid to heart the meaning of this triumphal entry, and its demonstration of where the power of the Master lay, would they have struck up such alliances with worldly powers and forms of force as, alas! have weakened and corrupted the Church for hundreds of years? Surely, surely, there is no more manifest condemnation of war and the warlike spirit, and of the spirit which finds the strength of Christ's Church in anything material and violent, than is that solitary instance of His assumption of royal state when thus He entered into His city. I need not say a word, brethren, about the nature of Christ's kingdom as embodied in His subjects, as represented in that shouting multitude that marched around Him. How Caesar in his golden house in Rome would have sneered and smiled at the Jewish peasant, on the colt, and surrounded by poor men, who had no banners but the leafy branches from the trees, and no pomp to strew in his way but their own worn garments! And yet these were stronger in their devotion, in their enthusiastic conviction that He was the King of Israel and of the whole earth, than Caesar, with all his treasures and with all his legions and their sharp swords. Christ accepts poor homage because He looks for hearts; and whatever the heart renders is sweet to Him. He passes on through the world, hailed by the acclamations of grateful hearts, needing no body-guard but those that love Him; and they need to bear no weapons in their hands, but their mission is to proclaim with glad hearts hosannas to the King that ''cometh in the name of the Lord.''

There is one more point that I may note. Another of the Evangelists tells us that it was when the humble cortège swept round the shoulder of Olivet, and caught sight of the city gleaming in the sunshine, across the Kedron valley, that they broke into the most rapurous of their hosannas, as if they would call to the city that came in view to rejoice and welcome its King. And what was the King doing when that sight burst upon Him, and while the acclamations eddied round Him? His thoughts were far away. His eyes with divine prescience looked on to the impending end, and then they dimmed, and filled with tears; and He wept over the city.

That is our King; a pauper King, a meek and patient King, a King that delights in the reverent love of hearts, a King whose armies have no swords, a King whose eyes fill with tears as He thinks of men's woes and cries. Blessed be such a King!

3. Lastly, we have the royal visitation of the Temple. Our Evangelist has no word to speak about the march of the procession down into the valley, and up on the other side, and through the gate, and into the narrow streets of the city that was "moved" as they passed through it. His language sounds as if he considered that our Lord's object in entering Jerusalem at all was principally to enter the Temple. He "looked round on all things" that were there. Can we fancy the keen observance, the recognition of the hidden bad and good, the blazing indignation, and yet dewy pity, in those eyes? His visitation of the Temple was its inspection by its Lord. And it was an inspection in order to cleanse. Today He looked; tomorrow He wielded the whip of small cords. His chastisement is never precipitate. Perfect knowledge wields His scourge, and pronounces condemnation.

Brethren, Jesus Christ comes to us as a congregation, to the church to which we belong, and to us individually, with the same inspection. He whose eyes are a flame of fire, says to His churches today, "I know thy works." What would He think if He came to us and tested us?

In the incident of my text He was fulfilling another ancient prophecy, which says, "The Lord shall suddenly come to His Temple, and . . . sit as a refiner of silver . . . like a refiner's fire and as fuller's soap . . . and He shall purify the sons of Levi. . . . Then shall the offering of Jerusalem be pleasant, as in the days of old."

We need nothing more, we should desire nothing more earnestly, than that He would come to us: "Search me, O Christ, and know me. And see if there be any wicked way in me, and lead me in the way everlasting." Jesus Christ is the King of England as truly as of Zion; and He is your King and mine. He comes to each of us, patient, meek, loving; ready to bless and to cleanse. Dear brother, do you open your heart to Him? Do you acknowledge Him as your King? Do you count it your highest honor if He will use you and your possessions, and condescend to say that He has need of such poor creatures as we are? Do you cast your garments in the way, and say: "Ride on, great Prince"? Do you submit yourself to His inspection, to His cleansing?

Remember, He came once on "a colt, the foal of an ass, meek, and having salvation." He will come "on the white horse, in righteousness to judge and to make war," and with power to destroy.

Oh! I beseech you, welcome Him as He comes in gentle love, that when He comes in judicial majesty you may be among the "armies of heaven that follow after," and from immortal tongues utter rapturous and undying hosannas.

Christ's Need of Us and Ours

. . . Say ye that the Lord hath need of him; and straightway he will send him hither. MARK 11:3.

You will remember that Jesus Christ sent two of His disciples into the village that looked down on the road from Bethany to Jerusalem, with minute instructions and information as to what they were to do and find there. The instructions may have one of two explanations—they suggest either superhuman knowledge or a previous arrangement. Perhaps, although it is less familiar to our thoughts, the latter is the explanation. There is a remarkable resemblance, in that respect, to another incident which lies close beside this one in time, when our Lord again sent two disciples to make preparation for the Passover, and, with similar minuteness, told them that they would find, at a certain point, a man bearing a pitcher of water. Him they were to accost, and he would take them to the room that had been prepared. Now the old explanation of both these incidents is that Jesus Christ knew what was going to happen. Another possible explanation, and in my view more probable and quite as instructive, is, that Jesus Christ had settled with the two owners what was to happen. Clearly, the owner of the colt was a disciple, because at once he gave up his property when the message was repeated, "the *Lord* hath need of him." Probably he had been one of the guests at the modest festival that had been held the night before, in the village close by, in Simon's house, and had seen how Mary had expended her most precious possession on the Lord, and, under the influence of the resurrection of Lazarus, he, too, perhaps, was touched, and was glad to arrange with Jesus Christ to have his colt waiting there at the crossroad for his Master's convenience. But, be that as it may, it seems to me that this incident, and especially these words that I have read for a text, carry very striking and important lessons for us, whether we look at them in connection with the incident itself, or whether we venture to give them a somewhat wider application. Let me take these two points in turn.

1. Now, what strikes one about our Lord's requisitioning the colt is this, that here is a piece of conduct on His part singularly unlike all the rest of His life. All through it, up to this last moment, His one care was to damp down popular enthusiasm, to put on the drag whenever there came to be the least symptom of it, to discourage any reference to Him as the Messiah-King of Israel, to shrink back from the coarse adulation of the crowd, and to glide quietly through the world, blessing and doing good. But now, at the end, He flings off all disguise. He deliberately sets Himself, at a time when popular enthusiasm ran highest and was most turbid and difficult to manage, at the gathering of the nation for the Passover in Jerusalem, to cast an effervescing element into the caldron. If He had planned to create a popular rising, He could not have done anything more certain to bring it about than what He did that morning when He made arrangements for a triumphal procession into the city, amidst the excited crowds gathered from every quarter of the land. Why did He do that? What was the meaning of it?

Then there is another point in this requisitioning of the colt. He not only deliberately set Himself to stir up popular excitement, but He consciously did what would be an outward fulfillment of a great Messianic prophecy. I hope you are wiser than to fancy that Zechariah's prophecy of the peaceful monarch who was to come to Zion, meek and victorious, and riding upon a "colt the foal of an ass," was fulfilled by the outward fact of Christ being mounted on this colt "whereon never man sat." That is only the shell, and if there had been no such triumphal entry, our Lord would as completely have fulfilled Zechariah's prophecy. The fulfillment of it did not depend on the petty detail of the animal upon which He sat when He entered the city, nor even on that entrance. The meaning of the prophecy was that to Zion, wherever and whatever it is, there should come that Messianic King, whose reign owed nothing to chariots and horses and weapons of war for its establishment, but who, meek and patient, pacing upon the humble animal used only for peaceful services, and not mounted on the prancing steed of the warrior, should inaugurate the reign of majesty and of meekness. Our Lord uses the external fact just as the prophet had used it, as of no value in itself, but as a picturesque emblem of the very spirit of His kingdom. The literal fulfillment was a kind of fingerpost for inattentive onlookers, which might induce them to look more closely, and so see that He was indeed the King-Messiah, because of more important correspondences with prophecy than His once riding on an ass. Do not so degrade these Old Testament prophecies as to fancy that their literal fulfillment is of chief importance. That is the shell: the kernel is the all-important thing, and Jesus Christ would have fulfilled the role, that was sketched for Him by the prophets of old, just as completely if there never had been this entrance into Jerusalem.

But, further, the fact that He had to borrow the colt was as significant as the choice of it. For so we see blended two things, the blending of which makes the unique peculiarity and sublimity of Christ's life: absolute authority, and meekness of poverty and lowliness. A King, and yet a pauper-King! A King claiming His dominion, and yet obliged to borrow another man's colt in order that He might do it! A strange kind of monarch!—and yet that remarkable combination runs through all His life. He had to be obliged to a couple of fishermen for a boat, but He sat in it, to speak words of divine wisdom. He had to be obliged to a lad in the crowd for barley loaves and fishes, but when He took them into His hands they were multiplied. He had to be obliged for a grave, and yet He rose from the borrowed grave the Lord of life and death. And so when He would pose as a King, He has to borrow the regalia, and to be obliged to this anonymous friend for the colt which made the emphasis of His claim. "Who, though He was rich, yet for our sakes became poor, that we through His poverty might be rich."

2. And now turn for a moment to the wider application of these words. "The Lord hath need of him." That opens the door to thoughts, that I cannot crowd into the few minutes that I have at my disposal, as to that great and wonderful truth that Christ cannot assume His kingdom in this world without your help, and that of the other people whose hearts are touched by His love. "The Lord hath need" of them. Though upon that Cross of Calvary He did all that was necessary for the redemption of the world and the salvation of humanity as a whole, yet for the bearing of that blessing into individual hearts, and for the application of the full powers that are stored in the Gospel and in Jesus, to their work in the world, the missing link is man. We "are fellow laborers with God." We are Christ's tools. The instruments by which He builds His kingdom are the souls that have already accepted His authority. "The Lord hath need of him," though, as the psalmist sings, "If I were hungry I would not tell thee, for all the beasts of the forest are Mine." Yes, and when the Word was made flesh, He had need of one of the humblest of the beasts. The Christ that redeemed the world needs us, to carry out and to bring into effect His redemption. "God mend all," said one, and the answer was, "We must help Him to mend it."

Notice again the authoritative demand, which does not contemplate the possibility of reluctance or refusal. "The Lord hath need of him." That is all. There is no explanation or motive alleged to induce surrender to the demand. This is a royal style of speech. It is the way in which, in despotic countries, kings lay their demands upon a poor man's whole plenishing and possession, and sweep away all.

Jesus Christ comes to us in like fashion, and brushes aside all our convenience and everything else, and says, "I want you, and that is enough." Is it not enough? Should it not be enough? If He demands, He has the right to demand. For we are His, "bought with a price." All the slave's possessions are his owner's property. The slave is given a little patch of garden ground, and perhaps allowed to keep a fowl or two, but the master can come and say, "Now *I* want them," and the slave has nothing for it but to give them up.

"The Lord hath need of him" is in the autocratic tone of One who has absolute power over us and ours. And that power, where does it come from? It comes from His absolute surrender of Himself to us, and because He has wholly given Himself for us. "He does not expect us to say one contrary word when He sends and says, I have need of you, or of yours."

Here, again, we have an instance of glad surrender. The last words of my text are susceptible of a double meaning. "Straightway he will send him hither"—who is "he"? It is usually understood to be the owner of the colt, and the clause is supposed to be Christ's assurance to the two messengers of the success of their errand. So understood, the words suggest the great truth that Love loosens the hand that grasps possessions, and unlocks our treasurehouses. There is nothing more blessed than to give in response to the requirement of love. And so, to Christ's authoritative demand, the only proper answer is obedience swift and glad, because it is loving. Many possibilities of joy and blessing are lost by us through not yielding on the instant to Christ's demands. Hesitation and delay are dangerous. In "straightway" complying are security and joy. If the owner had begun to say to himself that he very much needed the colt, or that he saw no reason why someone else's beast should not have been taken, or that he would send the animal very soon, but must have the use of him for an hour or two first, he would probably never have sent him at all, and so would have missed the greatest honor of his life. As soon as I know what Christ wants from me, without delay let me do it; for if I begin with delaying I shall probably end with declining. The psalmist was wise when he laid emphasis on the swiftness of his obedience, and said, "I made haste and delayed not, but made haste to keep Thy commandments."

But another view of the words makes them part of the message to the owner of the colt, and not of the assurance to the disciples. "Say ye that the Lord hath need of him, and that straightway (when He has done with him) He will send him back again." That is a possible rendering, and I am disposed to think it is the proper one. By it the owner is told that he is not parting with his property for good and all, that Jesus only wishes to borrow the animal for the morning, and that it will be returned in the afternoon. What does that view of the words suggest to us? Do you not think that that colt, when it did come back—for of course it came back some time or other —was a great deal more precious to its owner than it ever had been before, or ever could have been if it had not been lent to Christ, and Christ had not made His royal entry upon it? Can you not fancy that the man, if he was, as he evidently was, a disciple and lover of the Lord, would look at it, especially after the Crucifixion and the Ascension, and think, "What an honor to me, that I provided the mount for that triumphal entry!"? It is always so. If you wish anything to become precious, lend it to Jesus Christ, and when it comes back again, as it will come back, there will be a fragrance about it, a touch of His fingers will be left upon it, a memory that He has used it. If you desire to own yourselves, and to make yourselves worth owning, give yourselves to Christ. If you wish to get the greatest possible blessing and good out of possessions, lay them at His feet. If you wish love to be hallowed, joy to be calmed, perpetuated, and deepened, carry it to Him. "If the house be worthy, your peace shall rest upon it; if not," like the dove to the ark when it could find no footing in the turbid and drowned world, "it shall come back to you again." Straightway He will "send him back again," and that which I give to Jesus He will return enhanced, and it will be more truly and more blessedly mine, because I have laid it in His hands. This "altar" sanctifies the giver and the gift.

Nothing but Leaves

> *And seeing a fig tree afar off having leaves, He came, if haply He might find any thing thereon: and when He came to it, He found nothing but leaves; . . . 14. And Jesus . . . said unto it, No man eat fruit of thee hereafter for ever.* Mark 11:13, 14.

The date of this miracle has an important bearing on its meaning and purpose. It occurred on the Monday morning of the last week of Christ's ministry. That week saw His last coming to Israel, "if haply He might find any thing thereon." And if you remember the foot-to-foot duel with the rulers and representatives of the nation, and the words, weighty with coming doom, which He spoke in the Temple on the subsequent days, you will not doubt that the explanation of this strange and anomalous miracle is that it is an acted parable, a symbol of Israel in its fruitlessness and in its consequent barrenness to all coming time.

This is the only point of view, as it seems to me, from which the peculiarities of the miracle can either be warranted or explained. It is our

Lord's only destructive act. The fig tree grew by the wayside; probably, therefore, it belonged to nobody, and there was no right of property affected by its loss. He saw it from afar, "having leaves," and that was why, three months before the time, He went to look if there were figs on it. For experts tell us that in the fig tree the leaves accompany, and do not precede, the fruit. And so this one tree, brave in its show of foliage amidst leafless companions, was a hypocrite unless there were figs below the leaves. Therefore Jesus came, if haply he might find anything theron, and finding nothing, perpetuated the condition which He found, and made the sin its own punishment.

Now all that is plain symbol, and so I ask you to look with me, for a few moments, at these three things: What Christ sought and seeks; What He found and often finds; What He did when He found it.

1. What Christ sought and seeks. He came "seeking fruit." Now I may just notice, in passing, how pathetically and beautifully this incident suggests to us the true, dependent, weak manhood of that great Lord. In all probability He had just come from the home of Mary and Martha, and it is strange that having left their hospitable abode He should be "an hungered." But so it was. And even with all the weight of the coming crisis pressing upon His soul, He was conscious of physical necessities, as one of us might have been, and perhaps felt the more need for sustenance because so terrible a conflict was waiting Him. Nor, I think, need we shrink from recognizing another of the characteristics of humanity here, in the limitations of His knowledge and in the real expectation, which was disappointed, that He might find fruit where there were leaves. I do not want to plunge into depths far too deep for any man to find sure footing in, nor seek to define the undefinable, nor to explain how the divine inosculates with the human, but sure I am that Jesus Christ was not getting up a scene in order to make a parable out of His miracle; and that the hunger and the expectancy and the disappointment were all real, however they afterwards may have been turned by Him to a symbolical purpose. And so here we may see the weak Christ, the limited Christ, the true human Christ. But side by side, as is ever the case, with this manifestation of weakness, there comes an apocalypse of power. Wherever you have, in the history of our Lord, some signal exemplification of human infirmity, you have flashed out through "the veil, that is, His flesh," some beam of His glory. Thus this hungry Man could say, "No fruit grow on thee henceforward for ever"; and His bare word, the mere forth-putting and manifestation of His will, had power on material things. That is the sign and impress of divinity.

But I pass from that, which is not my special point now. What did

Christ seek? "Fruit." And what is fruit in contradistinction to leaves? Character and conduct like His. That is our fruit. All else is leafage. As the Apostle says, "Love, joy, hope, peace, righteousness in the Holy Ghost"; or, to put it into one word, Christ-likeness in our inmost heart and nature, and Christ-likeness, so far as it may be possible for us, in our daily life, that is the one thing that our Lord seeks from us.

We do not realize enough for ourselves, day by day, that it was for this end that Jeus Christ came. The cradle in Bethlehem, the weary life, the gracious words, the mighty deeds, the Cross on Calvary, the open grave, Olivet with His last footprints; His place on the throne, Pentecost, they were all meant for this, to make you and me good men, righteous people, bearing the fruits of holy living and conduct corresponding to His own pattern. Emotions of the selectest kind, religious experience of the profoundest and truest nature, these are blessed and good. They are the blossom which sets into fruit. And they come for this end, that by the help of them we may be made like Jesus Christ. He has yet to learn what is the purpose and the meaning of the Gospel who fixes upon anything else as its ultimate design than the production in us, as the results of the life of Christ dwelling in our hearts, of character and conduct like to His.

I suppose I ought to apologize for talking such commonplace platitudes as these, but, brethren, the most commonplace truths are usually the most important and the most impotent. And no "platitude" is a platitude until you have brought it so completely into your lives that there is no room for a fuller outworking of it. So I come to you, Christian men and women, real and nominal, now with this for my message, that Jesus Christ seeks from you this first and foremost, that you shall be good men and women "according to the pattern that has been showed us in the Mount," according to the likeness of His own stainless perfection.

And do not forget that Jesus Christ hungers for that goodness. That is a strange, and infinitely touching, and absolutely true thing. He is only "satisfied," and the hunger of His heart appeased, when "He sees of the travail of His soul" in the righteousness of His servants. I passed a day or two ago, in a country place, a great field on which there was stuck up a board that said, "___'s trial ground for seeds." This world is *Christ's* trial ground for seeds, where He is testing you and me to see whether it is worthwhile cultivating us any more, and whether we can bring forth any "fruit to perfection" fit for the lips and the refreshment of the Owner and Lord of the vineyard. Christ longs for fruit from us. And—strange, and wonderful, and yet true—the "bread" that He eats is the service of His servants. That, amongst other things, is what is meant by the ancient institution of sacrifice, "the food of the gods." Christ's food is the holiness and obedience of His children. He comes to us, as He came to that fig tree, seeking from *us* this fruit which He delights in receiving. Brethren, we cannot think too much of Christ's unspeakable gift in itself and in its consequences; but we may easily think too little, and I am sure that a great many of us do think too little, of Christ's demands. He is not an austere man, "reaping where He did not sow"; but having sowed so much, He does look for the harvest. He comes to us with the heart-moving appeal, "I have given all to thee; what givest thou to Me?" "My well-beloved hath a vineyard in a very fruitful hill; and he fenced it and planted it, and built a tower and a winepress in it"—and what then?—"and he looked that it should bring forth grapes." Christ comes to each of you professing Christians, and asks, "What fruit hast thou borne after all My sedulous husbandry?"

2. Now note, in the next place, what Christ found. "Nothing but leaves." I have already said that we are told that the habit of growth of these trees is that the fruit accompanies, and sometimes precedes, the leaves. Whether it is so or no, let me remind you that leaves are an outcome of the life as well as fruit, and that they benefit the tree, and assist in the production of the fruit which it ought to bear. And so the symbol suggests things that are good in themselves, ancillary and subsidiary to the production of fruit, but which sometimes tend to such disproportionate exuberance of growth as that all the life of the tree runs to leaf, and there is not a berry to be found on it.

And if you want to know what such things are, remember the condition of the rulers of Israel at that time. They prided themselves upon their nominal, external, hereditary connection with a system of revelation, they trusted in mere ritualisms, they had ossified religion into theology, and degraded morality into casuistry. They thought that because they had been born Jews, and circumcised, and because there was a daily sacrifice going on in the Temple, and because they had Rabbis who could split hairs *ad infinitum,* therefore they were the "temple of the Lord," and God's chosen.

And that is exactly what hosts of pagans, masquerading as Christians, are doing in all our so-called Christian lands, and in all our so-called Christian congregations. In any community of so-called Christian people there is a little nucleus of real, earnest, God-fearing folk, and a great fringe of people whose Christianity is mostly from the teeth outward, who have a nominal and external connection with religion, who have been "baptized" and are "communicants," who think that religion lies mainly in coming on a Sunday, and with more or less toleration and interest listening to a preacher's words and joining in external worship, and all the while the "weightier matters of the law"—righteousness, justice, and the love of God—they leave untouched. What describes such a type of religion with more piercing accuracy than "nothing but leaves"?

External connection with God's Church is a good thing. It is meant to make us better men and women. If it does not, it is a bad thing. Acts of worship, more or less elaborate—for it is not the elaboration of ceremonial, but the mistaken view of it, that does the harm—acts of worship may be helpful, or may be absolute barriers to real religious life. They are becoming so largely today. The drift and trend of opinion in some parts of so-called Christendom is in the direction of outward ceremonial. And I, for one, believe that there are few things doing more harm to the Christian character of people today than the preposterous recurrence to a reliance on the mere externals of worship. Of course, we Dissenters pride ourselves on having no complicity with the sacramentarian errors which underlie these. But there may be quite as much of a barrier between the soul and Christ, reared by the bare worship of Nonconformists, or by the no-worship of the Society of Friends. If the absence of form be converted into a form, as it often is, there may be as lofty and wide a barrier raised by these as by the most elaborate ritual of the highest ceremonial that exists in Christendom. And so I say to you, dear brethren, seeing that we are all in danger of cleaving to externals and substituting these which are intended to be helps to the production of godly life and character, it becomes us all to listen to the solemn word of exhortation that comes out of my text, and to beware lest our religion runs to leaf instead of setting into fruit.

It does so with many of us; that is a certainty. I am thinking about no individual, about no individuals, but I am only speaking common sense when I say that amongst as many people as I am now addressing there will be an appreciable proportion who have no notion of religion as anything beyond a more or less imperative and more or less unwelcome set of external observances.

3. And so, lastly, let me ask you to notice what Christ did. I do not need to trouble myself nor you with vindicating the morality of this miracle against the fantastic objections that often have been made against it; nor need I say a word more than I have already said about its symbolical meaning. Israel was in that week being asked for the last time to "bring forth fruit" to the Lord of the vineyard. The refusal bound barrenness on the synagogue and on the nation, if not absolutely forever, at all events until "it shall turn to the Lord," and partake again of "the root and fatness" from which it has been broken off. What thirsty lips since that week have ever got any good out of Rabbinism and Judaism? No "figs" have grown on that "thistle." The world has passed it by, and left all its subtle casuistries and painfully microscopic studies of the letter of Scripture—with utter oblivion of its spirit—left them all severely and wisely alone. Judaism is a dead tree.

And is there nothing else in this incident? "No man eat fruit of thee hereafter for ever"; the punishment of that fruitlessness was confirmed and eternal barrenness. *There* is the lesson that the punishment of any sin is to bind the sin upon the doer of it.

But, further, the church or the individual whose religion runs to leaf is useless to the world. What does the world care about the ceremonials and the externals of worship, and a painful orthodoxy, and the study of the letter of Scripture? Nothing. A useless church or a Christian, from whom no man gets any fruit to cool a thirsty, parched lip, is only fit for what comes after the barrenness, and that is, that every tree that bringeth "not forth good fruit is hewn down and cast into the fire." The churches of England, and we, as integral parts of these, have solemn duties lying upon us today; and if we cannot help our brethren, and feed and nourish the hungry and thirsty hearts and souls of mankind, then—then! the sooner we are plucked up and pitched over the vineyard wall, which is the fate of the barren vine, the better for the world and the better for the vineyard.

The fate of Judaism teaches, to all of us professing Christians, very solemn lessons. "If God spared not the natural branches, take heed lest He also spare not thee." What has become of the seven churches of Asia Minor? They hardened into chattering theological "orthodoxy," and all the blood of them went to the surface, so to speak. And so down came the Mohammedan power—which was strong then because it did believe in a God, and not in its own belief about a God—and wiped them off the face of the earth. And so, brethren, we have, in this miracle, a warning and a prophecy which it becomes all the Christian communities of this day, and the individual members of such, to lay very earnestly to heart.

But do not let us forget that the Evangelist who does not tell us the story of the blasted fig tree does tell us its analogue, the parable of the barren fig tree, and that in it we read that when the fiat of destruction had gone forth, there was one who said, "Let it alone this year also that I may dig about it, . . . and if it bear fruit, well! If not, after that thou shalt cut it down." So the barren tree may become a fruitful tree, though it has hitherto borne nothing but leaves. Your religion may have been all on the surface and in form, but you can come into touch with Him in whom is our life and from whom comes our fruitfulness. He has said to each of us, "As the branch cannot bear fruit of itself, except it abide in the vine, no more can ye, except ye abide in Me."

12

The Nearness of the Kingdom

Dishonest Tenants

And He began to speak unto them by parables. A certain man planted a vineyard, and set an hedge about it, and digged a place for the winevat, and built a tower, and let it out to husbandmen, and went into a far country. 2. And at the season he sent to the husbandmen a servant, that he might receive from the husbandmen of the fruit of the vineyard. 3. And they caught him, and beat him, and sent him away empty. 4. And again he sent unto them another servant; and at him they cast stones, and wounded him in the head, and sent him away shamefully handled. 5. And again he sent another; and him they killed, and many others; beating some, and killing some. 6. Having yet therefore one son, his well beloved, he sent him also last unto them, saying, They will reverence my son. 7. But those husbandmen said among themselves, This is the heir; come, let us kill him, and the inheritance shall be ours. 8. And they took him, and killed him, and cast him out of the vineyard. 9. What shall therefore the lord of the vineyard do! He will come and destroy the husbandmen, and will give the vineyard unto others. 10. And have ye not read this scripture; The stone which the builders rejected is become the head of the corner: 11. This was the Lord's doing, and it is marvelous in our eyes! 12. And they sought to lay hold on Him, but feared the people: for they knew that He had spoken the parable against them: and they left Him, and went their way. MARK 12:1–12.

The ecclesiastical rulers had just been questioning Jesus as to the authority by which He acted. His answer, a counter-question as to John's authority, was not an evasion. If they decided whence John came, they would not be at any loss as to whence Jesus came. If they steeled themselves against acknowledging the Forerunner, they would not be receptive of Christ's message. That keen-edged retort plainly indicates Christ's conviction of the rulers' insincerity, and in this parable He charges home on these solemn hypocrites their share in the hereditary rejection of messengers whose authority was unquestionable. Much they cared for even divine authority, as they and their predecessors had shown through centuries! The veil of parable is transparent here. Jesus increased in severity and bold attack as the end drew near.

1. The parable begins with a tender description of the preparation and allotment of the vineyard. The picture is based upon Isaiah's lovely apologue (Isaiah 5:1), which was, no doubt, familiar to the learned officials. But there is a slight difference in the application of the metaphor which in Isaiah means the nation, and in the parable is rather the theocracy as an institution, or, as we may put it roughly, the aggregate of divine revelations and appointments which constituted the religious prerogatives of Israel.

Our Lord follows the original passage in the description of the preparation of the vineyard, but it would probably be going too far to press special meanings on the wall, the winepress, and the watchman's tower. The fence was to keep off marauders, whether passersby or "the boar out of the wood" (Psalm 130:12,13); the winepress, for which Mark uses the word which means rather the vat into which the juice from the press proper flowed, was to extract and collect the previous liquid; the tower was for the watchman.

A vineyard with all these fittings was ready for profitable occupation. Thus abundantly had God furnished Israel with all that was needed for fruitful, happy service. What was true of the ancient Church is still more true of us who have received every requisite for holy living. Isaiah's solemn appeal has a still sharper edge for Christians: "Judge, I pray you, betwixt me and my vineyard. What could have been done more to my vineyard that I have not done in it?"

The "letting of the vineyard to husbandmen" means the committal to Israel and its rulers of these divine institutions, and the holding them responsible for their fruitfulness. It may be a question whether the tenants are to be understood as only the official persons, or whether, while these are primarily addressed, they represent the whole people. The usual interpretation limits the meaning to the rulers, but, if so, it is difficult to carry out the application, as the vineyard would then have to be regarded as being the nation, which confuses all. The language of Matthew (which threatens the taking of the vineyard and giving it to another nation) obliges us to regard the nation as included in the husbandmen, though primarily the expression is addressed to the rulers.

But more important is it to note the strong expressions for man's quasi-independence and responsibility. The Jew was invested with full possession of the vineyard. We all, in like manner, have entrusted to us, to do as we will with, the various gifts and powers of Christ's Gospel. God, as it were, draws somewhat apart from man, that he may have free play for his choice, and bear the burden of responsibility. The divine action was conspicuous at the time of founding the polity of Judaism, and then came long years in which there were no miracles, but all things continued as they were. God was as near as before, but He seemed far off. Thus Jesus has, in like manner, gone "into a far country to receive a kingdom and to return"; and we, the tenants of a richer vineyard than Israel's, have to administer what He has entrusted to us, and to bring near by faith Him who is to sense far off.

2. The next scenes paint the conduct of the dishonest vinedressers. We mark the stern, dark picture drawn of the continued and brutal violence, as well as the flagrant unfaithfulness, of the tenants. Matthew's version gives emphasis to the increasing harshness of treatment of the owner's messengers, as does Mark's. First comes beating, then wounding, then murder. The interpretation is self-evident. The "servants" are the prophets, mostly men inferior in rank to the hierarchy, shepherds, fig gatherers, and the like. They came to rouse Israel to a sense of the purpose for which they had received their distinguishing prerogatives, and their reward had been contempt and maltreatment. They "had trial of mockings and scourgings, of bonds and imprisonment: they were stoned, they were sawn asunder, they were slain with the sword."

The indictment is the same as that by which Stephen wrought the Sanhedrin into a paroxysm of fury. To make such a charge as Jesus did, in the very Temple courts, and with the already hostile priests glaring at Him while He spoke, was a deliberate assault on them and their predecessors, whose true successors they showed themselves to be. They had just been solemnly questioning Him as to His authority. He answers by thus passing in review the uniform treatment meted by them and their like to those who came with God's manifest authority.

If a mere man had spoken this parable, we might admire the magnificent audacity of such an accusation. But the Speaker is more than man, and we have to recognize the judicial calmness and severity of His tone. Israel's history, as it shaped itself before His "pure eyes and perfect judgment," was one long series of divine favors and of human ingratitude, of ample preparations for righteous living and of no result, of messengers sent and their contumelious rejection. We wonder at the sad monotony of such requital. Are we doing otherwise?

3. Then comes the last effort of the owner, the last arrow in the quiver of Almighty Love. Two things are to be pondered in this part of the parable. First, that wonderful glimpse into the depths of God's heart, in the hope expressed by the Owner of the vineyard, brings out very clearly Christ's claim, made there before all these hostile, keen critics, to stand in an altogether singular relation to God. He asserts His Sonship as separating Him from the class of prophets who are servants only, and as constituting a relationship with the Father prior to His coming to earth. His Sonship is no mere synonym for His Messiahship, but was a fact long before Bethlehem; and its assertion lifts for us a corner of the veil of cloud and darkness round the throne of God. Not less striking is the expression of a frustrated hope in "they will reverence My Son." Men can thwart God's purpose. His divine charity "hopeth all things." The mystery thus sharply put here is but that which is presented everywhere in the co-existence of God's purposes and man's freedom.

The other noteworthy point is the corresponding casting of the vine-dressers' thoughts into words. Both representations are due to the graphic character of parable; both crystallize into speech motives which were not actually spoken. It is unnecessary to suppose that even the rulers of Israel had gone the awful length of clear recognition of Christ's Messiahship, and of looking each other in the face and whispering such a fiendish resolve. Jesus is here dragging to light unconscious motives. The masses did wish to have their national privileges and to avoid their national duties. The rulers did wish to have their sway over minds and consciences undisturbed. They did resent Jesus' interference, chiefly because they instinctively felt that it threatened their position. They wanted to get Him out of the way, that they might lord it at will. They could have known that He was the Son, and they suppressed dawning suspicions that He was. Alas! they have descendants still in many of us who put away His claims, even while we secretly recognize them, in order that we may do as we like without His meddling with us!

The rulers' calculation was a blunder. As Augustine says, "They slew Him that they might possess, and, because they slew, they lost." So is it always. Whoever tries to secure any desired end by putting away his responsibility to render to God the fruit of his thankful service, loses the good which he would fain clutch at for his own. All sin is a mistake.

The parable passes from thinly veiled history to equally transparent prediction. How sadly and how unshrinkingly does the meek yet mighty Victim disclose to the conspirators His perfect knowledge of the murder which they were even now hatching in their minds! He foresees all, and will not lift a finger to prevent it. Mark puts the "killing" before the "casting out of the vineyard," while Matthew and Luke invert the order of the two things. The slaughtered corpse was, as a further indignity, thrown over the wall, by which is symbolically expressed His exclusion from Israel, and the vinedressers' delusion that they now had secured undisturbed possession.

4. The last point is the authoritative sentence on the evildoers. Mark's condensed account makes Christ Himself answer His own question. Probably we are to suppose that, with hypocritical readiness, some of the rulers replied, as the other Evangelists represent, and that Jesus then solemnly took up their words. If anything could have enraged the rulers more than the parable itself, the distinct declaration of the transference of Israel's prerogatives to more worthy tenants would do so. The words are heavy with doom. They carry a lesson for us. Stewardship implies responsibility, and faithlessness, sooner or later, involves deprivation. The only way to keep God's gifts is to use them for His glory. "The grace of God," says Luther somewhere, "is like a flying summer shower." Where are Ephesus and the other apocalyptic churches? Let us "take heed lest, if God spared not the natural branches, He also spare not us."

Jesus leaves the hearers with the old psalm ringing in their ears, which proclaimed that "the stone which the builders rejected becomes the head stone of the corner." Other words of the same psalm had been chanted by the crowd in the procession on entering the city. Their fervor was cooling, but the prophecy would still be fulfilled. The builders are the same as the vinedressers; their rejection of the stone is parallel with slaying the Son.

But though Jesus foretells His death, He also foretells His triumph after death. How could He have spoken, almost in one breath, the prophecy of His being slain and "cast out of the vineyard," and that of His being exalted to be the very apex and shining summit of the true Temple, unless He had been conscious that His death was indeed not the end, but the center, of His work, and His elevation to universal and unchanging dominion?

God's Last Arrow

Having yet therefore one son, his well-beloved, he sent him also last unto them. MARK 12:6.

Reference to Isaiah 5. There are differences in detail here which need not trouble us.

Isaiah's parable is a review of the theocratic history of Israel, and clearly the messengers are the prophets; here Christ speaks of Himself and His own mission to Israel, and goes on to tell of His death as already accomplished.

1. The Son who follows and surpasses the servants. Our Lord here places Himself in the line of the prophets as coming for a similar purpose. The mission *to Israel* was the same. The mission *of His life* was the same.

The last words of the lawgiver certainly point to a person (Deuteronomy 18:18): "A prophet shall the Lord your God raise up unto you like unto me. Him shall ye hear." How ridiculous the cool superciliousness with which modern historical criticism "pooh-poohs" that interpretation! But the contrast is quite as prominent as the resemblance. This saying is one which occurs in all the Synoptics, and is as full a declaration of Sonship as any in John's Gospel. It reposes on the scene at the baptism (Matthew 3): "This is My beloved Son!" Such a saying was well enough understood by the Jews to mean more than the "Messiah." It clearly involves kindred to the divine in a far other and higher sense than any prophet ever had it. It involves pre-existence. It asserts that He was the special object of the divine love, the "heir."

You cannot relieve the New Testament Christ of the responsibility of having made such assertions. There they are! He did deliberately declare that He was, in a unique sense, "*the* Son" on whom the love and complacency of the Father rested continually.

2. The aggravation of men's sins as tending to the enhancement of the divine efforts. The terrible Nemesis of evil is that it ever tends to reproduce itself in aggravated forms. Think of the influence of habit; the searing of conscience, so that we become able to do things that we would have shrunk from at an earlier stage. Remember how impunity leads to greater sin. So here the first servant is merely sent away empty, the second is wounded and disgraced, the third is killed. All evil is an inclined plane, a steady, downward progress. How beautifully the opposite principle of the divine love and patience is represented as striving with the increasing hate and resistance! According to Matthew, the householder sent other servants "*more than* the first," and the climax was that he sent his son. Mightier forces are brought to bear. This attraction *increases* as the square of the distance. The blacker the cloud, the brighter the sun; the thicker the ice, the hotter the flame; the harder the soil, the stronger the plowshare. Note, too, the undertone of sacrifice and of yearning for the son which may be discerned in the "householder's" words. The son is his "dearest treasure," his mightiest gift, than which is nothing higher.

The mission of Christ is the ultimate appeal of God to men.

In the primary sense of the parable Jesus does close the history of the divine strivings with Israel. After Christ, the last of the prophets, the divine voice ceases; after the blaze of that light all is dark. There is nothing more remarkable in the whole history of the world than that cessation in an instant, as it were, of the long, august series of divine efforts for Israel. Henceforeward there is an awful silence. "Forsaken Israel wanders lone."

And the principle involved for us is the same.

"Christ crucified" is more than Christ miracle-working. That "more" we have, as the Jews had. But if that avails not, then nothing else will.

He is "last" because highest, strongest, and all-sufficient.

He is "last" inasmuch as all since are but echoes of His voice and proclaimers of His grace.

He is "last" as the eternal and the permanent, the "same forever" (Hebrews 13:8). There are to be no new powers for the world; no new forces to draw men to God. God's quiver is empty, His last bolt shot, His most tender appeal made.

3. The unwearied divine charity. "They will reverence My Son." May we not say this is a divine hope? It is not worthwhile to make a difficulty of the bold representation. It is but parallel to all the dealings of God with men; and it sets forth the possibility that He *might* have won Israel back to God and to obedience. It suggests the good faith and the earnestness with which God sent Him, and He came, to bring Israel back to God. But we are not to suppose that this divine hope excluded the divine purpose of His death or was inconsistent with that, for He goes on to speak of His death as if it were past (verse 8). This shows how distinctly He foreknew it.

Its highest aspect is not here, for it was not needed for the parable. "With wicked hands ye have crucified," etc., is true, as well as "I lay it down of Myself."

Let us lay to heart the solemn love which warns by prophesying, tells what men are going to do in order that they may *not* do it (and what He will do in order that He may *not* have to do it). And let us yield ourselves to the power of Christ's death as God's magnet for drawing us all back to Him; and as certain to bring about at last the satisfaction of the Father's long-frustrated hope: "They will reverence my Son," and the fulfillment of the Son's long-unaccomplished prediction: "I, if I be lifted up from the earth, will draw all men unto Me."

Not Far and Not In

Thou art not far from the kingdom of God. MARK 12:34.

"A bruised reed He will not break, and the smoking flax He will not quench."

Here is Christ's recognition of the low beginnings of goodness and faith.

This is a special case of a man who appears to have fully discerned the spirituality and inwardness of law, and to have felt that the one bond between God and man was love. He needed only to have followed out the former thought to have been smitten by the conviction of his own sinfulness, and to have reflected on the latter to have discovered that he needed someone who could certify and commend God's love to him, and thereby to kindle his to God. Christ recognizes such beginnings and encourages him to persevere: but warns him against the danger of supposing himself in the kingdom, and against the prolongation of what is only good as a transition state.

This Scribe is an interesting study as being one who recognized the Law in its spiritual meaning, in opposition to forms and ceremonies. His intellectual convictions needed to be led on from recognition of the spirituality of the Law to recognition of his own failures. "By law is the knowledge of sin." His intellectual convictions needed to pass over into and influence his heart and life. He recognized true piety, and was earnestly striving after it, but entrance into the kingdom is by faith in the Saviour, who is "the Way." So Jesus' praise of him is but measured. For in him there was separation between knowing and doing.

1. Who are near? Christ's kingdom is near us all, whether we are heathen, infidel, profligate or not.

Here is a distinct recognition of two things—(*a*) degrees of approximation; (*b*) decisive separation between those who are, and those who are not, within the kingdom.

This Scribe was near, and yet not in, the kingdom, because, like so many in all ages, he had an intellectual hold of principles which he had never followed out to their intellectual issues, nor ever enthroned as, in their practical issues, the guides of his life. How constantly we find characters of similar incompleteness among ourselves!

How many of us have true thoughts concerning God's law and what it requires, which ought, in all reason, to have brought us to the consciousness of our own sin, and are yet untouched by one pang of penitence! How many of us have lying in our heads, like disused furniture in a storeroom, what we suppose to be beliefs of ours, which only need to be followed out to their necessary results to refurnish with a new equipment the whole of our religious thinking! How few of us do really take pains to bring our beliefs into clear sunlight, and to follow them wherever they lead us! There is no commoner fault, and no greater foe, than the hazy, lazy half-belief, of which its owner neither knows the grounds nor perceives the intellectual or the practical issues.

There are multitudes who have, or have had, convictions of which the only rational outcome is practical surrender to Jesus Christ by faith and love. Such persons abound in Christian congregations and in Christian homes. They are on the verge of "the great surrender," but they do not go beyond the verge, and so they perpetrate "the great refusal." And to all such the word of our text should sound as a warning note, which has also hope in its tone. "Not far from" is still "outside."

2. Why they are only near. The reason is not because of anything apart from themselves. The Christian Gospel offers immediate entrance into the Kingdom, and all the gifts which its King can bestow, to all and every one who will. So that the sole cause of any man's non-entrance lies with himself.

We have spoken of failure to follow out truths partially grasped, and that constitutes a reason which affects the intellect mainly, and plays its part in keeping men out of the Kingdom.

But there are other, perhaps more common, reasons, which intervene to prevent convictions being followed out into their properly consequent acts.

The two most familiar and fatal of these are:
(*a*) procrastination.
(*b*) lingering love of the world.

3. Such men cannot continue near. The state is necessarily transitional. It must pass over into—(*a*) either going on and into the Kingdom, or (*b*) going further away from it.

Christ warns here, and would stimulate to action, for—(*a*) convictions not acted on die; (*b*) truths not followed out fade; (*c*) impressions resisted are harder to be made again; (*d*) obstacles increase with time; (*e*) the habit of lingering becomes strengthened.

4. Unless you are in, you are finally shut out. "City of refuge." It was of no avail to have been *near*. "Strive to enter *in*."

Appeal to all such as are in this transition stage.

13

Belief and Watchfulness

The Credulity of Unbelief

Many shall come in My name, saying, I am Christ, and shall deceive many. MARK 13:6.

When the Son of Man cometh, shall He find faith on the earth? LUKE 18:8.

It was the same generation that is represented in these two texts as void of faith in the Son of Man, and as credulously giving heed to impostors. Unbelief and superstition are closely allied. Religion is so vital a necessity, that if the true form of it be cast aside, some false form will be eagerly seized in order to fill the aching void. Men cannot permanently live without some sort of a faith in the Unseen, but they can determine whether it shall be a worthy recognition of a worthy conception of that Unseen, or a debasing superstition. An epoch of materialism in philosophic thought has always been followed by violent reaction, in which quacks and fanatics have reaped rich harvests. If the dark is not peopled with one loved Face, our busy imagination will fill it with a crowd of horrible ones.

Just as a sailor, looking out into the night over a solitary, islandless sea, sees shapes; intolerant of the islandless expanse, makes land out of fogbanks; and, sick of silence, hears "airy tongues" in the moanings of the wind and the slow roll of the waves, so men shudderingly look into the dark unknown, and if they see not their Father there, will either shut their eyes or strain them in gazing it into shape. The sight of Him is religion, the closed eye is infidelity, the strained gaze is superstition. The second and the third are each so unsatisfying that they perpetually pass over into one another and destroy one another, as when I shut my eyes, I see slowly shaping itself a colored image of my eye, which soon flickers and fluctuates into black nothingness again, and then rises once more, once more to fade. Men, if they believe not in God, then do service to "them which by nature are no gods."

But let us come to more immediately Christian thoughts. Christ does what men so urgently require to be done, that if they do not believe in Him they will be forced to shape out for themselves some fancied ways of doing it. The emotions which men cherish towards Him so irrepressibly need an object to rest on, that if not He, then some far less worthy one, will be chosen to receive them.

It is just to the illustration of these thoughts that I seek to turn now, and in such alternatives as these—

1. Reception of Christ as the Revealer is the only escape from unmanly submission to unworthy pretenders. That function is one which the instincts of men teach them that they need.

Christ comes to satisfy the need as the visible true embodiment of the Father's love, of the Father's wisdom.

If He be rejected—what then? Why, not that the men who reject will contentedly continue in darkness—that is never possible; but that some manner or other of satisfying the clamant need will be had recourse to, and then that to it will be transferred the submission and credence that should have been His. If we have Him for our Teacher and Guide, then all other teachers and guides will take their right places. We shall not angrily repel their power, nor talk loudly about "the right of private judgment," and our independence of all men's thoughts. We are not so independent. We shall thankfully accept all help from all men wiser, better, more manly than ourselves, whether they give us uttered words of wisdom and beauty, having "grace poured into their lips," or whether they give us lives ennobled by strenuous effort, or whether they give us greater treasure than all these—the sight once more of a loving heart. All is good, all is helpful, all we shall receive; but in proportion to the felt obligations we are laid under to them will be the felt authority of that saying, "Call no man your master on earth, for One is your Master, even Christ." That command forbids our slavishly accepting any human domination over our faith, but it no less emphatically forbids our contemptuously rejecting any human helper of our joy, for it closes with "and all ye are brethren"—bound then to mutual observance, mutual helpfulness, mutual respect for each other's individuality, mutual avoidance of needless division. To have Him for his Guide makes the human guide gentle and tender among his disciples "as a nurse among her children," for he remembers "the gentleness of Christ," and he dare not be other than an imitator of Him. A Christian teacher's spirit will always be, "not for that we have dominion over your faith, but we are helpers of your joy"; his most earnest word, "I beseech you, therefore, brethren"; his constant desire, "He must increase. I must decrease." And to have Christ for our Guide makes the taught lovingly submissive to all who by largeness of gifts and graces are set by Him above them, and yet lovingly recalcitrant at any attempt to compel adhesion or force dogmas. The one freedom from undue dependence on men and men's opinions lies in this submission to Jesus. Then we can say, when need is, "I have a Master. To Him I submit; if *you* seek to be master, I demur: of them who seemed to be somewhat, whatsoever they were, it maketh no matter to me."

But the greatest danger is not that our guides shall insist on our submission, but that we shall insist on giving it. It is for all of us such a burden to have the management of our own fate, the forming of our own opinions, the fearful responsibility of our own destiny, that we are all only too ready to say to some man or other, from love or from laziness, "Where thou goest, I will go; thy people shall be my people, and thy God my God."

Few things are more strange and tragic than the eagerness with which people who are a great deal too enlightened to render allegiance to Jesus Christ will install some teacher of their own choosing as their authoritative master, will swallow his dicta, swear by him, and glory in being called by his name. What they think is derogatory to their mental independence to give to the Teacher of Nazareth, they freely give to their chosen oracle. It is not in "the last times" only that men who will not endure sound teaching "heap to themselves teachers after their own lusts," and have "the ears" which are fast closed to "the Truth" wide open "to fables."

On the small scale we see this melancholy perversity of conduct exemplified in every little coterie and school of unbelievers.

On the great scale Mohammedanism and Buddhism, with their millions of adherents, write the same tragic truth large in the history of the world.

2. Faith in the reconciling Christ is the only sure deliverance from debasing reliance on false means of reconciliation. In a very profound sense ignorance and sin are the same fact regarded under two different aspects. And in the depths of their natures men have the longing for some Power who shall put away sin, as they have the longing for one that will dispel ignorance. The consciousness of alienation from God lies in the human heart, dormant indeed for the most part, but like a coiled, hibernating snake, ready to wake and strike its poison into the veins. Christ by His great work, and specially by His sacrificial death, meets that universal need.

But closely as His work fits men's needs, it sharply opposes some of their wishes, and of their interpretations of their needs. The Jew "demands a sign,'' the Greek craves a reasoned system of ''wisdom,'' and both concur in finding the Cross an ''offense.''

But the rejection of Jesus as the Reconciler does not quiet the cravings, which make themselves heard at some time or other in most consciences, for deliverance from the dominion and from the guilt of sin. And men are driven to adopt other expedients to fill up the void which their turning away from Jesus has left. Sometimes they fall back on a vague reliance on a vague assertion that ''God is merciful''; sometimes they reason themselves into a belief—or, at any rate, an assertion—that the conception of sin is an error, and that men are not guilty. Sometimes they manage to silence the inward voice that accuses and condemns, by dint of not listening to it or drowning it by other noises.

But these expedients fail them some time or other, and then, if they have not cast the burden of their sin and their sins on the great Reconciler, they either have to weary themselves with painful and vain efforts to be their own redeemers, or they fall under the domination of a priest.

Hence the hideous penances of heathenism; and hence, too, the power of sacramentarian and sacerdotal perversions of evangelical truth.

3. Faith in Christ as the Regenerator is the only deliverance from baseless hopes for the world. The world is today full of moaning voices crying, ''Art thou He that should come, or do we look for another?'' and it is full of confident voices proclaiming other means of its regeneration than letting Christ ''make all things new.''

The conviction that society needs to be reconstituted on other principles is spread everywhere, and is often associated with intense disbelief in Christ the Regenerator.

Has not the past proved that all schemes for the regeneration of society which do not grapple with the fact of sin, and which do not provide a means of infusing into human nature a new impulse and direction, will end in failure, and are only too likely to end in blood? These two requirements are met by Jesus, and by Him only, and whoever rejects Him and His gift of pardon and cleansing, and His inbreathing of a new life into the individual, will fail in his effort, however earnest and noble in many aspects, to redeem society and bring about a fair new world.

It is pitiable to see the waste of high aspiration and eager effort in so many quarters today. But that waste is sure to attend every scheme which does not start from the recognition of Christ's work as the basis of the world's transformation, and does not crown Him as the King, because He is the Saviour, of mankind.

Authority and Work

For the Son of Man is as a man taking a far journey, who left his house, and gave authority to his servants, and to every man his work, and commanded the porter to watch. MARK 13:34.

Church order is not directly touched on in the Gospels, but the principles which underlie all Church order are distinctly laid down. The whole community of Christian people is a family or household, being brethren because possessors of a new life through Christ. In that household there is one "Master," and all its members are "servants." That name suggests the purpose for which they exist; the meaning of all their offices, dignities, etc.

1. The authority with which the servants are invested. We hear a great deal about the authority of the Church in these days, as a determiner of truth and as a prescriber of Christian action. It means generally official authority, the power of guidance and definition of the Church's action, etc., which some people think is lodged in the hands of preachers, pastors, priests, either individually or collectively. There is nothing of that sort meant here. Whatever this authority is, it belongs to the whole body of the servants, not to individuals among them. It is the prerogative of the whole *ecclesia,* not of some handful of them. "This honor," whatever it be, "have all the saints."

Explain by reference to "the kings of the earth exercise lordship over them"; "the greatest shall be your servant." It is then but another name for capacity for service, power to bless, etc.

And this idea is still further borne out if we go back to the parable of our text. A man leaves his house in charge of his servants. To them is committed the responsibility for his goods. His honor and interests are in their hands. They have control over his possessions. This is the analogy which our Lord suggests as presenting a vivid likeness to our position in the world.

Christ has committed the care of His kingdom, the glory of His name, the growth of His cause in the world to His Church, and has endowed it with all "talents" *i.e.* gifts needful for that work. Or, to put it in other words, they are His representatives in the world. They have to defend His honor. His name is scandalized or glorified by their actions. They have to see to His interests. They are charged with the carrying out of His mind and purposes.

The foundation of all is laid. Henceforth building on it is all, and that is to be done by men. Human lips and Christian effort—not without the divine Spirit in the word—are to be the means.

It is as when some commander plans his battle, and from an eminence overlooks the current of the fight, and marks the plunging legions as they struggle through the smoke. He holds all the tremendous machinery in his hands. The plan and the glory are his, but the execution of the plan lies with the troops.

In a still more true sense all the glory of the Christian conquest of the world is His, but still the instruments are ourselves. The whole counsel of God is on our side. We "go not a warfare at our own charges." Note the perfect consistency of this with all that we hold of the necessity of divine influence, etc.

His servants are entrusted with all His "goods." They have authority over the gifts which He has given them, *i.e.* Christian men are stewards of Christ's riches for others.

They have access to the free use of them all for themselves.

Thus the "authority" is all derived. It is all given for the sake of others. It is all capacity for service. Hence—

2. The authority with which the servants are invested blinds every one of them to hard work for Christ. "To every man his work."

(*a*) Gifts involve duties. That is the first great thought. To have received binds us to impart. "Freely ye have received, freely give."

All selfish possession of the gifts which Christ bestows is grave sin.

The price at which they were procured, that miracle and mystery of self-sacrifice, is the great pattern as well as the great motive for our service.

The purpose for which we have received them is plainly set forth: in the existence of the solidarity in which we are all bound; in the definite utterances of Scripture.

The need for their exercise is only too palpable in the condition of things around us.

(*b*) In this multitude of servants every one has his own task.

The universality of the great gift leads to a corresponding universality of obligation. All Christians have their gifts. Each of us has his special work marked out for him by character, relationship, circumstances, natural tastes, etc.

How solemn a divine call there is in these individual peculiarities which we often think of as unimportant accidents, or regard mainly in their bearing on our own ease and comfort! How reverently we should regard the diversities which are thus revelations of God's will concerning our tasks! How earnestly we should seek to know what it is that we are fitted for!

The importance of all protests against priestly assumption lies here, that they strengthen the force with which we proclaim that every man has his "work."

Ponder the variety of characters and gifts which Christ gives and desires His servants to use, and the indispensable need for them all. The ideal Church is the "body" of Christ, in which each member has its place and function.

Our fault in this matter.

(*c*) The duties are to be done in the spirit of hard toil.

The servant has "his work" allotted him, and the word implies that the work calls for effort. The race is not to be run without dust and sweat. Our Christian service is not to be regarded as a "by-product" or *parergon*. It is, so to speak, a *vocation,* not an *avocation*. It deserves and demands all the energy that we can put forth, continuity and constancy, plan and system. Nothing is to be done for God, any more than for ourselves, without toil. "In the sweat of thy brow shalt thou eat bread and give it to others."

3. To do this work, watchfulness is needed. The division of tasks between "servant" and "porter" is only part of the drapery of the parable. To show that watchfulness belongs to all, see the two following verses.

What is this watchfulness?

Not constant fidgety curiosity about the coming of the Lord; not hunting after apocalyptic dates. The modern impression seems to be that such study is "watchfulness." Christ says that the time of His coming is hidden (see previous verses). Ignorance of that is the very reason why we are to watch. Watchfulness, then, is just a profound and constant feeling of the transiency of this present. The mind is to be kept detached from it; the eye and heart are to be going out to things "unseen and eternal"; we are to be familiarizing ourselves with the thought that the world is passing away.

This watchfulness is an indispensable part of our "work." The true Christian thought of the transiency of the world sets us to work the more vigorously in it, and increases, not diminishes, our sense of the importance of time and of earthly things, and braces us to our tasks by the thought of the brevity of opportunity, as well as by guarding us against tastes and habits which eat all earnestness out of the soul.

Thus "working and watching," happy will be the servant whom his Lord will find "so doing," *i.e.* at work, not idly looking for Him. Our common duties are the best preparation for our Lord's coming.

14

The Guest Chamber and the Garden

The Alabaster Box

And Jesus said, Let her alone; why trouble ye her? she hath wrought a good work on Me. . . . 8. She hath done what she could: she is come aforehand to anoint My body to the burying. 9. Verily I say unto you, Wheresoever this gospel shall be preached throughout the whole world, this also that she hath done shall be spoken of for a memorial of her. MARK 14:6–9.

John's Gospel sets this incident in its due framework of time and place, and tells us the names of the actors. The time was within a week of Calvary, the place was Bethany, where, as John significantly reminds us, Jesus had raised Lazarus from the dead, thereby connecting the feast with that incident; the woman who broke the box of ointment and poured the perfume on the head and feet of Jesus was Mary; the first critic of her action was Judas. Selfishness blames love for the profusion and prodigality, which to it seem folly and waste. The disciples chimed in with the objection, not because they were superior to Mary in wisdom, but because they were inferior in consecration.

John tells us, too, that Martha was "amongst them that served." The characteristics of the two sisters are preserved. The two types of character which they respectively represent have great difficulty in understanding and doing justice to one another. Christ understands and does justice to them both. Martha, bustling, practical, utilitarian to the fingertips, does not much care about listening to Christ's words of wisdom. She has not any very high-strung or finely spun emotions, but she can busy herself in getting a meal ready; she loves Him with all her heart, and she takes her own way of showing it. But she gets impatient with her sister, and thinks that her sitting at Christ's feet is a dreamy waste of time, and not without a touch of selfishness, "taking no care for me, though I have got so much on my back." And so, in like manner, Mary is made out to be a monster of selfishness; ''Why was not this ointment sold for three hundred pence, and given to the poor?'' She could not serve, she would only have been in Martha's road if she had tried. But she had one precious thing which was her very own, and she caught it up, and in the irrepressible burst of her thankful love, as she saw Lazarus sitting there at the table beside Jesus, she poured the liquid perfume on His head and feet. He casts His shield over the poor, unpractical woman, who did such an utterly useless thing, for which a basin of water and a towel would have served far better. There are a great many useless things which, in Heaven's estimate, are more valuable than a great many apparently more practical ones. Christ accepts the service, and in His deep words lays down three or four principles which it would do us all good to carry with us into our daily lives. So I shall now try to gather from these utterances of our Lord's some great truths about Christian service.

1. The first of them is the motive which hallows everything. ''She hath wrought a good work on Me.'' Now that is pretty nearly a definition of what a good work is, and you see it is very unlike our conventional notions of what constitutes a ''good work.'' Christ implies that anything, no matter what are its other characteristics, that is ''on'' Him, that is to say, directed towards Him under the impulse of simple love to Him, is a ''good work''; and the converse follows, that nothing which has not that saving salt of reference to Him in it deserves the title. Did you ever think of what an extraordinary position that is for a man to take up? ''Think about Me in what you do, and you will do good. Do anything, no matter what, because you love Me, and it will be lifted up into high regions, and become transfigured; a good work.'' He took the best that any one could give Him, whether it was of outward possessions or of inward reverence, abject submission, and love and trust. He never said to any man, ''You are going over the score. You are exaggerating about Me. Stand up, for I also am a Man.'' He did say once, ''Why callest thou Me good?'' not because it was an incorrect attribution, but because it was a mere piece of conventional politeness. And in all other cases, not only does He accept as His rightful possession the utmost of reverence that any man can do Him, and bring Him, but He here implies, if He does not, as He almost does, specifically declare, that to be done for His sake lifts a deed into the region of ''good'' works.

Have you reflected what such an attitude implies as to the self-consciousness of the Man who took it, and whether it is intelligible, not to say admirable, or rather whether it is not worthy of reprobation, except upon one hypothesis—''Thou art the everlasting Son of the Father,'' and all men honor God when they honor the Incarnate Word? But that is aside from my present purpose.

Is not this conception, that the motive of reverence and love to him ennobles and sanctifies every deed, the very fundamental principle of Christian morality? All things are sanctified when they are done for His sake. You plunge a poor pebble into a brook, and as the sunlit ripples pass over its surface, the hidden veins of delicate color come out and glow, and the poor stone looks a jewel, and is magnified as well as glorified by being immersed in the stream. Plunge your work into Christ, and do it for Him, and the giver and the gift will be greatened and sanctified.

But, brethren, if we take this point of view, and look to the motive, and not to the manner or the issues, or the immediate objects, of our actions, as determining whether they are good or no, it will revolutionize a great many of our thoughts, and bring new ideas into much of our conventional language. ''A good work'' is not a piece of beneficence or benevolence, still less is it to be confined to those actions which conventional Christianity has chosen to dignify by the name. It is a designation that should not be clotted into certain specified corners of a life, but be extended over them all. The things which more specifically go under such a name, the kind of things that Judas wanted to have substituted for the utterly useless, lavish expenditure by this heart that was burdened with the weight of its own blessedness, come, or do not come, under the designation, according as there is present in them, not only natural charity to the poor whom ''ye have always with you,'' but the higher reference of them to Christ Himself. All these lower forms of beneficence are imperfect without that. And instead of, as we have been taught by authoritative voices of late years, the service of man being the true service of God, the relation of the two terms is precisely the opposite, and it is the service of God that will effloresce into all service of man. Judas did not do much for the poor, and a great many other people who are sarcastic upon the ''folly,'' the ''uncalculating impulses'' of Christian love, with its ''wasteful expenditure,'' and criticize us because we are spending time and energy and love upon objects which they think are moonshine and mist, do little more than he did, and what beneficence they do exercise has to be hallowed by this reference to Jesus before it can aspire to be beneficence indeed.

I sometimes wish that this generation of Christian people, amid its multifarious schemes of beneficence, with none of which would one interfere for a moment, would sometimes let itself go into manifestations of its love to Jesus Christ, which had no use at all except to relieve its own burdened heart. I am afraid that the lower motives, which are all right and legitimate when they are lower, are largely hustling the higher ones into the background, and that the river has got so many ponds to fill, and so many canals to trickle through, and so many plantations to irrigate and make verdant, that there is a danger of its falling low at its fountain, and running shallow in its course. One sometimes would like to see more things done for Him that the world would call "utter folly," and "prodigal waste," and "absolutely useless." Jesus Christ has a great many strange things in His treasurehouse—widows' mites, cups of water, Mary's broken vase—has He anything of yours? "She hath wrought a good work on Me."

2. Now, there is another lesson that I would gather from our Lord's apologizing for Mary, and that is the measure and the manner of Christian service. "She hath done what she could"; that is generally read as if it were an excuse. So it is, or at least it is a vindication of the manner and the direction of Mary's expression of love and devotion. But whilst it is an apologia for the form, it is a high demand in regard to the measure.

"She hath done what she could." Christ would not have said that if she had taken a niggardly spoonful out of the box of ointment, and dribbled that, in slow and half-grudging drops, on His head and feet. It was because it *all* went that it was to Him thus admirable. I think it is John Foster who says, "Power to its last particle is duty." The question is not how much have I done, or given, but could I have done or given more? We Protestants have indulgences of our own; the guinea or the hundred guineas that we give in a certain direction, we some of us seem to think, buy for us the right to do as we will with all the rest. But "she hath done what she could." It all went. And that is the law for us Christian people, because the Christian life is to be ruled by the great law of self-sacrifice, as the only adequate expression of our recognition of, and our being affected by, the great Sacrifice that gave Himself for us.

> Give all thou canst! High Heaven rejects the lore
> Of nicely calculated less or more.

But whilst thus there is here a definite demand for the entire surrender of ourselves and our activities to Jesus Christ, there is also the wonderful vindication of the idiosyncrasy of the worker, and the special manner of her gift. It was not Mary's *métier* to serve at the table, nor to do any practical thing. She did not know what there was for her to do; but something she *must* do. So she caught up her alabaster box, and without questioning herself about the act, let her heart have its way, and poured it out on Christ. It was the only thing she could do, and she did it. It was a very useless thing. It was an entirely unnecessary expenditure of the perfume. There might have been a great many practical purposes found for it, but it was her way.

Christ says to each of us, Be yourselves, take circumstances, capacities, opportunities, individual character, as laying down the lines along which you have to travel. Do not imitate other people. Do not envy other people; be yourselves, and let your love take its natural expression, whatever folk round you may snarl and sneer and carp and criticize. ''She hath done what she could,'' and so He accepts the gift.

Engineers tell us that the steam engine is a very wasteful machine, because so little of the energy is brought into actual operation. I am afraid that there are a great many of us Christian people like that, getting so much capacity, and turning out so little work. And there are a great many more of us who simply pick up the kind of work that is popular round us, and never consult our own bent, nor follow this humbly and bravely, wherever it will take us. ''She hath done what she could.''

3. And now the last thought that I would gather from these words is as to the significance and the perpetuity of the work which Christ accepts. ''She hath come beforehand to anoint My body to the burying.'' I do not suppose that such a thought was in Mary's mind when she snatched up her box of ointment, and poured it out on Christ's head. But it was a meaning that He, in His tender pity and wise love and foresight, put into it, pathetically indicating, too, how the near Cross was filling His thought, even whilst He sat at the humble rustic feast in Bethany village.

He puts meaning into the service of love which He accepts. Yes, He always does. For all the little bits of service that we can bring get worked up into the great whole, the issues of which lie far beyond anything that we conceive. ''Thou sowest not that body that shall be, but bare grain . . . and God giveth it a body as it hath pleased Him.'' We cast the seed into the furrows. Who can tell what the harvest is going to be? We know nothing about the great issues that may suddenly, or gradually, burst from, or be evolved out of, the small deeds that we do. So, then, let us take care of the end, so to speak, which is under our control, and that is the motive. And Jesus Christ will take care of the other end that is beyond our control, and that is the issue. He will bring forth what seemeth to Him good, and we shall be as much astonished ''when we get yonder'' at what has come out of what we did here, as poor Mary, standing there behind Him, was when He translated her act into so much higher a meaning than she had seen in it.

"Lord! when saw we Thee hungry and fed Thee?" We do not know what we are doing. We are like the Hindu weavers that are said to weave their finest webs in dark rooms; and when the shutters come down, and not till then, shall we find out the meanings of our service of love.

Christ makes the work perpetual as well as significant by declaring that "in the whole world this shall be preached for a memorial of her." Have not "the poor" got far more good out of Mary's box of ointment than the three hundred pence that a few of them lost by it? Has it not been an inspiration to the Church ever since? "The house was filled with the odor of the ointment." The fragrance was soon dissipated in the scentless air, but the deed smells sweet and blossoms for ever. It is perpetual in its record, perpetual in God's remembrance, perpetual in its results to the doer, and in its results in the world, though these may be indistinguishable, just as the brook is lost in the river and the river in the sea.

But did you ever notice that the Evangelist who records the promise of perpetual remembrance of the act does not tell us who did it, and that the Evangelists who tell us who did it do not record the promise of perpetual remembrance? Never mind whether your deed is labeled with your address or not. God knows to whom it belongs, and that is enough. As Paul says in one of his letters, "other my fellow laborers also, whose names are in the Book of Life." Apparently he had forgotten the names, or perhaps did not think it needful to occupy space in his letter with detailing them, and so makes that graceful, half-apologetic suggestion that they are inscribed on a more august page. The work and the worker are associated in that Book, and that is enough.

Brethren, the question of Judas is far more fitting when asked of other people than of Christians. "To what purpose is this waste?" may well be said to those of you who are taking mind, and heart, and will, capacity, and energy, and all life, and using it for lower purposes than the service of God, and the manifestation of loving obedience to Jesus Christ. "Why do ye spend money for that which is not bread?" Is it not waste to buy disappointments at the price of a soul and of a life? Why do ye spend that money thus? "Whose image and superscription hath it?" Whose name is stamped upon our spirits? To whom should they be rendered? Better for us to ask ourselves the question today about all the godless parts of our lives, "To what purpose is this waste?" than to have to ask it yonder! Everything but giving our whole selves to Jesus Christ is waste. It is not waste to lay ourselves and our possessions at His feet. "He that loveth his life shall lose it, and he that loseth his life for My sake, the same shall find it."

A Secret Rendezvous

And the first day of unleavened bread, when they killed the passover, His disciples said unto Him, Where wilt Thou that we go and prepare that Thou mayest eat the passover? 13. And He sendeth forth two of His disciples, and saith unto them, Go ye into the city, and there shall meet you a man bearing a pitcher of water: follow him. 14. And wheresoever he shall go in, say ye to the goodman of the house, The Master saith, Where is the guestchamber, where I shall eat the passover with My disciples? 15. And he will show you a large upper room furnished and prepared: there make ready for us. 16. And His disciples went forth, and came into the city, and found as He had said unto them; and they made ready the passover. MARK 14:12–16.

This is one of the obscurer and less noticed incidents, but perhaps it contains more valuable teaching than appears at first sight.

The first question is—Miracle or Plan? Does the incident mean supernatural knowledge or a preconcerted token, like the provision of the ass at the entry into Jerusalem? I think that there is nothing decisive either way in the narrative. Perhaps the balance of probability lies in favor of the latter theory. A difficulty in its way is that no communication seems to pass between the two disciples and the man by which he could know them to be the persons whom he was to precede to the house. There are advantages in either theory which the other loses; but, on the whole, I incline to believe in a preconcerted signal. If we lose the supernatural, we gain a suggestion of prudence and human adaptation of means to ends which makes the story even more startlingly real to us.

But whichever theory we adopt, the main points and lessons of the narrative remain the same.

1. The remarkable thing in the story is the picture it gives us of Christ as elaborately adopting precautions to conceal the place. They are at Bethany. The disciples ask where the passover is to be eaten. The easy answer would have been to tell the name of the man and his house. That is not given. The deliberate round-aboutness of the answer remains the same whether miracle or plan. The two go away, and the others know nothing of the place. Probably the messengers did not come back, but in the evening Jesus and the ten go straight to the house which only He knew.

All this secrecy is in strong contrast with His usual frank and open appearances.

What is the reason? To baffle the traitor by preventing him from acquiring previous knowledge of the place. He was watching for some quiet hour in Jerusalem to take Jesus. So Christ does not eat the passover at the house of any well-known disciple who had a house in Jerusalem, but goes to some man unknown to the Apostolic circle, and takes steps to prevent the place being known beforehand.

All this looks like the ordinary precautions which a man who knew of the plots against him would take, and might mean simply a wish to save his life. But is that the whole explanation? *Why* did He wish to baffle the traitor?

(*a*) Because of His desire to eat the passover with the disciples. His loving sympathy.

(*b*) Because of His desire to found the new rite of His kingdom.

(*c*) Because of His desire to bring His death into immediate connection with the Paschal sacrifice. There was no reason of a selfish kind, no shrinking from death itself.

The fact that such precautions only meet us here, and that they stand in strongest contrast with the rest of His conduct, emphasizes the purely voluntary nature of His death: how He *chose* to be betrayed, taken, and to die. They suggest the same thought as do the staggering back of His would-be captors in Gethsemane, at His majestic word, "I am He. . . . Let these go their way." The narrative sets Him forth as the Lord of all circumstances, as free, and arranging all events.

Judas, the priests, Pilate, the soldiers, were swept by a power which they did not know to deeds which they did not understand. The Lord of all gives Himself up in royal freedom to the death to which nothing dragged Him but His own love.

Such seem to be the lessons of this narrative in so far as it bears on our Lord's own thoughts and feelings.

2. We note also the authoritative claim which He makes. One reading is "my guest chamber," and that makes His claim even more emphatic; but apart from that, the language is strong in its expression of a right to this unknown man's "upper room." Mark the singular blending here, as in all His earthly life, of poverty and dignity—the lowliness of being obliged to a man for a room; the royal style, "The Master saith."

So even now there is the blending of the wonderful fact that He puts Himself in the position of needing anything from us, with the absolute authority which He claims over us and ours.

3. The answer and blessedness of the unknown disciple. (*a*) Jesus knows disciples whom the other disciples know not.

This man was one of the "secret" disciples. There is no excuse for shrinking from confession of His name; but it is blessed to believe that His eye sees many a "hidden one." He recognizes their faith, and gives them work to do. Add the striking thought that though this man's name is unrecorded by the Evangelist, it is known to Christ, was written in His heart, and, to use the prophetic image, "was graven on the palms of His hands."

(*b*) The true blessedness is to be ready for whatever calls He may make on us. These may sometimes be sudden and unlooked for. But the preparation for obeying the most sudden or exacting summons of His is to have our hearts in fellowship with Him.

(*c*) The blessedness of His coming into our hearts, and accepting our service.

How honored that man felt then! how much more so as years went on! how most of all now!

Our greatest blessedness that He does come into the narrow room of our hearts: "If any man open the door, I will sup with him."

The New Passover

And the first day of unleavened bread, when they killed the Passover, His disciples said unto Him, Where wilt Thou that we go and prepare that Thou mayest eat the Passover? 13. And He sendeth forth two of His disciples, and saith unto them, Go ye into the city, and there shall meet you a man bearing a pitcher of water: follow him. 14. And wheresoever he shall go in, say ye to the goodman of the house, The Master saith, Where is the guestchamber, where I shall eat the Passover with My disciples? 15. And he will show you a large upper room furnished and prepared: there make ready for us. 16. And His disciples went forth, and came into the city, and found as He had said unto them: and they made ready the Passover. 17. And in the evening He cometh with the twelve. 18. And as they sat and did eat, Jesus said, Verily I say unto you, One of you which eateth with Me shall betray Me. 19. And they began to be sorrowful, and to say unto Him one by one, Is it I? and another said, Is it I? 20. And He answered and said unto them, It is one of the twelve, that dippeth with Me in the dish. 21. The Son of Man indeed goeth, as it is written of Him: but woe to that man by whom the Son of Man is betrayed! good were it for that man if he had never been born. 22. And as they did eat, Jesus took bread, and blessed, and brake it, and gave to them, and said, Take, eat: this is My body. 23. And He took the cup, and when He had given thanks, He gave it to them: and they all drank of it. 24. And He said unto them, This is My blood of the new tes-

tament, which is shed for many. 25. *Verily I say unto you, I will drink no more of the fruit of the vine, until that day that I drink it new in the kingdom of God.* 26. *And when they had sung an hymn, they went out into the mount of Olives.* MARK 14:12–26.

This passage falls into three sections—the secret preparation for the Passover (verses 12–17), the sad announcement of the betrayer (verses 18–21), and the institution of the Lord's Supper (verses 22–26). It may be interesting to notice that in the two former of these, Mark's account approximates to Luke's, while in the third he is nearer Matthew's. A comparison of the three accounts, noting the slight, but often significant, variations, should be made. Nothing in the Gospels is trivial. "The dust of that land is gold."

1. The secret preparation for the Passover. The three Evangelists all give the disciples' question, but only Luke tells us that it was in answer to our Lord's command to Peter and John to go and prepare the Passover. They very naturally said "Where?" as they were all strangers in Jerusalem. Matthew may not have known of our Lord's initiative; but if Mark were, as he is, with apparent correctness, said to have been, Peter's mouthpiece in his Gospel, the reticence as to the prominence of that Apostle is natural, and explains the omission of all but the bare fact of the dispatch of the two. The curiously roundabout way in which they are directed to the "upper room" is only explicable on the supposition that it was intended to keep them in the dark till the last moment, so that no hint might leak from them to Judas. Whether the token of the man with the waterpot was a preconcerted signal or an instance of our Lord's supernatural knowledge and sovereign sway, his employment as a silent and probably unconscious guide testifies to Christ's wish for that last hour to be undisturbed. A man carrying a waterpot, which was woman's special task, would be a conspicuous figure even in the festival crowds. The message to the householder implies that he recognized "the Master" as his Master, and was ready to give up at His requisition even the chamber which he had prepared for his own family celebration of the feast.

Thus instructed, the two trusted Apostles left Bethany, early in the day, without a clue of their destination reaching Judas's hungry watchfulness. Evidently they did not return, and in the evening Jesus led the others straight to the place. Mark says that He came "with the twelve"; but he does not mean thereby to specify the number, but to define the class, of His attendants.

Each figure in this preparatory scene yields important lessons. Our

Lord's earnest desire to secure that still hour before pushing out into the storm speaks pathetically of His felt need of companionship and strengthening, as well as of His self-forgetting purpose to help His handful of bewildered followers and His human longing to live in faithful memories. His careful arrangements bring vividly into sight the limitations of His manhood, in that He, "by whom all things consist," had to contrive and plan in order to baffle for a moment His pursuers. And, side by side with the lowliness, as ever, is the majesty; for while He stoops to arrange, He sees with superhuman certitude what will happen, moves unconscious feet with secret and sovereign sway, and in royal tones claims possession of His servant's possessions.

The two messengers, sent out with instructions which would only guide them halfway to their destination, and obliged, if they were to move at all, to trust absolutely to His knowledge, present specimens of the obedience still required. He sends us out still on a road full of sharp turnings round which we cannot see. We get light enough for the first stage; and when it is traversed, the second will be plainer.

The man with the waterpot reminds us how little we may be aware of the Hand which guides us, or of our uses in His plans. "I girded thee, though thou hast not known Me,"—how little the poor water-bearer knew who were following, or dreamed that he and his load would be remembered for ever!

The householder responded at once, and gladly, to the authoritative message, which does not ask a favor, but demands a right. Probably he had intended to celebrate the Passover with his own family, in the large chamber on the roof, with the cool evening air about it, and the moonlight sleeping around. But he gladly gives it up. Are we as ready to surrender our cherished possessions for His use?

2. The sad announcement of the traitor (verses 18–21). As the Revised Version indicates more clearly than the Authorized, the purport of the announcement was not merely that the betrayer was an Apostle, but that he was to be known by his dipping his hand into the common dish at the same moment as our Lord. The prophetic psalm would have been abundantly fulfilled though Judas's fingers never touched Christ's; but the minute accomplishment should teach us that Jewish prophecy was the voice of divine foreknowledge, and embraced small details as well as large tendencies. Many hands dipped with Christ's, and so the sign was not unmistakably indicative, and hence was privately supplemented, as John tells us, by the giving of "the sop." The uncertainty as to the indication given by the token is reflected by the reiterated questions of the Apostles, which, in the Greek, are cast in a form that anticipates a negative answer: ''Surely not I?'' Mark omits the audacious hypocrisy of Judas's question in the same form, and Christ's curt, sad answer which Matthew gives. His brief and vivid sketch is meant to fix attention on the unanimous shuddering horror of these faithful hearts at the thought that they could be thus guilty—a horror which was not the child of presumptuous self-confidence, but of hearty, honest love. They thought it impossible, as they felt the throbbing of their own hearts—and yet—and yet—might it not be? As they probed their hearts deeper, they became dimly aware of dark gulfs of possible unfaithfulness half visible there, and so betook themselves to their Master, and strengthened their loyalty by the question, which breathed at once detestation of the treason and humble distrust of themselves. It is well to feel and speak the strong recoil from sin of a heart loyal to Jesus. It is better to recognize the sleeping snakes, the possibilities of evil in ourselves, and to take to Christ our ignorance and self-distrust. It is wiser to cry ''Is it I?'' than to boast, ''Although all shall be offended, yet will not I.'' ''Hold Thou me up, and I shall be safe.''

Our Lord answers the questions by a still more emphatic repetition of the distinctive mark, and then, in verse 21, speaks deep words of mingled pathos, dignity, and submission. The voluntariness of His death, and its uniqueness as His own act of return to His eternal home, are contained in that majestic ''goeth,'' which asserts the impotence of the betrayer and his employers, without the Lord's own consent. On the other hand, the necessity to which He willingly bowed is set forth in that ''as it is written of Him.'' And what sadness and lofty consciousness of His own sacred personality and judicial authority are blended in the awful sentence on the traitor! What was He that treachery to Him should be a crime so transcendent? What right had He thus calmly to pronounce condemnation? Did He see into the future? Is it the voice of a Divine Judge, or of a man judging in his own cause, which speaks this passionless sentence? Surely none of His sayings are more fully charged with His claims to pre-existence, divinity, and judicial authority, than this which He spoke at the very moment when the traitor's plot was on the verge of success.

3. The institution of the Lord's Supper (verses 22–26). Mark's account is the briefest of the three, and his version of Christ's words the most compressed. It omits the affecting ''Do this for remembering Me,'' which is presupposed by the very act of instituting the ordinance, since it is nothing if not memorial; and it makes prominent two things—the significance of the elements, and the command to partake of them. To these must be added Christ's attitude in ''blessing'' the bread and cup, and His distribution of them among the disciples. The Passover was to Israel the commemoration of their redemption from captivity and their birth as a nation. Jesus puts aside this divinely appointed and venerable festival to set in its stead the remembrance of Himself. That night, "to be much remembered of the children of Israel," is to be forgotten, and come no more into the number of the months; and its empty place is to be filled by the memory of the hours then passing. Surely His act was either arrogance or the calm consciousness of the unique significance and power of His death. Think of any mere teacher or prophet doing the like! The world would meet the preposterous claim implied with deserved and inextinguishable laughter. Why does it not do so with Christ's act?

Christ's view of His death is written unmistakably on the Lord's Supper. It is not merely that He wishes *it* rather than His life, His miracles, or words, to be kept in thankful remembrance, but that He desires one aspect of it to be held high and clear above all others. He is the true "Passover Lamb," whose shed and sprinkled blood establishes new bonds of amity and new relations, with tender and wonderful reciprocal obligations, between God and the "many" who truly partake of that sacrifice. The key words of Judaism—"sacrifice," "covenant," "sprinkling with blood"—are taken over into Christianity, and the ideas they represent are set in its center, to be cherished as its life. The Lord's Supper is the conclusive answer to the allegation that Christ did not teach the sacrificial character and atoning power of His death. What, then, did He teach when He said, "This is My blood of the covenant, which is shed for many"?

The Passover was a family festival, and that characteristic passes over to the Lord's Supper. Christ is not only the food on which we feed, but the Head of the family and distributor of the banquet. He is the feast and the Governor of the feast, and all who sit at that table are "brethren." One life is in them all, and they are one as partakers of One.

The Lord's Supper is a visible symbol of the Christian life, which should not only be all lived in remembrance of Him, but consists in partaking by faith of His life, and incorporating it in ours, until we come to the measure of perfect men, which, in one aspect, we reach when we can say, "I live; yet not I, but Christ liveth in me."

There is a prophetic element, as well as a commemorative and symbolic, in the Lord's Supper, which is prominent in Christ's closing words. He does not partake of the symbols which He gives; but there comes a time, in that perfected form of the kingdom, when perfect love shall make all the citizens perfectly conformed to the perfect will of God. Then, whatsoever associations of joy, of invigoration, of festal fellowship, clustered round the winecup here, shall be heightened, purified, and perpetuated in the calm raptures of the heavenly feast, in which He will be Partaker, as well as Giver and Food. "Thou shalt make them drink of the river of Thy pleasures." The King's lips will touch the golden cup filled with unfoaming wine, ere He commends it to His guests. And from that feast they will "go no more out," neither shall the triumphant music of its great "hymn" be followed by any Olivet or Gethsemane, or any denial, or any Calvary; but there shall be "no more sorrow, nor sin, nor death"; for "the former things are passed away," and He has made "all things new."

"Is It I?"

Is it I? MARK 14:19.

The scene shows that Judas had not as yet drawn any suspicion on himself.

Here the Apostles seem to be higher than their ordinary stature; for they do not take to questioning one another, or even to protest, "No!" but to questioning Christ.

1. The solemn prophecy. It seems strange at first sight that our Lord should have introduced such thoughts then, disturbing the sweet repose of that hallowed hour. But the terrible fact of the betrayal was naturally suggested by the emblems of His death, and still more by the very confiding familiarity of that hour. His household were gathered around Him, and the more close and confidential the intercourse, the bitterer that thought to Him, that one of the little band was soon to play the traitor. It is the cry of His wounded love, the wail of His unrequited affection, and, so regarded, is infinitely touching. It is an instance of that sad insight into man's heart which in His divinity He possessed. What a fountain of sorrow for His manhood was that knowledge! How it increases the pathos of His tenderness! Not only did He read hearts as they thought and felt in the present, but He read their future with more than a prophet's insight. He saw how many buds of promise would shrivel, how many would "go away and walk no more with Him."

That solemn prophecy may well be pondered by all Christian assemblies, and specially when gathered for the observance of the Lord's Supper. Perhaps never since that first institution has a community met to celebrate it without Him who "walks amid the candlesticks," with eyes as a flame of fire marking a Judas among the disciples. There is, I think, no doubt that Judas partook of the Lord's Supper. But be that as it may, he was among the number, and our Lord knew him to be "the traitor."

In its essence Judas's sin can be repeated still, and the thought of that possibility may well mingle with the grateful and adoring contemplations suitable to the act of partaking of the Lord's Supper. In the hour of holiest Christian emotion the thought that I may betray the Lord who has died for me will be especially hateful, and to remember the possibility then will do much to prevent its ever becoming a reality.

2. The self-distrustful question, "Is it I?" It suggests that the possibilities of the darkest sin are in each of us, and especially, that the sin of treason towards Christ is in each of us.

Think generally of the awful possibilities of sin in every soul.

All sin has one root, so it is capable of passing from one form to another as light, heat, and motion do, or like certain diseases that are protean in their forms. One sin is apt to draw others after it. "None shall want her mate." Wild beasts of "the desert" meet with wild beasts of "the islands." Sins are gregarious, as it were; they "hunt in couples." "Then goeth he, and taketh with him seven other spirits more wicked than himself."

The roots of all sin are in each. Men may think that they are protected from certain forms of sin by temperament, but identity of nature is deeper than varieties of temperament. The greatest sins are committed by yielding to very common motives. Love of money is not a rare feeling, but it led Judas to betray Jesus. Anger is thought to be scarcely a sin at all, but it often moves an arm to murder.

Temptations to each sin are round us all. We walk in a tainted atmosphere.

There is progress in evil. No man reaches the extreme of depravity at a bound. Judas's treachery was of slow growth.

So still there is the constant operation and pressure of forces and tendencies drawing us away from Jesus Christ. We, every one of us, know that, if we allowed our nature to have its way, we should leave Him and "make shipwreck of faith and of a good conscience." The forms in which we might do it might vary, but do it we should. We are like a man desperately clutching some rocky projection on the face of a precipice, who knows that if once he lets go, he will be dashed to pieces. "There goes John Bradford, but for the grace of God!" But for this same restraining grace, to what depths might we not sink? So, in all Christian hearts there should be profound consciousness of their own weakness. The man "who fears no fall" is sure to have one. It is perilous to march through an enemy's country in loose order, without scouts and rearguard. Rigorous control is ever necessary. Brotherly judgment, too, of others should result from our consciousness of weakness. Examples of others falling are not to make us say cynically, "We are all alike," but to set us to think humbly of ourselves, and to supplicate divine keeping, "Lord, save *me*, or I perish!"

3. The safety of the self-distrustful. When the consciousness of possible falling is brought home to us, we shall carry, if we are wise, all our doubts as to ourselves to Jesus. There is safety in asking Him, "Is it I?" To bare our inmost selves before Him, and not to shrink, even if that piercing gaze lights on hidden meannesses and incipient treachery, may be painful, but is healing. He will keep us from yielding to the temptation of which we are aware, and which we tell frankly to Him. The lowly sense of our own liability to fall, if it drives us closer to Him, will make it certain that we shall not fall.

While the other disciples asked, "Is it I?" John asked "Who is it?" The disciple who leaned on Christ's bosom was bathed in such a consciousness of Christ's love that treason against it was impossible. He, alone of the Evangelists, records his question, and he tells us that he put it, "leaning back as he was, on Jesus' breast." For the purpose of whispering his interrogation, he changed his attitude for a moment so as to press still closer to Jesus. How could one who was thus nestling nearer to that heart be the betrayer? The consciousness of Christ's love, accompanied with the effort to draw closer to Him, is our surest defense against every temptation to faithlessness or betrayal of Him.

Any other fancied ground of security is deceptive, and will sooner or later crumble beneath our deceived feet. On this very occasion, Peter built a towering fabric of profession of unalterable fidelity on such shifting ground, and saw it collapse into ruin in a few hours. Let us profit by the lesson!

That wholesome consciousness of our weakness need not shade with sadness the hours of communion, but it may well help us to turn them to their highest use in making them occasions for lowlier self-distrust and closer cleaving to Him. If we thus use our sense of weakness, the sweet security will enter our souls that belongs to those who have trusted in the great promise: "He shall not fall, for God is able to make him stand." The blessed ones who are kept from falling and "presented faultless before the presence of His glory," will hear with wonder the voice of the Judge ascribing to them deeds of service to Him of which they had not been conscious, and will have to ask once more the old question, but with a new meaning: "Lord, is it I? when saw we Thee an hungered, and fed Thee?"

"Strong Crying and Tears"

And they came to a place which was named Gethsemane: and He saith to His disciples, Sit ye here, while I shall pray.
33. And He taketh with Him Peter and James and John, and began to be sore amazed, and to be very heavy;
34. And saith unto them, My soul is exceeding sorrowful unto death: tarry ye here, and watch.
35. And He went forward a little, and fell on the ground, and prayed that, if it were possible, the hour might pass from Him.
36. And He said, Abba, Father, all things are possible unto Thee; take away this cup from Me: nevertheless not what I will, but what Thou wilt.
37. And He cometh, and findeth them sleeping, and saith unto Peter, Simon, sleepest thou? couldest not thou watch one hour?
38. Watch ye and pray, lest ye enter into temptation. The spirit truly is ready, but the flesh is weak.
39. And again He went away, and prayed, and spake the same words.
40. And when he returned, he found them asleep again, (for their eyes were heavy,) neither wist they what to answer Him.
41. And He cometh the third time, and saith unto them, Sleep on now, and take your rest: it is enough, the hour is come; behold, the Son of man is betrayed into the hands of sinners.
42. Rise up, let us go; lo, he that betrayeth Me is at hand. MARK 14:32–42.

The three who saw Christ's agony in Gethsemane were so little affected that they slept. We have to beware of being so little affected that we speculate and seek to analyze rather than to bow adoringly before that mysterious and heart-subduing sight. Let us remember that the place is "holy ground." It was meant that we should look on the Christ who prayed "with strong crying and tears," else the three sleepers would not have accompanied Him so far; but it was meant that our gaze should be reverent and from a distance, else they would have gone with Him into the shadow of the olives.

"Gethsemane" means "an oil press." It was an enclosed piece of ground, according to Matthew and Mark; a garden, according to John. Jesus, by some means, had access to it, and had "ofttimes resorted thither with His disciples." To this familiar spot, with its many happy associations, Jesus led the disciples, who would simply expect to pass the night there, as many Passover visitors were accustomed to bivouac in the open air.

The triumphant tone of spirit which animated His assuring words to His disciples, "I have overcome the world," changed as they passed through the moonlight down to the valley, and when they reached the garden deep gloom lay upon Him. His agitation is pathetically and most naturally indicated by the conflict of feeling as to companionship. He leaves the other disciples at the entrance, for He would fain be alone in His prayer. Then, a moment after, He bids the three, who had been on the Mount of Transfiguration and with Him at many other special times, accompany Him into the recesses of the garden. But again need of solitude overcomes longing for companionship, and He bids them stay where they were, while He plunges still further into the shadow. How human it is! How well all of us, who have been down into the depths of sorrow, know the drawing of these two opposite longings!

Scripture seldom undertakes to tell Christ's emotions. Still seldomer does He speak of them. But at this tremendous hour the veil is lifted by one corner, and He Himself is fain to relieve His bursting heart by pathetic self-revelation, which is in fact an appeal to the three for sympathy, as well as an evidence of His sharing the common need of lightening the burdened spirit by speech. Mark's description of Christ's feelings lays stress first on their beginning, and then on their nature as being astonishment and anguish. A wave of emotion swept over Him, and was in marked contrast with His previous demeanor.

The three had never seen their calm Master so moved. We feel that such agitation is profoundly unlike the serenity of the rest of His life, and especially remarkable if contrasted with the tone of John's account of His discourse in the upper room; and, if we are wise, we shall gaze on that picture drawn for us by Mark with reverent gratitude, and feel that we look at something more sacred than human trembling at the thought of death.

Our Lord's own infinitely touching words heighten the impression of the Evangelist's "My soul is exceeding sorrowful," or, as the word literally means, ringed round with sorrow." A dark orb of distress encompassed Him, and there was nowhere a break in the gloom which shut Him in. And this is He who, but an hour before, had bequeathed His "joy" to His servants, and had bidden them "be of good cheer," since He had "conquered the world."

Dare we ask what were the elements of that all-enveloping horror of great darkness? Reverently we may. That astonishment and distress no doubt were partly due to the recoil of flesh from death. But if that was their sole cause, Jesus has been surpassed in heroism, not only by many a martyr who drew his strength from Him, but by many a rude soldier and by many a criminal. No! The waters of the baptism with which He was baptized had other sources than that, though it poured a tributary stream into them.

We shall not understand Gethsemane at all, nor will it touch our hearts and wills as it is meant to do, unless, as we look, we say in adoring wonder, "The Lord hath made to meet on Him the iniquity of us all." It was the weight of the world's sin which He took on Him by willing identification of Himself with men, that pressed Him to the ground. Nothing else than the atoning character of Christ's sufferings explains so far as it can be explained, the agony which we are permitted to behold afar off.

How nearly that agony was fatal is taught us by His own word "unto death." A little more, and He would have died. Can we retain reverence for Jesus as a perfect and pattern man, in view of His paroxysm of anguish in Gethsemane, if we refuse to accept that explanation? Truly was the place named "The Olive Press," for in it His whole being was as if in the press, and another turn of the screw would have crushed Him.

Darkness ringed Him round, but there was a rift in it right overhead. Prayer was His refuge, as it must be ours. The soul that can cry, "Abba, Father!" does not walk in unbroken night. His example teaches us what our own sorrows should also teach us—to betake ourselves to prayer when the spirit is desolate. In that wonderful prayer we reverently note three things: there is unbroken consciousness of the Father's love; there is the instinctive recoil of flesh and the sensitive nature from the suffering imposed; and there is the absolute submission of the will, which silences the remonstrance of flesh. Whatever the weight laid on Jesus by His bearing of the sins of the world, it did not take from Him the sense of sonship. But, on the other hand, that sense did not take from Him the consciousness that the world's sin lay upon Him. In like manner, His cry on the Cross mysteriously blended the sense of communion with God and of abandonment by God. Into these depths we see but a little way, and adoration is better than speculation.

Jesus shrank from "this cup," in which so many bitter ingredients besides death were mingled, such as treachery, desertion, mocking, rejection, exposure to "the contradiction of sinners." There was no failure of purpose in that recoil, for the cry for exemption was immediately followed by complete submission to the Father's will. No perturbation in the lower nature ever caused His fixed resolve to waver. The needle always pointed to the pole, however the ship might pitch and roll. A prayer in which "remove this from me" is followed by that yielding "nevertheless" is always heard. Christ's was heard, for calmness came back, and His flesh was stilled and made ready for the sacrifice.

So He could rejoin the three, in whose sympathy and watchfulness He had trusted—and they all were asleep! Surely that was one ingredient of bitterness in His cup. We wonder at their insensibility; and how they must have wondered at it too, when after years taught them what they had lost, and how faithless they had been! Think of men who could have seen and heard that scene, which has drawn the worshipping regard of the world ever since, missing it all because they fell asleep! They had kept awake long enough to see Him fall on the ground and to hear His prayer, but, worn out by a long day of emotion and sorrow, they slept.

Jesus was probably rapt in prayer for a considerable time, perhaps for a literal "hour." He was specially touched by Peter's failure, so sadly contrasted with his confident professions in the upper room; but no word of blame escaped Him. Rather He warned them of swift-coming temptation, which they could only overcome by watchfulness and prayer. It was indeed near, for the soldiers would burst in, before many minutes had passed, polluting the moonlight with their torches and disturbing the quiet night with their shouts. What gracious allowance for their weakness and loving recognition of the disciples' imperfect good lie in His words, which are at once an excuse for their fault and an enforcement of His command to watch and pray! "The flesh is weak," and hinders the willing spirit from doing what it wills. It was an apology for the slumber of the three; it is a merciful statement of the condition under which all discipleship has to be carried on. "He knoweth our frame." Therefore we all need to watch and pray, since only by such means can weak flesh be strengthened and strong flesh weakened, or the spirit preserved in willingness.

The words were not spoken in reference to Himself, but in a measure were true of Him. His second withdrawal for prayer seems to witness that the victory won by the first supplication was not permanent. Again the anguish swept over His spirit in another foaming breaker, and again He sought solitude, and again He found tranquility—and again returned to find the disciples asleep. "They knew not what to answer Him" in extenuation of their renewed dereliction.

Yet a third time the struggle was renewed. And after that, He had no need to return to the seclusion, where He had fought, and now had conclusively conquered by prayer and submission. We too may, by the same means, win partial victories over self, which may be interrupted by uprisings of flesh; but let us persevere. Twice Jesus' calm was broken by recrudescence of horror and shrinking; the third time it came back, to abide through all the trying scenes of the passion, but for that one cry on the Cross, "Why hast Thou forsaken Me?" So it may be with us.

The last words to the three have given commentators much trouble. "Sleep on now, and take your rest," is not so much irony as "spoken with a kind of permissive force, and in tones in which merciful reproach was blended with calm resignation." So far as He was concerned, there was no reason for their waking. But they had lost an opportunity, never to return, of helping Him in His hour of deepest agony. He needed them no more. And do not we in like manner often lose the brightest opportunities of service by untimely slumber of soul, and is not "the irrevocable past" saying to many of us, "Sleep on now, since you can no more do what you have let slip from your drowsy hands"?

"It is enough" is obscure, but probably refers to the disciples' sleep, and prepares for the transition to the next words, which summon them to arise, not to help Him by watching, but to meet the traitor. They had slept long enough, He sadly says. That which will effectually end their sleepiness is at hand. How completely our Lord had regained His calm superiority to the horror which had shaken Him is witnessed by that majestic "Let us be going." He will go out to meet the traitor, and, after one flash of power, which smote the soldiers to the ground, will yield Himself to the hands of sinners.

The Man who lay prone in anguish beneath the olive trees comes forth in serene tranquility, and gives Himself up to the death for us all. His agony was endured for us, and needs for its explanation the fact that it was so. His victory through prayer was for us, that we too might conquer by the same weapons. His voluntary surrender was for us, that "by His stripes we might be healed." Surely we shall not sleep, as did these others, but, moved by His sorrows and animated by His victory, watch and pray that we may share in the virtue of His sufferings and imitate the example of His submission.

The Sleeping Apostle

Simon, sleepest thou? MARK 14:37.

It is a very old Christian tradition that this Gospel is in some sense the Apostle Peter's. There are not many features in the Gospel itself which can be relied on as confirming this idea. Perhaps one such may be found in this plaintive remonstrance, which is only preserved for us here. Matthew's Gospel, indeed, tells us that the rebuke was addressed to Peter, but blunts the sharp point of it as directed to him, by throwing it into the plural, as if spoken to all the three slumberers: "What, could ye not watch with Me one hour?" To Matthew, the special direction of the words was unimportant, but Peter could never forget how the Master had come out from the shadow of the olives to him lying there in the moonlight, and stood before him worn with His solitary agony, and in a voice yet tremulous from His awful conflict, had said to *him*, so lately loud in his professions of fidelity, "Sleepest *thou*?"

It was but an hour or two since he had been saying, and meaning, "I will lay down my life for Thy sake," and this was what all that fervor had come to. No wonder if there is almost a tone of surprise discernible in our

Lord's word, as if He who "marveled at the unbelief" of those who were not His followers, marveled still more at the imperfect sympathy of those who were, and marveled most of all at such a sudden ebb of such a flood of devotion. Surprise and sorrow, the pain of a loving heart thrown back upon itself, the sharp pang of feeling how much less one is loved than one loves, the pleading with His forgetful servant, rebuke without anger, all breathe through the question, so pathetic in its simplicity, so powerful to bow in contrition by reason of its very gentleness and self-restraint.

The record of this Evangelist proves how deep it sank into the impulsive, loving heart of the apostle, and yet the denials in the high priest's palace, which followed so soon, show how much less power it had on him on the day when it was spoken, than it gained as he looked back on it through the long vista of years that had passed, when he told the story to Mark.

The first lesson to be gathered from these words is drawn from the name by which our Lord here addresses the apostle: "*Simon*, sleepest thou?"

Now the usage of Mark's Gospel in reference to this apostle's name is remarkably uniform and precise. Both his names occur in Mark's catalogue of the Apostles: "Simon he surnamed Peter." He is never called by both again, but before that point he is always Simon, and after it he is always Peter, except in this verse. The other Evangelists show similar purpose, for the most part, in their interchange of the names. Luke, for instance, always calls him Simon up to the same point as Mark, except once where he uses the form "Simon Peter," and thereafter always Peter, except in Christ's solemn warning, "Simon, Simon, Satan hath desired to have you" and in the report of the tidings that met the disciples on their return from Emmaus, "The Lord hath appeared to Simon." So Matthew calls him Simon in the story of the first miraculous draught of fishes, and in the catalogue of Apostles, and afterwards uniformly Peter, except in Christ's answer to the apostle's great confession, where He names him "Simon Bar Jona," in order, as would appear, to bring into more solemn relief the significance of the immediately following words, "Thou art Peter." In John's Gospel, again, we find the two forms "Simon Peter" and the simple "Peter" used throughout with almost equal frequency, while "Simon" is only employed at the very beginning, and in the heart-piercing triple question at the end, "Simon, son of Jonas, lovest thou Me?"

The conclusion seems a fair one from these details that, on the whole, the name Simon brings into prominence the natural unrenewed humanity, and the name Peter suggests the Apostolic office, the bold confessor, the impulsive, warmhearted lover and follower of the Lord. And it is worth noticing that, with one exception, the instances in which he is called by his former name, after his designation to the apostolate, occur in words addressed to him by our Lord.

He had given the name, and surely His withdrawal of it was meant to be significant, and must have struck with boding, rebuking emphasis on the ear and conscience of the apostle. "Simon, Simon, Satan hath desired to have you": "Remember thy human weakness, and in the sore conflict that is before thee, trust not to thine own power." "Simon, sleepest thou?" "Can I call thee Peter now, when thou hast not cared for My sorrow enough to wake while I wrestled? Is this thy fervid love?" "Simon, son of Jonas, lovest thou Me?" "Thou wast Peter because thou didst confess Me; thou hast fallen back to thine old level by denying Me. It is not enough that in secret I should have restored thee to My love. Here before thy brethren, thou must win back thy forfeited name and place by a confession as open as the denial, and thrice repeated like it. Once thou hast answered, but still thou art 'Simon.' Twice thou hast answered, but not yet can I call thee 'Peter.' Thrice thou hast answered, by each reply effacing a former denial, and now I ask no more. Take back thine office; henceforth thou shalt be called 'Cephas' as before."

And so it was. In the Acts of the Apostles, and in Paul's letters, "Peter" or "Cephas" entirely obliterates "Simon." Only for ease in finding him, the messengers of Cornelius are to ask for him in Joppa by the name by which he would be known outside the Church, and his old companion James begins his speech to the council at Jerusalem by referring with approbation to what "Simeon" had said, as if he liked to use the old name, that brought back memories of the far-off days in Galilee, before they had known the Master.

Very touching, too, is it to notice how the apostle himself, while using the name by which he was best known in the Church, in the introduction to his first Epistle, calls himself "Simon Peter" in his second, as if to the end he felt that the old nature clung to him, and was not yet, "so long as he was in this tabernacle," wholly subdued under the dominion of the better self, which his Master had breathed into him.

So we see that a bit of biography and an illustration of a large truth are wrapped up for us in so small a matter as the apparently fortuitous use of one or other of these names. I do not suppose that in every instance where either of them occur, we can explain their occurrence by a reference to such thoughts. But still there is an unmistakable propriety in several instances in the employment of one rather than the other, and we may fairly suggest the lesson as put here in a picturesque form, which Paul gives us in definite words, "The flesh lusteth against the spirit, and the spirit against the flesh." The better and the worse nature contend in all

Christian souls, or, as our Lord says with such merciful leniency in this very context, ''The spirit is willing, but the flesh is weak.'' However real and deep the change which passes over us when ''Christ is formed in us,'' it is only by degrees that the transformation spreads through our being. The renewing process follows upon the bestowment of the new life, and works from its deep inward center outwards and upwards to the circumference and surface of our being, on condition of our own constant diligence and conflict.

True, ''If any man to be in Christ, he is a new creature''; but also, and precisely because he is, therefore the daily and hourly exhortation is, ''Put on the new man.'' The leaven is buried in the dough, and must be well kneaded up with it if the whole is to be leavened. Peter is still Simon, and sometimes seems to be so completely Simon that he has ceased to be Peter. He continues Simon Peter to his own consciousness to the very end, however his brethren call him. The struggle between the two elements in his nature makes the undying interest of his story, and brings him nearer to us than any of the other disciples are. We, too, have to wage the conflict between the old nature and the new; for us, too, the worse part seems too often to be the stronger, if not the only part. The Master has often to speak to us, as if His merciful all-seeing eye could discern in us nothing of our better selves which are in truth Himself and has to question our love. We, too, have often to feel how little those who think best of us know what we are. But let us take heart and remember that from every fall it is possible to rise by penitence and secret converse with Him, and that if only we remember to the end our lingering weakness, and ''giving all diligence,'' cleave to Him, ''an entrance shall be ministered unto us abundantly into His everlasting kingdom.''

We may briefly notice, too, some other lessons from this slumbering apostle.

Let us learn, for instance, to distrust our own resolutions. An hour or two at the most had passed since the eager protestation, ''Though all should deny Thee, yet will not I. I will lay down my life for Thy sake.'' It had been most honestly said, at the dictate of a very loving heart, which in its enthusiasm was overestimating its own power of resistance, and taking no due account of obstacles. The very utterance of the rash vow made him weaker, for some of his force was expended in making it. The uncalculating, impulsive nature of the man makes him a favorite with all readers, and we sympathize with him, as a true brother, when we hear him blurting out his big words, followed so soon by such a contradiction in deeds. He is the same man all through his story, always ready to push himself into dangers, always full of rash confidence, which passes at once into abject fear when the dangers which he had not thought about appear.

His sleep in the garden following close on his bold words in the upper chamber, is just like his eager wish to come to Christ on the water, followed by his terror. He desires to be singled out from the others; he desires to be beside his Master, and then as soon as he feels a dash of spray on his cheek, and the heaving at that uneasy floor beneath him, all his confidence collapses and he shrieks to Christ to save him. It is just like his thrusting himself into the high priest's palace—no safe place, and bad company for him by the coal fire—and then his courage oozing out at his fingers' ends as soon as a maidservant's sharp tongue questioned him. It is just like his hearty welcome of the heathen converts at Antioch, and his ready breaking through Jewish restrictions, and then his shrinking back into his old shell again, as soon as "certain came down from Jerusalem."

And in it all, he is one of ourselves. We have to learn to distrust all our own resolutions, and to be chary of our vows. "Better is it that thou shouldest not vow, than that thou shouldest vow and not pay." So, aware of our own weakness, and the flutterings of our own hearts, let us not mortgage the future, nor lightly say "I will"—but rather let us turn our vows into prayers,

> Nor confidently say,
> "I never will deny Thee, Lord!"
> But, "Grant I never may."

Let us note, too, the slight value of even genuine emotion. The very exhaustion following on the strained emotions which these disciples had been experiencing had sent them to sleep. Luke, in his physician-like way, tells us this, when he says that they "slept for sorrow." We all know how some great emotion which we might have expected would have held our eyes waking, lulls to slumber. Men sleep soundly on the night before their execution. A widow leaves her husband's deathbed as soon as he has passed away, and sleeps a dreamless sleep for hours. The strong current of emotion sweeps through us, and leaves us dry. Sheer exhaustion and collapse follow its intenser forms. And even in its milder, nothing takes so much out of a man as emotion. Reaction always follows, and people are in some degree unfitted for sober work by it. Peter, for example, was all the less ready for keeping awake, and for bold confession, because of the vehement emotions which had agitated him in the upper chamber. We have, therefore, to be chary, in our religious life, of feeding the flames of mere feeling. An unemotional Christianity is a very poor thing, and most probably a spurious and unreal thing. But a merely emotional Christianity is closely related to practical unholiness, and leads by a very short straight road to windy wordy insincerity and conscious hypocrisy. Emotion which is firmly based upon an intelligent grasp of God's truth, and which is at once translated into action, is good. But unless these two conditions be rigidly observed, it darkens the understanding and enfeebles the soul.

Lastly, notice how much easier it is to purpose and to do great things than small ones.

I have little doubt that if the Roman soldiers had called on Peter to have made good his boast, and to give up his life to rescue his Master, he would have been ready to do it. We know that he was ready to fight for Him, and in fact did draw a sword and offer resistance. He could die for Him, but he could not keep awake for Him. The great thing he could have done, the little thing he could not do.

Brethren, it is far easier once in a way, by a dead lift, to screw ourselves up to some great crisis which seems worthy of a supreme effort of enthusiasm and sacrifice, than it is to keep on persistently doing the small monotonies of daily duty. Many a soldier will bravely rush to the assault in a storming party, who would tremble in the trenches. Many a martyr has gone unblenching to the stake for Christ, who had found it far harder to serve Him in common duties. It is easier to die for Him than to watch with Him. So let us listen to His gentle voice, as He speaks to us, not as of old in the pauses of His agony, and His locks wet with the dews of the night, but bending from His throne, and crowned with many crowns: "Sleepest thou? Watch and pray, lest ye enter into temptation."

The Captive Christ and the Circle Round Him

And immediately, while He yet spake, cometh Judas, one of the twelve, and with him a great multitude with swords and staves, from the chief priests and the scribes and the elders. 44. And he that betrayed Him had given them a token, saying, Whomsoever I shall kiss, that same is He; take Him, and lead Him away safely. 45. And as soon as he was come, he goeth straightway to Him, and saith, Master, Master; and kissed Him. 46. And they laid their hands on Him, and took Him. 47. And one of them that stood by drew a sword, and smote a servant of the high priest, and cut off his ear. 48. And Jesus answered and said unto them, Are ye come out, as against a thief, with swords and with staves to take Me? 49. I was daily with you in the temple teaching, and ye took Me not: but the scriptures must be fulfilled. 50. And they all forsook Him, and fled. 51. And there followed Him a certain young man, having a linen cloth cast about his naked body; and the young man laid hold on Him: 52. And he left the linen cloth, and fled from them naked.

53. And they led Jesus away to the high priest: and with him were assembled all the chief priests and the elders and the scribes. 54. And Peter followed Him afar off, even into the palace of the high priest: and to eat with the servants, and warmed himself at the fire. MARK 14:43–54.

A comparison of the three first Gospels in this section shows a degree of similarity, often verbal, which is best accounted for by supposing that a common (oral?) "Gospel," which had become traditionally fixed by frequent and long repetition, underlies them all. Mark's account is briefest, and grasps with sure instinct the essential points; but, even in his brevity, he pauses to tell of the young man who so nearly shared the Lord's apprehension. The canvas is narrow and crowded; but we may see unity in the picture, if we regard as the central fact the sacrilegious seizure of Jesus, and the other incidents and persons as grouped round it and Him, and reflecting various moods of men's feelings towards Him.

1. The avowed and hypocritical enemies of incarnate love. Again we have Mark's favorite, "straightway," so frequent in the beginning of the Gospel, and occurring twice here, vividly painting both the sudden inburst of the crowd which interrupted Christ's words and broke the holy silence of the garden, and Judas's swift kiss. He is named—the only name but our Lord's in the section; and the depth of his sin is emphasized by adding "one of the twelve." He is not named in the next verse, but gibbeted for immortal infamy by the designation, "he that betrayed Him." There is no dilating on his crime, nor any bespattering him with epithets. The passionless narrative tells of the criminal and his crime with unsparing, unmoved tones, which have caught some echo beforehand of the Judge's voice. To name the sinner, and to state without cloak or periphrasis what his deed really was, is condemnation enough. Which of us could stand it?

Judas was foremost of the crowd. What did he feel as he passed swiftly into the shadow of the olives, and caught the first sight of Jesus? That the black depths of his spirit were agitated is plain from two things—the quick kiss, and the nauseous repetition of it. Mark says, "Straightway . . . he kissed Him much." Probably the swiftness and vehemence, so graphically expressed by these two touches, were due, not only to fear lest Christ should escape, and to hypocrisy overacting its part, but to a struggle with conscience and ancient affection, and a fierce determination to do the thing and have it over. Judas is not the only man who has tried to drown conscience by hurrying into and reiterating the sin from which conscience tries to keep him. The very extravagances of evil betray the divided and stormy spirit of the doer. In the darkness and confusion, the kiss was a surer token than a word or a pointing finger would have been; and simple convenience appears to have led to its selection. But what a long course of hypocrisy must have preceded, and how complete the alienation of heart must have become, before such a choice was possible! That traitor's kiss has become a symbol for all treachery cloaked in the garb of affection. Its lessons and warnings are obvious, but this other may be added—that such audacity and nauseousness of hypocrisy is not reached at a leap, but presupposes long underground tunnels of insincere discipleship, through which a man has burrowed, unseen by others, and perhaps unsuspected by himself. Much hypocrisy of the unconscious sort precedes the deliberate and conscious.

How much less criminal and disgusting was the rude crowd at Judas's heels! Most of them were mere passive tools. The Evangelist points beyond them to the greater criminals by his careful enumeration of all classes of the Jewish authorities, thus laying the responsibility directly on their shoulders, and indirectly on the nation whom they represented. The semitumultuous character of the crowd is shown by calling them "a multitude," and by the medley of weapons which they carried. Half-ignorant hatred, which had had ample opportunities of becoming knowledge and love, offended formalism, blind obedience to ecclesiastical superiors, the dislike of goodness—these impelled the rabble who burst into the garden of Gethsemane.

2. Incarnate love, bound and patient. We may bring together verses 46, 48, and 49, the first of which tells in simplest, briefest words the sacrilegious violence done to Jesus, while the others record His calm remonstrance. "They laid hands on Him." That was the first stage in outrage—the quick stretching of many hands to secure the unresisting prisoner. They "took Him," or, as perhaps we might better render, "They held Him fast," as would have been done with any prisoner. Surely, the quietest way of telling that stupendous fact is the best! It is easy to exclaim, and, after the fashion of some popular writers of lives of Christ, to paint fancy pictures. It is better to be sparing of words, like Mark, and silently to meditate on the patient longsuffering of the love which submitted to these indignities, and on the blindness which had no welcome but this for "God manifest in the flesh." Both are in full operation today, and the germs of the latter are in us all.

Mark confines himself to that one of Christ's sayings which sets in the clearest light His innocence and meek submissiveness. With all its calmness and patience, it is majestic and authoritative, and sounds as if spoken from a height far above the hubbub. Its question is not only an assertion of His innocence, and therefore of his captor's guilt, but also declares the impotence of force as against Him—"Swords and staves to take Me!" All that parade of arms was out of place, for He was no evildoer; needless, for He did not resist; and powerless, unless He chose to let them prevail. He speaks as the stainless, incarnate Son of God. He speaks also as Captain of "the noble army of martyrs," and His question may be extended to include the truth that force is in its place when used against crime, but ludicrously and tragically out of place when employed against any teacher, and especially against Christianity. Christ, in His persecuted confessors, puts the same question to the persecutors which Christ in the flesh put to His captors.

The second clause of Christ's remonstrance appeals to their knowledge of Him and His words, and to their attitude towards Him. For several days He had daily been publicly teaching in the Temple. They had laid no hands on him. Nay, some of them, no doubt, had helped to wave the palm branches and swell the hosannas. He does not put the contrast of then and now in its strongest form, but spares them, even while He says enough to bring an unseen blush to some cheeks. He would have them ask, "Why this change in us, since He is the same? Did He deserve to be hailed as King a few short hours ago? How, then, before the palm branches are withered, can He deserve rude hands?" Men change in their feelings to the unchanging Christ; and they who have most closely marked the rise and fall of the tide in their own hearts will be the last to wonder at Christ's captors, and will most appreciate the gentleness of His rebuke and remonstrance.

The third clause rises beyond all notice of the human agents, and soars to the divine purpose which wrought itself out through them. That divine purpose does not make them guiltless, but it makes Jesus submissive. He bows utterly, and with no reluctance, to the Father's will, which would be wrought out through unconscious instruments, and had been declared of old by half-understanding prophets, but needed the obedience of the Son to be clear-seeing, cheerful, and complete. We, too, should train ourselves to see the hand that moves the pieces, and to make God's will our will, as becomes sons. Then Christ's calm will be ours, and, ceasing from self, and conscious of God everywhere, and yielding our wills, which are the self of ourselves, to Him, we shall enter into rest.

3. Rash love defending its Lord with wrong weapons (verse 47). Peter may have felt that he must do something to vindicate his recent boasting, and, with his ritual headlong haste, stops neither to ask what good his sword is likely to do, nor to pick his man and take deliberate aim at him. If swords were to be used, they should do something more effectual than hacking off a poor servant's ear. There was love in the foolish deed, and a certain heroism in braving the chance of a return thrust or capture, which should go to Peter's credit. If he alone struck a blow for his Master, it was because the others were more cowardly, not more enlightened. Peter has had rather hard measure about this matter, and is condemned by some of us who would not venture a tenth part of what he ventured for his Lord then. No doubt, this was blind and blundering love, with an alloy of rashness and wish for prominence; but that is better than unloving enlightenment and caution, which is chiefly solicitous about keeping its own ears on. It is also worse than love which sees and reflects the image of the meek Sufferer whom it loves. Christ and His cause are to be defended by other weapons. Christian heroism endures and does not smite. Not only swords, but bitter words which wound worse than they, are forbidden to Christ's soldier. We are ever being tempted to fight Christ's battles with the world's weapons; and many a "defender of the faith" in later days, perhaps even in this very enlightened day, has repeated Peter's fault with less excuse than he, and with very little of either his courage or his love.

4. Cowardly love forsaking its Lord (verse 50). "They all forsook Him, and fled." And who will venture to say that he would not have done so too? The tree that can stand such a blast must have deep roots. The Christ whom they forsook was, to them, but a fragment of the Christ whom we know; and the fear which scattered them was far better founded and more powerful than anything which the easygoing Christians of today have to resist. Their flight may teach us to place little reliance on our emotions, however genuine and deep, and to look for the security for our continual adherence to Christ, not to our fluctuating feelings, but to His steadfast love. We keep close to Him, not because our poor fingers grasp His hand—for that grasp is always feeble, and often relaxed—but because His strong and gentle hand holds us with a grasp which nothing can loosen. Whoso trusts in his own love to Christ builds on sand, but whoso trusts in Christ's love to him builds on rock.

5. Adventurous curiosity put to flight (verses 51, 52). Probably this young man was Mark. Only he tells the incident, which has no bearing on the course of events, and was of no importance but to the person concerned. He has put himself unnamed in a corner of his picture, as monkish painters used to do, content to associate himself even thus with his Lord. His hastily cast-on covering seems to show that he had been roused from sleep. Mingled love and curiosity and youthful adventurousness made him bold to follow when Apostles had fled. No effort appears to have been made to stop their flight; but he is laid hold of, and, terrified at his own rashness, wriggles himself out of his captors' hands. The whole incident singularly recalls Mark's behavior on Paul's first missionary journey. There are the same adventurousness, the same inconsiderate entrance on perilous paths, the same ignominious and hasty retreat at the first whistle of the bullets. A man who pushes himself needlessly into difficulties and dangers without estimating their force is pretty sure to take to his heels as soon as he feels them, and to cut as undignified a figure as this naked fugitive.

6. Love frightened, but following (verse 54). Fear had driven Peter but a little way. Love soon drew him and John back. Sudden and often opposite impulses moved his conduct and ruffled the surface of his character, but, deep down, the core was loyal love. He followed, but afar off: though "afar off," he did follow. If his distance betrayed his terror, his following witnessed his bravery. He is not a coward who is afraid, but he who lets his fear hinder him from duty or drive him to flight. What is all Christian living but following Christ afar off? And do the best of us do more, though we have less apology for our distance than Peter had? "Leaving us an example, that ye should follow His steps," said he, long after, perhaps remembering both that morning and the other by the lake when he was bidden to leave other servants" tasks to the Master's disposal, and, for his own part, to follow Him.

His love pushed him into a dangerous place. He was in bad company among the inferior sort of servants huddled around the fire that cold morning, at the lower end of the hall; and as its light flickered on his face, he was sure to be recognized. But we have not now to do with his denial. Rather he is the type of a true disciple, coercing his human weakness and cowardice to yield to the attraction which draws him to his Lord, and restful in the humblest place where he can catch a glimpse of His face, and so be, as he long after alleged it as his chief title to authority to have been, "a witness of the sufferings of Christ."

The Condemnation Which Condemns the Judges

*And the chief priests and all the council sought for witness against
Jesus to put Him to death; and found none. 56. For many bare
false witness against Him, but their witness agreed not
together. 57. And there arose certain, and bare false witness
against Him, saying, 58. We heard Him say, I will destroy this
temple that is made with hands, and within three days I will build
another made without hands. 59. But neither so did their witness
agree together. 60. And the high priest stood up in their midst,*

and asked Jesus, saying, Answerest Thou nothing? what is it which these witness against Thee? 61. *But He held His peace, and answered nothing. Again the high priest asked Him, and said unto Him, Art Thou the Christ, the Son of the Blessed?* 62. *And Jesus said, I am: and ye shall see the Son of Man, sitting on the right hand of power, and coming in the clouds of heaven.* 63. *Then the high priest rent his clothes, and saith, What need we any further witnesses?* 64. *Ye have heard the blasphemy: what think ye? And they all condemned Him to be guilty of death.* 65. *And some began to spit on Him, and to cover His face, and to buffet Him, and to say unto Him, Prophesy: and the servants did strike Him with the palms of their hands.* MARK 14:55–65.

Mark brings out three stages in our Lord's trial by the Jewish authorities—their vain attempts to find evidence against Him, which were met by His silence; His own majestic witness to Himself, which was met by a unanimous shriek of condemnation; and the rude mockery of the underlings. The other Evangelists, especially John, supply many illuminative details; but the essentials are here. It is only in criticizing the Gospels that a summary and a fuller narrative are dealt with as contradictory. These three stages naturally divide this paragraph.

1. The judges with evil thoughts, the false witnesses, and the silent Christ (verses 55–61). The criminal is condemned before He is tried. The judges have made up their minds before they sit, and the Sanhedrin is not a court of justice, but a slaughterhouse, where murder is to be done under sanction of law. Mark, like Matthew, notes the unanimity of the "council," to which Joseph of Arimathea—the one swallow which does not make a summer—appears to have been the only exception; and he probably was absent, or, if present, was silent. He did "not consent"; but we are not told that he opposed. That ill-omened unanimity measures the nation's sin. Flagrant injustice and corruption in high places is possible only when society as a whole is corrupt or indifferent to corruption. This prejudging of a case from hatred of the accused as a destroyer of sacred tradition, and this hunting for evidence to bolster up a foregone conclusion, are preeminently the vices of ecclesiastical tribunals and not of Jewish Sanhedrin or Papal Inquisition only. Where judges look for witnesses for the prosecution, plenty will be found, ready to curry favor by lies. The eagerness to find witnesses against Jesus is witness for Him, as showing that nothing in His life or teaching was sufficient to warrant their murderous purpose. His judges condemn themselves in seeking grounds to condemn Him, for they thereby show that their real motive was personal spite, or, as Caiaphas suggested, political expediency.

The single specimen of the worthless evidence given may be either a piece of misunderstanding or of malicious twisting of innocent words; nor can we decide whether the witnesses contradicted one another or each himself. The former is the more probable, as the fundamental principle of the Jewish law of evidence (''two or three witnesses'') would, in that case, rule out the testimony. The saying which they garble, meant the very opposite of what they made it mean. It represented Jesus as the restorer of that which Israel should destroy. It referred to His body which is the true Temple; but the symbolic temple ''made with hands'' is so inseparably connected with the real, that the fate of the one determines that of the other. Strangely significant, therefore, is it, that the rulers heard again, though distorted, at that moment when *they* were on their trial, the far-reaching sentence, which might have taught them that in slaying Jesus they were throwing down the Temple and all which centered in it, and that by His resurrection, His own act, He would build up again a new polity, which yet was but the old transfigured, even ''the Church, which is His body.'' His work destroys nothing but ''the works of the devil.'' He is the restorer of the divine ordinances and gifts which men destroy, and His death and resurrection bring back in nobler form all the good things lost by sin, ''the desolations of many generations.'' The history of all subsequent attacks on Christ is mirrored here. The foregone conclusion, the evidence sought as an afterthought to give a colorable pretext, the material found by twisting His teaching, the blindness which accuses Him of destroying what He restores, and fancies itself as preserving what it is destroying, have all reappeared over and over again.

Our Lord's silence is not only that of meekness, ''as a sheep before her shearers is dumb.'' It is the silence of innocence, and, if we may use the word concerning Him, of scorn. He will not defend Himself to such judges, nor stoop to repel evidence which they knew to be worthless. But there is also something very solemn and judicial in His locked lips. They had ever been ready to open in words of loving wisdom; but now they are fast closed, and this is the penalty for despising, that He ceases to speak. Deaf ears make a dumb Christ. What will happen when Jesus and His judges change faces, as they will one day do? When He says to each, ''Answerest thou nothing? What is it which these, thy sins, witness against thee?'' each will be silent with the consciousness of guilt and of just condemnation by His all-knowing justice.

2. Christ's majestic witness to Himself received with a shriek of condemnation. What a supreme moment that was when the head of the hierarchy put this question and received the unambiguous answer! The veriest impostor asserting Messiahship had a right to have his claims examined; but a howl of hypocritical horror is all which Christ's evoke. The high priest knew well enough what Christ's answer would be. Why, then, did he not begin by questioning Jesus, and do without the witnesses? Probably because the council wished to find some pretext for His condemnation without bringing up the real reason; for it looked ugly to condemn a man for claiming to be Messiah, and to do it without examining His credentials. The failure, however, of the false witnesses compelled the council to "show their hands," and to hear and reject our Lord solemnly and, so to speak, officially, laying His assertion of dignity and office before them, as the tribunal charged with the duty of examining His proofs. The question is so definite as to imply a pretty full and accurate knowledge of our Lord's teaching about Himself. It embraces two points—office and nature; for "the Christ" and "the Son of the Blessed" are not equivalents. The latter title points to our Lord's declarations that He was the Son of God, and is an instance of the later Jewish superstition which avoided using the divine name. Loving faith delights in the name of the Lord. Dead formalism changes reverence into dread, and will not speak it.

Sham reverence, feigned ignorance, affected wish for information, the false show of judicial impartiality, and other lies and vices not a few, are condensed in the question; and the fact that the judge had to ask it and hear the answer, is an instance of a divine purpose working through evil men, and compelling reluctant lips to speak words the meaning and bearing of which they little know. Jesus could not leave such a challenge unanswered. Silence *then* would have been abandonment of His claims. It was fitting that the representatives of the nation should, at that decisive moment, hear Him declare Himself Messiah. It was not fitting that He should be condemned on any other ground. In that answer, and its reception by the council, the nation's rejection of Jesus is, as it were, focused and compressed. This was the end of centuries of training by miracle, prophet and psalmist—the saddest instance in man's long, sad history of his awful power to frustrate God's patient educating!

Our Lord's majestic "I am," in one word answers both parts of the question, and then passes on, with strange calm and dignity, to point onwards to the time when the criminal will be the judge, and the judges will stand at His bar. "The Son of Man," His ordinary designation of Himself, implies His true manhood, and His representative character, as perfect man, or, to use modern language, the "realized ideal" of humanity. In the present connection, its employment in the same sentence to His assertion that He is the Son of God goes deep into the mystery of His twofold nature, and declares that His manhood had a supernatural origin and wielded divine prerogatives. Accordingly there follows the explicit prediction of His assumption of the highest of these after His death. The Cross was as plain to Him as ever; but beyond it gleamed the crown and the throne. He anticipates ''sitting on the right hand of power,'' which implies repose, enthronement, judicature, investiture with omnipotence, and administration of the universe. He anticipates ''coming in the clouds of heaven,'' which distinctly claims to be the future Judge of the world. His hearers could scarcely fail to discern the reference to Daniel's prophecy.

Was ever the irony of history more pungently exemplified than in an Annas and Caiaphas holding up hands of horror at the ''blasphemies'' of Jesus? They rightly took His words to mean more than the claim of Messiahship as popularly understood. To say that He was the Christ was not ''blasphemy,'' but a claim demanding examination; but to say that He, the Son of Man, was of God and supreme Judge was so, according to their canons. How unconsciously the exclamation, ''What need we further witnesses?'' betrays the purpose for which the witnesses had been sought, as being simply His condemnation! They were ''needed'' to compass His death, which the council now gleefully feels to be secured. So with precipitate unanimity they vote. And this was Israel's welcome to their King, and the outcome of all their history! And it was the destruction of the national life. That howl of condemnation pronounced sentence on themselves and on the whole order of which they were the heads. The prisoner's eyes alone saw then what we and all men may see now—the handwriting on the wall of the high priest's palace: ''Weighed in the balance, and found wanting.''

3. The savage mockers and the patient Christ (verse 65). There is an evident antithesis between the ''all'' of verse 64 and the ''some'' of verse 65, which shows that the inflictors of the indignities were certain members of the council, whose fury carried them beyond all bounds of decency. The subsequent mention of the ''servants'' confirms this, especially when we adopt the more accurate rendering of the Revised Version, ''received Him with blows.'' Mark's account, then, is this: that, as soon as the unanimous howl of condemnation had been uttered, some of the ''judges''(!) fell upon Jesus with spitting and clumsy ridicule and downright violence, and that afterwards He was handed over to the underlings, who were not slow to copy the example set them at the upper end of the hall.

It was not an ignorant mob who thus answered His claims, but the leaders and teachers—the *crême de la crême* of the nation. A wild beast lurks below the Pharisee's long robes and phylacteries; and the more that men have changed a living belief in religion for a formal profession, the more fiercely antagonistic are they to every attempt to realize its precepts and hopes. The "religious" men who mock Jesus in the name of traditional religion are by no means an extinct species. It is of little use to shudder at the blind cruelty of dead scribes and priests. Let us rather remember that the seeds of their sins are in us all, and take care to check their growth. What a volcano of hellish passion bursts out here! Spitting expresses disgust; blinding and asking for the names of the smiters is a clumsy attempt at wit and ridicule; buffeting is the last unrestrained form of hate and malice. The world has always paid its teachers and benefactors in such coin; but all other examples pale before this saddest, transpondent instance. Love is repaid by hate; a whole nation is blind to supreme and unspotted goodness; teachers steeped in "law and prophets" cannot see Him at and for whom law and prophets witnessed and were, when He stands before them. The sin of sins is the failure to recognize Jesus for what He is. His person and claims are the touchstone which tries every beholder of what sort He is.

How wonderful the silent patience of Jesus! He withholds not His face "from shame and spitting." He gives "His back to the smiters." Meek endurance and passive submission are not all which we have to behold there. This is more than an uncomplaining martyr. This is the sacrifice for the world's sin; and His bearing of all that men can inflict is more than heroism. It is redeeming love. His sad, loving eyes, wide open below their bandage, saw and pitied each rude smiter, even as He sees us all. They were and are eyes of infinite tenderness, ready to beam forgiveness; but they were and are the eyes of the Judge, who sees and repays His foes, as those who smite Him will one day find out.

15

The King on the Cross

Christ and Pilate: The True King and His Counterfeit

And straightway in the morning the chief priests held a consulta-
tion with the elders and scribes and the whole council, and bound
Jesus, and carried Him away, and delivered Him to Pilate. 2. And
Pilate asked Him, Art Thou the King of the Jews? And He answering
said unto him, Thou sayest it. 3. And the chief priests accused Him
of many things: but He answered nothing. 4. And Pilate asked
Him again, saying, Answerest Thou nothing? behold how many things
they witness against Thee. 5. But Jesus yet answered nothing; so
that Pilate marveled. 6. Now at that feast he released unto them
one prisoner, whomsoever they desired. 7. And there was one
named Barabbas, which lay bound with them that had made insur-
rection with him, who had committed murder in the
insurrection. 8. And the multitude crying aloud began to desire
him to do as he had ever done unto them. 9. But Pilate answered
them, saying, Will ye that I release unto you the King of the
Jews? 10. For he knew that the chief priests had delivered Him for
envy. 11. But the chief priests moved the people, that he should
rather release Barabbas unto them. 12. And Pilate answered and
said again unto them, What will ye then that I shall do unto Him
whom ye call the King of the Jews? 13. And they cried out again,
Crucify Him. 14. Then Pilate said unto them, Why, what evil hath
He done? And they cried out the more exceedingly, Crucify
Him. 15. And so Pilate, willing to content the people, released
Barabbas unto them, and delivered Jesus, when he had scourged
Him, to be crucified. 16. And the soldiers led Him away into the
hall, called Prætorium; and they call together the whole
band. 17. And they clothed Him with purple, and platted a crown
of thorns, and put it about His head, 18. And began to salute Him,
Hail, King of the Jews! 19. And they smote Him on the head with
a reed, and did spit upon Him, and bowing their knees worshipped

Him. 20. And when they had mocked Him they took off the purple from Him, and put His own clothes on Him, and led Him out to crucify Him. MARK 15:1–20.

The so-called trial of Jesus by the rulers turned entirely on his claim to be Messiah; His examination by Pilate turns entirely on His claim to be king. The two claims are indeed one, but the political aspect is distinguishable from the higher one; and it was the Jewish rulers' trick to push it exclusively into prominence before Pilate, in the hope that he might see in the claim an incipient insurrection, and might mercilessly stamp it out. It was a new part for them to play to hand over leaders of revolt to the Roman authorities, and a governor with any common sense must have suspected that there was something hid below such unusual loyalty. What a moment of degradation and of treason against Israel's sacredest hopes that was when its rulers dragged Jesus to Pilate on such a charge! Mark follows the same method of condensation and discarding of all but the essentials, as in the other parts of his narrative. He brings out three points—the hearing before Pilate, the popular vote for Barabbas, and the soldiers' mockery.

1. The true King at the bar of the apparent ruler (verses 1–6). The contrast between appearance and reality was never more strongly drawn than when Jesus stood as a prisoner before Pilate. The One is helpless, bound, alone; the other invested with all the externals of power. But which is the stronger? and in which hand is the scepter? On the lowest view of the contrast, it is ideas *versus* swords. On the higher and truer, it is the incarnate God, mighty because voluntarily weak, and man "dressed in a little brief authority," and weak because insolently "making his power his god." Impotence, fancying itself strong, assumes sovereign authority over omnipotence clothed in weakness. The phantom ruler sits in judgment on the true King. Pilate holding Christ's life in his hand is the crowning paradox of history, and the mystery of self-abasing love. One exercise of the Prisoner's will and His chains would have snapped, and the governor lain dead on the marble "pavement."

The two hearings are parallel, and yet contrasted. In each there are two stages—the self-attestation of Jesus and the accusations of others; but the order is different. The rulers begin with the witnesses, and, foiled there, fall back on Christ's own answer. Pilate, with Roman directness and a touch of contempt for the accusers, goes straight to the point, and first questions Jesus. His question was simply as to our Lord's regal pretensions. He cared nothing about Jewish "superstitions" unless they threatened political disturbance. It was nothing to him whether or no one crazy fanatic more fancied himself "the Messiah," whatever that might be. Was He going to fight?—that was all which Pilate had to look after. He is the very type of the hard, practical Roman, with a "practical" man's contempt for ideas and sentiments, skeptical as to the possibility of getting hold of "truth," and too careless to wait for an answer to his question about it; loftily ignorant of and indifferent to the notions of the troublesome people that he ruled, but alive to the necessity of keeping them in good humor, and unscrupulous enough to strain justice and unhesitatingly to sacrifice so small a thing as an innocent life to content them.

What could such a man see in Jesus but a harmless visionary? He had evidently made up his mind that there was no mischief in Him, or he would not have questioned Him as to His kingship. It was a new thing for the rulers to hand over dangerous patriots, and Pilate had experience enough to suspect that such unusual loyalty concealed something else, and that if Jesus had really been an insurrectionary leader, He would never have fallen into Pilate's power. Accordingly, he gives no serious attention to the case, and his question has a certain half-amused, half-pitying ring about it. "Thou a king?"—poor helpless peasant! A strange specimen of royalty this! How constantly the same blindness is repeated, and the strong things of this world despise the weak, and material power smiles pityingly at the helpless impotence of the principles of Christ's Gospel, which yet will one day shatter it to fragments, like a potter's vessel! The phantom ruler judges the real King to be a powerless shadow, while himself is the shadow and the other the substance. There are plenty of Pilates today who judge and misjudge the King of Israel.

The silence of Jesus in regard to the eager accusations corresponds to His silence before the false witnesses. The same reason dictated both. His silence is His most eloquent answer. It calmly passes by all these charges by envenomed tongues as needing no reply, and as utterly irrelevant. Answered, they would have lived in the Gospels; unanswered, they are buried. Christ can afford to let many of His foes alone. Contradictions and confutations keep slanders and heresies above water, which the law of gravitation would dispose of if they were left alone.

Pilate's wonder might and should have led him further. It should have prompted to further inquiry, and that might have issued in clearer knowledge. It was the little glimmer of light at the far-off end of his cavern, which, traveled towards, might have brought him into free air and broad day. One great part of his crime was neglecting the faint monitions of which he was conscious. His light may have been dim, but it would have brightened; and he quenched it. He stands as a tremendous example of possibilities missed, and of the tragedy of a soul that has looked on Jesus, and has not yielded to the impressions made on him by the sight.

2. The people's favorite (verses 7–15). "Barabbas" means "son of the father." His very name is a kind of caricature of the "Son of the Blessed," and his character and actions present in gross form the sort of Messiah whom the nation really wanted. He had headed some one of the many small riots against Rome which were perpetually sputtering up and being trampled out by an armed heel. There had been bloodshed, in which he had himself taken part ("a murderer," Acts 3:14). And this coarse, red-handed desperado is the people's favorite, because he embodied their notions and aspirations, and had been bold enough to do what every man of them would have done if he had dared. He thought and felt, as they did, that freedom was to be won by the sword. The popular hero is as a mirror which reflects the popular mind. He echoes the popular voice, a little improved or exaggerated. Jesus had taught what the people did not care to hear, and given blessings which even the recipients soon forgot, and lived a life whose "beauty of holiness" oppressed and rebuked the common life of men. What chance had truth and kindness and purity against the sort of bravery that slashes with a sword, and is not elevated above the mob by inconvenient reach of thought or beauty of character? Even now, after nineteen centuries of Christ's influence have modified the popular ideals, what chance have they? Are the popular "heroes" of Christian nations saints, teachers, lovers of men, in whom their Christ-likeness is the thing venerated? The old saying that the voice of the people is the voice of God receives an instructive commentary in the vote for Barabbas and against Jesus. That was what a plebiscite for the discovery of the people's favorite came to. What a reliable method of finding the best man universal suffrage, manipulated by wirepullers like these priests, is! and how wise the people are who let it guide their judgments, or still wiser, who fret their lives out in angling for its approval! Better be condemned with Jesus than adopted with Barabbas.

That fatal choice revealed the character of the choosers, both in their hostility and admiration; for excellence hated shows what we ought to be and are not, and grossness or vice admired shows what we would fain be if we dared. It was the tragic sign that Israel had not learned the rudiments of the lesson which "at sundry times and in divers manners" God had been teaching them. In it the nation renounced its Messianic hopes, and with its own mouth pronounced its own sentence. It convicted them of insensibility to the highest truth, of blindness to the most effulgent light, of ingratitude for the richest gifts. It is the supreme instance of short-lived, unintelligent emotion, inasmuch as many who on Friday joined in the roar, "Crucify Him!" had on Sunday shouted "Hosanna!" till they were hoarse.

Pilate plays a cowardly and unrighteous part in the affair, and tries to make amends to himself for his politic surrender of a man whom he knew to be innocent, by taunts and sarcasm. He seems to see a chance to release Jesus, if he can persuade the mob to name Him as the prisoner to be set free, according to custom. His first proposal to them was apparently dictated by a genuine interest in Jesus, and a complete conviction that Rome had nothing to fear from this "King." But there are also in the question a sneer at such pauper royalty, as it looked to him, and a kind of scornful condescension in acknowledging the mob's right of choice. He consults their wishes for once, but there is haughty consciousness of mastery in his way of doing it. His appeal is to the people, as against the priests whose motives he had penetrated. But in his very effort to save Jesus he condemns himself; for, if he knew that they had delivered Christ for envy, his plain duty was to set the prisoner free, as innocent of the only crime of which he ought to take cognizance. So his attempt to shift the responsibility off his own shoulders is a piece of cowardice and a dereliction of duty. His second question plunges him deeper in the mire. The people had a right to decide which was to be released, but none to settle the fate of Jesus. To put that in their hands was an unconditional surrender by Pilate, and the sneer in "whom *ye* call the King of the Jews" is a poor attempt to hide from them and himself that he is afraid of them. Mark puts his finger on the damning blot in Pilate's conduct when he says that his motive for condemning Jesus was his wish to content the people. The life of one poor Jew was a small price to pay for popularity. So he let policy outweigh righteousness, and, in spite of his own clear conviction, did an innocent man to death. That would be his reading of his act, and, doubtless, it did not trouble his conscience much or long, but he would leave the judgment seat tolerably satisfied with his morning's work. How little he knew what he had done! In his ignorance lies his palliation. His crime was great, but his guilt is to be measured by his light, and that was small. He prostituted justice for his own ends, and he did not follow out the dawnings of light that would have led him to know Jesus. Therefore he did the most awful thing in the world's history. Let us learn the lesson which he teaches!

3. The soldiers' mockery (verses 16–20). This is characteristically different from that of the rulers, who jeered at His claim to supernatural enlightenment, and bade Him show His Messiahship by naming His smiters. The rough legionnaires knew nothing about a Messiah, but it seemed to them a good jest that this poor, scourged prisoner should have called Himself a King, and so they proceed to make coarse and clumsy merriment over it. It is like the wild beast playing with its prey before killing it. The laughter is not only rough, but cruel. There was no pity for the Victim "bleeding from the Roman rods," and soon to die. And the absence of any personal hatred made this mockery more hideous. Jesus was nothing to them but a prisoner whom they were to crucify, and their mockery was sheer brutality and savage delight in torturing. The sport is too good to be kept by a few, so the whole band is gathered to enjoy it. How they would troop the place! They get hold of some robe or cloth of the imperial color, and of some flexible shoots of some thorny plant, and out of these they fashion a burlesque of royal trappings. Then they shout, as they would have done to Caesar, "Hail, King of the Jews!" repeating again with clumsy iteration the stale jest which seems to them so exquisite. Then their mood changes, and naked ferocity takes the place of ironical reverence. Plucking the mock scepter, the reed, from His passive hand, they strike the thorn-crowned Head with it, and spit on Him, while they bow in mock reverence before Him, and at last, when tired of their sport, tear off the purple, and lead him away to the Cross.

If we think of who He was who bore all this, and of why He bore it, we may well bow not the knee but the heart, in endless love and thankfulness. If we think of the mockers—rude Roman soldiers, who probably could not understand a word of what they heard on the streets of Jerusalem—we shall do rightly to remember our Lord's own plea for them, "they know not what they do," and reflect that many of us with more knowledge do really sin more against the King than they did. Their insult was an unconscious prophecy. They foretold the basis of His dominion by the crown of thorns, and its character by the scepter of reed, and its extent by their mocking salutations; for His Kingship is founded in suffering, wielded with gentleness, and to Him every knee shall one day bow, and every tongue confess that the King of the Jews is monarch of mankind.

The Death Which Gives Life

And they compel one Simon a Cyrenian, who passed by, coming out of the country, the father of Alexander and Rufus, to bear His crown. 22. And they bring Him unto the place Golgotha, which is, being interpreted, The place of a skull. 23. And they gave Him to drink wine mingled with myrrh: but He received it not. 24. And when they had crucified Him, they parted His garments, casting lots upon them, what every man should take. 25. And it was the third hour, and they crucified Him. 26. And the superscription of His accusation was written over, THE KING OF THE JEWS. 27. And with Him they crucify two thieves; the one on His right hand, and the other on His left. 28. And the Scripture was fulfilled, which saith, And He was numbered with the transgressors. 29. And they that passed by railed on Him, wagging their heads, and saying, Ah, Thou that destroyest the temple, and buildest it in three days, 30. Save Thyself, and come down from the cross. 31. Likewise also the chief priests mocking said among themselves with the scribes, He saved others; Himself He cannot save. 32. Let Christ the King of Israel descend now from the cross, that we may see and believe. And they that were crucified with Him reviled Him. 33. And when the sixth hour was come, there was darkness over the whole land until the ninth hour. 34. And at the ninth hour Jesus cried with a loud voice, saying, Eloi, Eloi, lama sabachthani? which is, being interpreted, My God, My God, why hast Thou forsaken Me? 35. And some of them that stood by, when they heard it, said, Behold, He calleth Elias. 36. And one ran and filled a spunge full of vinegar, and put it on a reed, and gave Him to drink, saying, Let alone; let us see whether Elias will come to take him down. 37. And Jesus cried with a loud voice, and gave up the ghost. 38. And the veil of the temple was rent in twain from the top to the bottom. 39. And when the centurion, which stood over against Him, saw that He so cried out, and gave up the ghost, he said, Truly this man was the Son of God. MARK 15:21–39.

The narrative of the crucifixion is, in Mark's hands, almost entirely a record of what was done to Jesus, and scarcely touches what was done by Him. We are shown the executioners, the jeering rabble, the triumphant priests, the fellow sufferers reviling; but the only glimpses we get of Him are His refusal of the stupefying draught, His loud cries, and His giving up the ghost. The narrative is perfectly calm, as well as reverently reticent. It would have been well if our religious literature had copied the example, and treated the solemn scene in the same fashion. Mark's inartificial style of linking long paragraphs with the simple "and" is peculiarly observable here, where every verse but vv. 30 and 32, which are both quotations, begins with it. The whole section is one long sentence, each member of which adds a fresh touch to the tragic picture. The monotonous repetition of "and," "and," "and," gives the effect of an endless succession of the waves of sorrow, pain, and contumely which broke over that sacred head. We shall do best simply to note each billow as it breaks.

The first point is the impressing of Simon to bear the Cross. That was not dictated by compassion so much as by impatience. Apparently the weight was too heavy for Jesus, and the pace could be quickened by making the first man who could be laid hold of help to carry the load. Mark adds that Simon was the "father of Alexander and Rufus," whom he supposes to need no introduction to his readers. There is a Rufus mentioned in Romans 16:13 as being, with his mother, members of the Roman Church. Mark's Gospel has many traces of being primarily intended for Romans. Possibly these two Rufuses are the same; and the conjecture may be allowable that the father's fortuitous association with the crucifixion led to the conversion of himself and his family, and that his sons were of more importance or fame in the Church than he was. Perhaps, too, he is the "Simeon called Niger" (bronzed by the hot African sun) who was a prophet of Antioch, and stands by the side of a Cyrenian (Acts 13:1). It is singular that he should be the only one of all the actors in the crucifixion who is named; and the fact suggests his subsequent connection with the Church. If so, the seeking love of God found him by a strange way. On what apparently trivial accidents a life may be pivoted, and how much may depend on turning to right or left in a walk! In this bewildering network of interlaced events, which each ramifies in so many directions, the only safety is to keep fast hold of God's hand, and to take good care of the purity of our motives, and let results alone.

The next verse brings us to Golgotha, which is translated by the three Evangelists, who give it as meaning "the place of the skull." The name may have been given to the place of execution with grim suggestiveness; or, more probably, Conder's suggested identification is plausible, which points to a little, rounded, skull-shaped knoll, close outside the northern wall, as the site of the crucifixion. In that case, the name would originally describe the form of the height, and be retained as specially significant in view of its use as the place of execution. That was the "place" to which Israel led its King! The place of death becomes a place of life, and from the mournful soil where the bones of evildoers lay bleaching in the sun springs the fountain of water of life.

Arrived at that doleful place, a small touch of kindness breaks the monotony of cruelty, if it be not merely a part of the ordinary routine of executions. The stupefying potion would diminish, but would therefore protract, the pain, and was possibly given for the latter rather than the former effect. But Jesus "received it not." He will not, by any act of His, lessen the bitterness. He will drink to the dregs the cup which His Father hath given Him, and therefore He will not drink of the numbing draught. It is a small matter comparatively, but it is all of a piece with the greater things. The spirit of His whole course of voluntary, cheerful endurance of all the sorrows needful to redeem the world, is expressed in His silent turning away from the draught which might have alleviated physical suffering, but at the cost of dulling conscious surrender.

The act of crucifixion is but named in a subsidiary clause, as if the writer turned away, with eyes veiled in reverence, from the sight of man's utmost sin and Christ's utmost mystery of suffering love. He can describe the attendant circumstances, but his pen refuses to dwell upon the central fact. The highest art and the simplest natural feeling both know that the fewest words are the most eloquent. He will not expressly mention the indignity done to the sacred Body in which "dwelt all the fulness of the Godhead," but leaves it to be inferred from the parting of Christ's raiment, the executioner's perquisite. He had nothing else belonging to Him, and of even that poor property He is spoiled. According to John's more detailed account, the soldiers made an equal parting of His garments except the seamless robe, for which they threw lots. So the "parting" applies to one portion, and the "casting lots" to another. The incident teaches two things: on the one hand, the stolid indifference of the soldiers, who had crucified many a Jew, and went about their awful work as a mere piece of routine duty; and, on the other hand, the depth of the abasement and shame to which Jesus bowed for our sakes. "Naked shall I return thither" was true in the most literal sense of Him whose earthly life began with His laying aside His garments of divine glory, and ended with rude legionnaires parting "His raiment" among them.

Mark alone tells the hour at which Jesus was nailed to the Cross (verse 25). Matthew and Luke specify the sixth and ninth hours as the times of the darkness and of the death; but to Mark we owe our knowledge of the fact that for six slow hours Jesus hung there, tasting death drop by drop. At any moment of all these sorrow-laden moments He could have come down from the Cross, if He would. At each, a fresh exercise of His loving will to redeem kept Him there.

The writing on the Cross is given here in the most condensed fashion (verse 26). The one important point is that His "accusation" was— "King of the Jews." It was the official statement of the reason for His crucifixion, put there by Pilate as a double-barreled sarcasm, hitting both Jesus and the nation. The rulers winced under the taunt, and tried to get it softened; but Pilate sought to make up for his unrighteous facility in yielding Jesus to death, by obstinacy and jeers. So the inscription hung there, a truth deeper than its author or its angry readers knew, and a prophecy which has not received all its fulfillment yet.

The narrative comes back, in verse 27, to the sad catalogue of the insults heaped on Jesus. Verse 28 is probably spurious here, as the Revised Version takes it to be; but it truly expresses the intention of the crucifixion of the thieves as being to put Him in the same class as they, and to suggest that He was a ringleader, pre-eminent in evil. Possibly the two robbers may have been part of Barabbas' band, who had been brigands disguised as patriots; and, if so, the insult was all the greater. But, in any case, the meaning of it was to bring Him down, in the eyes of beholders, to the level of vulgar criminals. If a Cranmer or a Latimer had been bound to the stake with a housebreaker or a cutthroat, that would have been a feeble image of the malicious contumely thus flung at Jesus; but His love had identified Him with the worst sinners in a far deeper and more real way, and not a crime had stained these men's hands, but its weight pressed on Him. He numbered Himself with transgressors, that they may be numbered with His saints.

Then follows (verses 29–32) the threefold mockery by people, priests, and fellow sufferers. That is spread over three hours, and is all which Mark has to tell of them. Other Evangelists give us words spoken by Jesus; but this narrative has only one of the seven words from the Cross, and gives us the picture rather of the silent Sufferer, bearing in meek resolution all that men can lay on Him. Both pictures are true, for the words are too few to make notable breaches in the silence. The mockery harps on the old themes, and witnesses at once the malicious cruelty of the mockers and the innocence of the Victim, at whom even such malice could find nothing to fling except these stale taunts. The chance passengers, of whom there would be a stream to and from the adjacent city gate, "wag their heads" in gratified and fierce hate. The calumny of the discredited witnesses, although even the biased judges had not dared to treat it as true, has lodged in the popular mind, and been accepted as proved. Lies are not killed when they are shown to be lies. They travel faster than truth. Ears were greedily open for the false witnesses' evidence which had been closed to Christ's gracious teaching. The charge that He was a would-be destroyer of the Temple obliterated all remembrance of miracles and benefits, and fanned the fire of hatred in men whose zeal for the Temple was a substitute for religion. Are there any of them left nowadays—people who have no real hearthold of Christianity, but are fiercely antagonistic to supposed destroyers of its externals, and not overparticular to the evidence against them? These mockers thought that Christ's being fastened to the Cross was a *reductio ad absurdum* of His claim to build the Temple. How little they knew that it led straight to that rebuilding, or that they, and not He, were indeed the destroyers of the holy house which they thought that they were honoring, and were really making "desolate"!

The priests do not take up the people's mockery, for they know that it is based upon a falsehood; but they scoff at His miracles, which they assume to be disproved by His crucifixion. Their venomous gibe is profoundly true, and goes to the very heart of the Gospel. Precisely because "He saved others," therefore "Himself He cannot save"—not, as they thought, for want of power, but because His will was fixed to obey the Father and to redeem His brethren, and therefore He must die and cannot deliver Himself. But the necessity and inability both depend on His will. The priests, however, take up the other part of the people's scoff. They unite the two grounds of condemnation in the names "the Christ, the King of Israel," and think that both are disproved by His hanging there. But the Cross is the throne of the King. A sacrificial death is the true work of the Messiah of law, prophecy, and psalm; and because He did not come down from the Cross, therefore is He "crowned with glory and honor" in heaven, and rules over grateful and redeemed hearts on earth.

The midday darkness lasted three hours, during which no word or incident is recorded. It was nature divinely draped in mourning over the sin of sins, the most tragic of deaths. It was a symbol of the eclipse of the Light of the world; but ere He died it passed, and the sun shone on His expiring head, in token that His death scattered our darkness and poured day on our sad night. The solemn silence was broken at last by that loud cry, the utterance of strangely blended consciousness of possession of God and of abandonment by Him, the depths of which we can never fathom. But this we know: that our sins, not His, wove the veil which separated Him from His God. Such separation is the real death. Where cold analysis is out of place, reverent gratitude may draw near. Let us adore, for what we can understand speaks of a love which has taken on itself the iniquity of us all. Let us silently adore, for all words are weaker than that mystery of love.

The first hearers of that cry misunderstood it, or cruelly pretended to do so, in order to find fresh food for mockery. "Eloi" sounded like enough to "Elijah" to suggest to some of the flinty hearts around a travesty of the piteous appeal. They must have been Jews, for the soldiers knew nothing about the prophet; and if they were Scribes, they could scarcely fail to recognize the reference to the Twenty-second Psalm, and to understand the cry. But the opportunity for one more cruelty was too tempting to be resisted, and savage laughter was man's response to the most pitiful prayer ever uttered. One man in all that crowd had a small touch of human pity, and, dipping a sponge in the sour drink provided for the soldiers, reached it up to the parched lips. That was no stupefying draught, and was accepted. Matthew's account is more detailed, and represents the words spoken as intended to hinder even that solitary bit of kindness.

The end was near. The lips, moistened by the "vinegar," opened once more in that loud cry which both showed undiminished vitality and conscious victory; and then He "gave up the ghost," *sending away* His spirit, and dying, not because the prolonged agony had exhausted His energy, but because He chose to die. He entered through the gate of death as a conqueror, and burst its bars when He went in, and not only when He came out.

His death rent the Temple veil. The innermost chamber of the Divine Presence is open now, and sinful men have "access with confidence by the faith of Him," to every place whither He has gone before. Right into the secret of God's pavilion we can go, now and here, knowledge and faith and love treading the path which Jesus has opened, and coming to the Father by Him. Right into the blaze of the glory we shall go hereafter; for He has gone to prepare a place for us, and when He overcame the sharpness of death He opened the gate of heaven to all believers.

Jews looked on, unconcerned and unconvinced by the pathos and triumph of such a death. But the rough soldier who commanded the executioners had no prejudices or hatred to blind his eyes and ossify his heart. The sight made its natural impression on him; and his exclamation, though not to be taken as a Christian confession or as using the phrase "Son of God" in its deepest meaning, is yet the beginning of light. Perhaps, as he went thoughtfully to his barrack that afternoon, the process began which led him at last to repeat his first exclamation with deepened meaning and true faith. May we all gaze on that Cross, with fuller knowledge, with firm trust, and endless love!

Simon the Cyrenian

And they compel one Simon, a Cyrenian, who passed by, coming out of the country, the father of Alexander and Rufus, to bear His Cross. MARK 15:21.

How little these soldiers knew that they were making this man immortal! What a strange fate that is which has befallen those persons in the Gospel narrative, who for an instant came into contact with Jesus Christ. Like ships passing athwart the white ghost-like splendor of moonlight on the sea, they gleam silvery pure for a moment as they cross its broad belt, and then are swallowed up again in the darkness.

This man Simon, fortuitously, as men say, meeting the little procession at the gate of the city, for an instant is caught in the radiance of the light, and stands out visible forevermore to all the world; and then sinks into the blackness, and we know no more about him. This brief glimpse tells us very little, and yet the man and his act and its consequences may be worth thinking about.

He was a Cyrenian; that is, he was a Jew by descent, probably born, and certainly resident, for purposes of commerce, in Cyrene, on the North African coast of the Mediterranean. No doubt he had come up to Jerusalem for the Passover; and like very many of the strangers who flocked to the Holy City for the feast, met some difficulty in finding accommodation in the city, and so was obliged to go to lodge in one of the outlying villages. From this lodging he is coming in, in the morning, knowing nothing about Christ nor His trial, knowing nothing of what he is about to meet, and happens to see the procession as it is passing out of the gate. He is impressed by the centurion to help the fainting Christ to carry the heavy Cross. He probably thought Jesus a common criminal, and would resent the task laid upon him by the rough authority of the officer in command. But he was gradually touched into some kind of sympathy; drawn closer and closer, as we suppose, as he looked upon this dying meekness; and at last, yielded to the soul-conquering power of Christ.

Tradition says so, and the reasons for supposing that it was right may be very simply stated. The description of him in our text as "the father of Alexander and Rufus" shows that, by the time when Mark wrote, his two sons were members of the Christian community, and had attained some eminence in it. A Rufus is mentioned in the salutations in Paul's Epistle to the Romans, as being "elect in the Lord," that is to say, "eminent," and his mother is associated in the greeting, and commended as having been motherly to Paul as well as to Rufus. Now, if we remember that Mark's Gospel was probably written in Rome, and for Roman Christians, the conjecture seems a very reasonable one that the Rufus here was the Rufus of the Epistle to the Romans. If so, it would seem that the family had been gathered into the fold of the Church, and in all probability, therefore, the father with them.

Then there is another little morsel of possible evidence which may just be noticed. We find in the Acts of the Apostles, in the list of the prophets and teachers in the Church at Antioch, a "Simon, who is called Niger" (that is, black, the hot African sun having tanned his countenance, perhaps), and side by side with him one "Lucius of Cyrene," from which place we know that several of the original brave preachers to the Gentiles in Antioch came. It is possible that this may be our Simon, and that he who was the last to join the band of disciples during the Master's life and learned courage at the Cross was among the first to apprehend the world-wide destination of the Gospel, and to bear it beyond the narrow bounds of his nation.

At all events, I think we may, with something like confidence, believe that his glimpse of Christ on that morning and his contact with the suffering Saviour ended in his acceptance of Him as his Christ, and in his bearing in a truer sense the Cross after Him.

And so I seek now to gather some of the lessons that seem to me arise from this incident.

1. First, the greatness of trifles. If Simon had started from the little village where he lodged five minutes earlier or later, if he had walked a little faster or slower, if he had happened to be lodging on the other side of Jerusalem, or if the whim had taken him to go in at another gate, or if the centurion's eye had not chanced to alight on him in the crowd, or if the centurion's fancy had picked out somebody else to carry the Cross, then all his life would have been different. And so it is always. You go down one turning rather than another, and your whole career is colored thereby. You miss a train, and you escape death. Our lives are like the Cornish rocking stones, pivoted on little points. The most apparently insignificant things have a strange knack of suddenly developing unexpected consequences, and turning out to be, not small things at all, but great and decisive and fruitful.

Let us then look with ever fresh wonder on this marvelous contexture of human life, and on Him that molds it all to His own perfect purposes. Let us bring the highest and largest principles to bear on the smallest events and circumstances, for you can never tell which of these is going to turn out a revolutionary and formative influence in your life. And if the highest Christian principle is not brought to bear upon the trifles, depend upon it, it will never be brought to bear upon the mighty things. The most part of every life is made up of trifles, and unless these are ruled by the highest motives, life, which is divided into grains like the sand, will have gone by, while we are waiting for the great events which we think worthy of being regulated by lofty principles. "Take care of the pence and the pounds will take care of themselves."

Look after the trifles, for the law of life is like that which is laid down by the Psalmist about the Kingdom of Jesus Christ: "There shall be a handful of corn in the earth," a little seed sown in an apparently ungenial place "on the top of the mountains." Ay! but this will come of it, "The fruit thereof shall shake like Lebanon," and the great harvest of benediction or of curse, of joy or of sorrow, will come from the minute seeds that are sown in the great trifles of our daily life.

Let us learn the lesson, too, of quiet confidence in Him in whose hands the whole puzzling, overwhelming mystery lies. If a man once begins to think of how utterly incalculable the consequences of the smallest and most commonplace of his deeds may be, how they may run out into all eternity, and like divergent lines may enclose a space that becomes larger and wider the further they travel; if, I say, a man once begins to indulge in thoughts like these, it is difficult for him to keep himself calm and sane at all, unless he believes in the great loving Providence that lies above all, and shapes the vicissitude and mystery of life. We can leave all in His hands—and if we are wise we shall do so—to whom *great* and *small* are terms that have no meaning; and who looks upon men's lives, not according to the apparent magnitude of the deeds with which they are filled, but simply according to the motive from which, and the purpose towards which, those deeds were done.

2. Then, still further, take this other lesson, which lies very plainly here—the blessedness and honor of helping Jesus Christ. If we turn to the story of the Crucifixion, in John's Gospel, we find that the narratives of the three other Gospels are, in some points, supplemented by it. In reference to our Lord's bearing of the Cross, we are informed by John that when He left the judgment hall He was carrying it Himself, as was the custom with criminals under the Roman law. The heavy cross was laid on the shoulder, at the intersection of its arms and stem, one of the arms hanging down in front of the bearer's body, and the long upright trailing behind.

Apparently our Lord's physical strength, sorely tried by a night of excitement and the hearings in the High priest's palace and before Pilate, as well as by the scourging, was unequal to the task of carrying, albeit for that short passage, the heavy weight. And there is a little hint of that sort in the context. In the verse before my text we read, "They led Jesus out to crucify Him," and in the verse after, "they bring," or *bear* "Him to the place Golgotha," as if, when the procession began, they led Him, and before it ended they had to carry Him, His weakness having become such that He Himself could not sustain the weight of His cross or of His own enfeebled limbs. So, with some touch of pity in their rude hearts, or more likely with professional impatience of delay, and eager to get their task over, the soldiers lay hold of this stranger, press him into the service and make him carry the heavy upright, which trailed on the ground behind Jesus. And so they pass on to the place of execution.

Very reverently, and with few words, one would touch upon the physical weakness of the Master. Still, it does not do us any harm to try to realize how very marked was the collapse of His physical nature, and to remember that that collapse was not entirely owing to the pressure upon Him of the mere fact of physical death; and that it was still less a failure of His will, or like the abject cowardice of some criminals who have had to be dragged to the scaffold, and helped up its steps; but that the reason why His flesh failed was very largely because there was laid upon Him the mysterious burden of the world's sin. Christ's demeanor in the act of death, in such singular contrast to the calm heroism and strength of hundreds who have drawn all their heroism and strength from Him, suggests to us that, looking upon His sufferings, we look upon something the significance of which does not lie on the surface; and the extreme pressure of which is to be accounted for by that blessed and yet solemn truth of prophecy and Gospel alike—"The Lord hath laid on Him the iniquity of us all."

But, apart from that, which does not enter properly into my present contemplations, let us remember that though changed in form, very truly and really in substance, this blessedness and honor of helping Jesus Christ is given to us; and is demanded from us, too, if we are His disciples. He is despised and set at nought still. He is crucified afresh still. There are many men in this day who scoff at Him, mock Him, deny His claims, seek to cast Him down from His throne, rebel against His dominion. It is an easy thing to be a disciple, when all the crowd is crying "Hosanna!" It is a much harder thing to be a disciple when the crowd, or even when the influential cultivated opinion of a generation, is crying "Crucify Him! crucify Him!" And some of you Christian men and women have to learn the lesson that if you are to be Christians you must be Christ's companions when His back is at the wall as well as when men are exalting and honoring Him, that it is your business to confess Him when men deny Him, to stand by Him when men forsake Him, to avow Him when the avowal is likely to bring contempt upon you from some people, and thus, in a very real sense, to bear His Cross after Him. "Let us go forth unto Him without the camp, bearing His reproach"—the tail end of His Cross, which is the lightest! He has borne the heaviest end on His own shoulders; but we have to ally ourselves with that suffering and despised Christ if we are to be His disciples.

I do not dwell upon the lesson often drawn from this story, as if it taught us to "take up *our* cross daily and follow Him." That is another matter, and yet is closely connected with that about which I speak; but what I say is, Christ's Cross has to be carried today; and if we have not found out that it has, let us ask ourselves if we are Christians at all. There will be hostility, alienation, a comparative coolness, and absence of a full sense of sympathy with you, in many people, if you are a true Christian. You will come in for a share of contempt from the wise and the cultivated of this generation, as in all generations. The mud that is thrown after the Master will spatter your faces too, to some extent; and if you are walking with Him you will be, to the extent of your communion with Him, objects of the aversion with which many men regard Him. Stand to your colors.

Do not be ashamed of Him in the midst of a crooked and perverse generation.

And there is yet another way in which this honor of helping the Lord is given to us. As in His weakness He needed someone to aid Him to bear His Cross, so in His glory He needs our help to carry out the purposes for which the Cross was borne. The paradox of a man's carrying the Cross of Him who carried the world's burden is repeated in another form. He needs nothing, and yet He needs us. He needs nothing, and yet He needed that ass which was tethered at "the place where two ways met," in order to ride into Jerusalem upon it. He does not need man's help, and yet He does need it, and He asks for it. And though He bore Simon the Cyrenian's sins "in His own body on the tree," He needed Simon the Cyrenian to help Him to bear the tree, and He needs us to help Him to spread throughout the world the blessed consequences of that Cross and bitter Passion. So to us all is granted the honor, and from us all are required the sacrifice and the service, of helping the suffering Saviour.

3. Another of the lessons which may very briefly be drawn from this story is that of the perpetual recompense and record of the humblest Christian work. There were different degrees of criminality and different degrees of sympathy with Him, if I may use the word, in that crowd that stood round the Master. The criminality varied from the highest degree of violent malignity in the Scribes and Pharisees, down to the lowest point of ignorance, and therefore all but entire innocence, on the part of the Roman legionnaires, who were merely the mechanical instruments of the order given, and stolidly "watched Him there," with eyes which saw nothing.

On the other hand, there were all grades of service, and help and sympathy, from the vague emotions of the crowd who beat their breasts, and the pity of the daughters of Jerusalem, or the kindly meant help of the soldiers, who would have moistened the parched lips, to the heroic love of the women at the Cross, whose ministry was not ended even with His life. But surely the most blessed share in that day's tragedy was reserved for Simon, whose bearing of the Cross may have been compulsory at first, but became, ere it was ended, willing service. But whatever were the degrees of recognition of Christ's character, and of sympathy with the meaning of His sufferings, yet the smallest and most transient impulse of loving gratitude that went out towards Him was rewarded then, and is rewarded forever, by blessed results in the heart that feels it.

Besides these results, service for Christ is recompensed, as in the instance before us, by a perpetual memorial. How little Simon knew that "wherever in the whole world this gospel was preached, there also, this that *he* had done should be told for a memorial of *him*!" How little he understood when he went back to his rural lodging that night, that he had written his name high up on the tablet of the world's memory, to be legible forever. Why, men have fretted their whole lives away to win what this man won, and knew nothing of—one line in the chronicle of fame.

So we may say, it shall be always, "I will never forget any of their works." We may not leave our deeds inscribed in any records that men can read. What of that, if they are written in letters of light in the "Lamb's Book of Life," to be read out by Him before His Father and the holy angels, in that last great day? We may not leave any separable traces of our services, any more than the little brook that comes down some gulley on the hillside flows separate from its sisters, with whom it has coalesced, in the bed of the great river, or in the rolling, boundless ocean. What of that so long as the work, in its consequences, shall last? Men that sow some great prairie broadcast cannot go into the harvestfield and say, "I sowed the seed from which that ear came, and you the seed from which this one sprang." But the waving abundance belongs to them all, and each may be sure that his work survives and is glorified there—"that he that soweth and he that reapeth may rejoice together." So a perpetual remembrance is sure for the smallest Christian service.

4. The last lesson that I would draw is, let us learn from this incident the blessed results of contact with the suffering Christ. Simon the Cyrenian apparently knew nothing about Jesus Christ when the Cross was laid on his shoulders. He would be reluctant to undertake the humiliating task, and would plod along behind Him for a while, sullen and discontented, but by degrees be touched by more of sympathy, and get closer and closer to the Sufferer. And if he stood by the Cross when it was fixed, and saw all that transpired there, no wonder if, at last, after more or less protracted thought and search, he came to understand who He was that he had helped, and to yield himself to Him wholly.

Yes! dear brethren, Christ's great saying, "I, if I be lifted up, will draw all men unto Me," began to be fulfilled when He began to be lifted up. The centurion, the thief, this man Simon, by looking on the Cross, learned the Crucified.

And it is the only way by which any of us will ever learn the true mystery and miracle of Christ's great and loving Being and work. I beseech you, take your places there behind Him, near His Cross; gazing upon Him till your hearts melt, and you, too, learn that He is your Lord, and your Saviour, and your God. The Cross of Jesus Christ divides men into classes as the Last Day will. It, too, parts men—"sheep" to the right hand, "goats" to the left. If there was a penitent, there was an impenitent thief; if there was a convinced centurion, there were gambling soldiers; if there were hearts touched with compassion, there were mockers who took His very agonies and flung them in His face as a refutation of His claims. On the day when that Cross was reared on Calvary it began to be what it has been ever since, and is at this moment to every soul who hears the Gospel, "a savor of life unto life, or of death unto death." Contact with the suffering Christ will either bind you to His service, and fill you with His Spirit, or it will harden your hearts, and make you tenfold more selfish—that is to say, "tenfold more a child of hell"—than you were before you saw and heard of that divine meekness of the suffering Christ. Look to Him, I beseech you, who bears what none can help Him to carry, the burden of the world's sin. Let Him bear yours, and yield to Him your grateful obedience, and then take up your cross daily, and bear the light burden of self-denying service to Him who has borne the heavy load of sin for you and all mankind.

16

Love's Triumph

The Incredulous Disciples

And when the sabbath was past, Mary Magdalene, and Mary the
mother of James, and Salome, had bought sweet spices, that they
might come and anoint Him. 2. *And very early in the morning, the*
first day of the week, they came unto the sepulchre at the rising of the
sun. 3. *And they said among themselves, Who shall roll us away*
the stone from the door of the sepulchre? 4. *And when they looked,*
they saw that the stone was rolled away: for it was very
great. 5. *And entering into the sepulchre, they saw a young man*
sitting on the right side, clothed in a long white garment; and they
were affrighted. 6. *And he saith unto them, Be not affrighted: Ye*
seek Jesus of Nazareth, which was crucified: He is risen; He is not
here: behold the place where they laid Him. 7. *But go your way,*
tell his disciples and Peter that He goeth before you into Galilee:
there shall ye see Him, as He said unto you. 8. *And they went out*
quickly, and fled from the sepulchre; for they trembled and were
amazed: neither said they anything to any man; for they were
afraid. 9. *Now, when Jesus was risen early the first day of the*
week, He appeared first to Mary Magdalene, out of whom He had
cast seven devils. 10. *And she went and told them that had been*
with Him, as they mourned and wept. 11. *And they, when they*
had heard that He was alive, and had been seen of her, believed
not. 12. *After that He appeared in another form unto two of them,*
as they walked, and went into the country. 13. *And they went and*
told it unto the residue: neither believed they them. MARK
16:1–13.

It is not my business to discuss questions of harmonizing or of criticism. I have only to deal with the narrative as it stands. Its peculiar character is very plain. The manner in which the first disciples learned the fact of the Resurrection, and the disbelief with which they received it, much rather than the Resurrection itself, come into view in this section. The disciples, and not the risen Lord, are shown us. There is nothing here of the earthquake, or of the descending angel, or of the terrified guard, or of our Lord's appearance to the women. The two appearances to Mary Magdalene and to the travelers to Emmaus, which, in the hands of John and Luke, are so pathetic and rich, are here mentioned with the utmost brevity, for the sake chiefly of insisting on the disbelief of the disciples who heard of them. Mark's theme is mainly what they thought of the testimony to the Resurrection.

1. He shows us, first, bewildered love and sorrow. We leave the question whether this group of women is the same one as that of which Luke records that Joanna was one, as well as the other puzzle as to harmonizing the notes of time in the Evangelists. May not the difference between the time of starting and that of arrival solve some of the difficulty? When all the notes are more or less vague, and refer to the time of transition from dark to day, when every moment partakes of both and may be differently described as belonging to either, is precision to be expected? In the whirl of agitation of that morning, would anyone be at leisure to take much note of the exact minute? Are not these "discrepancies" much more valuable as confirmation of the story than precise accord would have been? It is better to try to understand the feelings of that little band than to carp at such trifles.

Sorrow wakes early, and love is impatient to bring its tribute. So we can see these three women, leaving their abode as soon as the doleful gray of morning permitted, stealing through the silent streets, and reaching the rock-cut tomb while the sun was rising over Olivet. Where were Salome's ambitious hopes for her two sons now? Dead, and buried in the Master's grave. The completeness of the women's despair, as well as the faithfulness of their love, is witnessed by their purpose. They had come to anoint the body of Him to whom in life they had ministered. They had no thought of a resurrection, plainly as they had been told of it. The waves of sorrow had washed the remembrance of His assurances on that subject clean out of their minds. Truth that is only half understood, however plainly spoken, is always forgotten when the time to apply it comes. We are told that the disbelief of the disciples in the Resurrection, after Christ's plain predictions of it, is "psychologically impossible." Such big words are imposing, but the objection is shallow. These disciples are not the only people who forgot in the hour of need the thing which it most concerned them to remember, and let the clouds of sorrow hide starry promises which would have turned mourning into dancing, and night into day. Christ's sayings about His resurrection were not understood in their, as it appears to us, obvious meaning when spoken. No wonder, then, that they were not expected to be fulfilled in their obvious meaning when He was dead. We shall have a word to say presently about the value of the fact that there was no anticipation of resurrection on the part of the disciples. For the present it is enough to note how these three loving souls confess their hopelessness by their errand. Did they not know, too, that Joseph and Nicodemus had been beforehand with them in their labor of love? Apparently not. It might easily happen, in the confusion and dispersion, that no knowledge of this had reached them; or perhaps sorrow and agitation had driven it out of their memories; or perhaps they felt that, whether others had done the same before or no, they must do it too, not because the loved form needed it, but because their hearts needed to do it. It was the love which must serve, not calculation of necessity, which loaded their hands with costly spices. The living Christ was pleased with the ''odor of a sweet smell,'' from the needless spices, meant to reanoint the dead Christ, and accepted the purpose, though it came from ignorance and was never carried out, since its deepest root was love, genuine, though bewildered.

The same absence of ''calm practical common sense'' is seen in the too late consideration, which never occurred to the three women till they were getting near the tomb, as to how to get into it. They do not seem to have heard of the guard; but they know that the stone is too heavy for them to move, and none of the men among the disciples had been taken into their confidence. ''Why did they not think of that before? what a want of foresight!'' says the cool observer. ''How beautifully true to nature!'' says a wiser judgment. To obey the impulse of love and sorrow without thinking, and then to be arrested on their road by a difficulty, which they might have thought of at first, but did not till they were close to it, is surely just what might have been expected of such mourners. Mark gives a graphic picture in that one word ''looking up,'' and follows it with picturesque present tenses. They had been looking down or at each other in perplexity, when they lifted their eyes to the tomb, which was possibly on an eminence. What a flash of wonder would pass through their minds when they saw it open! What that might signify they would be eager to hurry to find out; but, at all events, their difficulty was at an end. When love to Christ is brought to a stand in its venturous enterprises by difficulties occurring for the first time to the mind, it is well to go close up to them; and it often happens that when we do, and look steadily at them, we see that they are rolled away, and the passage cleared which we feared was hopelessly barred.

2. The calm herald of the Resurrection and the amazed hearers. Apparently Mary Magdalene had turned back as soon as she saw the opened tomb, and hurried to tell that the body had been carried off, as she supposed. The guard had also probably fled before this; and so the other two women enter the vestibule, and there find the angel. Sometimes one angel, sometimes two, sometimes none, were visible there. The variation in their numbers in the various narratives is not to be regarded as an instance of "discrepancy." Many angels hovered round the spot where the greatest wonder of the universe was to be seen, "eagerly desiring to look into" that grave. The beholder's eye may have determined their visibility. Their number may have fluctuated. Mark does not use the word "angel" at all, but leaves us to infer what manner of being he was who first proclaimed the Resurrection.

He tells of his youth, his attitude, and his attire. The angelic life is vigorous, progressive, buoyant, and alien from decay. Immortal youth belongs to them who "excel in strength," because they "do his commandments." That waiting minister shows us what the children of the Resurrection shall be, and so his presence as well as his speech expounds the blessed mystery of our life in the risen Lord. His serene attitude of sitting "on the right side" is not only a vivid touch of description, but is significant of restfulness and fixed contemplation, as well as of the calmness of a higher life. That still watcher knows too much to be agitated; but the less he is moved, the more he adores. His quiet contrasts with and heightens the impression of the storm of conflicting feelings in the women's tremulous natures. His garments symbolize purity and repose. How sharply the difference between heaven and earth is given in the last words of verse 5! They were "amazed," swept out of themselves in an ecstasy of bewilderment in which hope had no place. Terror, surprise, curiosity, wonder, blank incapacity to know what all this meant, made chaos in them.

The angel's words are a succession of short sentences, which have a certain dignity, and break up the astounding revelation he has to make into small pieces, which the women's bewildered minds can grasp. He calms their tumult of spirit. He shows them that he knows their errand. He adoringly names his Lord and theirs by the names recalling His manhood, His lowly home, and His ignominious death. He lingers on the thought, to him covering so profound a mystery of divine love, that his Lord had been born, had lived in the obscure village, and died on the Cross. Then, in one word, he proclaims the stupendous fact of His resurrection as His own act—"He is risen." This crown of all miracles, which brings life and immortality to light, and changes the whole outlook of humanity, which changes the Cross into victory, and without which Christianity is a dream and a ruin, is announced in a single word—the mightiest ever spoken save by Christ's own lips. It was fitting that angel lips should proclaim the Resurrection, as they did the Nativity, though in either "He taketh not hold of angels," and they had but a secondary share in the blessings. Yet that empty grave opened to ''principalities and powers in heavenly places'' a new unfolding of the manifold wisdom and love of God.

The angel—a true evangelist—does not linger on the wondrous intimation, but points to the vacant place, which would have been so dreary but for his previous words, and bids them approach to verify his assurance, and with reverent wonder to gaze on the hallowed and now happy spot. A moment is granted for feeling to overflow, and certainty to be attained, and then the women are sent on their errand. Even the joy of that gaze is not to be selfishly prolonged, while others are sitting in sorrow for want of what they know. That is the law for all the Christian life. First make sure work of one's own possession of the truth, and then hasten to tell it to those who need it.

''And Peter''—Mark alone gives us this. The other Evangelists might pass it by; but how could Peter ever forget the balm which that message of pardon and restoration brought to him, and how could Peter's mouthpiece leave it out? Is there anything in the Gospels more beautiful, or fuller of longsuffering and thoughtful love, than that message from the risen Saviour to the denier? And how delicate the love which, by calling him Peter, not Simon, reinstates him in his official position by anticipation, even though in the subsequent full restoration scene by the lake he is thrice called Simon, before the complete effacement of the triple denial by the triple confession!

Galilee is named as the rendezvous, and the word employed, ''goeth before you,'' is appropriate to the Shepherd in front of His flock. They had been ''scattered,'' but are to be drawn together again. He is to ''precede'' them there, thus lightly indicating the new form of their relations to Him, marked during the forty days by a distance which prepared for his final withdrawal. Galilee was the home of most of them, and had been the field of His most continuous labors. There would be many disciples there, who would gather to see their risen Lord (''five hundred at once''); and there, rather than in Jerusalem which had slain Him, was it fitting that He should show Himself to His friends. The appearances in Jerusalem were all within a week (if we except the Ascension), and the connection in which Mark introduces them (if verse 14 be his) seems to treat them as forced on Christ by the disciples' unbelief, rather than as His original intention. It looks as if He meant to show Himself in the city only to one or two, such as Mary, Peter, and some others, but to reserve His more public appearance for Galilee.

How did the women receive the message? Mark represents them as trembling in body and in an ecstasy in mind, and as hurrying away silent with terror. Matthew says that they were full of ''fear and great joy,'' and went in haste to tell the disciples. In the whirl of feeling, there were opposites blended or succeeding one another; and the one Evangelist lays hold of one set, and the other of the other. It is as impossible to catalogue the swift emotions of such a moment as to separate and tabulate the hues of sunrise. The silence which Mark tells of can only refer to their demeanor as they "fled." His object is to bring out the very imperfect credence which, at the best, was given to the testimony that Christ was risen, and to paint the tumult of feeling in the breasts of its first recipients. His picture is taken from a different angle from Matthew's; but Matthew's contains the same elements, for he speaks of "fear," though he completes it by "joy."

3. The incredulity of the disciples. The two appearances to Mary Magdalene and the travelers to Emmaus are introduced mainly to record the unbelief of the disciples. A strange choice that was, of the woman who had been rescued from so low a debasement, to be first to see Him! But her former degradation was the measure of her love. Longing eyes, that have been washed clean by many a tear of penitent gratitude, are purged to see Jesus; and a yearning heart ever brings Him near. The unbelief of the story of the two from Emmaus seems to conflict with Luke's account, which tells that they were met by the news of Christ's appearance to Simon. But the two statements are not contradictory. If we remember the excitement and confusion of mind in which they were, we shall not wonder if belief and unbelief followed each other, like the flow and recoil of the waves. One moment they were on the crest of the billows, and saw land ahead; the next they were down in the trough, and saw only the melancholy surge. The very fact that Peter was believed, might make them disbelieve the travelers; for how could Jesus have been in Jerusalem and Emmaus at so nearly the same time?

However the two narratives be reconciled, it remains obvious that the first disciples did not believe the first witnesses of the Resurrection, and that their unbelief is an important fact. It bears very distinctly on the worth of their subsequent conviction. It has special bearing on the most modern form of disbelief in the Resurrection, which accounts for the belief of the first disciples on the ground that they expected Christ to rise, and that they then persuaded themselves, in all good faith, that He had risen. That monstrous theory is vulnerable at all points, but one sufficient answer is—the disciples did not expect Christ to rise again, and were so far from it that they did not believe that He had risen when they were told it. Their original unbelief is a strong argument for the reliableness of their final faith. What raised them from the stupor of despair and incredulity? Only one answer is "psychologically" reasonable: they at last believed because they saw. It is incredible that they were conscious deceivers; for such lives as they lived, and such a Gospel as they preached, never came from liars. It is as incredible that they were unconsciously mistaken; for they were wholly unprepared for the Resurrection, and sturdily disbelieved all witnesses for it, till they saw with their own eyes, and had "many infallible proofs." Let us be thankful for their unbelief and its record, and let us seek to possess the blessing of those "that have not seen, and yet have believed!"

Perpetual Youth

And entering into the sepulchre, they saw a young man sitting on the right side, clothed in a long, white garment. MARK 16:5.

Many great truths concerning Christ's death, and its worth to higher orders of being, are taught by the presence of that angel form, clad in the whiteness of his own God-given purity, sitting in restful contemplation in the dark house where the body of Jesus had lain. "Which things the angels desire to look into." Many precious lessons of consolation and hope, too, lie in the wonderful words which he spake from his Lord and theirs to the weeping, waiting women. But to touch upon these ever so slightly would lead us too far from our more immediate purpose.

It strikes one as very remarkable that this superhuman being should be described as a "*young* man." Immortal youth, with all of buoyant energy and fresh power which that attribute suggests, belongs to those beings whom Scripture faintly shows as our elder brethren. No waste decays their strength, no change robs them of forces which have ceased to increase. For them there never comes a period when memory is more than hope. Age cannot wither them. As one of our modern mystics has said, hiding imaginative spiritualism under a crust of hard, dry matter-of-fact, "In heaven the oldest angels are the youngest."

What is true of them is true of God's children, who are "accounted worthy to obtain that world and the resurrection from the dead," for "they are equal unto the angels." For believing and loving souls, death too is a birth. All who pass through it to God, shall, in deeper meaning than lay in the words at first, "return unto the days of their youth"; and when the end comes, and they are "clothed with their house from heaven," they shall stand by the throne, like him who sat in the sepulchre, clothed with lustrous light and radiant with unchanging youth.

Such a conception of the condition of the dead in Christ may be followed out in detail into many very elevating and strengthening thoughts. Let me attempt to set forth some of these now.

1. The life of the faithful dead is eternal progress towards infinite perfection. For body and for spirit the life of earth is a definite whole, with distinct stages, which succeed each other in a well-marked order. There are youth, and maturity, and decay—the slow climbing to the narrow summit, a brief moment there in the streaming sunshine, and then a sure and gradual descent into the shadows beneath. The same equable and constant motion urges the orb of our lives from morning to noon, and from noon to evening. The glory of the dawning day, with its golden clouds and its dewy freshness, its new awakened hopes and its unworn vigor, climbs by silent, inevitable stages to the hot noon. But its ardors flame but for a moment; but for a moment does the sun poise itself on the meridian line, and the short shadow point to the pole. The inexorable revolution goes on, and in due time come the mists and dying purples of evening and the blackness of night. The same progress which brings April's perfumes burns them in the censer of the hot summer, and buries summer beneath the falling leaves, and covers its grave with winter's snow.

Everything that grows
Holds in perfection but a little moment.

So the life of man, being under the law of growth, is, in all its parts, subject to the consequent necessity of decline. And very swiftly does the direction change from ascending to descending. At first, and for a little while, the motion of the dancing stream, which broadens as it runs, and bears us past fields each brighter and more enameled with flowers than the one before it, is joyous; but the slow current becomes awful as we are swept along when we would fain moor and land—and to some of us it comes to be tragic and dreadful at last, as we sit helpless, and see the shore rush past and hear the roar of the falls in our ears, like some poor wretch caught in the glassy smoothness above Niagara, who has flung down the oars, and, clutching the gunwale with idle hands, sits effortless and breathless till the plunge comes. Many a despairing voice has prayed as the sands ran out, and joys fled, "Sun, stand thou still on Gibeon; and thou, Moon, in the valley of Ajalon," but in vain. Once the wish was answered; but, for all other fighters, the twelve hours of the day must suffice for victory and for joy. Time devours his own children. The morning hours come to us with full hands and give, the evening hours come with empty hands and take; so that at the last "naked shall he return to go as he came." Our earthly life runs through its successive stages, and for it, in body and mind, old age is the child of youth.

But the perfect life of the dead in Christ has but one phase, youth. It is growth without a limit and without decline. To say that they are ever young is the same thing as to say that their being never reaches its climax, that it is ever but entering on its glory; that is, as we have said, that the true conception of their life is that of eternal progress towards infinite perfection.

For what is the goal to which they tend? The likeness of God in Christ—all His wisdom, His love, His holiness. He is all theirs, and His whole perfection is to be transfused into their growing greatness. ''He is made unto them of God, wisdom, and righteousness, and salvation and redemption,'' nor can they cease to grow till they have outgrown Jesus and exhausted God. On the one hand is infinite perfection, destined to be imparted to the redeemed spirit. On the other hand is a capability of indefinite assimilation to, by reception of, that infinite perfection. We have no reason to set bounds to the possible expansion of the human spirit. If only there be fitting circumstances and an adequate impulse, it may have an endless growth. Such circumstances and such impulses are given in the loving presence of Christ in glory. Therefore we look for an eternal life which shall never reach a point beyond which no advance is possible. ''The path of the just'' in that higher state ''shineth more and more,'' and never touches the zenith. Here we float upon a landlocked lake, and on every side soon reach the bounding land; but there we are on a shoreless ocean, and never hear any voice that says, ''Hitherto shalt thou come, and no farther.'' Christ will be ever before us, the yet unattained end of our desires; Christ will be ever above us, fairer, wiser, holier, than we; after unsummed eternities of advance there will yet stretch before us a shining way that leads to Him. The language, which was often breathed by us on earth in tones of plaintive confession, will be spoken in heaven in gladness, ''Not as though I had attained, either were perfect, but I follow after.'' The promise that was spoken by Him in regard to our mortality will be repeated by Him in respect to our celestial being, ''I am come that they might have life, and that they might have it *more abundantly*.'' And as this advance has no natural limit, either in regard to our Pattern or to ourselves, there will be no reverse direction to ensue. Here the one process has its two opposite parts; the same impulse carries up to the summit and forces down from it. But it is not so then. There growth will never merge into decay, nor exacting hours come to recall the gifts, which their free-handed sisters gave.

They who live in Christ, beyond the grave, begin with a relative perfection. They are thereby rendered capable of more complete Christ-likeness. The eye, by gazing into the day, becomes more recipient of more light; the spirit cleaves closer to a Christ more fully apprehended and more deeply loved; the whole being, like a plant reaching up to the sunlight, grows by its yearning towards the light, and by the light towards which it yearns—lifts a stronger stem and spreads a broader leaf, and opens into immortal flowers tinted by the sunlight with its own colors. This blessed and eternal growth towards Him whom we possess, to begin with, and never can exhaust, is the perpetual youth of God's redeemed.

We ought not to think of those whom we have loved and lost as if they had gone, carrying with them declining powers, and still bearing the marks of this inevitable law of stagnation, and then of decay, under which they groaned here. Think of them rather as having, if they sleep in Jesus, reversed all this, as having carried with them, indeed, all the gifts of matured experience and ripened wisdom which the slow years bring, but likewise as having left behind all the weariness of accomplished aims, the monotony of a formed character, the rigidity of limbs that have ceased to grow. Think of them as receiving again from the hands of Christ much of which they were robbed by the lapse of years. Think of them as then crowned with lovingkindness and satisfied with good, so that "their youth is renewed like the eagle's." Think of them as again joyous, with the joy of beginning a career, which has no term but the sum of all perfection in the likeness of the infinite God. They rise like the songbird, aspiring to the heavens, circling round, and ever higher, which "singing still doth soar, and soaring ever singeth"—up and up through the steadfast blue to the sun! "Even the youths shall faint and be weary, and the young men shall utterly fall; but they that wait upon the Lord shall renew their strength." They shall lose the marks of age as they grow in eternity, and they who have stood before the throne the longest shall be likest him who sat in the sepulchre young with immortal strength, radiant with unwithering beauty.

2. The life of the faithful dead recovers and retains the best characteristics of youth. Each stage of our earthly course has its own peculiar characteristics, as each zone of the world has its own vegetation and animal life. And, for the most part, these characteristics cannot be anticipated in the preceding stage, nor prolonged into the succeeding. To some small extent they will bear transplanting, and he is nearest a perfect man who carries into each period of his life some trace of the special beauty of that which went before, making "the child the father of the man," and carrying deep into old age the simple self-forgetfulness of the child and the energy of the youth. But this can only be partially done by any effort; and even those whose happily constituted temperaments make it comparatively easy for them, do often carry the weakness rather than the strength of the earlier into the later epochs. It is easier to be always childish than to be always childlike. The immaturity and heedlessness of youth bear carriage better than the more precious vintages of that sunny land—its freshness of eye and heart, its openness of mind, its energy of hand. Even when these are in any measure retained—beautiful as they are in old age—they are but too apt to be associated with an absence of the excellences more proper to the later stages of life, and to involve a want of patient judgment, of sagacious discrimination, of rooted affections, of prudent, persistent action. Beautiful indeed it is when the grace of the child and the strength of the young man live on in the fathers, and when the last of life encloses all that was good in all that went before. But miserable it is, and quite as frequent a case, when gray hairs cover a childish brain, and an aged heart throbs with the feverish passion of youthful blood. So for this life it is difficult, and often not well, that youth should be prolonged into manhood and old age.

But the thought is none the less true, that the perfection of our being requires the reappearance and the continuance of all that was good in each successive stage of it in the past. The brightest aspects of youth will return to all who live in Jesus, beyond the grave, and will be theirs for ever. Such a consideration branches out into many happy anticipations, which we can but very cursorily touch on here.

For instance—Youth is the time for hope. The world then lies all before us, fair and untried. We have not learned our own weakness by many failures, nor the dread possibilities that lie in every future. The past is too brief to occupy us long, and its furthest point too near to be clothed in the airy purple, which draws the eye and stirs the heart. We are conscious of increasing powers which crave for occupation. It seems impossible but that success and joy shall be ours. So we live for a little while in a golden haze; we look down from our peak upon the virgin forests of a new world, that roll away to the shining waters in the west, and then we plunge into their mazes to hew out a path for ourselves, to slay the wild beasts, and to find and conquer rich lands. But soon we discover what hard work the march is, and what monsters lurk in the leafy coverts, and what diseases hover among the marshes, and how short a distance ahead we can see, and how far off it is to the treasure cities that we dreamed of; and if at last we gain some cleared spot whence we can look forward, our weary eyes are searching at most for a place to rest, and all our hopes have dwindled to hopes of safety and repose. The day brings too much toil to leave us leisure for much anticipation. The journey has had too many failures, too many wounds, too many of our comrades left to die in the forest glades, to allow of our expecting much. We plod on, sometimes ready to faint, sometimes with lighter hearts, but not any more winged by hope as in the golden prime—unless indeed for those of us who have fixed our hopes on God, and so get through the march better, because, be it rough or smooth, long or short, He moves before us to guide, and all our ways lead to Him. But even for these there comes, before very long, a time when they are weary of hoping for much more here, and when the light of youth fades into common day. Be it so! They will get the faculty and the use of it back again in far nobler fashion, when death has taken them away from all that is transient, and faith has through death given for their possession and their expectation, the certitudes of eternity. It will be worthwhile to look forward again, when we are again standing at the beginning of a life. It will be possible once more to hope, when disappointments are all past. A boundless future stretching before us, of which we know that it is all blessed, and that we shall reach all its blessedness, will give back to hearts that have long ceased to drink of the delusive cup which earthly hope offered to their lips, the joy of living in a present, made bright by the certain anticipation of a yet brighter future. Losing nothing by our constant progress, and certain to gain all which we foresee, we shall remember and be glad, we shall hope and be confident. With "the past unsighed for, and the future sure," we shall have that magic gift, which earth's disappointments dulled, quickened by the sure mercies of the heavens.

Again, youth has mostly a certain keenness of relish for life which vanishes only too soon. There are plenty of our young men and women too, of this day, no doubt, who are as *blasé* and wearied before they are out of their teens as if they were fifty. So much the sadder for them, so much the worse for the social state which breeds such monsters. For monsters they are: there ought to be in youth a sense of fresh wonder undimmed by familiarity, the absence of satiety, a joy in joyful things because they are new as well as gladsome. The poignancy of these early delights cannot long survive. Custom stales them all, and wraps everything in its robe of ashen gray. We get used to what was once so fresh and wonderful, and do not care very much about anything any more. We smile pitying smiles—sadder than any tears—at "boyish enthusiasm," and sometimes plume ourselves on having come to "years which bring the philosophic mind"; and all the while we know that we have lost a great gift, which here can never come back any more.

But what if that eager freshness of delight may yet be ours once again? What if the eternal youth of the heavens means, among other things, that *there* are pleasures which always satisfy but never cloy? What if, in perpetual advance, we find and keep forever that ever new gladness, which here we vainly seek in perpetual distraction? What if constant new influxes of divine blessedness, and constant new visions of God, keep in constant exercise that sense of wonder, which makes so great a part of the power of youth? What if, after all that we have learned and all that we have received, we still have to say, "It doth not yet appear what we shall be"? Then, I think, in a very profound and blessed sense, heaven would be perpetual youth.

I need not pause to speak of other characteristics of that period of life—such as its enthusiasm, its life by impulse rather than by reason, its buoyant energy and delight in action. All these gifts, so little cared for when possessed, so often misused, so irrevocably gone with a few brief years, so bitterly bewailed, will surely be found again, where God keeps all the treasures that He gives and we let fall. For transient enthusiasm, heaven will give us back a fervor of love like that of the seraphs, that have burned before His throne unconsumed and undecaying for unknown ages. For a life of instinctive impulse, we shall then receive a life in which impulse is ever parallel with the highest law, and, doing only what we would, we shall do only what we ought. For energy which wanes as the years wax, and delight in action which is soon worn down into mechanical routine of toil, there will be bestowed strength akin to His "who fainteth not, neither is weary." All of which maturity and old age robbed us is given back in nobler form. All the limitation and weakness which they brought, the coldness, the monotony, the torpor, the weariness, will drop away. But we shall keep all the precious things which they brought us. None of the calm wisdom, the ripened knowledge, the full-summed experience, the powers of service acquired in life's long apprenticeship, will be taken from us.

All will be changed indeed. All will be cleansed of the impurity which attaches to all. All will be accepted and crowned, not by reason of its goodness, but by reason of Christ's sacrifice, which is the channel of God's mercy. Though in themselves unworthy, and having nothing fit for the heavens, yet the souls that trust in Jesus, the Lord of Life, shall bear into their glory the characters which by His grace they wrought out here on earth, transfigured and perfected, but still the same. And to make up that full-summed completeness, will be given to them at once the perfection of all the various stages through which they passed on earth. The perfect man in the heavens will include the graces of childhood, the energies of youth, the steadfastness of manhood, the calmness of old age; as on some tropical trees, blooming in more fertile soil and quickened by a hotter sun than ours, you may see at once bud, blossom, and fruit—the expectancy of spring, and the maturing promise of summer, and the fulfilled fruition of autumn—hanging together on the unexhausted bough.

3. The faithful dead shall live in a body that cannot grow old. Scripture assures us, I believe, that the dead in Christ are now in full, conscious enjoyment of His presence, and of all the blessedness that to dwell in Christ can bring to a spirit. All, then, which we have been saying applies to the present condition of those who sleep in Jesus. As concerning toil and trouble they take rest in sleep, as concerning contact with an outer world they slumber untroubled by its noise; but as concerning their communion with their Lord they, like us, "whether we wake or sleep, live together with Him." But we know too, from Scripture, that the dead in Christ wait for the resurrection of the body, without which they cannot be perfected, nor restored to full activity of outward life in connection with an external creation.

The lesson which we venture to draw from this text enforces the familiar teaching of Scripture as to that body of glory—that it cannot decay, nor grow old. In this respect, too, eternal youth may be ours. Here we have a bodily organization which, like all other living bodies, goes through its appointed series of changes, wastes in effort, and so needs reparation by food and rest, dies in growing, and finally waxes old and dissolves. In such a house, a man cannot be ever young. The dim eye and shaking hand, the wrinkled face and thin gray hairs cannot but age the spirit, since they weaken its instruments.

If the redeemed of the Lord are to be always young in spirit, they must have a body which knows no weariness, which needs no repose, which has no necessity of dying impressed upon it. And such a body Scripture plainly tells us will belong to those who are Christ's, at His coming. Our present acquaintance with the conditions of life makes that great promise seem impossible to many learned men amongst us. And I know not that anything but acquaintance with the sure word of God and with a risen Lord will make that seeming impossibility again a great promise for us. If we believe it at all, I think we must believe it because the resurrection of Jesus Christ says so, and because the Scriptures put it into articulate words as the promise of His resurrection. "Ye do err," said Christ long ago, to those who denied a resurrection, "not knowing the Scriptures nor the power of God." Then knowledge of the Scriptures leads to belief in the resurrection of the dead, and the remembrance of our ignorance of the power of God disposes of all the doubts which are raised on the supposition that His present works are the pattern of His future ones, or the limits of His unexhausted energy.

We are content then to fall back on Scripture words, and to believe in the resurrection of the dead simply because it is, as we believe, told us from God.

For all who accept the message, this hope shines clear, of a *building* of God imperishable and solid, when contrasted with the *tent* in which we dwell here—of a body "raised in incorruption," "clothed with immortality," and so, as in many another phrase, declared to be exempt from decay, and therefore vigorous with unchanging youth. How that comes we cannot tell. Whether because that body of glory has no proclivity to mutation and decay, or whether the perpetual volition and power of God counteract such tendency and give, as the Book of Revelation says, "to eat of the tree of life which is in the midst of the paradise of God"—matters not at all. The truth of the promise remains, though we have no means of knowing more than the fact, that we shall receive a body, fashioned like His who dieth no more. There shall be no weariness nor consequent need for repose—"they rest not day nor night." There shall be no faintness nor consequent craving for sustenance—"they shall hunger no more neither thirst any more." There shall be no disease—"the inhabitant thereof shall no more say, I am sick," "neither can they die any more, for they are equal unto the angels."

And if all this is true, that glorious and undecaying body will then be the equal and fit instrument of the perfected spirit, not, as it is now, the adequate instrument only of the natural life. The deepest emotions then will be capable of expression, nor as now, like some rushing tide, choke the floodgates through whose narrow aperture they try to press, and be all tossed into foam in the attempt. We shall then seem what we are, as we shall also be what we ought. All outward things will then be fully and clearly communicated to the spirit, for that glorious body will be a perfect instrument of knowledge. All that we desire to do we shall then do, nor be longer tortured with tremulous hands which can never draw the perfect circle that we plan, and stammering lips that will not obey the heart, and throbbing brain that *will* ache when we would have it clear. The ever-young spirit will have for true yokefellow a body that cannot tire, nor grow old, nor die.

The aged saints of God shall rise then in youthful beauty. More than the long-vanished comeliness shall on that day rest on faces that were haggard with anxiety, and pinched with penury and years. There will be no more palsied hands, no more scattered gray hairs, no more dim and horny eyes, no more stiffened muscles and slow throbbing hearts. "It is sown in weakness, it is raised in power." It is sown in decaying old age, it is raised in immortal youth. His servants shall stand in that day among "the young-eyed cherubim," and be like them forever. So we may think of the dead in Christ.

But do not forget that Christian faith may largely do for us here what God's grace and power will do for us in heaven, and that even now we may possess much of this great gift of perpetual youth. If we live for Christ by faith in Him, then may we carry with us all our days the energy, the hope, the joy of the morning tide, and be children in evil while men in understanding. With unworn and fresh heart we may "bring forth fruit in old age,'' and have the crocus in the autumnal fields as well as in the springtime of our lives. So blessed, we may pass to a peaceful end, because we hold His hand who makes the path smooth and the heart quiet. Trust yourselves, my brethren, to the immortal love and perfect work of the Divine Saviour, and by His dear might your days will advance by peaceful stages, whereof each gathers up and carries forward the blessings of all that went before, to a death which shall be a birth. Its chill waters will be as a fountain of youth from which you will rise, beautiful and strong, to begin an immortality of growing power. A Christian life on earth solves partly, a Christian life in heaven solves completely, the problem of perpetual youth. For those who die in His faith and fear, ''better is the end than the beginning, and the day of one's death than the day of one's birth.'' Christ keeps the good wine until the close of the feast.

Such is Thy banquet, dearest Lord;
O give us grace, to cast
Our lot with Thine, to trust Thy word,
And keep our best till last.

The Angel in the Tomb

. . . They saw a young man sitting on the right side, clothed in a long white garment; and they were affrighted. 6. And he saith unto them, Be not affrighted. Ye seek Jesus of Nazareth, which was crucified: He is risen; He is not here: behold the place where they laid Him. MARK 16:5, 6.

Each of the four Evangelists tells the story of the Resurrection from his own special point of view. None of them has any record of the actual fact, because no eye saw it. Before the earthquake and the angelic descent, before the stone was rolled away, while the guards perhaps slept, and before Love and Sorrow had awakened, Christ rose. And deep silence covers the event. But in treating of the subsequent portion of the narrative, each Evangelist stands at his own point of view. Mark has scarcely anything to say about our Lord's appearance after the Resurrection. His object seems mainly to be to describe rather the manner in which the report of the Resurrection affected the disciples, and so he makes prominent the bewildered astonishment of the women. If the latter part of this chapter be his, he passes by the appearance of our Lord to Mary Magdalene and to the two travelers to Emmaus with just a word for each—contrasting singularly with the lovely narrative of the former in John's Gospel and with the detailed account of the latter in Luke's. He emphasizes the incredulity of the Twelve after receiving the reports, and in like manner he lays stress upon the unbelief and hardness of heart which the Lord rebuked.

So, then, this incident, the appearance of the angel, the portion of his message to the women which we have read, and the way in which the first testimony to the Resurrection affected its hearers, may suggest to us some thoughts which, though subsidiary to the main teaching of the Resurrection, may yet be important in their place.

1. Note the first witness to the Resurrection. There are singular diversities in the four Gospels in their accounts of the angelic appearances, the number, occupation, and attitude of these superhuman persons, and contradictions may be spun, if one is so disposed, out of these varieties. But it is wiser to take another view of them, and to see in the varying reports, sometimes of one angel, sometimes of two, sometimes of one sitting outside the sepulchre, sometimes one within, sometimes none, either different moments of time or differences produced by the different spiritual condition of the beholders. Who can count the glancing wings of the white-winged flock of seabirds as they sail and turn in the sunshine? Who can count the numbers of these "bright-harnessed angels," sometimes more, sometimes less, flickering and fluttering into and out of sight, which shone upon the vision of the weeping onlookers? We know too little about the laws of angelic appearances; we know too little about the relation in that high region between the seeing eye and the objects beheld to venture to say that there is contradiction where the narratives present variety. Enough for us to draw the lessons that are suggested by that quiet figure sitting there in the inner vestibule of the grave, the stone rolled away and the work done, gazing on the tomb where the Lord of men and angels had lain.

He was a youth. "The oldest angels are the youngest", says a great mystic. The angels "excel in strength" because they "delight to do His commandments, hearkening unto the voice of His word." The lapse of ages brings not age to them who "wait on the Lord" in the higher ministries of heaven, and run unwearied, and walk unfainting, and when they are seen by men are radiant with immortal youth. He was "clothed in a long white garment," the sign at once of purity and of repose; and he was sitting in rapt contemplation and quiet adoration there, where the body of Jesus had lain.

But what had he to do with the joy of Resurrection? It delivered *him* from no fears, it brought to him no fresh assurance of a life which was always his. Wherefore was he there? Because that Cross strikes its power upwards as well as downwards; because He that had lain there is the Head of all creation, and the Lord of angels as well as of men; because that Resurrection following upon that Cross, ''unto the principalities and powers in heavenly places,'' opened a new and wonderful door into the unsounded and unfathomed abyss of divine love; because into these things ''angels desire to look,'' and looking, are smitten with adoring wonder and flushed with the illumination of a new knowledge of what God is, and of what man is to God. The Resurrection of the Prince of Life was no mystery to the angel. To him the mystery was in His death. To us the death is not a mystery, but the Resurrection is. That gazing figure looks from the other side upon the grave which we contemplate from this side of the gulf of death; but the eyes of both orders of Being fix upon the same hallowed spot—they in adoring wonder that there a God should have lain; we in lowly thankfulness that thence a man should have risen.

Further, we see in that angel presence not only the indication that Christ is his King as well as ours, but also the mark of his and all his fellows' sympathetic participation in whatsoever is of so deep interest to humanity. There is a certain tone of friendship and oneness in his words. The trembling women were smitten into an ecstasy of bewildered fear (as one of the words, ''affrighted,'' might more accurately be rendered), and his consolation to them, ''Be not affrighted, ye seek Jesus,'' suggests that, in all the great sweep of the unseen universe, whatsoever beings may people that to us apparently waste and solitary space, howsoever many they may be, ''thick as the autumn leaves in Vallambrosa,'' or as the motes that dance in the sunshine, they are all friends and allies and elder brethren of those who seek for Jesus with a loving heart. No creature that owns His sway can touch or injure or need terrify the soul that follows after Christ. ''All the servants of our King in heaven and earth are one,'' and He sends forth His brightest and loftiest to be brethren and ministers to them who shall be ''heirs of salvation.'' So we may pass through the darkest spaces of the universe and the loveliest valleys of the shadow of death, sure that whosoever may be there will be our friend if we are the friends of Christ.

2. Note, secondly, the triumphant light cast upon the cradle and the Cross. There is something very remarkable, because for purposes of identification plainly unnecessary, in the minute particularity of the designation which the angel lips give to Jesus Christ. ''Jesus, the Nazarene, who was crucified.'' Do you not catch a tone of wonder and a tone of triumph in this threefold particularizing of the humanity, the lowly residence, and the ignominious death? All that lowliness, suffering, and shame are brought into comparison with the rising from the dead. That is to say, when we grasp the fact of a risen Christ, we look back upon all the story of His birth, His lowly life, His death of shame, and see a new meaning in it, and new reasons for triumph and for wonder. The cradle is illuminated by the grave, the Cross by the empty sepulchre. As at the beginning there is a supernatural entrance into life, so at the end there is a supernatural resumption of it. The birth corresponds with the resurrection, and both witness to the divinity. The lowly life culminates in the conquest over death; the Nazarene despised, rejected, dwelling in a place that was a byword, sharing all the modest lowliness and self-respecting poverty of the Galilean peasants, has conquered death. The Man that was crucified has conquered death. And the fact that He has risen explains and illuminates the fact that He died.

Brethren, let us lay this to heart, that unless we believe in the Resurrection of Jesus Christ, the saying ''He was crucified'' is the saddest word that can be spoken about any of the great ones of the past. If Jesus Christ be lying in some nameless grave, then all the power of His death is gone, and He and it are nothing to me, or to you, or to any of our fellow men, more than a thousand deaths of the mighty ones of old. But Easter day transfigures the gloom of the day of the Crucifixion, and the rising sun of its morning gilds and explains the Cross. Now it stands forth as the great redeeming power of the world, where my sins and yours and the whole world's have been expiated and done away. And now, instead of being ignominy, it is glory, and instead of being defeat it is victory, and instead of looking upon that death as the lowest point of the Master's humiliation, we may look upon it as He Himself did, as the highest point of His glorifying. For the Cross then becomes His great means of winning men to Himself, and the very throne of His power. On the historical fact of a Resurrection depend all the worth and meaning of the death of Christ. ''If He be not risen our preaching is vain, and your faith is also vain.'' ''If Christ be not risen, ye are yet in your sins.'' But if what this day commemorates be true, then upon all His earthly life is thrown a new light; and we first understand the Cross when we look upon the empty grave.

3. Again, notice here the majestic announcement of the great fact, and its confirmation. ''He is risen; He is not here.'' The first preacher of the Resurrection was an angel, a true ev-angel-ist. His message is conveyed in these brief sentences, unconnected with each other, in token, not of abruptness and haste, but of solemnity. ''He is risen'' is one word in the original—a sentence of one word, which announces the mightiest miracle that ever was wrought upon earth, a miracle which opens the door wide enough for all supernatural events recorded of Jesus Christ to find an entrance to the understanding and the reason.

"He is risen." The Resurrection of Jesus Christ is declared by angel lips to be His own act; not, indeed, as if He were acting separately from the Father, but still less as if in it He were merely passive. Think of that; a dead Christ raised Himself. That is the teaching of the Scripture. I do not dwell here, at this stage of my sermon, on the many issues that spring from such a conception, but this only I urge, Jesus Christ was the Lord of life; held life and death, His own and others', at His beck and will. His death was voluntary; He was not passive in it, but He died because He chose. His resurrection was His act; He rose because He willed. "I have power to lay it down, I have power to take it again." No one said to Him, "I say unto Thee, arise!" The divine power of the Father's will did not work upon Him as from without to raise Him from the dead; but He, the embodiment of divinity, raised Himself, even though it is also true that He was raised from the dead by the glory of the Father. These two statements are not contradictory, but the former of them can only be predicated of Him; and it sets Him on a pedestal immeasurably above, and infinitely apart from, all those to whom life is communicated by a divine act. He Himself is "the Life," and it was not possible that Life should be holden of Death; therefore He burst its bonds, and, like the ancient Jewish hero, though in far nobler fashion, our Samson enters into the city which is a prison, and on His strong shoulders bears away the gates, that none may ever there be prisoners without hope.

Now, then, note the confirmation of this stupendous fact. "He is risen; He is not here." The grave was empty, and the trembling women were called upon to look and see for themselves that the body was not there. One remark is all that I wish to make about this matter—viz. this, all theories, ancient or modern, which deny the Resurrection, are shattered by this one question, What became of Jesus Christ's body? We take it as a plain historical fact, which the extremest skepticism has never ventured to deny, that the grave of Christ was empty. The trumped-up story of the guards sufficiently shows that. When the belief of a resurrection began to be spread abroad, what would have been easier for Pharisees and rulers than to have gone to the sepulchre and rolled back the stone, and said, "Look there! there is your risen Man, lying moldering, like all the rest of us." They did not do it. Why? Because the grave was empty. Where was the body? They had it not, else they would have been glad to produce it. The disciples had it not, for if they had, you come back to the discredited and impossible theory that, having it, and knowing that they were telling lies, they got up the story of the Resurrection. Nobody believes that nowadays—nobody can believe it who looks at the results of the preaching of this, by hypothesis, falsehood. "Men do not gather grapes of thorns, nor figs of thistles." And whether the disciples were right or wrong, there can be no question in the mind of anybody who is not prepared to swallow impossibilities compared to which miracles are easy, that the first disciples heartily believed that Jesus Christ was risen from the dead. As I say, one confirmation of the belief lies in the empty grave, and this question may be put to anybody that says "I do not believe in your Resurrection": "What became of the sacred body of Jesus Christ?"

Now, note the way in which the announcement of this tremendous fact was received. With blank bewilderment and terror on the part of these women, followed by incredulity on the part of the Apostles and of the other disciples. These things are on the surface of the narrative, and very important they are. They plainly tell us that the first hearers did not believe the testimony which they themselves call upon us to believe. And, that being the state of mind of the early disciples in the Resurrection day, what becomes of the modern theory, which seeks to explain the fact of the early belief in the Resurrection by saying, "Oh, they had worked themselves into such a fever of expectation that Jesus Christ would rise from the dead that the wish was father to the thought, and they said that He did because they expected that He would"? No! they did not expect that He would; it was the very last thing that they expected. They had not in their minds the soil out of which such imaginations would grow. They were perfectly unprepared to believe it, and, as a matter of fact, they did not believe until they had seen. So I think that that one fact disposes of a great deal of pestilent and shallow talk in these days that tries to deny the Resurrection and to save the character of the men that witnessed it.

4. And now, lastly, note here the summons to grateful contemplation. "Behold the place where they laid Him." To these women the call was simply one to come and see what would confirm the witness. But we may, perhaps, permissibly turn it to a wider purpose, and say that it summons us all to thankful, lowly, believing, glad contemplation of that empty grave as the basis of all our hopes. Look upon it and upon the Resurrection which it confirms to us as an historical fact. It sets the seal of the divine approval on Christ's work, and declares the divinity of His person and the all-sufficiency of His mighty sacrifice. Therefore let us, laden with our sins and seeking for reconciliation with God, and knowing how impossible it is for us to bring an atonement or a ransom for ourselves, look upon that grave and learn that Christ has offered the sacrifice which God has accepted, and with which He is well pleased.

"Behold the place where they laid Him," and, looking upon it, let us think of that Resurrection as a prophecy, with a bearing upon us and upon all the dear ones that have trod the common road into the great darkness. Christ has died, therefore they live; Christ lives, therefore we shall never die. His grave was in a garden—a garden indeed. The yearly miracle of the returning "life reorient out of dust," typifies the mightier miracle which He works for all that trust in Him, when out of death He leads them into life. The graveyard has become "God's acre"; the garden in which the seed sown in weakness is to be raised in power, and sown corruptible is to be raised in incorruption.

"Behold the place where they laid Him," and in the empty grave read the mystery of the Resurrection as the pattern and the symbol of our higher life; that, "like as Christ was raised from the dead by the glory of the Father, even so we also should walk in newness of life." Oh to partake more and more of that power of His Resurrection!

In Christ's empty grave is planted the true "tree of life, which is in the midst of the 'true' Paradise of God." And we, if we truly trust and humbly love that Lord, shall partake of its fruits, and shall one day share the glories of His risen life in the heavens, even as we share the power of it here and now.

Love's Triumph Over Sin

Tell His disciples and Peter that He goeth before you into Galilee. MARK 16:7.

The prevailing tradition of Christian antiquity ascribes this Gospel to John Mark, sister's son to Barnabas, and affirms that in composing it he was in some sense the "interpreter" of the Apostle Peter. Some confirmation of this alleged connection between the Evangelist and the Apostle may be gathered from the fact that the former is mentioned by the latter as with him when he wrote his First Epistle. And, in the Gospel itself, there are some little peculiarities which seem to look in the same direction. A certain speciality is traceable here and there, both in omissions of incidents in the Apostle's life recorded by some of the other Evangelists, and in the addition of slight facts concerning him unnoticed by them.

Chief among these is the place which his name holds in this very remarkable message, delivered by the angels to the women who came to Christ's tomb on the Resurrection morning. Matthew, who also reports the angels' words, has only "tell His disciples." Mark adds the words, which must have come like wine and oil to the bruised heart of the denier, "tell His disciples *and Peter.*" To the others, it was of little importance that his name should have been named then; to him it was life from the dead, that he should have been singled out to receive a word of forgiveness and a summons to meet his Lord; as if He had said through His angel messengers—"I would see them all; but whoever may stay behind, let not *him* be absent from our glad meeting again."

We find, too, that the same individualizing of the Apostle, which led to his being thus greeted in the first thoughts of his risen Lord, led also to an interview with Him on that same day, about which not a syllable of detail is found in any Gospel, though the fact was known to the whole body of the disciples. For when the two friends who had met Christ at Emmaus came back in the night with their strange tidings, their eagerness to tell their joyful news is anticipated by the eagerness of the brethren to tell *their* wonderful story: "The Lord is risen indeed, and hath appeared to Simon." Paul, too, gives that meeting, when the Lord was alone with the penitent, the foremost place in his list of the evidences of Christ's resurrection, "He was seen of Cephas." What passed then is hidden from all eyes. The secrets of that hour of deep contrition and healing love Peter kept secretly curtained from sight, in the innermost chamber of his memory. But we may be sure that then forgiveness was sought and granted, and the bond that fastened him to his Lord was welded together again, where it had snapped, and was the stronger because it had been broken, and at the point of fracture.

The man must be first reunited to his Saviour, before the Apostle can be reinstated in his functions. In secrecy, not beheld by any, is the personal act of restoration to love and friendship effected; and then in public, before his brethren, who were concerned in his official position, but not in his personal relation to his Lord, the reappointment of the pardoned disciple to his apostleship takes place. His sin had had a public aspect, and his threefold denial must, in so far as it was an outward act, be effaced by his threefold confession. Then he becomes again "Peter"—not merely "Simon Bar Jonas"; and, as the Book of the Acts shows, never ceases to hear the divine commissions, "Feed My sheep," "Follow Me"; nor ever forgets the lessons he had learned in these bitter hours of self-loathing, and in the rapturous moments when again he saw his Lord.

Putting all these things together—this message from Christ, the interview which followed it, and the subsequent history of the Apostle—we have a connected series of facts which may illustrate for us, better than many dry words of mine could do, the triumph over sin of the forgiving love of Christ.

1. Notice, then, first, the loving message with which He beckons the wanderer back. If we try to throw ourselves back into the Apostle's black thoughts during the interval between his denial and the Resurrection morning, we shall better feel what this love-token from the grave must have been to him. His natural character, as well as his real love for his Master, ensured that his lies could not long content him. They were uttered so vehemently because they were uttered in spite of inward resistance. Overpowered by fear, beaten down from all his vainglorious self-confidence by a womanservant's sharp tongue and mocking eye, he lied—and then came the rebound. The same impulsive vehemence which had hurried him into the fault, would swing him back again to quick penitence when the cock crew, and that Divine Face, turning slowly from before the judgment seat with the sorrow of wounded love upon it, silently said, "Remember." We can fancy how that bitter weeping, which began so soon, grew more passionate and more bitter when the end came. We are singularly happy if we do not know the pang of remembering some fault to the loved dead—some hasty word, some momentary petulance, some selfish disregard of their happiness, some sullen refusal of their tenderness. How the thought that it is all irrevocable now embitters the remorse! How passionately we long that we could have one of the moments again, which seemed so trivial while we possessed them, that we might confess and be forgiven, and atone! And this poor, warm-hearted, penitent denier had to think that his very last act to the Lord whom he loved so well had been such an act of cowardly shrinking from acknowledging Him; and that henceforward his memory of that dear face was to be forever saddened by that last look! That they should have parted so! that that sad gaze was to be the last he should ever have, and that *it* was to haunt him for the rest of his life! We can understand how heavily the hours passed on that dreary Saturday. If, as seems probable, he was with John in his home, whither the latter had led the mother of our Lord, what a group were gathered there, each with a separate pang from the common sorrow!

Into this sorrow come the tidings that all was not over, that the irrevocable was not irrevocable, that perhaps new days of loyal love might still be granted, in which the doleful failure of the past might be forgotten; and then, whether before or after his hurried rush to the grave we need not here stay to inquire, follows the message of our text, a word of forgiveness and reconciliation, sent by the Lord as the herald and outrider of His own coming, to bring gladness and hope ere He Himself draws near.

Think of this message as a revelation of love that is stronger than death.

The news of Christ's resurrection must have struck awe, but not necessarily joy, into the disciples' hearts. The dearest ones suffer so solemn a change to our apprehensions when they pass into the grave, that to many a man it would be maddening terror to meet those whom he loved and still loves. So there must have been a spasm of fear even among Christ's friends when they heard of Him as risen again, and much confusing doubt as to what would be the amount of resemblance to His old self. They probably dreaded to find Him far removed from their familiar love, forgetful perhaps of much of the old life, with other thoughts than before, with the atmosphere of the other world round about Him, which glorified Him indeed, but separated Him too from those whose grosser lungs could live only in this thick air. These words of our text would go far to scatter all such fears. They link on the future to the past, as if His first thought when He rose had been to gather up again the dropped threads of their intercourse, and to carry on their ancient concord and companionship as though no break had been at all. For all the disciples, and especially for him who is especially named, they confirm the identity of Christ's whole disposition towards them now, with those which He had before. Death has not changed Him at all. Much has been done since He left them; the world's history has been changed, but nothing which has happened has had any effect on the reality of His love, and on the inmost reality of their companionship. In these respects they are where they were, and even Calvary and the tomb are but as a parenthesis. The old bonds are all reknit, and the junction is all but imperceptible.

This is how we have to think of our Lord now, in His attitude towards us. We, too, may have our share in that message, which came like morning twilight before He shone upon the apostles' darkness. To them it proclaimed a love which was stronger than death. To us it may declare a love which is stronger than all change of circumstances. He is no more parted from us by the Throne than from them by the Cross. He descended into "the lower parts of the earth," and His love lived on, and so it does now, when He has "ascended up far above all heavens." Love knows no difference of place, conditions, or functions. From out of the blazing heart of the Glory the same tender face looks that bent over sick men's pallets, and that turned on Peter in the judgment hall. The hand that holds the scepter of the universe is the hand that was nailed to the Cross, and that was stretched out to that same Peter when he was ready to sink. The breast that is girt with the golden girdle of priestly sovereignty is the same tender home on which John's happy head rested in placid contentment. All the love that ever flowed from Christ flows from Him still. To Him, "whose nature and whose name are Love," it matters nothing whether He is in the house at Bethany, or in the upper room, or hanging on the Cross, or lying in the grave, or risen from the dead, or seated on the right hand of God. He is the same everywhere and always. "I have loved thee with an everlasting love."

Again, this message is the revelation of a love that is not turned away by our sinful changes.

Peter may have thought that he had, with his own words, broken the bond between him and his Lord. He had renounced his allegiance; was the renunciation to be accepted? He had said, "I am not one of them"; did Christ answer, "Be it so; one of them thou shalt no more be"? The message from the women's lips settled the question, and let him feel that, though his grasp of Christ had relaxed, Christ's grasp of him had not. He might change, he might cease for a time to prize his Lord's love, he might cease either to be conscious of it or to wish for it; but that love could not change. It was unaffected by his unfaithfulness, even as it had not been originated by his fidelity. Repelled, it still lingered beside him. Disowned, it still asserted its property in him. Being reviled, it blessed; being persecuted, it endued; being defamed, it entreated; and, patient through all wrongs and changes, it loved on till it had won back the erring heart, and could fill it with the old blessedness again.

And is not that same miracle of long-enduring love presented before every one of us, as in Christ's heart for us? True, our sin interferes with our sense of it, and modifies the form in which it must deal with us; but, however real and disastrous may be the power of our evil in troubling the communion of love between us and our Lord, and in compelling Him to smite before He binds up, never forget that our sin is utterly impotent to turn away the tide that sets to us from the heart of Christ. Earthborn vapors may hang about the low levels, and turn the gracious sun himself into a blood-red ball of lurid fire; but they reach only a little way up, and high above their region is the pure blue, and the blessed light pours down upon the upper surface of the white mist, and thins away its opaqueness, and dries up its clinging damp, and at last parts it into filmy fragments that float out of sight, and the dwellers on the green earth see the sun, which was always there even when they could not behold it, and which, by shining on, has conquered all the obstructions that veiled its beams. Sin is mighty, but one thing sin cannot do, and that is to make Christ cease to love us. Sin is mighty, but one other thing sin cannot do, and that is to prevent Christ from manifesting His love to us sinners, that we may learn to love and so may cease to sin. Christ's love is not at the beck and call of our fluctuating affections. It has its source deeper than in the springs in our hearts, namely in the depths of His own nature. It is not the echo or the answer to ours, but ours is the echo to His; and that being so, our changes do not reach to it, any more than earth's seasons affect the sun. Forever and ever He loves. Whilst we forget Him, He remembers us. Whilst we repay Him with neglect or with hate, He still loves. If we believe not, He still abides faithful to His merciful purpose, and, in spite of all that we can do, will not deny Himself, by ceasing to be the incarnate Patience, the perfect Love. He is Himself the great example of that "charity" which His Apostle painted; He is not easily provoked; He is not soon angry; He beareth all things; He hopeth all things. We cannot get away from the sweep of His love, wander we ever so far. The child may struggle in the mother's arms, and beat the breast that shelters it with its little hand; but it neither hurts or angers that gentle bosom, nor loosens the firm but loving grasp that holds it fast. He carries, as a nurse does, His wayward children, and, blessed be His name! His arm is too strong for us to shake it off, His love too divine for us to dam it back.

And still further, here we see a love which sends a special message because of special sin.

If one was to be singled out from the little company to receive by name the summons of the Lord to meet Him in Galilee, we might have expected it to have been that faithful friend who stood beneath the Cross, till his Lord's command sent him to his own home; or that weeping mother whom he then led away with him; or one of the two who had been turned from secret disciples into confessors by the might of their love, and had laid His body with reverent care in the grave in the garden. Strange reward for true love that they should be merged in the general message, and strange recompense for treason and cowardice that Peter's name should be thus distinguished! Is sin, then, a passport to His deeper love? Is the murmur true after all, "Thou never gavest me a kid, but as soon as this thy son is come, which hath devoured thy living with harlots, thou hast killed for him the fatted calf"? Yes, and no. No, inasmuch as the unbroken fellowship hath in it calm and deep joys which the returning prodigal does not know, and all sin lays waste and impoverishes the soul. Yes, inasmuch as He, who knows all our needs, knows that the denier needs a special treatment to bring him back to peace, and that the further a poor heart has strayed from Him, the mightier must be the forthputting of manifested love, it if is to be strong enough to travel across all the dreary wastes, and draw back again, to its orbit among its sister planets, the wandering star. The depth of our need determines the strength of the restorative power put forth. They who had not gone away would come at the call addressed to them all, but he who had sundered himself from them and from the Lord would remain in his sad isolation, unless some special means were used to bring him back. The more we have sinned, the less can we believe in Christ's love; and so the more we have sinned, the more marvelous and convincing does He make the testimony and operations of His love to us. It is ever to the poor bewildered sheep, lying panting in the wilderness, that He comes. Among His creatures, the race which has sinned is that which receives the most stupendous proof of the seeking divine love. Among men, the publicans and the harlots, the denying Peters and the persecuting Pauls, are they to whom the most persuasive entreaties of His love are sent, and on whom the strongest powers of His grace are brought to bear. Our sin cannot check the flow of His love. More marvelous still, our sin occasions a mightier burst of the manifestation of His love, for eyes blinded by selfishness and carelessness, or by fear and despair, need to see a brightness beyond the noonday sun, ere they can behold the amazing truth of His love to them; and what they need, they get. "Go, tell Peter."

Here, too, is the revelation of a love which singles out a sinful man by name.

Christ does not deal with us in the mass, but soul by soul. Our finite minds have to lose the individual in order to grasp the class. Our eyes see the wood far off on the mountainside, but not the single trees, nor each fluttering leaf. We think of "the race"—the twelve hundred millions that live today, and the uncounted crowds that have been, but the units in that inconceivable sum are not separate in our view. But He does not generalize so. He has a clear individualizing knowledge of each; each separately has a place in his mind or heart. To each He says, "I know thee by name: He loves the world, because He loves every single soul with a distinct love. And His messages of blessing are as specific and individualizing as the love from which they come. He speaks to each of us as truly as He singled out Peter here, as truly as when His voice from heaven said, "Saul, Saul." English names are on His lips as really as Jewish ones. He calls to *thee* by *thy* name—thou hast a share in His love. To thee the call to trust Him is addressed, and to thee forgiveness, help, purity, life eternal are offered. Thou hast sinned; that only infuses deeper tenderness into His beseeching tones. Thou hast gone further from Him than some of thy fellows; that only makes His recovering energy greater. Thou hast denied His name; that only makes Him speak thine with more persuasive invitation.

Look, then, at this one instance of a love stronger than death, mightier than sin, sending its special greeting to the denier, and learn how deep the source, how powerful the flow, how universal the sweep, of that river of the love of God, which streams to us through the channel of Christ His Son.

2. Notice, second, the secret meeting between our Lord and the Apostle. That is the second stage in the victorious conflict of divine love with man's sin. As I have said, that interview took place on the day of the Resurrection, apparently before our Lord joined the two sorrowful travelers to Emmaus, and certainly before He appeared to the company gathered by night in the closed chamber. The fact was well known, for it is referred to by Luke and by Paul, but nothing beyond the fact seems to have been known, or at all events is made public by them. All this is very significant and very beautiful.

What tender consideration there is in meeting Peter alone, before seeing him in the companionship of the others! How painful would have been the rush of the first emotions of shame awakened by Christ's presence, if their course had been checked by any eye but His own beholding them! How impossible it would have then been to have poured out all the penitent confessions with which his heart must have been full, and how hard it would have been to have met for the first time, and not to have poured them out! With most loving insight, then, into the painful embarrassment, and dread of unsympathizing bystanders, which must have troubled the contrite Apostle, the Lord is careful to give him the opportunity of weeping his fill on His own bosom, unrestrained by any thought of others, and will let him sob out his contrition to His own ear alone. Then the meeting in the upper chamber will be one of pure joy to Peter, as to all the rest. The emotions which he has in common with them find full play, in that hour when all are reunited to their Lord. The experience which belongs to himself alone has its solitary hour of unrecorded communion. The first to whom He, who is "separate from sinners," appeared was "Mary Magdalene, out of whom He had cast seven devils." The next were the women who bore this message of forgiveness; and probably the next was the one among all the company who had sinned most grievously. So wondrous is the order of His preferences, coming ever nearest to those who need Him most.

And may we not regard this secret interview as representing for us what is needed on our part to make Christ's forgiving love our own? There must be the personal contact of my soul with the loving heart of Christ, the individual act of my own coming to Him, and, as the old Puritans used to say, "my transacting" with Him. Like the ocean of the atmosphere, His love encompasses me, and in it I "live, and move, and have my being," But I must let it flow into my spirit, and stir the dormant music of my soul. I can shut it out, sealing my heart love-tight against it. I do shut it out, unless by my own conscious, personal act I yield myself to Him, unless by my own faith I come to Him, and meet Him, secretly and really as did the penitent Apostle, whom the message, that proclaimed the love of his Lord, emboldened to meet the Lord who loved, and by His own lips to be assured of forgiveness and friendship. It is possible to stumble at noontide, as in the dark. A man may starve, outside of barns filled with plenty, and his lips may be parched with thirst, though he is within sight of a broad river flowing in the sunshine. So a soul may stiffen into the death of self and sin, even though the voice that wakes the dead to a life of love be calling to it. Christ and His grace are yours if you will, but the invitations and beseechings of His mercy, the constant drawings of His love, the all-embracing offers of His forgiveness, may be all in vain, if you do not grasp them and hold them fast by the hand of faith.

That personal act must be preceded by the message of His mighty love. Ever He sends such messages as heralds of His coming, just as He prepared the way for His own approach to the Apostle, by the words of our text. Our faith must follow His word. Our love can only be called forth by the manifestation of His. But His message must be followed by that personal act, else His word is spoken in vain, and there is no real union between our need and His fullness, nor any cleansing contact of His grace with our foulness.

Note, too, the intensely individual character of that act of faith by which a man accepts Christ's grace. Friends and companions may bring the tidings of the risen Lord's loving heart, but the actual closing with the Lord's mercy must be done by myself, alone with Him.

As if there were not another soul on earth, I and He must meet, and in solitude deep as that of death, each man for himself must yield to Incarnate Love, and receive eternal life. The flocks and herds, the wives and children, have all to be sent away, and Jacob must be left alone, before the mysterious Wrestler comes whose touch of fire lames the whole nature of sin and death, whose inbreathed power strengthens to hold Him fast till He speaks a blessing, who desires to be overcome, and makes our yielding to Him our prevailing with Him. As one of the old mystics called prayer "the flight of the lonely man to the only God," so we may call the act of faith the meeting of the soul alone with Christ alone. Do you know anything of that personal communion? Have you, your own very self, by your own penitence for your own sin, and your own thankful faith in the Love which thereby becomes truly yours, isolated yourself from all companionship, and joined yourself to Christ? Then, through that narrow passage where we can only walk singly, you will come into a large place. The act of faith, which separates us from all men, unites us for the first time in real brotherhood, and they who, one by one, come to Jesus and meet Him alone, next find that they "are come to the city of God, to an innumerable company, to the festal choirs of angels, to the Church of the Firstborn to the spirits of just men made perfect."

3. Notice, finally, the gradual cure of the pardoned Apostle. He was restored to his office, as we read in the supplement to John's Gospel. In that wonderful conversation, full as it is of allusions to Peter's fall, Christ asks but one question, "Lovest thou Me?" That includes everything. "Hast thou learned the lesson of My mercy? hast thou responded to My love? then thou art fit for My work, and beginning to be perfected.'' So the third stage in the triumph of Christ's love over man's sin is, when we, beholding that love flowing towards us, and accepting it by faith, respond to it with our own, and are able to say, ''Thou knowest that I love Thee.''

The all-embracing question is followed by an equally comprehensive command, ''Follow thou Me,'' a two-worded compendium of all morals, a precept which naturally results from love, and certainly leads to absolute perfectness. With love to Christ for motive, and Christ Himself for pattern, and following Him for our one duty, all things are possible, and the utter defeat of sin in us is but a question of time.

And the certainty, as well as the gradual slowness, of that victory, are well set forth by the future history of the Apostle. We know how his fickleness passed away, and how his vehement character was calmed and consolidated into resolved persistency, and how his love of distinction and self-confidence were turned in a new direction, obeyed a divine impulse, and became powers. We read how he started to the front; how he guided the Church in the first stage of its development; how whenever there was danger he was in the van, and whenever there was work his hand was first on the plow; how he bearded and braved rulers and councils; how—more difficult still for him— he lay quietly in prison sleeping like a child, between his guards, on the night before his execution; how—most difficult of all—he acquiesced in Paul's superiority; and, if he still needed to be withstood and blamed, could recognize the wisdom of the rebuke, and in his calm old age could speak well of the rebuker as his ''beloved brother Paul.'' Nor was the cure a change in the great lines of his character. These remain the same, the characteristic excellences possible to them are brought out, the defects are curbed and cast out. The ''new man'' is the ''old man'' with a new direction, obeying a new impulse, but retaining its individuality. Weaknesses become strengths; the sanctified character is the old character sanctified; and it is still true that ''every man hath his proper gift of God, one after this manner, and another after that.''

It is very instructive to observe how deeply the experiences of his fall, and of Christ's mercy then, had impressed themselves on Peter's memory, and how constantly they were present with him all through his afterlife. His Epistles are full of allusions which show this. For instance, to go a step further back in his life, he remembered that the Lord had said to him, ''Thou art Peter,'' ''a stone,'' and that his pride in that name had helped to his rash confidence, and so to his sin. Therefore, when he is cured of these, he takes pleasure in sharing his honor with his brethren, and writes, ''Ye also, as living stones, are built up.'' He remembered the contempt for others and the trust in himself with which he had said,

"Though all should forsake Thee, yet will not I"; and, taught what must come of that, he writes, "Be clothed with humility, for God resisteth the proud, and giveth grace to the humble." He remembered how hastily he had drawn his sword and struck at Malchus, and he writes, "If when ye do well and suffer for it, ye take it patiently, this is acceptable with God." He remembered how he had been surprised into denial by the questions of a sharp-tongued maidservant, and he writes, "Be ready always to give an answer to every man that asketh you a reason of the hope that is in you, with meekness." He remembered how the pardoning love of his Lord had honored him unworthy, with the charge, "Feed My sheep," and he writes, ranking himself as one of the class to whom he speaks—"The elders I exhort, who am also an elder . . . feed the flock of God." He remembered that last command, which sounded ever in his spirit, "Follow thou Me," and discerning now, through all the years that lay between, the presumptuous folly and blind inversion of his own work and his Master's which had lain in his earlier question, "Why cannot I follow Thee now? I will lay down my life for Thy sake"—he writes to all, "Christ also suffered for us, leaving us an example, that ye should follow His steps."

So well had he learned the lesson of his own sin, and of that immortal love which had beckoned him back, to peace at its side and purity from its hand. Let us learn how the love of Christ, received into the heart, triumphs gradually but surely over all sin, transforms character, turning even its weakness into strength, and so, from the depths of transgression and very gates of hell, raises men to God.

To us all this divine message speaks. Christ's love is extended to us; no sin can stay it; no fall of ours can make Him despair. He will not give us up. He waits to be gracious. This same Peter once asked, "How oft shall my brother sin against me and I forgive him?" And the answer, which commanded unwearied brotherly forgiveness, revealed inexhaustible divine pardon—"I say not unto thee until seven times, but until seventy times seven." The measure of the divine mercy, which is the pattern of ours, is completeness ten times multiplied by itself; we know not the numbers thereof. "Let the wicked forsake his way . . . and let him return unto the Lord, for He will have mercy upon him; and to our God, for He will multiply to pardon."

"First to Mary"

. . . He appeared first to Mary Magdalene, out of whom He had cast seven devils. MARK 16:2.

A great pile of legend has been built on the one or two notices of Mary Magdalene in Scripture. Art, poetry, and philanthropy have accepted and inculcated these, till we almost feel as if they were bits of the Bible. But there is not the shadow of a foundation for them. She has generally been identified with the woman in Luke's Gospel "who was a sinner." There is no reason at all for that identification. On the contrary, there is a reason against it, in the fact that immediately after that narrative she is named as one of the little band of women who ministered to Jesus.

Here is all that we know of her: that Christ cast out the seven devils; that she became one of the Galilean women, including the mothers of Jesus and of John, who "ministered to Him of their substance"; that she was one of the Marys at the Cross and saw the interment; that she came to the sepulchre, heard the angel's message, went to John with it, came back and stood without at the sepulchre, saw the Lord, and, having heard His voice and clasped His feet, returned to the little company, and then she drops out of the narrative and is no more named. That is all. It is enough. There are large lessons in this fact which Mark (or whoever wrote this chapter) gives with such emphasis, "He appeared first to Mary Madalene."

Think what the Resurrection is—how stupendous and wonderful! Who *might* have been expected to be its witnesses? But see! the first eye that beholds is this poor sin-stained woman's. What a distance between the two extremes of her experience—devil-ridden and gazing on the Risen Saviour!

1. An example of the depth to which the soul of man can descend. This fact of possession is very obscure and strange. I doubt whether we can understand it. But I cannot see how we can bring it down to the level of mere disease without involving Jesus Christ in the charge of consciously aiding in upholding what, if it be not an awful truth, is one of the grimmest, ghastliest superstitions that ever terrified men.

In all ways He gives in His adhesion to the fact of demoniacal possession. He speaks *to* the demons, and *of* them, rebukes them, holds conversations with them, charges them to be silent. He distinguishes between possession and diseases. "Heal the sick, cleanse the lepers, raise the dead"—these commands bring together forms of sickness running its course; why should He separate from them His next command and endowment, "cast out devils," unless because He regarded demoniacal possession as separate from sickness in any form? He sees in His casting of them out the triumph over the personal power of evil. "I beheld Satan as lightning fall from heaven." But while the fact seems to be established, the thing is only known to us by its signs. These were madness, melancholy, sometimes dumbness, sometimes fits and convulsions; the man was dominated by an alien power; there was a strange, awful double consciousness; ''We are many,'' ''My name is Legion.'' There was absolute control by this alien power, which like some parasitical worm had rooted itself within the poor wretch, and there lived upon his blood and life juices—only that it lived in the spirit, dominated the will, and controlled the nature.

Probably there had always been the yielding to the impulse to sin of some sort, or at any rate the man had opened the door for the devil to come in.

This woman had been in the deepest depths of this awful abyss. ''Seven'' is the numerical symbol of completeness, so she had been utterly devil-ridden. And she had once been a little child in some Galilean home, and parents had seen her budding beauty and early, gentle, womanly ways. And now, think of the havoc! the distorted face, the foul words, the blasphemous thoughts!

And is this worse than our sinful case? Are not the devils that possess us as real and powerful?

2. An example of the cleansing power of Christ. We know nothing about how she had come under His merciful eye, nor any of the circumstances of her healing; but only that this woman, with whom the serpent was so closely intertwined, as in some pictures of Eve's temptation, was not beyond His reach, and was set free. Note—

There is *no* condition of human misery which Christ cannot alleviate.

None is so sunk in sin that He cannot redeem them.

For all in the world there is hope.

Look on the extremest forms of sin. We can regard them all with the assurance that Christ can cleanse them—prostitutes, thieves, respectable worldlings.

None is so bad as to have lost His love.

None is so bad as to be excluded from the purpose of His death.

None is so bad as to be beyond the reach of His cleansing power.

None has wandered so far that he cannot come back.

Think of the earliest believers—a thief, a ''woman that was a sinner,'' this Mary, a Zacchæus, a persecuting Paul, a rude, rough jailer, etc.

Remember Paul's description of a class of the Corinthian saints— ''such were some of you.''

As long as man is man, so long is God ready to receive him back. There is no place where sun does not shine. No heart is given over to irremediable hardness. None ever comes to Christ in vain.

The Saviour is greater than all our sins.

The deliverance is more than sufficient for the worst.

''God is able of these stones to raise up children to Abraham.''

Ezekiel's vision of dry bones.

3. An example of how the remembrance of past and pardoned sin may be a blessing. Mary evidently tried always to be beside Him. The cure had been perfect, but perhaps there was a tremulous fear, as in the man that prayed ''that he might be with Him.''

And so, look how all the notices give us one picture of a heart set on Him. There were:

(*a*) Consciousness of weakness, that made her long for His presence as a security.

(*b*) Deep love, that made her long for His presence as a joy.

(*c*) Thankful gratitude, that made her long for opportunities to serve Him.

And this is what the remembrance of Jesus should be to us.

4. An example of how the most degraded may rise highest in fellowship with Christ. ''First'' to her, because she needed Him and longed for Him.

Now this is but an illustration of the great principle that by God's mercy sin when it is hated and pardoned may be made to subserve our highest joys.

It is not sin which separates us from God, but it is unpardoned sin. Not that the more we sin the more we are fit for Him, for all sin is loss. There are ways in which even forgiven and repented sin may injure a man. But there is nothing in it to hinder our coming close to the Saviour and enjoying all the fullness of His love, so that if we use it rightly it may become a help.

If it leads us to that clinging of which we have just spoken, then we shall come nearer to God for it.

The divine presence is always given to those who long for it.

Sin may help to kindle such longings.

He who has been almost dead in the wilderness will keep near the guide. The man that has been starved with cold in Arctic night will prize the glory and grace of sunshine in fairer lands.

Instances in Church history—Paul, Augustine, Bunyan.

''Publicans and harlots go into the kingdom before you.''

The noblest illustration is in heaven, where men lead the song of Redemption.

God uses sin as a black background on which the brightest rainbow tints of His mercy are displayed.

You can come to this Saviour whatever you have been. I say to no man, "Sin, for it does not matter." But I do say, "If you are conscious of sin, deep, dark, damning, that makes no barrier between you and God. You may come all the nearer for it if you will let your past teach you to long for His love and to lean on Him."

"He appeared first to Mary Magdalene," and those who stand nearest the throne and lead the anthems of heaven, and look up with undazzled angels' faces to the God of their joy, whose name blazes on their foreheads, all these were guilty, sinful men. But they "have washed their robes and made them white." There will be in heaven some of the worst sinners that ever lived on earth. There will not be one out of whom He has not "cast seven devils."

The Worldwide Commission

Every creature. MARK 16:15.

The missionary enterprise has been put on many bases. People do not like commandments, but yet it is a great relief and strength to come back to one, and answer all questions with "He bids me!"

Now, these words of our Lord open up the whole subject of the Universality of Christianity.

1. The divine audacity of Christianity. Take the scene. A mere handful of men, whether "the twelve" or "the five hundred brethren" is immaterial.

How they must have recoiled when they heard the sweeping command, "Go ye into all the world"! It is like the apparent absurdity of Christ's quiet word: "They need not depart; give ye them to eat," when the only visible stock of food was "five loaves and two small fishes." As on that occasion, so in this final commandment they had to take Christ's presence into account. "I am with you."

So note the obviously worldwide extent of Christ's claim of dominion. He had come into the world, to begin with, that "the world through Him might be saved." "If any man thirst, let him come." The parables of the kingdom of heaven are planned on the same grand scale. "I will draw all men unto Me." It cannot be disputed that Jesus "lived and moved and had His being" in this vision of universal dominion.

Here emerges the great contrast of Christianity with Judaism. Judaism was intolerant, as all merely monotheistic faiths must be, and sure of future universality, but it was not proselytizing—not a missionary faith. Nor is it so today. It is exclusive and unprogressive still.

Mohammedanism in its fiery youth, because monotheistic, was aggressive, but it enforced outward profession only and left the inner life untouched. So it did not scruple to persecute as well as to proselytize. Christianity is alone in calmly setting forth a universal dominion, and in seeking it by the Word alone. ''Put up thy sword into its sheath.''

2. The foundations of this bold claim. Christ's sole and singular relation to the whole race. There are profound truths embodied in this relation.

(*a*) There is implied the adequacy of Christ for all. He is *for* all, because He is the only and all-sufficient Saviour. By His death He offered satisfaction for the sins of the whole world. ''Look unto Me, and be ye saved, all the ends of the earth, for I am God, and there is none else.'' ''Neither is there salvation in any other, for there is none other name,'' etc.

(*b*) The divine purpose of mercy for all. ''God will have all men to be saved, and to come to a knowledge of the truth.''

(*c*) The adaptation of the Gospel message to all. It deals with all men as on one level. It addresses universal humanity. ''Unto you, O men, I call, and My voice is to the sons of men.'' It speaks the same language to all sorts of men, to all stages of society, and in all ages. Christianity has no esoteric doctrine, no inner circle of the ''initiated.'' Consequently it introduces a new notion of the unity of humanity, and knows nothing of privileged classes.

Note the history of Christianity in its relation to slavery, and to inferior and downtrodden races. Christianity has no belief in the existence of ''irreclaimable outcasts,'' but proclaims and glories in the possibility of winning any and all to the love which makes godlike. There is one Saviour, and so there is only one Gospel for ''all the world.''

3. Its vindication in facts. The history of the diffusion of the Gospel at first is significant. Think of the varieties of civilization it approached and absorbed. See how it overcame the bonds of climate and language, etc. How unlike the Europe of today is to the Europe of Paul's time!

In this twentieth century Christianity does not present the marks of an expiring superstition.

Note, further, that the history of missions vindicates the worldwide claim of the Gospel. Think of the wonderful number of converts in the first fifty years of Gospel preaching. The Roman empire was Christianized in three centuries! Recall the innumerable testimonies down to date; *e.g.* the absolute abandonment of idols in the South Sea Islands, the weakening of caste in India, the romance of missions in Central Africa, etc. etc.

The character, too, of modern converts is as good as was that of Paul's. The Gospel in this century produces everywhere fruits like those which it brought forth in Asia and Europe in the first century. The success has been in every field. None has been abandoned as hopeless. The Moravians in Greenland. The Hottentots. The Patagonians (Darwin's testimony). Christianity has constantly appealed to all classes of society. Not many "noble," but some in every age and land.

4. The practical duty. "Go ye and preach." The matter is literally left in our hands. Jesus has returned to the throne. Ere departing He announces the distinct command. There it is, and it is age-long in its application—"Preach!" that is the one Gospel weapon. Tell of the name and the work of "God manifest in the flesh." First "evangelize," then "disciple the nations." Bring *to* Christ, then build up *in* Christ. There are no other orders. Let there be boundless trust in the divine Gospel, and it will vindicate itself in every mission field. Let us think imperially of "Christ and the Church." Our anticipations of success should be world-wide in their sweep.

As when they kindle the festival lamps round the dome of St. Peter's, there is a first twinkling spot here and another there, and gradually they multiply till they outline the whole in an unbroken ring of light, so "one by one" men will enter the kingdom, till at last "every knee shall bow, and every tongue confess that Jesus is Lord."

He shall reign from shore to shore,
With illimitable sway.

The Enthroned Christ

So then after the Lord had spoken unto them, He was received up into heaven, and sat on the right hand of God. MARK 16:19.

How strangely calm and brief is this record of so stupendous an event! Do these sparing and reverent words sound to you like the product of devout imagination, embellishing with legend the facts of history? To me their very restrainedness, calmness, matter-of-factness, if I may so call it, are a strong guarantee that they are the utterance of an eyewitness, who verily saw what he tells so simply. There is something sublime in the contrast between the magnificence and almost inconceivable grandeur of the thing communicated, and the quiet words, so few, so sober, so wanting in all detail, in which it is told.

That stupendous fact of Christ sitting at the right hand of God is the one that should fill the present for us all, even as the Cross should fill the past, and the coming for Judgment should fill the future. So for us the one central thought about the present, in its loftiest relations, should be the throned Christ at God's right hand. It is to that thought of the session of Jesus by the side of the Majesty of the Heavens that I wish to turn now, to try to bring out the profound teaching that is in it, and the practical lessons which it suggests. I desire to emphasize very briefly four points, and to see, in Christ's sitting at the right hand, the revelation of these things: The exalted Man, the resting Saviour, the interceding Priest, and the ever-active Helper.

1. First, then, in that solemn and wondrous fact of Christ's sitting at the right hand of God, we have the exalted Man. We are taught to believe, according to His own words, that in His ascension Christ was but returning whence He came, and entering into the "glory which He had with the Father before the world was." And that impression of a return to His native and proper abode is strongly conveyed to us by the narrative of His ascension. Contrast it, for instance, with the narrative of Elijah's rapture, or with the brief reference to Enoch's translation. The one was taken by God up into the region and a state which he had not formerly traversed; the other was borne by a fiery chariot to the heavens; but Christ slowly sailed upwards, as it were, by His own inherent power, returning to His abode, and ascending up where He was before.

But while this is one side of the profound fact, there is another side. What was new in Christ's return to His Father's bosom? This, that He took His Manhood with Him. It was "the Everlasting Son of the Father," the Eternal Word, which from the beginning "was with God and was God," that came down from heaven to earth, to declare the Father; but it was the Incarnate Word, the Man Christ Jesus, that went back again. This most blessed and wonderful truth is taught with emphasis in His own words before the Council, "Ye shall see the Son of *Man* sitting on the right hand of power." Christ, then, today, bears a human body, not, indeed, the "body of His humiliation," but the body of His glory, which is none the less a true corporeal frame, and necessarily requires a locality. His ascension, whithersoever He may have gone, was the true carrying of a real humanity, complete in all its parts, Body, Soul, and Spirit, up to the very throne of God.

Where that locality is it is bootless to speculate. Scripture says that He ascended up "far above all heavens"; or, as the Epistle to the Hebrews has it, in the proper translation, the High Priest ''is passed *through* the heavens,'' as if all this visible material creation was rent asunder in order that He might soar yet higher beyond its limits wherein reign mutation and decay. But wheresoever that place may be, there *is* a place in which now, with a human body as well as a human spirit, Jesus is sitting ''at the right hand of God.''

Let us thankfully think how, in the profound language of Scripture, ''the Forerunner is for us entered''; how, in some mysterious manner, of which we can but dimly conceive, that entrance of Jesus in His complete humanity into the highest heavens is the preparation of a place for us. It seems as if, without His presence there, there were no entrance for human nature within that state, and no power in a human foot to tread upon the crystal pavements of the celestial City, but where He is, there the path is permeable, and the place native, to all who love and trust Him.

We may stand, therefore, with these disciples, and looking upwards as the cloud receives Him out of our sight, our faith follows Him, still our Brother, still clothed with humanity, still wearing a bodily frame; and we say, as we lose Him from our vision, ''What is man''? Capable of being lifted to the most intimate participation in the glories of divinity, and though he be poor and weak and sinful here, yet capable of union and assimilation with the Majesty that is on high. For what Christ's Body is, the bodies of them that love and serve Him shall surely be, and He, the Forerunner, is entered there for us; that we too, in our turn, may pass into the light and walk in the full blaze of the divine glory; as of old the children in the furnace were; unconsumed because companioned by ''One like unto the Son of Man.''

The exalted Christ, sitting at the right hand of God, is the Pattern of what is possible for humanity, and the prophecy and pledge of what will be actual for all that love Him and bear the image of Him upon earth, that they may be conformed to the image of His glory, and be with Him where He is. What firmness, what reality, what solidity this thought of the exalted bodily Christ gives to the else dim and vague conceptions of a Heaven beyond the stars and beyond our present experience! I believe that no doctrine of a future life has strength and substance enough to survive the agonies of our hearts when we part from our dear ones, the fears of our spirits when we look into the unknown, inane future of ourselves; except only this which says Heaven is Christ and Christ is Heaven, and points to Him and says, ''Where He is, there and that also shall His servants be.''

2. Now, second, look at Christ's sitting at the right hand of God as presenting to our view the Resting Saviour. That session expresses the idea of absolute repose after sore conflict. It is the same thought which is expressed in those solemn Egyptian colossal statues of deified conquerors, elevated to mysterious union with their gods, and yet men still, sitting before their temples in perfect stillness, with their mighty hands lying quiet on their restful limbs; with calm faces out of which toil and passion and change seem to have melted, gazing out with open eyes as over a silent, prostrate world. So, with the Cross behind, with all the agony and weariness of the arena, the dust and the blood of the struggle, left beneath, He "sitteth at the right hand of God the Father Almighty."

The rest of the Christ after His Cross is parallel with and carries the same meaning as the rest of God after the Creation. Why do we read "He rested on the seventh day from all His works"? Did the Creative Arm grow weary? Was there toil for the divine nature in the making of a universe? Doth He not speak and it is done? Is not the calm, effortless forthputting of His will the cause and the means of Creation? Does any shadow of weariness steal over that life which lives and is not exhausted? Does the bush consume in burning? Surely not. He rested from His works, not because He needed to recuperate strength after action by repose, but because the works were perfect, and in sign and token that His ideal was accomplished, and that no more was needed to be done.

And, in like manner, the Christ rests after His Cross, not because He needed repose even after that terrible effort, or was panting after His race, and so had to sit there to recover, but in token that His work was finished and perfected, that all which He had come to do was done; and in token, likewise, that the Father, too, beheld and accepted the finished work. Therefore, the session of Christ at the right hand of God is the proclamation from Heaven of what He cried with His last dying breath upon the Cross: "It is finished!" It is the declaration that the world has had all done for it that Heaven can do for it. It is the declaration that all which is needed for the regeneration of humanity has been lodged in the very heart of the race, and that henceforward all that is required is the evolving and the development of the consequences of that perfect work which Christ offered upon the Cross. So the writer of the Epistle to the Hebrews contrasts the priests who stood "daily ministering and offering oftentimes the same sacrifices" which "can never take away sin," with "this Man who, after He had offered one sacrifice for sins for ever, sat down at the right hand of God"; testifying thereby that His Cross is the complete, sufficient, perpetual atonement and satisfaction for the sins of the whole world. So we have to look back to that past as interpreted by this present, to that Cross as commented upon by this Throne, and to see in it the perfect work which any human soul may grasp, and which all human souls need, for their acceptance and forgiveness. The Son of Man set at the right hand of God is Christ's declaration, "I have finished the work which Thou gavest Me to do," and is also God's declaration, "This is My beloved Son, in whom I am well pleased."

3. Once more, we see here, in this great fact of Christ sitting at the right hand of God, the interceding Priest. So the Scripture declares. The Epistle to the Hebrews over and over again reiterates that thought that we have a Priest who has "passed into the heavens," there to "appear in the presence of God for us." And the Apostle Paul, in that great linked climax in the eighth chapter of the Epistle to the Romans, has it, "Christ that died, yea rather, that is risen again, who is even at the right hand of God, who also maketh intercession for us." There are deep mysteries connected with that thought of the intercession of Christ. It does not mean that the divine heart needs to be won to love and pity. It does not mean that in any mere outward and formal fashion Christ pleads with God, and softens and placates the Infinite and Eternal love of the Father in the heavens. It, at least, plainly means this, that He, our Saviour and Sacrifice, is forever in the presence of God; presenting His own blood as an element in the divine dealing with us, modifying the incidence of the divine law, and securing through His own merits and intercession the outflow of blessings upon our heads and hearts. It is not a complete statement of Christ's work for us that He died for us. He died that He might have somewhat to offer. He lives that He may be our Advocate as well as our propitiation with the Father. And just as the High Priest once a year passed within the curtain, and there in the solemn silence and solitude of the holy place sprinkled the blood that he bore thither, not without trembling, and but for a moment permitted to stay in the awful Presence, thus, but in reality and forever, with the joyful gladness of a Son in His "own calm home, His habitation from eternity," Christ *abides* in the Holy Place; and, at the right hand of the Majesty of the Heavens, lifts up that prayer, so strangely compact of authority and submission: "Father, I *will* that these whom Thou hast given Me be with Me where I am." The Son of Man at the right hand of God is our Intercessor with the Father. "Seeing, then, that we have a great High Priest that is passed through the heavens, let us come boldly to the Throne of Grace."

4. Lastly, this great fact sets before us the everactive Helper. The "right hand of God" is the Omnipotent energy of God: and howsoever certainly the language of Scripture requires for its full interpretation that we should firmly hold that Christ's glorified body dwells in a place, we are not to omit the other thought that to sit at the right hand also means to wield the immortal energy of that divine nature, over all the field of the

Creation, and in every province of His dominion. So that the ascended Christ is the ubiquitous Christ; and He who is ''at the right hand of God'' is wherever the power of God reaches throughout His whole Universe.

Remember, too, that it was once given to a man to look through the opened heavens (through which Christ had ''passed'') and to ''see the Son of Man standing''—not sitting—''at the right hand of God.'' Why to the dying protomartyr was there granted that vision thus varied? Wherefore was the attitude changed but to express the swiftness, the certainty of His help, and the eager readiness of the Lord, who starts to His feet, as it were, to succor and to sustain His dying servant?

And so, dear friends, we may take that great joyful truth that both as receiving ''gifts for men'' and bestowing gifts upon them, and as working by His providence in the world, and on the wider scale for the well-being of His children and of the Church, the Christ who sits at the right hand of God wields, ever with eager cheerfulness, all the powers of omnipotence for our well-being, if we love and trust Him. We may look quietly upon all perplexities and complications, because the hands that were pierced for us hold the helm and the reins, because the Christ who is our Brother is the King, and sits supreme at the center of the Universe. Joseph's brethren, that came up in their hunger and their rags to Egypt, and found their brother next the throne, were startled with a great joy of surprise, and fears were calmed, and confidence sprang in their hearts. Shall not we be restful and confident when our Brother, the Son of Man, sits ruling all things? ''We see not yet all things put under'' us, ''but we see Jesus,'' and that is enough.

So the ascended Man, the resting Saviour and His completed work, the interceding Priest, and the everactive Helper, are all brought before us in this great and blessed thought, ''Christ sitteth at the right hand of God.'' Therefore, dear friends, set your affection on things above. Our hearts travel where our dear ones are. Oh how strange and sad it is that professing Christians whose lives, if they are Christians at all, have their roots and are hid with Christ in God, should turn so few, so cold thoughts and loves thither! Surely ''where your treasure is there will your heart be also.'' Surely if Christ is your Treasure you will feel that with Him is home, and that this is a foreign land. ''Set your affection,'' then, ''on things above,'' while life lasts, and when it is ebbing away, perhaps to our eyes, too, Heaven may be opened, and the vision of the Son of Man standing to receive and to welcome us may be granted. And when it has ebbed away, His will be the first voice to welcome us, and He will lift us to share in His glorious rest, according to His own wondrous promise, ''To him that overcometh will I grant to sit with Me in My Throne, even as I also overcame, and am set down with My Father in His Throne.''